Contents

HAV

For use in the Library only

WITHDRAWN

Hampshire
County Council

CL14 2/03 20k

A directory of organisations and resources in
adult continuing education and training

supported by

Local Government Association

Department for
**Innovation,
Universities** &
Skills

Published by The National Institute of Adult
Continuing Education (England and Wales)
21 De Montfort Street
Leicester LE1 7GE, UK
Website: www.niace.org.uk

Registered charity number 1002775
A company limited by guarantee,
registration number 2603322

ISBN 978 1 86201 380 3

Typeset by Kerrypress Ltd, Luton, Bedfordshire
Printed and Bound in Great Britain by B&B Press Ltd, Rotherham

Whilst every effort is made to ensure the accuracy
of entries we are not liable for omissions or incorrect
insertion, whether as to wording, space or position of
entry. Email addresses and websites also often change.

The National Institute of Adult Continuing Education (England and Wales) (NIACE)

Renaissance House
20 Princess Road West
Leicester LE1 6TP
Tel: 0116 204 4200
Fax: 0116 285 4514
Email: enquiries@niace.org.uk
Website: www.niace.org.uk
Registered Charity no. 1002775
Company Limited by Guarantee no.
2603322

NIACE Dysgu Cymru
35 Cathedral Road
Cardiff CF11 9HB
Tel: 0292 0370900
Fax: 0292 0370909
Email: enquiries@niacedc.org.uk
Website: www.niacedc.org.uk

NIACE Object and Functions

NIACE is the national membership organisation for adult learning in England and Wales. It is a registered charity and a company limited by guarantee.

The main aim of the Institute is to promote the study and general advancement of adult continuing education by improving the quality of opportunities available, by increasing the number of adults engaged in formal and informal learning; and by widening access for those communities under-represented in current provision.

NIACE works with all the many interests active in the education and training of adults. It undertakes advocacy and policy work with national, regional and local agencies; provides information and advice to organisations and individuals; carries out research and development projects; organises conferences and seminars; publishes journals, books and directories; and co-ordinates a major national promotion of education and training for adults through Adult Learners' Week.

NIACE also works in partnership with Scottish and Northern Ireland adult education and plays a full part in the development of ideas and practice internationally through the European Association for the Education of Adults, the International Council for Adult Education, the Organisation for Economic Co-operation and Development, the Commonwealth Association for the Education and Training of Adults, the Council of Europe, UNESCO, and the British Council.

On 1 July 2000 the functions of the Institute in Wales came under the oversight of NIACE Dysgu Cymru/Learning Wales, a multi-agency partnership open to all who can sign up to its mission "to support and promote the development of lifelong learning in Wales".

Company Board of Directors and Trustees

NIACE Dysgu Cymru Management Group

Sian Cartwright, Bryn Davies (Chair),
Viv Davies, Jeff Greenidge, Gerry Jenson,
Graham Price,
Prof. Danny Saunders, Dr Joan Smith,
Joanne Thomas, Alan Watkin,
Annie Williams (Vice Chair), Jane Williams

NIACE Staff, Departments and Email Addresses

Directorate

Director: Alan Tuckett
Director for Commission of Inquiry:
Tom Schuller
Director (CROW) Stephen McNair
Director for LLN and Workplace:
Carol Taylor
Director for Programmes and Policy:
Sue Meyer
Director for Research, Development and
Information: Peter Lavender
Director for Resources: Margaret Conner
Director for Wales: Richard Spear
Associate Director (Further Education):
Paul Mackney
Associate Director (ICT and Learning):
Alan Clarke
Associate Director (International):
Jan Eldred
Associate Director (Regions):
Mark Ravenhall

Business Development Unit

Development and Research Project
Co-ordinator: Dana McLaughlin
Fund Raising Officer: Gary Mawby
Fund Raising Support Assistant:
Steve Hartshorn

Research

Development Officer (Research):
Fiona Aldridge
Research Fellow (CROW): Tony Maltby
Senior Research Officer: Helen Plant
Research Officers: Lorraine Casey,
Rachel Spacey, Sara Bosley
Research Assistants: Hayley Lamb,
Lovemore Muchenje, Swati Nettleship
Commission of Inquiry Co-ordinator:
Hanya Gordon
Research Administrator: Emily Jones
Administrative Secretary: Sue Parkins

Campaigns and Promotions

Senior Campaigns Officer: Rachel Thomson
Press Officer: Ed Melia
Assistant Press Officer: Marie Koupparis
Marketing and Sales Officer: Shona Gibson
Regional Campaigns and Promotions
Manager: Jo Knight
Assistant Marketing Co-ordinator:
Victoria Thompson
Advocacy and Campaigns Officer:
Claire Clarke
Campaigns Assistants: Emma Cliffe,
Lucy Crowe
Assistant Campaigns Co-ordinator (LLN):
Claire Woodward
Campaigns Officer (ALW): Kamy Basra
Assistant Publicity Co-ordinator:
Barry Norris
Administrator (Awards): Lucy Herbert
South East Learning Co-ordinator:
Pauline Roussos
Campaigns Officer (LLN): Richard Crabb
Regions and Partnership Co-ordinator:
Raksha Mistry
Administrative Assistants: Allison Parkes,
Mariyam Sidik, Silvia Errington,
Gareth Laity

Email: alw@niace.org.uk

Community Learning

Senior Development Officer: Jane Ward
Development Officer (Quality Improvement): Kate Watters
Development Officer (Voluntary and Community Sector): Cheryl Turner
Lead Development Officer: Mick Murray
Senior Project Officer and Information Manager: Mandy Thomas
Administrative Co-ordinator: Hanako Beeson
Research Officer: Anthea Rose
Administrative Assistant: Rachel Hughes

Conferences, Seminars and Training Courses

Team Leader: Averil Coutinho
Senior Co-ordinator: Jane Cattell
Data Analyst: Richard Briggs
Senior Conference Organisers: Philippa Cattell, Celestine Harris, Carl Liquorish, Kate Howe
Conference Organisers: Joanne Barrett, Kajal Samat, Matthew Jones, Simon Hoza
Events Adminstrator: Raksha Kanani
Events Assistant: Natalie Ayres
Design Adminstrator: Karima Ejaz
Promotions and Publicity Adminstrators: Annabel Mwagalanyi
Conference Assistant: Gurjit Kaur
Administrative Assistant: Ursula Wallace
Packing Assistant: Lloyd Weaver

Email: conferences@niace.org.uk

Core Services

Finance
Director for Resources: Margaret Conner
Financial Controller: Gordon Proctor
Financial Accountant: Noeline Joseph
Assistant Financial Accountant: Zaffer Sumra
Project Accountants: Kumar Vyas, Bindi Rakhra
Assistant Project Accountant: Nafissa Burani
Project Assistant: Masood Shahid Ahmed
Finance Assistants: Akil Moledina, Birju Khunti, Christine Barry, Harshila Karaji, Tracey Siniane
Administrative Assistant: Juliana Hancock

Personnel
Corporate Services Manager: Catherine Potts
Senior HR Officer: Emma Hodgkinson
HR and Training Officer: David Naylor
HR Administrator: Laura Hayes
HR Adminstrative Assistant: Amy Tanner

Office Services
Facilities Manager: Martin McDonnell
Office Co-ordinator: Tracey Morris
Team Leader, Central Support: Amy Curtis
Facilities Co-ordinators: Graham Allen, Gordon Carnachan
Receptionists: Lois Ambler, Danika Foster, Robena Hanslod
Handymen: Geoff Hall, Ron Stevens

Credit and Qualifications

Development Officer: Peter Wilson
Administrator, UALL: Lucy Bate

Directorate Support Unit

Policy and Communications Officer: Helen Prew
Personal Assistants: Jenny Sherrard, Margaret Dunn, Amy Smyth
Member Liaison Administrator: Roger Marvin
Administrator: Funso Akande

Equalities and Migration

Senior Development Officer, Equalities: Joyce Black
Development Officer, Race Equality: Lenford White
Regional Development Officer (Equalities & Migration): Jane Watts
Project Officer (EQUAL): Ljaja Sterland
Development Officer: David Ewens
Project Administrator: Raxa Chauhan

Family Learning

Lead Development Officer: Penny Lamb
Project Officers: Clare Meade, Karen Fairfax-Cholmeley
Administrative Assistants: Clare Chisolm, Gill Aird

Financial Education

Head of Financial Literacy: Claire Robinson
Research Fellow: Howard Gannaway
Research Assistants: Suzi Challenger,
Rebecca Czechowicz
Development Officer: Leonora Miles
Administrative Assistants: Gill Aird,
Sadia Samed

Government, Advocacy, Members

Senior Policy Officer: Alastair Thomson
Policy Assistant: Lucia Quintero
Editor, Adults Learning: Paul Stanistreet
Administrator: Rachel Pierce

Health and Disability Equality

Development Officer (Learning Difficulties):
Yola Jacobsen
Development Officer (Learning Difficulties):
Viv Berkeley
Development Officer (Learning and Health):
Kathryn James
Development Officer (General Projects):
David Ewens
Communications and Information Officer:
Liz Stevens
Research Assistant: Caroline Law
Administrators: Bhupinder Nijjar, Sue Rees
Secretarial Assistant: Anne Agius

ICT and Learning

Associate Director for ICT and Learning:
Alan Clarke
Personal Assistant to the Associate Director:
Linda Faulkner
Senior Development Officer: Alastair Clark
Development Officers: Eta De Cicco,
Angela Sanders, Mary Moss, Patsy Quinn
Senior Project Officers: Sally Betts,
Susan Easton, Ali Close, Barbara Nance
Project Officers: Jackie Essom,
Lisa Englebright,
Shubhanna Hussain-Ahmed, Claudia Hesse,
Ewa Luger
Communications Officer:
Gemma Hammond

Research Assistants: Munira Arkate,
Sarah Perry, Simon Sheldrake, Sonya Bovell,
Tracy Slawson
Administrator/Research Assistants:
Ian Pettit, Stephen Walker
Administrative Assistants: Delona Sweeney,
Leahnie Bennett, David Newman
Secretarial Assistants: Susan Charlish,
Odelle Lewis
IT Technicians: Ian Ball, Aidan Whiterow

Information Services

IT Manager: Kevin Stevens
Network Operations Manager:
Anthony Ludlow
IT Trainers: Louise Hill, Steve Bott
IT Project Officers: Mike Broadhurst,
Russell Oldham
Website Co-ordinator: Phil Hughes
Web Developer: Dan Seagrave
Database Developer: Mick Hardy
PC Helpdesk Support: Scott Clements
IT (E-Learning) Technician: Ian Ball,
Aidan Whiterow
IT Apprentices: Ashley Aldwinckle,
Jamie Clements
Administrative Assistant: Neil Goodall
Librarian: Helen Kruse
Information Co-ordinator: Andy Kail
Information Officers: Kathryn Butler,
Alison Gundle, Carolyn Winkless,
Dee Whitaker
Clerical Assistant: Sue Allen
Database Administrator: Clare Newton
Database Assistant: Harmandeep Kaur

Email: information@niace.org.uk

International

Development Officer (European Policies):
Sue Waddington

Literacy, Language and Numeracy

Senior Assistant Directors: Brenda Ainsley, Jenny Cobley, Lynn Carpenter, Sue Nicholson
Assistant Directors: Miriam Sampson, Martin Rose, Ned Ratcliffe
Senior Development Officer, Equalities: Joyce Black
Development Officer (Basic Skills): Chris Taylor
Development Officer (Basic Skills, Army): Paul Yarrien
Development Officers (CPD for Faith Leaders): Annette Williamson, Derek Owens-Rawle
Development Officer (Dyslexia): Rachel Davies
Development Officer (Literacy, Numeracy and ESOL): Sue Southwood
Development Officer (Literacy, Language and Numeracy): Anita Hallam
Development Officers (Workplace): Anne Hansen
Senior Project Officer: Susan Quinn (HMPS)
Project Officers: Linda Dixon, Robert Gray, Sally Croft, Alistair Lockhart-Smith
Personal Assistant: Amy Smyth
Research Assistant: Emily Bowman
Administrative Co-ordinator: Sarah Wright
Administrators: Jacqueline Kemp, Jasbinder Sangha
Administrative Assistants: Euphemia Mupinga, Rebecca Czechowicz
Secretarial Assistants: Emma Tierney, Hazel Power
Project Administrator: Annette Williamson

Publications

Head of Publications: David Shaw
Senior Publications Editor: Alec McAulay
Production Editors: Paul Hammonds, Sarah Bennett
Administrator: Cory Schouten
Assistant Marketing Co-ordinator: Michael Lyden

Email: publications@niace.org.uk

Regions

Associate Director (Regions): Mark Ravenhall
Senior Regional Development Officer (Development and Research): Jane Ward
Regional Development Officer (North East): Patricia Whaley
Regional Development Officer (South West): Simon Mauger
Regional Development Officer (London): Judith Gawn
Regional Development Officer (London): Simon Beer
Regional Development Officer (Eastern): Sue O'Gorman
Regional Development Officer (South East): Jenny Williams
Regional Development Officer (Midlands): Ian Yarroll
Regional Development Officer for Language, Literacy and Numeracy (North East/Yorkshire and Humberside): Jan Novitzky
Regional Development Officer for Language, Literacy and Numeracy (Midlands): Anne O'Grady
Regional Development Officer (Yorkshire and Humberside): John Lawton
Regional Development Officer (North West): Marie Kerwin
Regional Development Officer (Projects): Pamela Lumsden
Regional Programme Officer for Mental Health (East of England): Catina Barrett
Regional Programme Officer for Mental Health (North West): Clare Worrall
Regional Programme Officer for Mental Health (South East): Jenny Gartland
Regional Programme Officer for Mental Health (West Midlands): Lesley Talbot-Strettle
Regional Programme Officer for Mental Health (Yorkshire & Humberside): Tricia Clark
Regional Programme Officer for Mental Health (London): Victoria Sturdy
Regional Project Officer for Mental Health (North East): Ann Creed
Regional Project Officer for Mental Health (East Midlands): Carol Anne Taylor

Regional Project Officer for Mental Health (South West): Lin Westmoreland
Research Officer (Article 6): Kate Kelsey
Administrative Co-ordinator: Hanako Beeson
Administrator: James Tullett
Administrative Support: Catherine Dunn
Administrative Assistant: Farhat Majid

Workplace Learning

Development Officer: Anne Hansen
Research Assistant: Emily Bowman

Young Adult Learners' Partnership (YALP)

Development Officer: Bethia McNeil
Projects Officer: Nicola Aylward
Administrator: Clare Holland

NIACE Dysgu Cymru

Director for Wales: Richard Spear
Campaigns Officer: Kay Smith
Regional Co-ordinator (North Wales): Rachel Jones
Regional Agent: Essex Havard
Senior Campaigns Officer: Rhydian Thomas
Project and Policy Officer: Jenny Mackay
Development Officer: Cerys Furlong
Senior Project Officer (Older and Bolder): Eirwen Malin
Project Worker (Digital Storytelling): John Morris
Administration and Information Assistant (Older Learners): Rachel Lewis
Office Manager: Wendy Ellaway-Lock
Web and Communications Assistant: Stephen Martin
Administrative Assistants: Holly Barratt, Steve Johnson

Email: enquiries@niacedc.org.uk

NIACE Membership

NIACE is an independent membership body. The membership comprises corporate organisations, who are education providers or agencies concerned with adult learning, as well as individual members who work within adult learning fields, on a paid or unpaid basis. Honorary life members are given their honorary status because of their commitment to, and work for adult learners. The Company of Members holds an Annual General Meeting and one other general meeting each year. In addition, there are two open Assembly meetings each year to debate matters of educational policy and practice. All LEAs are members of NIACE, which receives support from local authorities through top-sliced Rate Support Grant. The following organisations are in membership of the Institute:

Adult and Community Education

ACE Adult Community Education Wigan Ltd; Adult College Lancaster; Adult College of Barking and Dagenham; Bolton Community College; Bromley Adult Education College; Choices 4 All; Coleg Harlech WEA (North Wales); Comberton Village College; County Durham Learning; Derbyshire Learning and Development Consortium; East London Advanced Technology Training; The Elthorne Learning Centre; Foleshill Women's Training; Hampstead Garden Suburb Institute; Kent Adult Education Service; The Mary Ward Centre; Medway Adult Learning Service; Merton Adult Education; Nash College of Further Education; Open Doors Cumbria; Oxfordshire Adult Learning; Redbridge Institute of Adult Education; Richmond Adult Community College; RMET Ruskin Mill College; Southend Adult Community College; Sutton College of Learning for Adults; Swarthmore Education Centre; Thurrock Adult Community College; Walsall College of Continuing Education; Westminster Adult Education Service; Workers' Educational Association; Workers' Educational Association South Wales

Awarding Bodies

City & Guilds; Edexcel; FAVA; National Open College Network; Open College of the North West; Open College Network Wales; Open College Network Yorkshire and Humber Region

Educational and Allied Organisations

Art Shape; Arts Council of England; Arts Council of Wales; Association for Education and Ageing; Association of Teachers of Lipreading to Adults; British Association for Literacy in Development; Campaign for Learning; Centre for Enterprise; Church of England Education Division; Crewe and Nantwich Lifelong Learning Partnership; Cyfanfyd; E-mpirical Ltd.; Employers' Forum on Age; Foundation for Community Dance; Granada Learning; Home Learning College; Kalyx Services; Learning and Skills Network (LSN); Learning South West; Life Academy; MacIntyre; McKenley-Simpson Ltd; The Marine Society and Sea Cadets; National Extension College; National Maritime Museum; National Youth Agency; Nautical Archaelogy Society; Open and Distance Learning Quality Council; Open College of the Arts; Open Doors International Language School; Skill: National Bureau for Students with Disabilities; Southwark Muslim Women's Association; (TWICS) Training for Work in Communities; YMCA George Williams College

Further Education

Association of Colleges; Barking College; Barnet College; Barnsley College; Bedford College; Blackburn College; Bournemouth and Poole College; Bracknell and Wokingham College; Bradford College; Bridgend College; Brooklands College; Brooksby Melton College; Burnley College; Burton College; Cambridge Regional College; Chichester College; City and Islington College; City College Brighton & Hove; City College Norwich; City Lit; City of Bath College; City of Bristol College; City of Wolverhampton College; Colchester Institute; Coleg Glan Hafren; Coleg Gwent; Coleg Meirion-Dwyfor; Coleg Menai; Coleg Morgannwg; Coleg Powys; Coleg Sir Gâr;

College of North East London; College of West Anglia; Croydon College; Dearne Valley College; Deeside College; Derby College; Doncaster College; Ealing, Hammersmith and West London College; East Surrey College; Exeter College; FFORWM; Franklin College; Gloucestershire College of Arts and Technology; Gorseinon College; Greenwich Community College; Guildford College of Further and Higher Education; Hackney Community College; Harrow College; Herefordshire College of Technology; Hereward College; Hull College; Huntingdonshire Regional College; Isle of Man College; Kensington and Chelsea College; Leeds Thomas Danby; Leicester College; Lewisham College; Llandrillo College; Loughborough College; Milton Keynes College; Morley College; National Star College; Neath Port Talbot College; New College Durham; New College Telford; Newbury College; North East Worcestershire College; North Warwickshire and Hinckley College; Northampton College; Oaklands College; The Oldham College; Park Lane College; Pembrokeshire College; Peterborough Regional College; Redbridge College; Redcar & Cleveland College; Riverside College Halton; Rotherham College of Arts and Technology; Royal National College for the Blind; Salford College; Shipley College; Solihull College; South Birmingham College; South Leicestershire College; South Thames College; Southgate College; Southwark College; Stafford College; Stockton Riverside College; Stroud College in Gloucestershire; Suffolk New College; Telford College of Arts & Technology; Trafford College; Tower Hamlets College; Truro and Penwith College; Tyne Metropolitan College; Warrington Collegiate; Warwickshire College; West Suffolk College; Westminster-Kingsway College; Worcester College of Technology; Working Men's College; Yale College; York College; Ystrad Mynach College

Government and Publicly Funded National Bodies

Birmingham and Solihull Mental Health Trust; Becta; Hertfordshire Learning and Skills Council; The Home Office; Learning and Skills Council; Learning Connections; Local Government Association; Ministry of Defence (Navy); NHS, Yorkshire and the Humber; Office for Standards in Education, Children's Services and Skills; Rampton Hospital; Scottish Further Education Unit; Tees, Esk and Wear Valleys NHS Trust; Welsh Joint Education Committee; Welsh Local Government Association

Higher Education

Bangor University; Birkbeck College; Cardiff University; GuildHE; London South Bank University; Manchester Metropolitan University; Northumbria University; The Open University; Open University Students Association; Sheffield Hallam University; Staffordshire University; Standing Conference on University Teaching and Research in the Education of Adults (SCUTREA); Universities Association for Lifelong Learning (UALL); Universities UK; University of Bradford; University of Cambridge; University of Chichester; University of Cumbria; University of East Anglia; University of Hull; University of Leeds; University of Leicester; University of Northampton; University of Nottingham; University of Oxford; University of Reading; University of Sunderland; University of Sussex; University of Teeside; University of Wales, Aberystwyth; University of Wales Institute, Cardiff (UWIC); University of Wales, Lampeter; University of Wales Swansea; University of Warwick; University of Wolverhampton; University of York; Waterford Institute of Technology

Learning Guidance

CRAC: The Career Development Organisation; Future Prospects; Nextstep London; Prospects Services Ltd; Skillset

Media

BBC Learning; Channel Four Television (Education); Granada Learning; OFCOM; Tribal Learning and Publishing; Voice of the Listener and Viewer

Residential Education

Adult Residential Colleges Association; Alston Hall College; Co-operative College Trust; Denman College; Dillington House; Fircroft College; Hillcroft College; Northern College; Residential Colleges Committee; Ruskin College

Voluntary and Community Organisations

TAEN – The Age and Employment Network; Centrepoint; The Bridge Project; The Connection at St Martins; DEA; The Disabled People's Electronic Village Hall; Educational Centres Association; Learning Plus; Lifeline Community Projects; Linkage Community Trust; NATECLA; National Federation of Women's Institutes; Opening Doors Cumbria; Pembrokeshire Association of Voluntary Services; Pre-School Learning Alliance; Preston Road Neighbourhood Development Company; South Craven Community Action; SOVA Head Office; Third Age Trust.

Workplace-led Learning

Accounting for Safety Ltd; Creating Careers Ltd; DC Accountancy Services Ltd; FDA; Ford EDAP; GMB Learning; M-R College; Partnerships London Region; Joint Society of Business Practitioners and Managing and Marketing Association; Learning Skills Wales – Dysgu'r Ddawn Cymru; Public and Commercial Services Union; South East London Lifelong Learning Network; South West Lifelong Learning Network; UCU University and College Union; UfI Ltd.; Unionlearn; UNISON; ViSTA; Workforce Solutions Ltd

For further details concerning NIACE membership:
Email: members@niace.org.uk

Government

Central Government

Government Departments

Department for Innovation, Universities and Skills
66–74 Victoria Street
London SW1E 6SW
Tel: 020 7215 5555
Website: www.dius.gov.uk
Secretary of State for Innovation,
Universities and Skills:
The Rt Hon John Denham MP
Minister of State for Science and Innovation:
Lord Drayson
Minister of State for Higher Education and
Intellectual Property: David Lammy MP
Parliamentary Under Secretary of State for
Further Education: Siôn Simon MP
Parliamentary Under Secretary of State for
Skills and Apprenticeships: Lord Young

Department for Children, Schools and Families
Sanctuary Buildings
Great Smith Street
London SW1P 3BT
Tel: 0870 000 2288
Website: www.dcsf.gov.uk
Secretary of State for Children, Schools and
Families: The Rt Hon Ed Balls MP
Minister of State for Schools and Learners:
Jim Knight MP
Minister of State for Children, Young People
and Families:
The Rt Hon Beverley Hughes MP
Parliamentary Under Secretary of State for
Schools and Learners:
Sarah McCarthy-Fry MP
Parliamentary Under Secretary of State for
Children, Young People and Families:
Baroness Delyth Morgan

Department for Work and Pensions
Richmond House
79 Whitehall
London SW1A 2NS
Website: www.dwp.gov.uk
Secretary of State for Work and Pensions:
The Rt Hon James Purnell MP
Minister of State for Employment and
Welfare Reform:
The Rt Hon Tony McNulty MP
Minister of State for Pensions and the
Ageing Society:
The Rt Hon Rosie Winterton MP
Minister for Disabled People:
Jonathan Shaw MP
Parliamentary Under Secretary of State
(Commons): Kitty Ussher MP
Parliamentary Under Secretary of State
(Lords): Lord McKenzie of Luton

Department for Business, Enterprise and Regulatory Reform
1 Victoria Street
London SW1H 0ET
Tel: 020 7215 5000
Website: www.berr.gov.uk
Secretary of State for Business, Enterprise
and Regulatory Reform:
The Rt Hon Lord Mandelson

Cabinet Office
70 Whitehall
London SW1A 2AS
Tel: 020 7276 1234
Website: www.cabinetoffice.gov.uk
Minister for the Cabinet Office and
Chancellor of the Duchy of Lancaster:
Liam Byrne MP
Parliamentary Secretary (Minister for the
Third Sector): Kevin Brennan MP
Parliamentary Secretary: Tom Watson MP
Minister for Economic Competitiveness and
Small Businesses: Baroness Vadera
Minister of State for the Olympics and
London: The Rt Hon Tessa Jowell MP

Department for Communities and Local Government
Eland House
Bressenden Place
London SW1E 5DU
Tel: 020 7944 4400
Website: www.communities.gov.uk
Secretary of State for Communities and
Local Government: Hazel Blears MP
Minister for Local Government:
John Healey MP
Minister for Housing, attending Cabinet:
Margaret Beckett MP
Parliamentary Under Secretary of State:
Ian Wright MP
Parliamentary Under Secretary of State:
Sadiq Khan MP
Parliamentary Under Secretary of State:
Baroness Kay Andrews OBE

Department for Culture, Media and Sport
2–4 Cockspur Street
London SW1Y 5DH
Tel: 020 7211 6000
Email: enquiries@culture.gov.uk
Website: www.culture.gov.uk
Secretary of State for Culture, Media and
Sport: The Rt Hon Andy Burnham MP
Minister for Culture, Creative Industries and
Tourism: Barbara Follett MP
Minister for Sport: Gerry Sutcliffe MP
Minister for Communications, Technology
& Broadcasting: Baron Carter of Barnes CBE

Ministry of Defence
Main Building
Whitehall
London SW1A 2HB
Tel: 020 7218 9000
Website: www.mod.uk
Secretary of State for Defence:
The Rt Hon John Hutton MP

Ministry of Defence (Army)
ETS3 SO2 Ed Dev at HQ DETS (A)
Trenchard Lines
Upavon, Pewsey
Wiltshire SN9 6BE
Tel: 01980 618701 or 618730
Fax: 01980 618705
Email: enquiries@detsa.co.uk
Director of Educational and Training
Services (Army): Brigadier A W E Brister

Ministry of Defence (Navy)
Naval Training and Education
Mail Point 3.4, Leach Building
Whale Island
Portsmouth PO2 8BY
Tel: 023 9262 5687
Fax: 023 9262 5736
Email: issy.emery979@mod.uk
ACOS Naval Training and Education

Ministry of Defence (Royal Air Force)
Headquarters Training Group Defence
Agency
Learning Forces (Room S84)
Royal Air Force Innsworth
Gloucester GL3 1EZ
Tel: 01452 712612
Fax: 01452 510854
Email: sllf@learning-forces.org.uk
Website: www.learning-forces.org.uk
Training Development Policy: Squadron
Leader, Learning Forces

Department of Energy and Climate Change
3–8 Whitehall Place
London SW1A 2HH
Tel: 0300 060 4000
Website: www.decc.gov.uk
Secretary of State for Energy and Climate
Change: The Rt Hon Ed Miliband MP

Department for Environment, Food and Rural Affairs
Nobel House
17 Smith Square
London SW1P 3JR
Tel: 020 7238 6000
Helpline Tel: 0845 933 5577
Fax: 020 7238 6591
Email: helpline@defra.gsi.gov.uk
Website: www.defra.gov.uk
Secretary of State for Environment, Food
and Rural Affairs:
The Rt Hon Hilary Benn MP

Foreign and Commonwealth Office
King Charles Street
London SW1A 2AH
Tel: 020 7008 1500
Website: www.fco.gov.uk
Secretary of State for Foreign and
Commonwealth Affairs:
The Rt Hon David Miliband MP

Department of Health
Richmond House
79 Whitehall
London SW1A 2NS
Website: www.dh.gov.uk
Tel: 020 7210 4850
Email: dhmail@dh.gsi.gov.uk
Website: www.dh.gov.uk
Secretary of State for Health:
The Rt Hon Alan Johnson MP

Home Office
2 Marsham Street
London SW1P 4DF
Tel: 020 7035 4848
Email:
public.enquiries@homeoffice.gsi.gov.uk
Website: www.homeoffice.gov.uk
Home Secretary:
The Rt Hon Jacqui Smith MP

Department for International Development
1 Palace Street
London SW1E 5HE
Tel: 0845 300 4100
Email: enquiry@dfid.gov.uk
Website: www.dfid.gov.uk
Secretary of State for International
Development:
The Rt Hon Douglas Alexander MP

Ministry of Justice
Selbourne House
54 Victoria Street
London SW1E 6QW
Tel: 020 7210 8500
Email: general.queries@justice.gsi.gov.uk
Website: www.justice.gov.uk
Secretary of State for Justice and
Lord Chancellor:
The Rt Hon Jack Straw MP

Northern Ireland Office
11 Millbank
London SW1P 4PN
Tel: 028 9052 0700
Website: www.nio.gov.uk
Secretary of State for Northern Ireland:
The Rt Hon Shaun Woodward MP

Scotland Office
Dover House
Whitehall
London SW1A 2AU
Tel: 020 7270 6754
Website: www.scotlandoffice.gov.uk
Secretary of State for Scotland:
The Rt Hon Jim Murphy MP

Department of Transport
Great Minster House
76 Marsham Street
London SW1P 4DR
Tel: 020 7944 8300
Website: www.dft.gov.uk
Secretary of State for Transport:
The Rt Hon Geoff Hoon MP

HM Treasury
1 Horseguards Road
London SW1A 2HQ
Tel: 020 7270 5000
Email: public.enquiries@hm-treasury.gov.uk
Website: www.hm-treasury.gov.uk
Chancellor of the Exchequer:
The Rt Hon Alastair Darling MP

Wales Office
Gwydyr House
Whitehall
London SW1A 2ER
Tel: 020 7270 0534
Email: wales.office@walesoffice.gsi.gov.uk
Website: www.walesoffice.gov.uk
Secretary of State for Wales:
The Rt. Hon. Paul Murphy MP

Other Government Offices and Public Bodies

COI Communications
Hercules House
Hercules Road
London SE1 7DU
Tel: 020 7928 2345
Fax: 020 7928 5037
Website: www.coi.gov.uk

Equality and Human Rights Commission
3 More London
Riverside Tooley Street
London SE1 2RG
Tel: 020 3117 0235
Email: info@equalityhumanrights.com
Website: www.equalityhumanrights.com
Chair: Trevor Philips
Chief Executive: Dr Nicola Brewer

UK Statistics Authority
Cardiff Road
Newport
South Wales NP10 8XG
Tel: 0845 601 3034
Fax: 01633 652747
Email: info@statistics.gov.uk
Website: www.statistics.gov.uk

Local Government

Local Government Association (LGA)
Local Government House
Smith Square
London SW1P 3HZ
Tel: 020 7664 3000
Fax: 020 7664 3030
Website: www.lga.gov.uk
Chief Executive: Paul Coen
Elected Member: Cllr. Graham Lane

The LGA represents local councils in England and Wales, and is the single voice for local government in representing views to government, the media and other organisations. It serves the interests of those elected to represent local communities as well as the officials who work to provide the services to residents, voluntary organisations and businesses on which they rely. The LGA promotes better local government and advocates the provision of high quality educational services in the cities, towns and rural areas of the UK, stressing the importance in a civilised society of lifelong learning opportunities that can enhance the quality of life for citizens of all ages.

Government Offices for the Regions

Government Office for the North East
Citygate
Gallowgate
Newcastle upon Tyne NE1 4WH
Tel: 0191 202 3300
Fax: 0191 202 3998
Email: jackie.doughty@gone.gsi.gov.uk
Website: www.go-ne.gov.uk
Director, Children and Learners:
Jackie Doughty

Government Office for the North West
City Tower
Piccadilly Plaza
Manchester M1 4BE
Tel: 0161 952 4000
Fax: 0161 952 4099
Website: www.gos.gov.uk/gonw
Director, Children and Learners:
Nigel Burke

Government Office for Yorkshire and the Humber
Lateral
8 City Walk
Leeds
West Yorkshire LS11 9AT
Tel: 0113 341 3000
Email: yhenquiries@goyh.gsi.gov.uk
Website: www.goyh.gov.uk
Regional Director: Felicity Everiss
Email: feveriss.goyh@go-regions.gov.uk
Director, Children and Learners:
Helen McMullen

Government Office for the West Midlands
5 St Philips Place
Colmore Row
Birmingham B3 2PW
Tel: 0121 352 5050
Email: enquiries.team@gowm.gsi.gov.uk
Website: www.gos.gov.uk/gowm
Director, Children and Learners:
Clive Wilkinson

Government Office for the East Midlands
The Belgrave Centre
Stanley Place
Talbot Street
Nottingham NG1 5GG
Tel: 0115 971 9971
Fax: 0115 971 2404
Email: enquiries@goem.gsi.gov.uk
Website: www.goem.gov.uk

Government Office for the East of England
Eastbrook
Shaftesbury Road
Cambridge CB2 8DF
Tel: 01223 372500
Email: enquiries.goeast@goeast.gsi.gov.uk
Website: www.go-east.gov.uk
Director, Children and Learners:
Hilary Cooper

Government Office for the South West
2 Rivergate
Temple Quay
Bristol BS1 6EH
Tel: 0117 900 1700
Fax: 0117 900 1900
Website: www.gosw.gov.uk

Government Office for the South East
Bridge House
1 Walnut Tree Close
Guildford
Surrey GU1 4GA
Tel: 01483 882255
Fax: 01483 882259
Website: www.gose.gov.uk
Director, Children and Learners:
Peter Weston

Government Office for London
Riverwalk House
157–161 Millbank
London SW1P 4RR
Tel: 020 7217 3151
Fax: 020 7217 3036
Website: www.gos.gov.uk/gol
Director, Children and Learners:
Jennifer Izekor

Regional Development Agencies

One North East
Stella House
Goldcrest Way
Newburn Riverside
Newcastle upon Tyne NE15 8NY
Tel: 0191 229 6200
Fax: 0191 229 6201
Email: enquiries@onenortheast.co.uk
Website: www.onenortheast.co.uk
Chairman: Margaret Fay OBE
Chief Executive: Alan Clarke

North West Development Agency
PO Box 37
Renaissance House
Centre Park
Warrington WA1 1XB
Tel: 01925 400100
Fax: 01925 400151
Email: info@nwda.co.uk
Website: www.nwda.co.uk
Chairman: Bryan Gray
Chief Executive: Steven Broomhead
Executive Director, Enterprise and
Development: Mark Hughes

Yorkshire Forward
Victoria House
2 Victoria Place
Leeds
West Yorkshire LS11 5AE
Tel: 0113 394 9600
Fax: 0113 243 1088
Email:
helen.thomson@yorkshire-forward.com
Website: www.yorkshire-forward.com
Chairman: Terry Hodgkinson
Chief Executive: Tom Riordan
Regional Learning and Skills Manager:
Ruth Adams

Advantage West Midlands
3 Priestley Wharf
Holt Street
Aston Science Park
Birmingham B7 4BN
Tel: 0121 380 3500
Fax: 0121 380 3501
Website: www.advantagewm.co.uk
Chairman: Nick Paul
Chief Executive: Mick Laverty

East Midlands Development Agency
Apex Court
City Link
Nottingham NG2 4LA
Tel: 0115 988 8300
Fax: 0115 853 3666
Email: info@emd.org.uk
Website: www.emda.org.uk
Chairman: Bryan Jackson OBE
Chief Executive: Jeff Moore
Director of Executive Business Services:
Michael Carr

East of England Development Agency
The Business Centre
Station Road
Histon
Cambridge CB4 9LQ
Tel: 01223 713900
Fax: 01223 713940
Email: knowledge@eeda.org.uk
Website: www.eeda.org.uk
Chief Executive: Deborah Cadman
Chair: Richard Ellis
Executive Director, Skills and Economic
Participation: Alison Webster

South West of England Regional Development Agency
Sterling House
Dix's Field
Exeter
Devon EX1 1QA
Tel: 01392 214747
Fax: 01392 214848
Email: enquiries@southwestrda.org.uk
Website: www.southwestrda.org.uk
Chairman: Juliet Williams
Chief Executive: Jane Henderson
Executive Director, People and Skills:
Suzanne Bond

South East England Development Agency
SEEDA Headquarters
Cross Lanes
Guildford
Surrey GU1 1YA
Tel: 01483 484200
Fax: 01483 484247
Email: seeda@seeda.co.uk
Website: www.seeda.co.uk
Chairman: James Brathwaite CBE

London Development Agency
Palestra
197 Blackfriars Road
London SE1 8AA
Tel: 020 7593 9000
Fax: 020 7593 8001
Email: info@lda.gov.uk
Website: www.lda.gov.uk
Chair: Harvey McGrath

National Education Agencies

Learning and Skills Council
Cheylesmore House
Quinton Road
Coventry
West Midlands CV1 2WT
Website: www.lsc.gov.uk
Chair: Chris Banks
Chief Executive: Mark Haysom

Detailed entry in the Learning and Skills
Council and Inspection chapter
(see page 18)

Higher Education Funding Council for England (HEFCE)
Northavon House
Coldharbour Lane
Bristol BS16 1QD
Tel: 0117 931 7317
Fax: 0117 931 7203
Email: hefce@hefce.ac.uk
Website: www.hefce.ac.uk
Chairman: Tim Melville-Ross CBE
Chief Executive: Prof. David Eastwood
Director, Education and Participation:
Dr John Selby

Office for Fair Access
Northavon House
Coldharbour Lane
Bristol BS16 1QD
Tel: 0117 931 7171
Fax: 0117 931 7479
Email: enquiries@offa.org.uk
Website: www.offa.org.uk
Director: Sir Martin Harris
Assistant Director: David Barrett
Operations and Research Manager:
Jean Arnold

The Office for Fair Access (OFFA) is an
independent, non departmental public body
which aims to promote and safeguard fair
access to higher education for
under-represented groups in light of the
introduction of variable tuition fees in
2006–07.

**Office for Standards in Education,
Children's Services and Skills**
Alexandra House
33 Kingsway
London WC2B 6SE
Tel: 0845 640 4045
Email: enquiries@ofsted.gov.uk
Website: www.ofsted.gov.uk
HM Chief Inspector of Schools (England):
Christine Gilbert
Divisional Manager Post-Sixteen:
John Landeryou

Qualifications and Curriculum Authority
83 Piccadilly
London W1J 8QA
Tel: 020 7509 5555
Fax: 020 7509 6975
Website: www.qca.org.uk
Chairman: Sir Anthony Greener
Email: greenera@qca.org.uk
Chief Executive: Dr Ken Boston AO

**Quality Assurance Agency for
Higher Education**
Southgate House
Southgate Street
Gloucester GL1 1UB
Tel: 01452 557000
Fax: 01452 557070
Email: comms@qaa.ac.uk
Website: www.qaa.ac.uk
Chairman: Sam Younger
Chief Executive: Peter Williams

**UK Commission for Employment and
Skills (UKCES)**
3 Callflex Business Park
Golden Smithies Lane
Wath-upon-Dearne
Rotherham
South Yorkshire S63 7ER
Tel: 01709 774800
Fax: 01709 774801
Email: info@ukces.org.uk
Website: www.uckes.org.uk
Chief Executive: Chris Humphries

Other Publicly Funded National Bodies

Becta
Milburn Hill Road
Science Park
Coventry
West Midlands CV4 7JJ
Tel: 024 7641 6994
Fax: 024 7641 1418
Email: becta@becta.org.uk
Website: www.becta.org.uk
Chief Executive: Stephen Crowne

Learning and Skills Network (LSN)
Regent Arcade House
19–25 Argyll Street
London W1F 7LS
Tel: 020 7297 9000
Fax: 020 7297 9001
Email: enquiries@lsneducation.org.uk
Website: www.lsneducation.org.uk
Chief Executive: John Stone

Learning and Skills Improvement Service (LSIS)
Friars House
Manor House Drive
Coventry CV1 2TE
Tel: 0870 1620 632
Fax: 0870 1620 633
Email: info@lsis.org.uk
Website: www.lsis.org.uk
Chair: Dame Ruth Silver
Chief Executive: Roger McClure

The Learning and Skills Improvement Service (LSIS) came into operation on 1 October 2008. Combining the best aspects of two different and highly successful sector bodies – the Centre for Excellence in Leadership (CEL) and the Quality Improvement Agency (QIA) – LSIS will focus on learners and on developing excellent and sustainable further education and skills provision across the sector. Leadership development will underpin and form an important part of the organisation's strategic role in the sector.

LSIS was established after consultations with sector leaders identified a strong desire for an organisation that would be sector-led. As a sector-owned public body, LSIS will be owned, directed and governed by FE and skills colleges and providers, and will be dedicated to supporting excellence, leadership development and self-regulation in the FE sector.

LSIS will be consulting with the sector during autumn 2008 and spring 2009 about its priorities and remit. While this is taking place, the activities and services of CEL and QIA will continue under joint branding; more information about their range of activities is available on their respective websites.

Ufi Ltd
Dearing House
1 Young Street
Sheffield S1 4UP
Tel: 0114 291 5000
Fax: 0114 291 5001
Website: www.ufi.com
Chief Executive: Sarah Jones
Executive Director: Pablo Lloyd
Chairman: John Weston

Learning and Skills Council and Inspection – England

Learning and Skills Council

Learning and Skills Council
Cheylesmore House
Quinton Road
Coventry
West Midlands CV1 2WT
Website: www.lsc.gov.uk
Chair: Chris Banks
Chief Executive: Mark Haysom
National Director – Strategy,
Communications and Learning: Rob Wye
National Director of Skills: David Way
Director of Resources Group: David Russell

Regional Directors:
Regional Director, North East:
Chris Roberts
Tel: 0191 492 6351
Email: chris.roberts@lsc.gov.uk

Regional Director, North West:
John Korzeniewski
Tel: 0161 261 0533
Email: john.korzeniewski@lsc.gov.uk

Regional Director, Yorkshire and
Humberside: Margaret Coleman
Tel: 01274 444100
Email: margaret.coleman@lsc.gov.uk

Regional Director, West Midlands:
David Cragg
Tel: 0121 345 4543
Email: david.cragg@lsc.gov.uk

Regional Director, East Midlands:
Tom Crompton
Tel: 0116 228 1874
Email: tom.crompton@lsc.gov.uk

Regional Director, East of England:
Caroline Neville
Tel: 01473 883010
Email: caroline.neville@lsc.gov.uk

Regional Director, South East:
Marinos Paphitis
Tel: 0118 908 2149
marinos.paphitis@lsc.gov.uk

Regional Director, South West:
Malcolm Gillespie
Tel: 0117 372 6407
Email: malcolm.gillespie@lsc.gov.uk

Regional Director, London: David Hughes
Tel: 0207 904 0803
Email: david.hughes@lsc.gov.uk

Widening Adult Participation Team
Lifelong Learning Director: Louise Proctor
Tel: 024 7682 3484

Senior Policy Manager: Jerry O'Shea
Tel: 024 7682 3305

Senior Policy Manager: Karen Milner
Tel: 024 7682 3356

Senior Policy Manager: Ray Plummer
Tel: 024 7682 5603

Senior Policy Manager: Chris Jones
Tel: 024 7682 3326

Team Administrator: Charlotte Male
Tel: 024 7682 3326

Skills for Life Team
Employee Development Director:
Anne Jones
Tel: 024 7682 3572

Senior Policy Manager: Leigh Smith
Tel: 024 7682 3444

Senior Policy Manager: Jo Mylrea
Tel: 024 7682 5810

Policy Advisor: Peter Coady
Tel: 024 7682 5858

Team Administrator: Esther Tull
Tel: 024 7682 5735

The Learning and Skills Council (LSC) was established on 2 April 2001 and is responsible for funding and planning education and training for over 16-year-olds in England. This includes further education colleges; school sixth forms; work-based training for young people; workforce development; adult and community learning; information, advice and guidance for adults; and education links. It does not include the university sector. The LSC operates through a national office and 47 local arms. The LSC's key tasks, as set in the Secretary of State's remit letter of 9 November 2000 are:

- to raise participation and achievement by young people;
- to increase demand for learning by adults, and equalise opportunities through better access to learning;
- to engage employers in improving skills for employability and national competitiveness;
- to raise the quality of education and training delivery; and
- to improve effectiveness and delivery.

Regional Learning and Skills Councils

North East

Learning and Skills Council North East
Moongate House
5th Avenue Business Park
Team Valley
Gateshead
Tyne and Wear NE11 0HF
Tel: 0845 019 4181
Fax: 0191 492 6398
Email: tyneandwearinfo@lsc.gov.uk
Regional Director, North East:
Chris Roberts
Tel: 0845 019 4181
Director of Area North: John Wayman
Regional Director of Skills: Gillian Miller
Regional Director of Learning, Planning and Performance: Dorothy Smith
Regional Director of Financing and Resourcing: John Smith
Head of Marketing and Communications: Julie Calvert

North West

Learning and Skills Council North West
9th Floor, Arndale House
Arndale Centre
Manchester M4 3AQ
Tel: 0845 019 4142
Fax: 0161 261 0370
Email: GrManchesterinfo@lsc.gov.uk
Regional Director North West:
John Korzeniewski
Director of Area for Greater Manchester:
John Temple
Regional Director of Finance and Resourcing: Chris Griffin
Regional Director of Skills: Paul Holme
Regional Director of Learning, Planning and Performance: Jane Cowell
Director of Area, Lancashire: Ian Haworth
Director of Area, Greater Merseyside:
Helen France
Director of Area, Greater Manchester North: John Rawsthorne
Director of Area, Greater Manchester South: Jane Bracewell
Director of Area, Cheshire and Warrington: Liz Davis
Director of Area for Cumbria: Emer Clarke

Yorkshire and Humberside

Learning and Skills Council Yorkshire and the Humber
Mercury House
4 Mancester Road
Bradford BD5 0QL
Tel: 0845 019 4169
Fax: 01274 444005
Email: westyorkshireinfo@lsc.gov.uk
Regional Director: Margaret Coleman
Regional Director of Skills: David Hodges
Regional Director of Learning, Planning and Performance: Andy Brown
Regional Director of Finances and Resources: Karen Sherry
Director of Area , LSC North Yorkshire:
Liz Burdett
Director of Area, LSC The Humber:
Jane Lyon
Director of Area, LSC West Yorkshire:
Mike Lowe

Director of Area, LSC South Yorkshire:
Nick Wilson
Head of Marketing and Communications
LSC Yorkshire and Humber: Gary Rae

West Midlands

Learning and Skills Council
West Midlands
NT1 Building
15 Bartholomew Row
Birmingham
West Midlands B5 5JU
Tel: 0845 019 4143
Email: BirminghamSolihullInfo@lsc.org.uk
Regional Director: David Cragg
Area Director, Birmingham and Solihull:
Peter Brammall
Area Director, Black Country: Mike Bell
Area Director, Coventry and Warwickshire:
Kim Thorneywork
Area Director, Hereford and Worcestershire
and Shropshire: Sharon Gray
Area Director, Staffordshire:
Christine Doubleday

East Midlands

Learning and Skills Council
East Midlands
17a Meridian East
Meridian Business Park
Leicester LE19 1UU
Tel: 0845 019 4177
Email: eastmidlandsinfo@lsc.gov.uk
Regional Director East Midlands:
Tom Crompton
Regional Director Learning, Planning and
Performance: Paul Williamson
Regional Director of Skills:
Karen Woodward
Regional Director of Finance and Resources:
Peter Newson
Regional Director of Marketing and
Communications: Margaret Warren
Director of Area, Derbyshire and
Nottinghamshire: Mick Brown
Director of Area, Leicestershire:
Mary Rogers
Director of Area, Lincolnshire and Rutland:
Nick Rashley
Director of Area, Northamptonshire:
Liz Searle

Eastern

East of England Learning and
Skills Council
Felaw Maltings
42 Felaw Street
Ipswich IP2 8SJ
Tel: 0845 019 4108
Fax: 01473 883090
Regional Director: Caroline Neville
Regional Director of Skills: Laurie Kay
Regional Director of Finance and Resources:
Paul McGuire
Head of Marketing and Communications:
Val Cumberland
Area Director, Bedfordshire and Luton:
Suzie Webb
Area Director, Cambridgeshire: Dr Jon Noy
Area Director, Essex: Jackie Logie
Area Director, Hertfordshire: Liam Sammon
Area Director, Norfolk: Graham Brough
Area Director, Suffolk: Judith Mobbs

South West

Learning and Skills Council South West
St Lawrence House
29–31 Broad Street
Bristol BS99 7YJ
Tel: 0845 019 4168
Email: westofengland@lsc.gov.uk
Regional Director South West:
Malcolm Gillespie
Area Director, Devon, Cornwall and West of
England: John Chudley
Area Director, LSC South West: Trish Taylor

South East

Learning and Skills Council South East
Princes House
53 Queens Road
Brighton BN1 3BX
Tel: 01273 783555
Fax: 01273 783507
Email: info@lsc.gov.uk

Learning and Skills Council South East
Pacific House
Imperial Way
Reading RG2 0FT
Tel: 0845 019 4147
Fax: 0118 908 2109
Email: info@lsc.gov.uk
Regional Director: Marinos Paphitis
Regional Director of Skills: Peter Marsh
Regional Director of Learning Planning and
Performance: Sue Samson
Regional Director of Finances and
Resources: Pauline Tiller
Area Director, Thames Valley: Bob Walding
Area Director, Sussex and Surrey:
David Smith
Area Director, LSC Kent and Medway:
Tony Allen
Area Director, Hampshire and Isle of Wight:
Martin Lamb

London

Learning and Skills Council London Region
Centre Point
103 New Oxford Road
London WC1A 1DR
Tel: 0845 019 4144
Email: londoninfo@lsc.gov.uk
LSC London Regional Director:
David Hughes

Regional Director Regeneration:
Mary Conneely
Regional Director of Skills:
Philippa Langton
Regional Director of Learning, Planning and
Performance: Doug Norris
Area Director, LSC London West:
Clare Arnold
Area Director, LSC London South:
Vic Grimes
Area Director, LSC London Central:
Jill Lowery
Area Director, LSC London East:
Mike Pettifer
Area Director, LSC London North:
Mary Vine-Morris

Inspection

Office for Standards in Education, Children's Services and Skills
Alexandra House
33 Kingsway
London WC2B 6SE
Tel: 08456 404045
Email: enquiries@ofsted.gov.uk
Website: www.ofsted.gov.uk
HM Chief Inspector of Schools (England):
Christine Gilbert
Director, Learning and Skills: Melanie Hunt

Adult Education Development Organisations – England

National Adult Education Development Organisations

Adult Residential Colleges Association (ARCA)
6 Bath Road
Felixstowe
Suffolk IP11 7JW
Tel: 01394 278161
Fax: 01394 271083
Email: arcasec@aol.com
Website: www.arca.uk.net
Secretary: Janet Dann
Chair of ARCA: Lisa Railton

ARCA is a well-established association of residential colleges for adult education. Its members provide a wide range of short-stay courses for the general public. All share a professional approach to education in a residential setting and are wholeheartedly committed to the principle of "life-long learning"; learning for personal satisfaction and enjoyment.

Adults Learning Mathematics (ALM)
187 Stranmills Road
Belfast BT9 5EE
Tel: 028 9066 5878
Email: info@alm-online.org
Website: www.alm-online.net
Company Secretary: Valerie Seabright

Adults Learning Mathematics (ALM) is an international research forum bringing together researchers and practitioners in adult mathematics/numeracy teaching and learning, in order to promote the learning of mathematics by adults. ALM is a company limited by guarantee (No.3901346), registered in England and Wales and a registered charity (No.1079462). Its objectives are the advancement of education through the development of an international research forum in the lifelong learning of mathematics and numeracy by adults, through encouraging research into adults learning mathematics at all levels and disseminating the results of this research; promoting and sharing knowledge, awareness and understanding of adults learning mathematics at all levels, to encourage the development of the teaching of mathematics to adults at all levels, for the public benefit. ALM welcomes new members, and participation in its annual conferences.

AoC NILTA
2–5 Stedham Place
London WC1A 1HU
Tel: 020 7034 9900
Fax: 020 7034 9900
Website: www.aoc.co.uk
Policy and Practice Manager: John Perks
Senior Technology and E-Learning Officer: Matt Dean

A membership organisation that exists to represent and support those using new technologies in the provision of further education and lifelong learning.

Association for College Management
35 The Point
Market Harborough
Leicestershire LE16 7QU
Tel: 01858 461110
Fax: 01858 461366
Email: administration@acm.uk.com
Website: www.acm.uk.com
General Secretary/Chief Executive: Peter Pendle
Head of Policy: Nadine Cartner
Head of Employment Relations: David Green
Head of Corporate Services: Sara Shaw

The Association for College Management is a TUC affiliated trade union and professional association which represents managers of post-16 education and training.

Association for Learning Technology (ALT)
Gipsy Lane
Headington
Oxford OX3 0BP
Tel: 01865 484125
Fax: 01865 484165
Email: admin@alt.ac.uk
Website: www.alt.ac.uk
Chief Executive: Seb Schmoller
Director of Development:
Mark van Harmelen
Director of Operations: Marion Samler

ALT provides a website with contacts in UK universities, FE colleges and commercial and government organisations who are working on the application of technology in teaching and learning. It organises conferences and training events, responds to policy consultations and publishes a quarterly web and print-based newsletter, a tri-annual peer-reviewed journal, and books. ALT-C 2009 will take place in Manchester.

Association of Colleges (AoC)
2–5 Stedham Place
London WC1A 1HU
Tel: 020 7034 9900
Fax: 020 7034 9950
Email: enquiries@aoc.co.uk
Website: www.aoc.co.uk
Chief Executive: Martin Doel

AoC's role is to provide leadership within the new culture of lifelong learning. It lobbies for the resources its learners and colleges need.

Association of Learning Providers
Colenso House
46 Bath Hill
Keynsham
Bristol BS31 1HG
Tel: 0117 986 5389
Fax: 0117 986 6196
Website: www.learningproviders.org
Chairman: Martin Dunford
Chief Executive: Graham Hoyle

ALP represents providers of quality work-based and other vocational learning, and works with government and others, to develop and implement effective workforce development policies.

Becta
Millburn Hill Road
Science Park
Coventry
West Midlands CV4 7JJ
Tel: 024 7641 6994
Fax: 024 7641 1418
Email: becta@becta.org.uk
Website: www.becta.org.uk
Chief Executive: Stephen Crowne

Becta is a government agency leading the national drive to ensure the effective and innovative use of technology throughout learning. Its ambition is to utilise the benefits of technology to create a more exciting, rewarding and successful experience for learners of all ages and abilities, enabling them to achieve their potential.

The British Institute for Learning and Development
Trym Lodge
1 Henbury Road
Westbury-on-Crym
Bristol BS39 3HQ
Tel: 0117 959 6517
Fax: 0117 959 6518
Email: info@thebild.org
Website: www.thebild.org
Business Manager: Sarah Wills

The new British Institute for Learning and Development builds on the success of the British Learning Association and will address the needs and raise the status of all those involved in learning and development (both organisations and individuals). With a focus on professionalism and performance improvement, it will provide coherence to a sector that embraces corporate, work-based and lifelong learning and vocational training.

Campaign for Learning

19 Buckingham Street
London WC2N 6EF
Tel: 020 7930 1111
Fax: 020 7930 1551
Email: info@cflearning.org.uk
Website: www.campaign-for-learning.org.uk
Chair: Simon Fuchs
Chief Executive: Tricia Hartley

The Campaign for Learning is working for a society where:

- everyone has the right to learn
- everyone understands and values learning
- everyone has chances to learn throughout their lives.

It has existed since 1996, helping to stimulate learning which excites, supports, develops and involves people all through their lives.

Centre for Economic and Social Inclusion

3rd Floor, Camelford House
89 Albert Embankment
London
Tel: 020 7582 7221
Fax: 020 7582 6391
Email: info@cesi.org.uk
Website: www.cesi.org.uk
Director: Dave Simmonds
Directors: Craig Watt, Jo Casebourne

The Centre for Economic and Social Inclusion is the UK's leading not-for-profit company dedicated to tackling disadvantage and promoting social justice.

It delivers cutting-edge research and innovative policy solutions, organises and manages events, including conferences and training, and publishes policy e-briefings and the journal 'Working Brief'.

It offers research and policy services, tailored consultancy and bespoke and in-house training, running a wide range of conferences and events.

Its key areas of social policy expertise are welfare to work, learning and skills, regeneration, homelessness, criminal justice and social exclusion.

The Centre works with the government, the public sector, interest groups and business to develop policy and strategy, and to implement ideas.

Chartered Institute of Personnel and Development

151 The Broadway
London SW19 1JQ
Tel: 020 8612 6200
Email: cipd@cipd.co.uk
Website: www.cipd.co.uk
Chief Executive Officer: Jackie Orme

The Chartered Institute of Personnel and Development (CIPD) is the pre-eminent professional body in the field of people management and development with over 130,000 members. The Institute was formed from the Institute of Personnel Management and the Institute of Training and Development, which were united on 1 July 1994. It received its Royal Charter in July 2000. The CIPD offers a wide range of services including over 130 training events, various levels of membership, a professional education scheme, books, consultancy and a full library and information service.

Citizens Advice

Central Office for England and Wales
Myddleton House
115–123 Pentonville Road
London N1 9LZ
Tel: 020 7833 2181
Fax: 020 7833 4371
Website: www.citizensadvice.org.uk
Chief Executive: David Harker

The Citizens Advice Service helps people resolve their legal, money, consumer and other problems by providing free information and advice and by influencing policymakers. Every Citizens Advice Bureau (CAB) is a registered charity. For online advice visit www.adviceguide.org.uk

ContinYou

Unit C1, Grovelands Court
Grovelands Estate
Longford Road
Exhall
Coventry CV7 9NE
Tel: 024 7658 8440
Fax: 024 7658 8441
Email: info.coventry@continyou.org.uk
Website: www.continyou.org.uk
Chief Executive Officer: Laurence Blackhall
Senior Administrator: Sharon Barker

ContinYou believes in the power of learning as a means of achieving social justice. It uses learning to tackle inequality and build social inclusion. It creates learning programmes and services that offer fresh opportunities to people who have gained least from formal education and training. ContinYou is one of the UK's leading community learning organisations.

DEA

CAN Mezzanine
32–36 Loman Street
London SE1 0EH
Tel: 020 7922 7930
Fax: 020 7922 7929
Email: info@dea.org.uk
Website: www.dea.org.uk
Director: Hetan Shah

DEA is an education charity that promotes global learning. Its national network of member organisations and supporters share the conviction that the role of education today is crucial in shaping a better tomorrow.
  For learners and society to flourish in a world which faces issues such as global poverty, climate change and racial and religious tensions, the DEA believes that education should put learning in a global context, fostering: critical thinking and creative thinking, self-awareness and open-mindedness towards difference; understanding of global issues and power relationships, and optimism and action for a better world.
  It works to change both what people learn and how they learn, through influencing policy and improving educator's practice, primarily focusing on schools and teacher training, and global youth work.

Educational Centres Association (ECA)

21 Ebbisham Drive
Norwich NR4 6HQ
Tel: 08442 495594
Fax: 01603 469292
Email: info@e-c-a.ac.uk
Website: www.e-c-a.ac.uk
Chief Executive: Bernard Godding
President:
Prof. Emeritus Brian Groombridge
Regional Contact, North: Walt Crowson
Email: walt.crowson@ntlworld.com
Regional Contact, West: Paul Olver
Email: paulolver@hotmail.com

The ECA is a practice-based, membership organisation representing a wide range of learners and providers in adult education. It is involved in citizenship education, widening participation, intergenerational learning, sustainability, staff development and social inclusion, and is the voice of adult learning in the Community Sector Coalition. Students, teachers, managers and governors from across the sector are active in responding to consultations and organising regional and national conferences, some sponsored by DIUS. The ECA is a UK-wide organisation with strong links to Europe. It was founded in 1920 and current projects include 'Every Action Counts', promoting environmental sustainability, and its acclaimed Grundtvig projects are 'Teach' active citizenship training and 'Teddy Bear' linking reminiscence by older people with activities in the primary school.

ENTO

Kimberley House
47 Vaughan Way
Leicester LE1 4SG
Tel: 0116 251 7979
Fax: 0116 251 1464
Email: info@ento.co.uk
Website: www.ento.co.uk
Managing Director: Tony Green
Director of Sales and Marketing:
David Morgan

ENTO is the guardian of standards responsible for representing people who work in learning and development, personnel, health and safety, trade unions and advice, guidance and counselling. This includes responsibility for developing the National Occupational Standards that form the basis of S/NVQ's in these areas.

Forum for Access and Continuing Education (FACE)
University of East London
Docklands Campus
4–6 University Way
London E16 2RD
Tel: 020 8223 4936
Fax: 020 8223 3394
Website: www.f-a-c-e.org.uk
Chair: John Storan
Partnership Support Officer: Jackie Leach

The Forum for Access and Continuing Education (FACE) is a charitable organisation established to support, promote and further develop continuing education opportunities. As an inclusive body, FACE members are to be found in higher education, further education, employer organisations, funding councils and many other related bodies. Members' benefits include a quarterly bulletin; conference and seminars; a compendium of research/consultancy contacts; representation of members' interest on national policy development; access to FACE development funds and website.

Further Education Research Association
Lifelong Learning Office
University of Worcester
Henwick Grove
Worcester WR2 6AJ
Tel: 01905 855145
Fax: 01905 855132
Email: g.elliott@worc.ac.uk
Website: www.fera.uk.net
Chairperson: Prof. Geoffrey Elliott

The Further Education Research Association sponsors the *Journal of Research in Post-Compulsory Education*, and through

conferences, sponsors research and information, dissemination on current issues and developments in further education. Chairperson is Geoffrey Elliott, University College Worcester.

GuildHE
Woburn House
20 Tavistock Square
London WC1H 9HB
Tel: 020 7387 7711
Fax: 020 7387 7712
Email: info@guildhe.ac.uk
Website: www.guildhe.ac.uk
Chief Executive: Alice Hynes

GuildHE is a recognised representative organisation within the higher education sector. Its members comprise higher education colleges, specialist institutions and some universities.

HOLEX
PO Box 145
Childswickham
Broadway
Worcestershire WR12 7ZQ
Tel: 01386 443 550
Fax: 01386 858 635
Email: holexbp@aol.com
Chief Officer: Bob Powell

A national network of local adult learning providers, operated as an unincorporated society and designed to facilitate networking, mutual support and information exchange between members, and to act as a "single voice" in representing members' interests to government, LSC and other national agencies. Recognised by the DIUS and LSC as part of formal consultative arrangements, the HOLEX network is supported by a national office, and holds regular meetings and ad hoc workshops and events. Membership (via subscription) is open to all local authority-maintained, voluntary and community sector organisations that deliver local learning opportunities for adults.

Leadership Foundation for Higher Education

88 Kingsway
London WC2B 6AA
Tel: 020 7841 2804
Fax: 020 7681 6219
Email: tricia.wombell@lfhe.ac.uk
Website: www.lfhe.ac.uk
Director of Marketing and
Communications: Tricia Wombell

The Leadership Foundation for Higher Education provides a dedicated service of support and advice on leadership, governance and management for all the UK's Universities and Higher Education Colleges.

Learning and Skills Improvement Service (LSIS)

Friars House
Manor House Drive
Coventry CV1 2TE
Tel: 0870 1620 632
Fax: 0870 1620 633
Email: info@lsis.org.uk
Website:www.lsis.org.uk
Chair: Dame Ruth Silver
Chief Executive: Roger McClure

The Learning and Skills Improvement Service (LSIS) came into operation on 1 October 2008. Combining the best aspects of two different and highly successful sector bodies – the Centre for Excellence in Leadership (CEL) and the Quality Improvement Agency (QIA) – LSIS will focus on learners and on developing excellent and sustainable further education and skills provision across the sector. Leadership development will underpin and form an important part of the organisation's strategic role in the sector.

LSIS was established after consultations with sector leaders identified a strong desire for an organisation that would be sector-led. As a sector-owned public body, LSIS will be owned, directed and governed by FE and skills college and skills colleges and providers, and will be dedicated to supporting excellence, leadership development and self-regulation in the FE sector.

LSIS will be consulting with the sector during autumn 2008 and spring 2009 about its priorities and remit. While this is taking place, the activities and services of CEL and QIA will continue under joint branding; more information about their range of activities is available on their respective websites.

Learning and Skills Network (LSN)

5th Floor
120 Holborn
London EC1N 2AD
Tel: 020 7297 9000
Fax: 020 7297 9001
Email: enquiries@lsneducation.org.uk
Website: www.lsneducation.org.uk
Chief Executive: John Stone

The Learning and Skills Network (LSN) is an independent not-for-profit organisation committed to making a difference to learning and skills.

LSN aims to do this by delivering quality improvement and staff development programmes that support specific government initiatives, through research, training and consultancy; and by supplying services directly to schools, colleges and training organisations.

LSN is one of the two successor organisations of the Learning and Skills Development Agency (LSDA).

Find out more about LSN by visiting the website www.LSNeducation.org.uk

Lifelong Learning UK

5th Floor, St Andrew's House
18–20 St. Andrew Street
London EC4A 3AY
Tel: 0870 757 7890
Fax: 0870 757 7889
Email: enquiries@lluk.org
Website: www.lluk.org
Chief Executive: David Hunter

Lifelong Learning UK is responsible for the professional development of all those working in libraries, archives and information services, work-based learning, higher education, further education and community learning and development.

LLU+

London South Bank University
103 Borough Road
London SE1 0AA
Tel: 020 7815 6290
Fax: 020 7815 6296
Email: lluplus@lsbu.ac.uk
Website: www.lsbu.ac.uk/lluplus
Director: Madeline Held MBE

LLU+ is a national consultancy and professional development centre for staff working in the areas of literacy, numeracy, dyslexia, family learning and English for Speakers of Other Languages. It is the main centre for training the teacher trainers in LLN and Adult Dyslexia Support throughout the UK. It also has specialists in learning support, language and maths, workplace LLN and the application of learning styles approaches to teaching and learning. Within these fields the unit offers consultancy and advice, project development, teacher and teacher trainer education, research and development and professional development networks. The unit also has an extensive list of publications and training videos developed through its work.

NAMSS (National Association for Managers of Student Services)

PO Box 529
Weston-super-Mare
North Somerset BS23 9EQ
Tel: 01934 811275
Fax: 01934 811275
Website: www.namss.ac.uk
Chair: Barry Hansford
Vice Chair: Stuart Darke

NAMSS aims to advance the education of college students – in particular, post-16 students and learners – by the development of high quality services which promote, enhance and support the learning opportunities available to them.

NATECLA

South Birmingham College
Room HB110
Hall Green Campus
Cole Bank Road
Hall Green
Birmingham B28 8ES
Tel: 0121 688 8121
Fax: 0121 694 5062
Email: co-ordinator@natecla.fsnet.co.uk
Website: www.natecla.org.uk
Co-Chair: Irene Austin
Co-Chair: Anne McKeown

NATECLA (the National Association for Teaching English and other Community Languages to Adults) is the national forum for English and community language issues. NATECLA campaigns for educational opportunities for adults from ethnic minorities and for anti-racist education and training; educational rights and opportunities for refugees and asylum seekers; and evaluation and recognition of overseas qualifications. NATECLA represents members through a variety of consultative bodies and is consulted by national organisations and decision makers on the needs of ESOL learners.

National Association for Voluntary and Community Action (NAVCA)

The Tower
2 Furnival Square
Sheffield
South Yorkshire S1 4QL
Tel: 0114 278 6636
Fax: 0114 278 7004
Email: navca@navca.org.uk
Website: www.navca.org.uk
Chief Executive: Kevin Curley
Interim Learning and Development Manager: Shaun Masterman

NAVCA is the national voice of local voluntary and community sector infrastructure in England. Its 360 members work with 160,000 local community groups and voluntary organisations which provide services, regenerate neighbourhoods, increase volunteering and tackle discrimination, in partnership with local public bodies.

National Council for Voluntary Organisations (NCVO)
Regents Wharf
8 All Saints Street
London N1 9RL
Tel: 020 7713 6161
Fax: 020 7713 6300
Email: ncvo@ncvo-vol.org.uk
Website: www.ncvo-vol.org.uk
Chief Executive: Stuart Etherington

Established in 1919 as the representative body for the voluntary sector in England, NCVO has over 3,750 members involved in all areas of voluntary and social action on a national, regional and local basis. It is also in daily contact with thousands of other voluntary bodies and groups, as well as government departments, local authorities and the business sector. NCVO believes that the voluntary sector enriches society and needs to be promoted and supported. NCVO champions the cause of the sector to government and policy makers to improve its effectiveness and provides services to support the organisations within it. Publications include a wide range of guides and good practice material, plus the *Engage* magazine.

National Literacy Trust
68 South Lambeth Road
London SW8 1RL
Tel: 020 7587 1842
Email: contact@literacytrust.org.uk
Website: www.literacytrust.org.uk
Head of Information: Sam Brookes

The National Literacy Trust is an independent charity that changes lives through literacy. It links home, school and the wider community to inspire learners and create opportunities for everyone. It supports those who work with learners through innovative programmes, information and research. Programmes supporting adult learners include Prison Reading Champions and the Vital Link

reader development project, which links libraries and adult basic skills (delivered by The Reading Agency in partnership with the NLT).

National Open College Network
The Quadrant
Parkway Business Park
99 Park Avenue
Sheffield S9 4WG
Tel: 0114 227 0500
Fax: 0114 227 0501
Email: nocn@nocn.org.uk
Website: www.nocn.org.uk
Chief Executive: Jill Brunt

National Open College Network (NOCN) is the leading credit and unit-based Awarding Body in the UK. There are 2,500 centres nationally offering NOCN qualifications, which collectively certificate around 600,000 successful learners every year. Its mission is to widen participation and access to high quality and flexible education, training and learning. It promotes social inclusion and works to ensure that learner achievement is recognised, valued and understood through a national framework of credit and qualifications.

NOCN licenses nine regional Open College Networks in England, one in Wales and one in Northern Ireland and together work in partnership with organisations to develop learning that will enable people to participate and succeed. Its provision is relevant to learners and employers, underpinned by robust standards, achievable goals and offers progression opportunities for all.

National Research and Development Centre for Adult Literacy and Numeracy
Institute of Education
20 Bedford Way
London WC1H 0AL
Tel: 020 7612 6476
Fax: 020 7612 6671
Email: info@nrdc.org.uk
Website: www.nrdc.org.uk
Director: Helen Casey
Director: John Vorhaus
Publications and Communications Officer: Fiona Freel

The National Research and Development Centre (NRDC) for Adult Literacy and Numeracy is the national centre dedicated to research and development on adult literacy, language and numeracy. It was established as part of *Skills for Life*, the national strategy for improving adult literacy and numeracy skills. The centre aims to improve practice and inform policy through the generation of knowledge, by creating a strong research culture and by developing professional practice.

National Youth Agency
Eastgate House
19–23 Humberstone Road
Leicester LE5 3GJ
Tel: 0116 242 7350
Fax: 0116 242 7444
Email: nya@nya.org.uk
Website: www.nya.org.uk
Chief Executive: Fiona Blacke

The National Youth Agency (NYA) aims to advance youth work to promote young people's personal and social development, as well as their voice, influence and place in society. Funded primarily by the Local Government Association and government departments it works to improve and extend youth services and youth work; enhance and demonstrate youth participation in society; and to promote effective youth policy and provision. It provides resources to improve work with young people and its management; creates and demonstrates innovation in services and methods; supports the leadership of organisations to deliver 'best value' and manage change; influences public perception and policy; and secures standards of education and training for youth work.

Open and Distance Learning Quality Council
16 Park Crescent
London W1B 1AH
Tel: 020 7612 7090
Fax: 020 7612 7092
Email: info@odlqc.org.uk
Website: www.odlqc.org.uk
Chief Executive: Dr David Morley

The Council, established in 1968, is the national organisation responsible for setting standards of tuition, education and training carried out by distance learning methods, for investigating these and, where appropriate, granting accreditation. It seeks to protect the interests of students, colleges and the general public; further the development of distance education and training techniques; and, where appropriate, to link correspondence courses with other forms of further education and training. An information leaflet, listing the accredited colleges and the courses offered, is available from the above address free of charge.

Research and Practice in Adult Literacy Group (RaPAL)
Literacy Research Centre
Institute for Advanced Studies
Lancaster University
Lancaster LA1 4YD
Tel: 01524 510828
Fax: 01524 510855
Website: www.literacy.lancs.ac.uk/rapal
Contact: Kathryn James

RaPAL is an independent network of learners, teachers, managers and researchers in adult basic education and literacy across the post-16 sector. Established in 1985, it is supported by membership subscription only. RaPAL encourages collaborative and reflective research that is closely linked with practice. It works in partnership with others committed to developing a learning democracy, campaigning for the rights of all adults to have access to the full range of literacies in their lives. RaPAL produces a journal three times a year and other occasional publications. It organises an annual conference and contributes to national debates about literacy, actively challenging public preconceptions and publicising alternative views.

Residential Colleges Committee
Ruskin College
Walton Street
Oxford OX1 2HE
Tel: 01865 517824
Fax: 01865 554372
Email: enquiries@ruskin.ac.uk
Secretary: Chris Wilkes

The Residential Colleges Committee
includes the six long-term residential
colleges providing courses for adult students.
The member colleges are Coleg Harlech,
Hillcroft College (women), Fircroft College,
the Northern College, Ruskin College and
Newbattle Abbey College. Students on
one-year full-time courses are eligible for
grants under an Adult Education Bursaries
Scheme. The colleges also accept a
proportion of overseas students who may be
awarded scholarships through
voluntary organisations.

Skill: National Bureau for Students with Disabilities
Chapter House
18–20 Crucifix Lane
London SE1 3JW
Tel: 020 7450 0620
Fax: 020 7450 0650
Email: skill@skill.org.uk
Website: www.skill.org.uk
Chief Executive: Barbara Waters

Skill is a national voluntary organisation
that aims to develop opportunities for
people with disabilities and learning
difficulties in post-16 education, training,
employment and volunteering. We run an
information service; provide good practice
advice and produce leaflets and publications;
run conferences and events, undertake
research and consultancy work; and liaise
with policy makers and other service
providers.
Information Service (Tuesday
11.30am–1.30pm and Thursday
1.30–3.30pm)
Tel: 0800 328 5050 or 020 7657 2337
Textphone: 0800 068 2422
Email: info@skill.org.uk

UCU University and College Union
27 Britannia Street
London WC1X 9JP
Tel: 020 7837 3636
Fax: 020 7837 4403
Email: hq@ucu.org.uk
Website: www.ucu.org.uk
General Secretary: Sally Hunt
Senior National Official: Dan Taubman
Tel: 020 7520 3230
Email: dtaubman@natfhe.org.uk

The largest trade union and professional
association for lecturers, trainers,
researchers and managers working in adult,
further and higher education throughout
England, Wales, Scotland and Northern
Ireland.

Ufi Ltd
Dearing House
1 Young Street
Sheffield S1 4UP
Tel: 0114 291 5000
Fax: 0114 291 5001
Website: www.ufi.com
Chief Executive: Sarah Jones
Deputy Chief Executive: Pablo Lloyd
Chairman: John Weston

Ufi is the organisation behind learndirect –
the largest e-learning network of its kind in
the world. Established in 1999 to take
forward the concept of a 'university for
industry', Ufi's mission is to use technology
to transform the skills and employability of
the working population to improve the UK's
productivity. Through the three strands of its
service, learndirect courses, learndirect
business and learndirect advice, Ufi has
enabled millions of people across England,
Wales and Northern Ireland to access
learning and acquire new skills.

UK Commission for Employment and Skills (UKCES)
3 Callflex Business Park
Golden Smithies Lane
Wath-upon-Dearne
Rotherham
South Yorkshire S63 7ER
Tel: 01709 774 800

Fax: 01709 774 801
Email: info@ukces.org.uk
Website: www.uckes.org.uk
Chief Executive: Chris Humphries

UK Workforce Hub
Regents Wharf
8 All Saints Street
London N1 9RL
Tel: 020 7520 2490
Fax: 020 7713 6300
Email:
workforcehub@ukworkforcehub.org.uk
Website: www.ukworkforcehub.org.uk
Head of Workforce Hub in England:
Janet Fleming

The UK Workforce Hub works to promote
skills development and good employment
practice and represents the interests of the
third sector on these issues to government
and other key stakeholders in the learning
and skills arena.

Universities Association for
Lifelong Learning
21 De Montfort Street
Leicester LE1 7GE
Tel: 0116 285 9702
Email: admin@uall.ac.uk
Website: www.uall.ac.uk
Chair: Prof. Peter Scott
Administrator: Lucy Bate
Secretary: Prof. Katherine Leni Oglesby

UALL (formerly UACE) is an association
which represents the lifelong learning
interests of the higher education sector.
UALL plays a leading role in national and
international policy formulation, advocacy,
research and practice in lifelong learning and
continuing education. It has well-
established links with all major agencies in
lifelong learning and higher education
including Funding Councils, UK
Government, Education and Lifelong
Learning Departments, University and
College Associations, Quality Assurance
Bodies, as well as other national and
international organisations. Membership of
UALL is open to all institutions providing
higher education opportunities in the field of

adult and continuing education.
Membership is open to international as well
as UK institutions and to individual
members. The Association is affiliated to its
USA sister body, UCEA. Activities include
the annual conference, other conferences,
events and workshops. The Association
publishes papers and represents the sector to
policy making bodies.

Universities UK
Woburn House
20 Tavistock Square
London WC1H 9HQ
Tel: 020 7419 4111
Fax: 020 7388 8649
Email: info@universitiesuk.ac.uk
Website: www.universitiesuk.ac.uk
President: Prof. Rick Trainor
Chief Executive: Baroness Diana Warwick
Information Officer: Susan Bradley

Universities UK is the essential voice of UK
universities, promoting their interests and
supporting their work. It represents all UK
universities and some higher education
institutions. Its members are the executive
heads of these institutions. Universities UK
was formerly known as the Committee of
Vice-Chancellors and Principals (CVCP).

Workers' Educational Association
70 Clifton Street
London EC2A 4HB
Tel: 020 7426 3450
Fax: 020 7426 3451
Email: national@wea.org.uk
Website: www.wea.org.uk
General Secretary: Richard Bolsin

The Workers' Educational Association
(WEA) is the largest voluntary sector
provider of adult education in Britain and
provides learning opportunities for over
80,000 people each year. It operates in all
nine English regions and in Scotland and
employs over three thousand part-time
tutors.
   The WEA creates and delivers courses in
response to local need, often in partnership
with community groups, local charities and
other organisations. The WEA believes that

education is life-long and should continue beyond school, college and university in order to help people develop their full human potential in society.

The WEA has always been committed to democratic practice in its teaching and learning, planning and governance. It values the experience and interests of its learners and sees its historic commitment to an educated democracy as very relevant to modern British society, communities and individuals.

Regional Adult Development Organisations

North East

Alliance SSP
Unit H1 B, Mill 3
Pleasley Vale Business Park
Pleasley Vale
Mansfield
Nottinghamshire NG19 8RL
Tel: 01623 811 223
Fax: 01623 812 611
Email: info@alliancessp.co.uk
Website: www.alliancessp.co.uk
Chief Executive: Andrew Street
Strategic Partnership Manager:
Stephanie Stubbs

County Durham Lifelong Learning Partnership
Learning Links
Canterbury Road
Newton Hall
Durham DH1 5QY
Tel: 0191 3706 400
Fax: 0191 386 9472
Email: paula.davidson@durham.gov.uk
Support Officer: Paula Davidson
Skills for Life Co-ordinator: Cath Button
Skills for Life Policy Officer:
Michelle Graham

Tyne and Wear Learning Partnership
1st Floor, City Library Building
Fawcett Street
Sunderland SR1 1RE
Tel: 0191 443 2857
Fax: 0191 553 2506
Email: lynda.brown@sunderland.gov.uk
Head of Standards, Children's Services:
Lynda Brown
Director of Children's Services:
Dr Helen Paterson

North West

Bolton Lifelong Learning Unit
c/o Bolton Council
Room 17
5th Floor, Civic Centre
Le Mans Crescent
Bolton BL1 1SA
Tel: 01204 337204
Fax: 01204 337285
Website: www.bolton.gov.uk
Assistant Director, Adult and Community
Services: Stephanie Crossley
Email: stephanie.crossley@bolton.gov.uk

Bury Learning Partnership
Hilton House
Irwell
Bury
Lancashire BL9 0HZ
Tel: 0161 253 5631
Fax: 0161 253 6144

Oldham Local Learning Partnership
Policy and Commissioning Unit
Oldham Metropolitan Borough Council
PO Box 335
Civic Centre
West Street
Oldham OL1 1XL
Tel: 0161 911 4188/3275
Fax: 0161 911 4162
Email: jon.bloor@oldham.gov.uk
Co-ordinator: Jon Bloor
Skills for Life Co-ordinator: Alison Wells

Rochdale Workbased and Community Learning Service

Floor 7, Municipal Offices
Smith Street
Rochdale
Lancashire OL16 1YD
Tel: 01706 925 167
Email: paul.gibson@rochdale.gov.uk
Team Leader: Paul Gibson

Salford Economic Development, Learning and Skills Partnership

Minerva House
Pendlebury Road
Swinton
Manchester M27 4EQ
Tel: 0161 778 0471
Fax: 0161 278 6234
Website: www.partnersinsalford.org.uk
Head of Learning and Skills: Steve Garner
Skills for Life Co-ordinator: Anne Beattie
Skills Contact: Emily Kynes

Stockport Learning and Skills Partnership

c/o Peter Roberts (Chair)
Principal of Stockport College
Wellington Road South
Stockport
Cheshire SK1 3UQ
Tel: Heidi Walker on 0161 958 3405

Tameside Learning Partnership

Post 16 Learning, Tameside MBC
Council Offices
Wellington Road
Ashton-under-Lyne
Lancashire OL6 6DL
Tel: 0161 342 3297
Email: jean.quinn@tameside.gov.uk
Website: www.tameside.gov.uk
 Principal Adult Learning Officer:
Jean Quinn

Warrington Learning, Skills and Enterprise Partnership

c/o Strategic Director, Community Services
Bewsey Old School
Lockton Lane
Warrington WA5 0BF
Partnership Co-ordinator: Marie Hoyles

Wirral Learning Partnership

Wirral Education Centre, Room G1A
Acre Lane
Bromborough
Wirral
Merseyside CH62 7BZ
Tel: 0151 346 6615
Fax: 0151 346 6607
Email: sarahhowarth@wirral.gov.uk

Yorkshire and Humberside

Barnsley Adult Learning Forum

Priory Campus
Pontefract Road
Lundwood
Barnsley
South Yorkshire S71 5PN
Tel: 01226 248761
Fax: 01226 770467
Learning and Skills Manager: Lesley Rudd
Email: lesley.rudd@priory-campus.co.uk

East Riding of Yorkshire Learning Partnership

3 North Bar Within
Beverley
North Humberside HU17 8AP
Tel: 01482 881639
Email:
learning.partnership@eastriding.gov.uk
Website: www.erlp.co.uk
The Learning Partnership Manager:
Sara Harrop

Kirklees Lifelong Learning Partnership

c/o Kirklees MBC
Room 513
5th Floor, Oldgate House
Huddersfield
West Yorkshire HD1 6QW
Tel: 01484 225016
Fax: 01484 225315
Email: denis.grainger@kirklees.gov.uk
Senior Improvement Manager:
Denis Grainger

Learning City York – York Lifelong Learning Partnership
Merchant House
11a Piccadilly
York YO1 9WB
Tel: 01904 656655
Fax: 01904 631435
Manager: Julia Massey

Learning Partnership, Bradford and District
Room 40E, Executive Office
c/o Bradford College
Westbook Building
Great Horton Road
Bradford
West Yorkshire BD7 1AY
Tel: 01274 433025
Fax: 01274 436386
Email: c.richardson@bradfordcollege.ac.uk
Website:
www.bradfordlearningpartnership.org.uk
Learning Partnership Manager:
Cynthia Richardson

Previously called Bradford Lifelong Learning Partnership

Leeds Learning Partnership
Leeds Initiative Office
40 Great George Street
Leeds LS1 3DL
Tel: 0113 247 8931
Fax: 0113 247 8988
Website: www.leedsinitiative.org

North Yorkshire Learning Partnership
York and North Yorkshire Partnership Unit
12 Clifton Moor Business Village
James Nicholson Link
Clifton Moor
York YO30 4XG
Tel: 01904 477970
Fax: 01904 477977
Email: julie.chandler@ynypu.org.uk
Learning Partnership Manager:
Julie Chandler

Rotherham Learning Partnership
Scent
Sheffield Road
Templeborough
Rotherham
South Yorkshire S60 1DX
Tel: 01709 336743
Email: collette.bailey@rotherham.gov.uk
Director, Learning Partnership:
Collette Bailey

Wakefield Skills, Enterprise and Work Partnership (SEWP)
Room D16, Newton Bar
Leeds Road
Wakefield
West Yorkshire WF1 1XS
Tel: 01924 306826
Website: www.wakefield.gov.uk
SEWP Manager: Catherine Lunn

West Midlands

Shropshire Learning Network County Forum
c/o Martin Ward
Shewsbury Sixth Form College
Priory Road
Shrewsbury SY1 1RH
Tel: 01743 235491

Solihull Adult Learning and Skills
Solihull Metropolitan Borough Council
Community Economic Regeneration
Council House Complex
Solihull
West Midlands B91 9QS
Tel: 0121 704 6972
Email: mgibbs@solihull.gov.uk
Website: www.solihull.gov.uk
Lifelong Learning Co-ordinator:
Mary Gibbs

Telford and Wrekin Lifelong Learning Partnership
Telford and Wrekin Council
Civic Offices
PO Box 59
Telford
Shropshire TF3 4WZ
Tel: 01952 382880
Fax: 01952 382327
Lifelong Learning Manager: Richard Probert

Walsall Lifelong Learning Alliance
c/o College of Continuing Education
Hawbush Centre
Beeches Road
Leamore
Walsall WS3 1AG
Tel: 01922 714850
Email: robinsonc@walsall.gov.uk
Website: www.wlla.co.uk
Lifelong Learning Officer: Colin Robinson

Wolverhampton Learning Partnership
Newhampton Centre
Newhampton Road East
Wolverhampton
West Midlands WV1 4AP
Tel: 01902 821937
Fax: 01902 821941
Email: rod_shep@yahoo.co.uk
Website: www.wlpukonline.co.uk
Co-ordinator: Rod Sheppard

Worcestershire Learning and Skills Partnership
Adult and Community Services Directorate
Worcestershire County Council
County Hall
Spetchley Road
Worcester WR5 2NP
Tel: 01905 728537
Fax: 01905 728993
Website: www.worcestershire.gov.uk
Partnerships and Inclusion Manager:
Annette Wright

East Midlands

EMFEC (East Midlands Further Education Council)
Robins Wood House
Robins Wood Road
Aspley
Nottingham NG8 3NH
Tel: 0115 854 1616
Fax: 0115 854 1617
Email: enquiries@emfec.co.uk
Website: www.emfec.co.uk
Chief Executive: Jennie Gardiner

EMFEC is an independent, not-for-profit company limited by guarantee with charitable status which delivers high quality support services to providers of vocational education and training in the post-14 sector.

Greater Nottingham Employment and Skills Board
Castle Heights
72 Maid Marion Way
Nottingham NG1 6BJ
Tel: 0115 950 6371
Fax: 0115 950 2173
Website: www.gnesb.org.uk
Employment and Skills Board:
Nicky Church
Employment and Skills Board:
David Kirkham
Making the Connection: Matt Lockley

Leicestershire and Leicester City Learning Partnership
Business Box
Unit 2, Brailsford Industrial Estate
Oswin Road
Leicester LE3 1HR
Tel: 0116 279 5036
Email: rflude@llclp.org.uk
Website: www.llclp.org.uk
Partnership Manager: Dr Ray Flude
Deputy Partnership Manager: Sue Grogan

Northamptonshire Learning Partnership
Royal Pavilion
Summerhouse Road
Moulton Park Industrial Estate
Redhouse Road
Northampton NN3 6BJ
Tel: 01604 671403
Email:
learningpartnership@northamptonshirelp.org
Manager: David Southron

Eastern

Association of Colleges in the Eastern Region (ACER)
Suite 1, Lancaster House
Meadow Lane
St Ives
Huntingdon
Cambridgeshire PE27 4LG
Tel: 01480 468198
Fax: 01480 468601
Email: general@acer.ac.uk
Website: www.acer.ac.uk
Chief Executive: Veronica Windmill

ACER is based in the East of England and its main purpose is to serve the needs of its member colleges (general FE, specialist colleges and sixth-form colleges) and other providers in the learning and skills sector. ACER provides a range of services including regional networks and forums, management development, training, conferences and consultancy. It also manages a number of projects, often with member colleges as partners. ACER's provision is open to all and many participants are from outside the region. ACER is the regional office for the Association of Colleges (AoC) and represents the FE system in the region. Much of ACER's work is carried out in collaboration with key regional partners and stakeholders.

CP Learning Trust
South Fens Business Centre
L21–L22 Fenton Way
Chatteris
Cambridgeshire PE16 6TT
Tel: 01354 691000
Fax: 01354 691658
Email: info@cpltrust.net
Website: www.cpltrust.net
Project Team Manager: Sue Besant

**Hertfordshire Adult
Learning Partnership**
4 Bishops Square Business Park
Hatfield
Hertfordshire AL10 9NE
Tel: 01707 398400
Fax: 01707 398430
Email: david.browne@halp.co.uk
Website: www.halp.co.uk
Partnership Manager: David Brown
Administrator: Vanessa MacDonald

**The Learning Partnership –
Bedfordshire and Luton Ltd**
Calibration House
1 Sunbeam Road
Woburn Road Industrial Estate
Kempston
Bedford MK42 7BZ
Tel: 01234 851154
Fax: 01234 856854
Email: info@learning-partnership.co.uk
Website: www.learningcommunities.co.uk
Learning Partnership: Stephen Ferris

Norfolk Learning Partnership
Henderson Business Centre
Ivy Road
Norwich NR5 8BF
Tel: 01603 251759
Fax: 01603 251703
Email: office@thenlpteam.com
Website:
www.norfolklearningpartnership.com
Chair: Fiona McDiarmid
Manager: Andy Hodgson

Thurrock Learning Partnership
Children, Education and Families
Civic Offices
New Road
Grays
Essex RM17 6SL
Tel: 01375 652918
Fax: 01375 652550
Email:
learning.partnership@thurrock.gov.uk
Website:
www.thurrocklearningpartnership.org.uk
Manager: Maureen Wilcox

South West

**Bath and North East Somerset Lifelong
Learning Partnership**
26 Devonshire Buildings
Bath BA2 4SU
Tel: 01225 333149
Fax: 01225 333149
Partnership Co-ordinator: Jacqui Buffton

Bristol Learning Partnership
c/o West of England Learning and Skills
Council
St Lawrence's House
29–31 Broad Street
Bristol BS1 2HF
Tel: 0845 0194168
Manager: John Chudley

**Learning for Skills Group,
North Somerset**
Up Line
Station Mead
Chilcompton
Radstock BA3 4FD
Tel: 01761 233260
Fax: 01761 233260
Email: john@cocksj1.freeserve.co.uk
Lifelong Learning Partnership Manager:
John Cocks

**Learning Partnership for Cornwall and
the Isles of Scilly**
The Lodge
Trevenson Road
Pool
Redruth
Cornwall TR15 3RD
Email:
pskinner@cornwall-learning-partnership.org
Website:
www.cornwall-learning-partnership.org
Director: Polly Skinner

Learning South West
Bishops Hull House
Bishops Hull Road
Taunton
Somerset TA1 5EP
Tel: 01823 335 491
Fax: 01823 323 388
Email: enquiries@learning-southwest.org.uk
Website: www.learning-southwest.org.uk
Chief Executive: Tim Boyes-Watson

Learning South West is a membership
organisation working to support the
learning and skills and youth work sectors
across the region.

South East

**Association of South East
Colleges (AOSEC)**
Building 11, University of Reading
London Road
Reading
Berkshire RG1 5AQ
Tel: 0118 378 6325
Fax: 0118 378 6324
Email: enquiries@aosec.org.uk
Website: www.aosec.org.uk
Chief Executive: Janet Eldrich
Chair: Barry Hicks

**Brighton and Hove
Learning Partnership**
3rd Floor, Brighton Town Hall
Bartholomew Square
Brighton BN1 1JR
Tel: 01273 294920
Fax: 01273 294924
Email:
paul.wadsworth@brighton-hove.gov.uk
Website: www.bhlp.org.uk
Learning Partnership Manager:
Daniel Shelley

**Buckinghamshire Economic and
Learning Partnership**
Friars Court
Friarage Passage
Aylesbury
Buckinghamshire HP20 1QS
Tel: 01296 619200
Fax: 01296 434142
Email: info@belp.co.uk
Website: www.bucks-ep.co.uk
Chief Executive: Graham Grover

Isle of Wight Learning Partnership
Innovation Centre
St Cross Business Park
Monks Brook
Newport
Isle of Wight PO30 5WB
Tel: 01983 535839
Email: bridget.welling@iwep.com
Area Manager: Andrew Preskey
Learning Partnership Co-ordinator:
Bridget Welling

Milton Keynes Economy and Learning Partnership

Central Business Exchange II
406–412 Midsummer Boulevard
Milton Keynes MK9 2EA
Tel: 01908 660101
Email: info@mkelp.co.uk
Executive Director: Colin Fox

Royal Borough of Windsor and Maidenhead Learning Partnership

c/o Town Hall
St Ives Road
Maidenhead
Berkshire SL6 1RF
Tel: 01628 796684
Fax: 01628 796907
Email: angela.wellings@rbwm.gov.uk
Website: www.discoversuccess.org.uk
Head of Extended Schools: Angela Wellings

Surrey Lifelong Learning Partnership

Unit 211, Lansbury Estate
102 Lower Guildford Road
Knaphill
Woking
Surrey GU21 2EP
Tel: 01483 487892
Email: kevin.delf@surreyllp.org.uk
Website: www.surreyllp.org.uk
Chief Executive: Kevin Delf

West Sussex Learning Network

County Hall
West Street
Chichester
West Sussex PO19 1RF
Tel: 01243 777034
Fax: 01243 777211
Website: www.westsussexlearning.net
General Adviser, Community Learning:
Anne Parkinson
Email: anne.parkinson@westsussex.gov.uk

Wokingham Learning Partnership

Wokingham District Council
PO Box 156

Shute End
Wokingham
Berkshire RG40 1WQ
Tel: 0118 974 6164
Fax: 0118 974 6259
Email: alan.bennett@wokingham.gov.uk
Learning Manager: Alan Bennett

London

Central London Learning Partnership

c/o Red Kite Learning
207 Waterloo Road
London SE1 8XD
Tel: 020 7928 2439 ext 218
Fax: 020 7633 9105
Email: cllpinfo@cllp.org.uk
Website: www.cllp.org.uk
Chair: Brendan Tarring
Manager: Ania Oprawska

North London Training Partnership

Dumayne House
1 Fox Lane
Palmers Green
London N13 4AB
Tel: 020 8929 1893
Fax: 020 8882 5931
Manager: Michelle Keady

South London Learning Partnership

c/o Prospects
7th Floor, Grosvenor House
125 High Street
Croydon
Surrey CR0 9XP
Tel: 020 8649 6421
Fax: 020 8649 6445
Email: sllp@prospects.co.uk
Website: www.sllp.org.uk
Manager: Janice Pigott

Local Authority Adult Education – England

North East

Darlington Borough Council
Children's Services
Town Hall
Darlington DL1 5QT
Tel: 01325 349634
Email: ruth.bernstein@darlington.gov.uk
Website: www.darlington.gov.uk
Director of Children's Services: Murray Rose
Head of Libraries and Community Learning:
Ruth Bernstein

Libraries and Community Learning Service
based at:
Crown Street Library
Darlington DL1 1ND

Durham County Council
Education in the Community
County Hall
Durham DH1 5UJ
Tel: 0191 383 3881
Fax: 0191 383 3288
Email: anne.adams@durham.gov.uk
Website: www.durham.gov.uk
Adult Education Manager: Anne Adams

Gateshead Council
Dryden Centre
Evistones Road
Lowfell
Gateshead
Tyne and Wear NE9 5UR
Tel: 0191 433 8646
Fax: 0191 491 1394
Email: adultlearning@gateshead.gov.uk
Website:
www.gateshead.gov.uk/adultlearning
Group Director, Learning Children's
Services: Maggie Atkinson
Adult Learning and Skills Manager:
Kevin Pearson

Hartlepool Borough Council
Adult Education
Golden Flatts
Seaton Lane
Hartlepool TS25 1HN
Tel: 01429 868616
Fax: 01429 891673
Email: maggie.heaps@hartlepool.gov.uk
Website: www.hartlepool.gov.uk
Director of Adult and Community Services:
Nicola Bailey
Adult Education Co-ordinator:
Maggie Heaps
Hartlepool Adult Education website:
www.haded.org.uk

Middlesbrough Borough Council
Acklam Adult Education Centre
Hall Drive
Middlesbrough
Cleveland TS5 7JZ
Tel: 01642 818480
Fax: 01642 821300
Email: acklam@maes.ac.uk
Website: www.maes.ac.uk
Corporate Director of Children, Families
and Learning: Gill Rollings
Community Education Manager:
Rose Bickle

Newcastle upon Tyne City Council
Civic Centre
Barras Bridge
Newcastle upon Tyne NE1 8PU
Tel: 0191 232 8520
Fax: 0191 211 4983
Website:
www.newcastle.gov.uk/lifelonglearning
Executive Director of Children's Services:
Catherine Fitt
Head of Adult Learning: Caroline Miller
Basic Skills Adviser: Doreen McCarthy

North Tyneside Council

Children, Young People and Learning
North Tyneside Adult Learning Alliance
Stephenson House
Stephenson Street
North Shields
Tyne and Wear NE30 1QA
Tel: 0191 200 5381
Fax: 0191 200 5060
Email: generaloffice@northtyneside.gov.uk
Director of Children, Young People and
Learning: Gill Alexander
Head of Education, Innovation and Skills:
Steve Rutland
Manager, Skills for Life: Joan Brown
Manager, Adult Community Learning:
Phil Knowles
Manager, Work Based Learning:
Peter Walley

Northumberland County Council

Adult Learning Service
Education Development Centre
Hepscott Park
Morpeth
Northumberland NE61 6NF
Tel: 01670 534 821
Fax: 01670 533 592
Email:
childrensservices@northumberland.gov.uk
Website: www.northumberland.gov.uk
Executive Director of Children's Services:
Trevor Doughty
Director of Schools and Family Support:
Robin Casson
Principal Adult Education Officer:
Heather Thomas
Tel: 01670 534821
Email: hthomas@northumberland.gov.uk

Redcar and Cleveland Borough Council

Redcar and Cleveland Adult Learning
Service
c/o Redcar Education Development Centre
Corporation Road
Redcar TS10 1HA
Tel: 01642 490409
Fax: 01642 492388
Email:
adult_education@redcar-cleveland.gov.uk
Website: www.redcar-cleveland.gov.uk
Director of Adult and Children's Services:
Mike Dillon
Principal Officer: John Harris
Strategy Manager: Denise Bollands

South Tyneside Borough Council

Adult and Community Learning Service
Central Library
Prince George Square
South Shields
Tyne and Wear NE33 5BU
Website: www.southtyneside.info
Executive Director, Children and Young
People's Services: Helen Watson
Assistant Head of Service – Enterprise and
Skills, Transition and Wellbeing:
Shashi Chopra

Stockton-on-Tees Borough Council

Children, Education and Social Care
Stockton Adult Education Service
PO Box 228
Municipal Buildings
Church Road
Stockton-on-Tees TS18 1XE
Tel: 01642 526416
Email: adult.education@stockton.gov.uk
Website: www.stockton.gov.uk/adulted
Corporate Director of Children, Education
and Social Care: Ann Baxter
Manager of Community Education:
Marc Mason
Email: marc.mason@stockton.gov.uk
Principal Officer: Gail Henegan
Principal Adult Education Officer:
Jocelyn McIntyre

Sunderland City Council
Family, Adult and Community Learning
The Stannington Centre
Stannington Grove
Sunderland SR2 9JT
Tel: 0191 553 2620
Fax: 0191 553 2617
Email: acl.info@sunderland.gov.uk
Website:
www.sunderland-learnersfirst.org.uk
Director of Education: Helen Paterson
Quality Improvement Manager: Judith Allen
Family, Adult and Community Learning
Manager: Sandra Kenny

North West

Blackburn with Darwen Borough Council
Lifelong Learning
Regeneration, Housing and
Neighbourhoods Department
J Floor, Tower Block
King William Street
Blackburn
Lancashire BB1 7DY
Tel: 01254 585851
Fax: 01254 692189
Website: www.blackburn.gov.uk
Director; Regeneration, Housing and
Neighbourhoods: Adam Scott
Lifelong Learning Manager: Heather Taylor

Blackpool Council
Culture and Communities
Progress House
Clifton Road
Blackpool
Lancashire FY4 4US
Tel: 01253 478131
Fax: 01253 478059
Email: adult.learning@blackpool.gov.uk
Website: www.blackpool.gov.uk
Director of Culture and Communities:
Paul Walker
Head of Adult and Community Learning:
Gwen Harris

Bolton Council
Lifelong Learning Unit
5th Floor, Paderborn House
Civic Centre
Bolton BL1 1JW
Tel: 01204 332821
Website: www.bolton.gov.uk
Assistant Director of Adult and Community
Services: Stephanie Crossley
Room 17
5th Floor, Civic Centre
Le Mans Crescent
Bolton BL1 1SA

Bury Metropolitan Borough Council
Libraries and Adult Learning
Bury Adult Learning Centre
18 Haymarket Street
Bury
Lancashire BL9 0AQ
Tel: 0161 253 6077
Fax: 0161 763 6267
Website:
www.bury.gov.uk/educationandlearning
Director of Environment and Development
Services (EDS): Graham Atkinson
Assistant Director of Arts, Libraries and
Adult Learning: John Carter
Head of Libraries and Adult Learning
Service: Diana Sorrigan
Assistant Head of Libraries and Adult
Learning (Skills for Life): Julie Kenrick

Cheshire County Council
Cheshire Lifelong Learning Service
Community Services
County Hall
Chester CH1 1SQ
Tel: 01244 602469
Fax: 01244 603 088
Website: www.cheshire.gov.uk
Director of Community Services: John
Weeks
Principal Officer – Lifelong Learning and
Inclusion: Hazel Manning

Cumbria County Council
Adult Learning, Children's Services
5 Portland Square
Carlisle CA1 1PU
Tel: 01228 226924
Fax: 01228 606896
Email:
charles.searle@cumbriaadulteducation.org
Website: www.cumbria.gov.uk/education/
adult-education
Deputy County Manager, Continuous
Learning: Dr Charles Searle
Skills Manager: Amanda Towers
Family Learning Manager: Sue Doyle
Planning and Resource Manager:
Terry Rowe
Area Operations Manager: Gill Mitchell

Halton Borough Council
Municipal Building
Kingsway
Widnes
Cheshire WA8 7QF
Tel: 0151 907 8300
Website: www.halton.gov.uk
Executive Director, Environment: Dick
Tregea
Head of Adult Learning and Skills
Development Service: Siobhan Saunders

Adult Learning
Kingsway Learning Centre
Victoria Road
Widnes
Cheshire WA8 7QY
Tel: 0151 471 7486
Fax: 0151 907 8366
Email: acornlll@halton.gov.uk

Knowsley Metropolitan Borough Council
Education Office
Huyton Hey Road
Huyton
Liverpool L36 5YH
Tel: 0151 443 4561
Fax: 0151 443 4533
Website: www.knowsleyface.co.uk
Executive Director of Children and Family
Services: Damian Allen
Head of Adult and Community Education:
Angie Feeney

Lancashire County Council
PO Box 61
County Hall
Preston
Lancashire PR1 8RJ
Tel: 0845 053 0000
Website: www.lancashire.gov.uk
Executive Director: Ged Fitzgerald

Liverpool City Council
Adult Learning Service
c/o Municipal Building
Dale Street
Liverpool L2 2DH
Tel: 0151 233 2784
Fax: 0151 233 3282
Website: www.liverpool.gov.uk
Executive Director: Tony Hunter

Manchester City Council
Manchester Adult Education Service
Plymouth Grove Adult Learning Centre
Hathersage Road
Longsight
Manchester M13 0BY
Tel: 0161 255 8206
Fax: 0161 255 8212
Website: www.manchester.gov.uk
Head of Service: Julie Rushton
Resource and Finance Manager: Mark Law
Districts and Partnerships Manager:
Sarah Watson

Metropolitan Borough of Wirral
Children and Young People's Services
Professional Excellence Centre
Acre Lane
Bromborough
Wirral
Merseyside CH62 7BZ
Fax: 0151 346 6607
Email: educ@wirral.gov.uk
Website: www.wirral.gov.uk
Director of Children's Services: Howard
Cooper
Head of Branch, Learning and Achievement:
Mark Parkinson
Lifelong Learning Adviser: Sarah Howarth

Oldham Council

Lifelong Learning
Greaves Street
Oldham OL1 1AL
Tel: 0161 911 4260
Fax: 0161 911 3222
Website: www.oldham.gov.uk
Executive Director Children, Young People
and Families: Janet Donaldson
Service Director, Learning, Development and
Localities: Jane Doherty
Head of Service: Lynda Fairhurst
Area and Finance Co-ordinator:
Glenys Bentley
Quality, MIS and Marketing Manager:
Caroline Ballard
Staff Development Co-ordinator:
Chiaka Ebizie
Skills for Life and Curriculum Co-ordinator:
Mary Grainger
Area and Learner Services Co-ordinator:
Karen Royle
Inclusion and Access Co-ordinator:
Steve Titley

Rochdale Metropolitan Borough Council

Learn Local
PO Box 70
Floor 7, Municipal Offices
Smith Street
Rochdale
Lancashire OL16 1YD
Tel: 01706 925168
Email: learnlocal@rochdale.gov.uk
Website: www.rochdale.gov.uk
Quality and Equality Manager:
Cindy Drinkwater
Adult and Community Learning Manager:
Christine Kay

St Helens Council

Children and Young People's Services
Atlas House
Corporation Street
St Helens
Merseyside WA9 1LD
Tel: 01744 455321
Fax: 01744 455319
Email: adultlearning@sthelens.gov.uk
Website: www.sthelens.gov.uk
Director of Children and Young People's
Service: Susan Richardson
Tel: 01744 671801
Head of Adult and Community Learning:
Pam Meredith
Skills for Life Contact: Pat O'Brien
Adult and Community Learning
Newton Campus
Crow Lane East
Newton le Willows
Merseyside WA12 9TT
Tel: 01744 677314
Fax: 01744 677676

Salford City Council

Children's Services
Minerva House
Pendlebury Road
Swinton
Manchester M27 4EQ
Tel: 0161 778 0123
Fax: 0161 728 6156
Website: www.salford.gov.uk
Director of Children's Services: Jill Baker
Head of Learning and Skills: Steve Garner
Family, Adult and Community Learning
Manager: Miranda Clarke
Tel: 0161 778 6456

Sefton Metropolitan Borough Council
Children's Services
9th Floor, Merton House
Stanley Road
Bootle
Merseyside L20 3JA
Tel: 0151 934 3326/3201
Fax: 0151 934 3520
Website: www.sefton.gov.uk
Strategic Director, Children's Services:
Brynley Marsh
Head of Family and Community Learning:
Olive Carey
Family and Community Learning Officer:
Pat Ashton-Smith

Stockport Metropolitan Borough Council
Children and Young People's Directorate
Continuing Education Services
Victoria House
Town Hall
Stockport
Cheshire SK1 3XE
Tel: 0161 474 3864
Fax: 0161 355 6968
Email: richard.mortimer@stockport.gov.uk
Website: www.stockport.gov.uk
Corporate Director: Andrew Webb
Head of Continuing Education:
Richard Mortimer
Service Manager for Curriculum and
Quality: Gerard Hynes
Service Manager, Performance and
Development: Sean Burke

Tameside Metropolitan Borough Council
Services for Children and Young People
Council Offices
Wellington Road
Ashton-under-Lyne OL6 6DL
Tel: 0161 342 8355
Fax: 0161 342 3260
Website: www.tameside.gov.uk
Executive Director, Services for Children and
Young People: Ian Smith
Principal Adult Learning Officer:
Jean Quinn
Tel: 0161 342 2190
Email: jean.quinn@tameside.gov.uk

Adult Learning delivered at:
Tameside Adult Learning
Learn @ St Ann's
Burlington Street
Ashton-under-Lyne OL6 7DG
Tel: 0161 343 8889

Trafford Council
Community Learning Trafford
c/o Trafford College, Room 155
Talbot Road
Stretford
Sale
Cheshire M33 0XH
Tel: 0161 912 1530
Fax: 0161 912 1351
Website: www.trafford.gov.uk
Community Learning Manager:
Wendy Diamond
Team: Natalie Gibson, Alison Tyrer,
Wendy Hanley, Sue Eaton, Sandra Barber,
Jane McKenzie, Trevor Eaton
Commissioning Officer: Carol Jones

Warrington Borough Council
Lifelong Learning Section
Community Floor
Halliwell Jones Stadium
Winwick Road
Warrington WA2 7NE
Tel: 01925 246490
Fax: 01925 248891
Website: www.warrington.gov.uk
Strategic Director: Helen Sumner
Adult and Family Learning Co-ordinator:
Susan Baker

Wigan Metropolitan Borough Council
Children and Young People's Services
Progress House
Westwood Park Drive
Wigan
Lancashire WN3 4HH
Tel: 01942 486123
Fax: 01942 486213
Email: education@wiganmbc.gov.uk
Website: www.wiganmbc.gov.uk
Director of Adult Services: Bernard Walker
Assistant Director of Adult Services:
Steve Peddie
Service Manager, Learning and Guidance:
Sheila Gallagher

Yorkshire and Humberside

Barnsley Metropolitan Borough Council
Education Services
Berneslai Close
Barnsley
South Yorkshire S70 2HS
Tel: 01226 773500
Fax: 01226 773599
Website: www.barnsley.gov.uk
Executive Director of Children, Young
People and Families: Edna Sutton
Assistant Executive Director for
Performance, Infrastructure and
Development: Steven Mair

**Calderdale Metropolitan
Borough Council**
Town Hall
Crossley Street
Halifax
West Yorkshire HX1 1UJ
Head of Service: Eileen Fawcett

Adult Learning is based at:
Horton House
Horton Street
Halifax HX1 1PU
Tel: 01422 392820
Email: cyps.cal@calderdale.gov.uk

**City of Bradford Metropolitan
District Council**
Department of Services for Skills for Work
1st Floor
Jacobs Well
Bradford
West Yorkshire BD1 5RW
Tel: 01274 434598
Fax: 01274 437656
Website: www.bradford.gov.uk
Director, Services for Children and Young
People: Kath Tunstall
Service Manager, Skills for Work:
Avril Austerberry

City of York Council
Learning, Culture and Children's Services
Mill House
North Street
York YO1 6JD
Tel: 01904 613161
Fax: 01904 554206
Website: www.york.gov.uk
Director of Learning, Culture and Children's
Services: Pete Dwyer
Head of Adult and Community Education:
Alistair Gourlay
Email: alistair.gourlay@york.gov.uk
Family Learning Manager: Lorna Batten
Email: lorna.batten@york.gov.uk

**Doncaster Metropolitan
Borough Council**
Directorate of Education Standards
PO Box 266
The Council House
College Road
Doncaster
South Yorkshire DN1 3AD
Tel: 01302 862688
Fax: 01302 872519
Website: www.doncaster.gov.uk
Director of Education Standards:
Steve Chew
Head of Service: Ruth Brook

East Riding of Yorkshire Council
Children, Family and Adult Services
Directorate
County Hall
Cross Street
Beverley
North Humberside HU17 9BA
Tel: 01482 392000
Fax: 01482 392829
Website:
www.eastriding.gov.uk/education/adult
Director of Children, Family and Adult
Services: Alison Waller
Learning and Skills Manager: Angie Bulter

Kingston upon Hull City Council
Children and Young People's Services
Guildhall
Alfred Guilder Street
Hull HU2 2AA
Tel: 01482 616325
Fax: 01482 616327
Website: www.hullcc.gov.uk
Director of Adult Education: Kevin l'Anson
Head of Learning, Leisure and Achievement:
Judith Harwood

Kirklees Council
Children and Young People's Services
Oldgate House
2 Oldgate
Huddersfield HD1 6QW
Tel: 01484 225005
Fax: 01484 225315
Website: www.kirklees.gov.uk
Director of Children and Young People's
Services: Alison O'Sullivan
Adult Lifelong Learning Manager:
Kate Fleming
Senior Improvement Manager:
Denis Grainger

Leeds City Council
Adult Learning
1st Floor, Technology Family Learning
Centre
9 Harrogate Road
Leeds LS7 3NB
Tel: 0113 395 0497
Fax: 0113 395 2041
Website: www.leeds.gov.uk
Director of Environment and
Neighbourhoods: Neil Evans
Head of Jobs and Skills: Val Snowden
Adult Learning Manager: Jane Hopkins
Email: jane.hopkins@leeds.gov.uk
Tel: 0113 247 5863

North East Lincolnshire Council
Adult Community Learning Service
39 Heneage Road
Grimsby
North East Lincolnshire DN32 9ES
Tel: 01472 323260
Fax: 01472 323267
Email: adult.ed@nelincs.gov.uk
Executive Director for Children's Services:
Andrew Samson
Skills for Life Co-ordinator: Kate Esmond
Tel: 01472 326261

North Lincolnshire Council
Learning Schools and Communities
PO Box 35
Hewson House
Station Road
Brigg
North Lincolnshire DN20 8XJ
Tel: 01724 297240
Fax: 01724 297242
Website: www.northlincs.gov.uk
Head of Learning, Schools and
Communities: David Lea
Head of Service: Andy Boak
Adult Education Manager:
Chriss Tomlinson
Adult Education Manager, Brumby Centre:
Carol Hughes
Adult Education Manager, Barton and Brigg:
Judy Skelton

North Yorkshire County Council
Children and Young People's Service
Adult Learning Service
County Hall
Northallerton
North Yorkshire DL7 8AE
Tel: 01609 532664
Fax: 01609 778772
Website: www.northyorks.gov.uk
Corporate Director, Children and Young
People's Service: Cynthia Welbourn
Principal Education Officer (Adult
Learning): Fran Lett

**Rotherham Metropolitan
Borough Council**
Education Department
1st Floor, Norfolk House
Walker Place
Rotherham
South Yorkshire S65 1AS
Tel: 01709 382121
Fax: 01709 372056
Website: www.rotherham.gov.uk
Senior Executive Director, Children and
Young People's Services: Dr Sonia Sharp
Adult and Family Learning Manager:
Gavin Baldauf-Good
Community Learning Manager: Helen Shaw

Sheffield City Council
Lifelong Learning and Skills Service
145 Crookesmoor Road
Sheffield S6 3FP
Tel: 0114 266 7503
Fax: 0114 266 7092
Email: educinformation@sheffield.gov.uk
Website: www.sheffield.gov.uk
Executive Director, Children and Young
People: Dr Sonia Sharp
Head of Lifelong Learning and Skills Service:
Tony Tweedy
Senior Manager, Learning, Skills and
Employment: Jayne Hawley

**Wakefield Metropolitan
Borough Council**
Adult and Community Education Service
Manygates Education Centre
Manygates Lane
Wakefield
West Yorkshire WF2 7DQ
Tel: 01924 303302
Fax: 01924 303342
Email: aces@wakefield.gov.uk
Website: www.wakefield.gov.uk
Corporate Director, Family Services:
Elaine McHale
Service Director, Schools and Lifelong
Learning: Paul Makin
Principal Adult Education Officer:
Sian Dodderidge
website: www.wakefieldaes.org.uk

West Midlands

Birmingham City Council
Adult Education
Louisa Ryland House
44 Newhall Street
Birmingham B3 3PL
Tel: 0121 303 2682
Fax: 0121 464 0333
Email: adult.education@birmingham.gov.uk
Website: www.bgfl.org
Head of Adult Learning: Bob Malloy

Coventry City Council
Adult Education Service
Central District
Southfields Old School
South Street
Coventry CV1 5EJ
Tel: 024 7678 5574
Fax: 024 7663 2573
Head of Adult Education: Alan Newbold

Dudley Metropolitan Borough Council
Council House
Priory Road
Dudley
West Midlands DY1 1HF
Tel: 01384 812345
Website: www.dudley.gov.uk
Head of Adult and Community Learning:
Ros Partridge
Assistant Director, Libraries, Archives and
Adult Learning: Kate Millin

Adult and Community Learning Team is
now based at:
8 Parton Street
Dudley DY1 1JJ
Tel: 01384 813976

Herefordshire Council
Economic and Community Services
PO Box 4
Plough Lane
Hereford HR4 0XH
Tel: 01432 260637
Fax: 01432 383031
Email: lllearning@herefordshire.gov.uk
Website: www.herefordshire.gov.uk
Lifelong Learning Development Manager:
Peter Ding

Sandwell Metropolitan Borough Council
Children and Young People's Services
Shaftesbury House
402 High Street
West Bromwich B70 9LT
Tel: 0121 569 8100
Website: www.sandwell.gov.uk
Executive Director of Children and Young
People's Services: Roger Crouch
Director of Learning: Penny Penn-Howard
Principal Advisor for Extended and Lifelong
Learning: James Wells

Shropshire County Council
Adult and Community Learning Services
The Gateway
Chester Street
Shrewsbury SY1 1NB
Tel: 01743 355159
Fax: 01743 358951
Website: www.shropshire.gov.uk
Acting Corporate Director, Community
Services: Liz Nicholson
ACL Manager: Sarah Bromley
Family Learning Manager: Hilary Blakely

Solihull Metropolitan Borough Council
Community Services Directorate
Council House
PO Box 19
Solihull
West Midlands B91 3QS
Tel: 0121 704 6000
Website: www.solihull.gov.uk
Corporate Director of Community Services:
Jim Harte

Staffordshire County Council
Children and Lifelong Learning
Tipping Street
Stafford ST16 2DH
Tel: 01785 223121
Fax: 01785 278764
Email: acl@staffordshire.gov.uk
Website: www.staffordshire.gov.uk
Corporate Director of Children and Lifelong
Learning: Peter Traves
Head of Adult and Community Learning:
Steve Lapworth

Stoke-on-Trent City Council
Community Services
Adult and Community Learning
Civic Centre
Glebe Street
Stoke-on-Trent ST4 1RU
Tel: 01782 236878
Fax: 01782 232217
Website: www.stoke.gov.uk
Director: Ken Ivatt
Head of Adult and Community Learning:
Carol Smith

Telford and Wrekin Council
Community Services
PO Box 59
Telford
Shropshire TF3 4WZ
Tel: 01952 382880
Fax: 01952 382327
Website: www.telford.gov.uk
Head of Community and Neighbourhoods:
Pete Jackson
Lifelong Learning Manager: Richard Probert

Walsall Metropolitan Borough Council
12th Floor, Tameway Tower
48 Bridge Street
Walsall WS1 1JZ
Tel: 01922 650000
Fax: 01922 722322
Email: info@walsall.gov.uk
Website: www.walsall.gov.uk
Executive Director, Neighbourhood
Directorate: Jamie Morris
Assistant Director, Leisure, Culture and
Lifelong Learning: Tim Challans
Principal of the College of Continuing
Education: Terry Bell

Warwickshire County Council
Adult, Health and Community Services
Adult and Community Learning Service
Orion House
Athena Drive
Tachbrook Park
Warwick CV34 6RQ
Tel: 01926 731228
Fax: 01926 731106
Website: www.warwickshire.gov.uk
Strategic Director: Graeme Betts
Head of Service: Peter Sutton

Wolverhampton City Council
Adults and Community Directorate
Wolverhampton Adult Education Service
Old Hall Street
Wolverhampton WV1 3AU
Tel: 01902 558180
Fax: 01902 558170
Email:
enquiries@aes.wolverhampton.gov.uk
Website: www.wolverhampton.gov.uk
Director of Adults and Community:
Sarah Norman
Head of Service: Christine Parsons

Worcestershire County Council
Libraries and Learning Service
County Hall
Spetchley Road
Worcester WR5 2NP
Tel: 01905 728537
Fax: 01905 728993
Email: kkirk@worcestershire.gov.uk
Website: www.worcestershire.gov.uk
Director of Adult and Community Services:
Eddie Clarke
Strategic Libraries and Learning Manager:
Kathy Kirk

East Midlands

Derby City Council
Allen Park Centre
Allen Street
Allenton
Derby DE24 9DE
Tel: 01332 706849
Fax: 01332 706841
Email: cath-harcula@derbyals.org
Website: www.adult-learning-derby.org.uk
Director of Children and Young People's
Services: Andrew Flack
Head of Adult Learning Service:
Cath Harcula
Basic Skills Contact: Anne Fraser
Learning Difficulties Contact: Lynda Raven

Derbyshire County Council
County Hall
Matlock
Derbyshire DE4 3AG
Tel: 01629 580000
Fax: 01629 580350
Website: www.derbyshire.gov.uk
Strategic Director, Children and Younger
Adults Department: Bruce Buckley
Assistant Director, Engagement and Skills:
Donald Rae
Head of Service, Adult Community
Education: Lesley Harry
Read On – Write Away!
Email: info@rowa.co.uk
Website: www.rowa.co.uk
Director: Sarah Birkinshaw

Leicester City Council
Adult Skills and Learning Service
10 York Road
Leicester LE1 5TS
Tel: 0116 233 4343
Email: info@laec.ac.uk
Website: www.leicester.gov.uk
Corporate Director of Adults and Housing:
Sheila Lock
Interim Head of Adult Skills and Learning:
Mary Harrison
Website: www.lasals.co.uk

Leicestershire County Council
Leicestershire Adult Learning Service
G16, County Hall
Glenfield
Leicester LE3 8RF
Tel: 0116 265 6563
Fax: 0116 265 6398
Website: www.leics.gov.uk/golearn
Director of Children and Young People's
Service: Gareth Williams
Principal Adult Learning Officer:
Peter Sapsford
Email: psapsford@leics.gov.uk
Community Regeneration Officer:
Wendy Manning
Quality and Workforce Development
Officer: Sharon Cope
Curriculum Development Officer:
Peter Cantle
Family Learning Strategy Officer:
Yvonne Casswell
Learning Support Strategy Officer:
Alison Doggett
Skills for Life Strategy Officer:
Colleen Molloy

Lincolnshire County Council
Communities Directorate – Culture and
Adult Education
County Offices
Newland
Lincoln LN1 1YL
Tel: 01522 552839
Fax: 01522 552811
Website: www.lincolnshire.gov.uk
Head for Communities: Ian Anderson
Learning Managers: Jill Hill and
Wendy Bond
Head of Libraries, Learning and Inclusion:
John Pateman

Northamptonshire County Council
Customer Services
PO Box 216
John Dryden House
8–10 The Lakes
Northampton NN4 7DD
Tel: 01604 236236
Fax: 01604 237441
Website: www.northamptonshire.gov.uk
Director of Customer Services:
Paul Blanthern
County Adult Learning Manager:
Allan Chesney

Nottinghamshire County Council
Communities Department
County Hall
West Bridgford
Nottingham NG2 7QP
Tel: 0115 977 2875
Fax: 0115 977 3859
Email: sue.green@nottscc.gov.uk
Website: www.nottinghamshire.gov.uk
Strategic Director of Communities:
Steve Calvert
Adult and Community Learning Service
Manager: Sue Green

Rutland County Council
Children and Young People's Service
Catmose
Oakham
Rutland LE15 6HP
Tel: 01572 722577
Fax: 01572 758479
Email: enquiries@rutland.gov.uk
Website: www.rutland.gov.uk
Director of Children and Young People's
Service: Carol Chambers
Service Manager: Jill Haigh

Eastern

Bedfordshire County Council
Room 515
County Hall
Cauldwell Street
Bedford MK42 9AP
Tel: 01234 363222
Fax: 01234 228993
Website: www.bedfordshire.gov.uk
Head of Adult and Community Learning:
Frances Darlow

Cambridgeshire County Council
ET 1020
Castle Court
Shire Hall
Cambridge CB3 0AP
Tel: 01223 717952
Fax: 01223 717997
Email:
sarah.bedward@cambridgeshire.gov.uk
Website: www.cambridgeshire.gov.uk
Deputy Chief Executive: Brian Smith
Director of Community Learning and
Development: Mike Hosking
Head of Strategy – Adult Learning:
Shelagh Rumbelow

Essex County Council
Adult Community Learning
PO Box 47
County Hall
Chelmsford
Essex CM2 6WN
Tel: 01245 436 132
Fax: 01245 436 319
Email: michael.bowes@essexcc.gov.uk
Website: www.essexcc.gov.uk/adultlearning
Director of Adult Leaning and Libraries:
Susan Carragher

Hertfordshire County Council
Children, Schools and Families Service
Room 145, County Hall
Pegs Lane
Hertford SG13 8DF
Tel: 01992 555 915
Fax: 01992 588 583
Website: www.hertsdirect.org
Director of Children, Schools and Families:
John Harris
Head of Adult, Family and Community
Learning: Marianne Stevenson

Luton Borough Council
Housing and Community Living
Luton Adult and Community Learning
Unity House
111 Stuart Street
Luton
Bedfordshire LU1 5NP
Tel: 01582 547 500
Fax: 01582 547 733
Website: www.luton.gov.uk
Director of Housing and Community Living:
Penny Furness-Smith
Head of Leisure and Community:
Peter Jones
Service Manager: Roger Cannon

Norfolk County Council
County Hall
Martineau Lane
Norwich
Norfolk NR1 2DL
Tel: 01603 222146
Fax: 01603 232119
Website: www.norfolk.gov.uk
Director of Corporate Resources and
Cultural Services: Paul Adams
Head of Service: Beverley Evans
Skills for Life, Curriculum Faculty Manager:
Julia Richards
Assistant Head of Service: Denise Saadvandi

Adult Education delivered at:
Wensum Lodge
169 King Street
Norwich
Norfolk NR1 1WQ
Tel: 01603 306582
Fax: 01603 306626
Email:
centraladmin.adulteducation@norfolk.gov.uk

Peterborough City Council
Education Department
College of Adult Education
Brook Street
Peterborough PE1 1TU
Tel: 01733 761 361
Fax: 01733 708 067
Website: www.pcae.ac.uk
Head of Adult Learning/Principal:
Dr Graham Winton
Deputy Principal: David Roxburgh

Southend on Sea Borough Council
Children and Learning
PO Box 6
5th Floor
Civic Centre
Southend on Sea
Essex SS2 6ER
Tel: 01702 215890
Fax: 01702 351090
Website: www.southend.gov.uk
Director of Children and Learning:
Paul Greenhalgh

Southend Adult Community College
Ambleside Drive
Southend on Sea SS1 2UP
Tel: 01702 445700
Email: info@southend-adult.co.uk

Suffolk County Council
Adult and Community Services
Endeavour House
8 Russell Road
Ipswich IP1 2BX
Tel: 01473 583000
Fax: 01473 216853
Website: www.suffolkcc.gov.uk
Head of Service, Community Learning and
Skills Development: Janet Bloomfield
Learning Support and Resource Manager:
Steve Pike
Locality Learning Manager: Simon Holmes
Learning Standards and Curriculum
Development Manager: Sally Butcher

Thurrock Council
Adult Education Service
Thurrock Adult Community College
Richmond Road
Grays
Essex RM17 6DN
Tel: 01375 372 476
Fax: 01375 394 104
Website: www.thurrock.gov.uk
Head of Resources, Development and
Lifelong Learning: Peter Mooney
Principal: Sharon Walsh

South West

Bath and North East Somerset Council
Community Learning Service
The Hollies
High Street
Midsomer Norton
Bath BA3 2DP
Tel: 01225 396450
Fax: 01225 396739
Website: www.bathnes.gov.uk
Community Learning Manager: Jan Walker

Borough of Poole
Education Service
Civic Centre
Poole
Dorset BH15 2RU
Tel: 01202 633633
Fax: 01202 633706
Website: www.poole.gov.uk
Strategic Director, Education: John Nash
Head of Culture and Community Learning:
Kevin McErlane
Adult Learning Manager: Lesley Ann Spain
Tel: 01202 262300
Fax: 01202 262307
Email: infopal@poole.gov.uk

Bournemouth Borough Council
Bournemouth Adult Learning
Bournemouth Learning Centre
Ensbury Avenue
Bournemouth BH10 4HG
Tel: 01202 451950
Fax: 01202 451989
Email: bal.enquiries@bournemouth.gov.uk
Website:
www.bournemouth.gov.uk/adultlearning
Head of Information, Culture and
Community Learning: Shelagh Levett
Strategy Manager – Curriculum and Learner
Services: Lorraine Holmes

Bristol City Council

The Learning Communities Team
The Park
Daventry Road
Knowle
Bristol BS4 1DQ
Tel: 0117 903 9750
Fax: 0117 903 9751
Website: www.bristol-city.gov.uk
Programme Director, Partnerships and
Localities: Paul Taylor
Strategy Leader, Parents and Learning
Communities: Jane Taylor

Cornwall County Council

County Hall
Truro
Cornwall TR1 3AY
Tel: 01872 274778
Fax: 01872 274781
Email: aecentral@cornwall.gov.uk
Website: www.cornwall.gov.uk
Head of Service: John Hall

Adult Education Services based at:
Treru
The Leats
Truro
Cornwall TR1 3AG

Council of the Isles of Scilly

Town Hall
St Mary's
Isles of Scilly TR21 0LW
Tel: 01720 422537
Fax: 01720 424017
Secretary for Education: Philip S Hygate
Email: phygate@scilly.gov.uk
Lifelong Learning Officer: Lesley Hopkins

Devon County Council

Adult and Community Services
County Hall
Topsham Road
Exeter EX2 4QD
Tel: 0845 155 1015
Fax: 0845 155 1003
Website: www.devon.gov.uk
Director of Adult and Community Services:
David Johnstone
Head of Service: Margaret Davidson

All contacts are based at: ACL (Adult and
Community Learning)
Buckland House
Park Five
Sowton
Exeter EX2 7ND
Tel: 01392 386580
Fax: 01392 385726

Dorset County Council

Adult and Community Services Directorate
County Hall
Dorchester
Dorset DT1 1XJ
Tel: 01305 251000
Fax: 01305 224499
Email: adult.ed@dorsetcc.gov.uk
Website: www.adult-ed.co.uk
Director of Adult and Community Services:
Steve Pitt
Service Manager, Dorset Adult Learning:
Marion Pymar

Gloucestershire County Council

Community and Adult Care Directorate
Shire Hall
Westgate Street
Gloucester GL1 2TG
Tel: 01452 425418
Fax: 01452 425396
Website: www.gloucestershire.gov.uk
Executive Director: Margaret Sheather
Head of Adult Education: Jim Austin
Head of Quality & LIS: Mark Hewlett

North Somerset Council
Adult Social Services and Housing
Directorate
Community Learning Team
PO Box 51
Town Hall
Weston-super-Mare
Somerset BS23 1ZZ
Tel: 01275 884309
Fax: 01275 888316
Email: lesley.dale@n-somerset.gov.uk
Website: www.n-somerset.gov.uk
Director of Adult Social Services and
Housing: Jane Smith
Widening Participation Manager:
Lesley Dale

Plymouth City Council
Children's Services
Plymouth Adult and Community Services
Civic Centre
Royal Parade
Plymouth PL1 2AA
Tel: 01752 668000
Fax: 01752 304880
Website: www.plymouth.gov.uk
Acting Senior Adult Education Officer:
Tracy Hewett
Tel: 01752 601114
website: www.plymouthoncourse.com

Somerset County Council
County Hall
Taunton
Somerset TA1 4DY
Tel: 01823 355933
Fax: 01823 356183
Website: www.learnsomerset.co.uk
Chief Executive: Alan Jones
Group Manager, Somerset Skills and
Learning: Steve Lay
Senior Manager, Skills: Margaret Luck
Senior Manager, Foundation:
Susie Simon-Norris
Senior Manager, Leisure Learning:
Holly Cole
Organisational Performance Manager:
Dave Watson

South Gloucestershire Council
Community Learning Service
The Ridgewood Centre
244 Station Road
Yate
Bristol BS37 4AF
Tel: 01454 863275
Fax: 01454 863309
Director of Community Services:
Steve Evans

Swindon Borough Council
Premier House
Station Road
Swindon SN1 1TZ
Tel: 01793 463 261
Fax: 01793 466 484
Website: www.swindon.gov.uk
Director of Community: Chris Sivers

Torbay Council
Children's Services Directorate
Oldway
Torquay Road
Paignton
Devon TQ3 2TE
Tel: 01803 208208
Fax: 01803 208225
Website: www.torbay.gov.uk
Strategic Director for Children's Services:
Margaret Dennison

Adult Education delivery is contracted to
South Devon College

Wiltshire County Council
Department for Children and Education
County Hall
Bythesea Road
Trowbridge
Wiltshire BA14 8JB
Tel: 01225 713000
Fax: 01225 713812
Website: www.wiltshire.gov.uk
Director: Carolyn Godfrey
Head of Extended Community Learning:
Debbie Rusbridge

South East

Bracknell Forest Borough Council
Social Care and Learning
Seymour House
38 Broadway
Bracknell
Berkshire RG12 1AU
Tel: 01344 354000
Fax: 01344 354001
Email: scl@bracknell-forest.gov.uk
Website www.bracknell-forest.gov.uk
Director of Social Care and Learning:
Lesley Heale
Senior Lifelong Learning Officer:
David Jones

Brighton and Hove City Council
Children, Families and Schools
Brighton Town Hall
Bartholomew Square
Brighton BN1 1JA
Tel: 01273 294920
Fax: 01273 294924
Director, Children and Young People's Trust:
Di Smith
Adult Skills and Learning Manager:
Dan Shelley

Buckinghamshire County Council
Buckinghamshire Culture and Learning
Gallery Suite
County Hall
Aylesbury
Buckinghamshire HP20 1UU
Tel: 01296 383549
Fax: 01296 382259
Website: www.adultlearningbcc.ac.uk
Head of Culture and Learning:
Amanda Brooke-Webb

East Sussex County Council
Chief Executive Department
County Hall
St Anne's Crescent
Lewes
East Sussex BN7 1UE
Tel: 01273 481731
Fax: 01273 481500
Email: adult.education@eastsussex.gov.uk
Website: www.eastsussex.gov.uk
Adult Learning and Skills Manager:
Christine Gervis

Hampshire County Council
Recreation and Heritage Department
Hampshire Learning
Mottisfont Court
High Street
Winchester
Hampshire SO23 8ZF
Tel: 01962 846002
Fax: 01962 820350
Email: adult.learning@hants.gov.uk
Website:
www.hampshireadultlearning.co.uk
Director of Recreation and Heritage:
Yinnon Ezra
Head of Adult and Family Learning:
Beverley Jones

Isle of Wight Council
County Hall
High Street
Newport
Isle of Wight PO30 1TY
Tel: 01983 821000
Fax: 01983 823841
Website: www.iwight.com
Director of Children's Services: Steve Beynon
Director of Adult and Community Services:
Sarah Mitchell
Adult and Community Learning Manager:
Jo Treagus
Community and Family Learning Manager:
Sarah Teague

Community and Family Learning
Westridge
Brading Road
Isle of Wight PO33 1QS
Tel: 01983 817280
Fax: 01983 817281

Kent County Council
Communities Directorate
Invicta House
County Hall
Maidstone
Kent ME14 1XX
Tel: 01622 671411
Fax: 01622 221764
Website: www.kent.gov.uk
Managing Director Communities:
Amanda Honey
Head of Service: Ian Forward
Tel: 01795 415901
Fax: 01795 435493

Medway Council
Children and Adults
Learning and Caring Directorate
Gun Wharf
Dock Road
Chatham
Kent ME4 4TR
Tel: 01634 306000
Fax: 01634 333465
Website: www.medway.gov.uk
Director: Rose Collinson
Adult Learning Manager: Malcolm Tite

Milton Keynes Council
Learning and Development Directorate
Milton Keynes Central Library
555 Silbury Boulevard
Milton Keynes MK9 3HL
Tel: 01908 254074
Fax: 01908 254089
Learning and Skills Manager:
Deborah Cooper
Lifelong Learning Officer: Claire Griffin

Oxfordshire Adult Learning
L18, Cricket Road Centre
Cricket Road
Oxford OX4 3DW
Tel: 01865 456738
Fax: 01865 458793
Email: adult.learning@oxfordshire.gov.uk
Website: www.oxfordshire.gov.uk
Director for Social and Community Services:
John Jackson
Head of Community Services:
Richard Munro
Head of Adult Learning: Jane Dixon

Portsmouth City Council
Directorate of Children, Families and
Learning
Civic Offices
Guildhall Square
Portsmouth
Hampshire PO1 2EA
Tel: 023 9284 1709
Fax: 023 9284 1208
Website: www.learnportsmouth.org.uk
Strategic Director: Lynda Fisher
Head of Community Learning:
Andrew Olive

Reading Borough Council
Education and Children's Services
PO Box 2623
Reading RG1 7WA
Tel: 0118 939 0900
Fax: 0118 958 0675
Website: www.reading.gov.uk
Director of Education and Children's
Services: Anna Wright
Head of Service, New Directions:
Lesley Reilly

**Royal Borough of Windsor
and Maidenhead**
Education Department
Lifelong Learning
Town Hall
St Ives Road
Maidenhead
Berkshire SL6 1RF
Tel: 01628 796584
Fax: 01628 796366
Email: adult.education@rbwm.gov.uk
Website: www.rbwm.gov.uk
Corporate Director of Learning and Care:
Jim Gould
Head of Extended Schools: Angela Wellings

Slough Borough Council
Community and Well Being
Town Hall
Bath Road
Slough
Berkshire SL1 3UQ
Tel: 01753 875741
Fax: 01753 875419
Website: www.slough.gov.uk
Strategic Director, Community and Well
Being: Jane Wood
Head of Lifelong Learning: Philip Wright

Southampton City Council
Directorate of Children's Services and
Learning
Frobisher House
Nelsons Gate
Southampton SO15 1BZ
Tel: 023 8083 2771
Fax: 023 8083 3221
Website: www.southampton.gov.uk
Executive Director for Children's Services
and Learning: Clive Webster
Senior Adult and Community Learning
Manager: John Bridge

Surrey County Council
Children and Young People's Service
County Hall
Penrhyn Road
Kingston upon Thames
Surrey KT1 2DJ
Tel: 020 8541 8800
Fax: 020 8541 9003
Website: www.surreycc.gov.uk
Strategic Director, Families: Andy Roberts
Adult Learning Manager: Paul Hoffman
Head of Cultural Services: Yvonne Rees

West Berkshire Council
Adult and Community Learning Team
Avonbank House
West Street
Newbury
Berkshire RG14 1BZ
Tel: 01635 519060
Fax: 01635 519811
Website: www.westberks.gov.uk
Principal Adult and Community Learning
Officer: Sarah Hanson

West Sussex County Council
Adult and Community Learning Department
County Hall
Chichester
West Sussex PO19 1RF
Tel: 01243 777770
Fax: 01243 777211
Website:
www.westsussex.gov.uk/adulteducation
Director of Adult and Children: John Dixon
Head of Adult and Community Learning:
Ros Parker

Wokingham Borough Council
Place and Neighbourhood Services
PO Box 156
Shute End
Wokingham
Berkshire RG40 1WN
Tel: 0118 974 6000
Fax: 0118 974 6135
Email: wokinghambc@wokingham.gov.uk
Website: www.wokingham.gov.uk
Learning Manager: Alan Bennett

London

City of London
Adult and Community Service
PO Box 270
Guildhall
London EC2P 2EJ
Tel: 020 7332 1750
Fax: 020 7332 1621
Email: education@cityoflondon.gov.uk
Website: www.cityoflondon.gov.uk
Head of Adult and Community Learning:
Barbara Hamilton

**London Borough of Barking
and Dagenham**
Department of Regeneration
Town Hall
Barking
Essex IG11 7LU
Tel: 020 8227 3181
Fax: 020 8227 3471
Email: sandra.thomson@lbbd.gov.uk
Website: www.barking-dagenham.gov.uk
Corporate Director of Regeneration:
Jennifer Dearing
Head of Skills, Learning and Enterprise:
Alan Lazell
Head of College: Patricia Cooney

London Borough of Barnet
Children's Services
Building 5
North London Business Park
Oakleigh Road South
London N11 1NP
Tel: 020 8359 2000
Fax: 087 0889 6779
Website: www.barnet.gov.uk
Chief Education Officer: Martin Baker

London Borough of Bexley

Children and Young People's Services
Hill View
Hill View Drive
Welling
Kent DA16 3RY
Tel: 020 8303 7777
Fax: 020 8319 4302
Website: www.bexley.gov.uk
Director of Children and Young People's
Services: Deborah Absalom
Principal: Malcolm Tite

London Borough of Brent

Children and Families Department
Chesterfield House
9 Park Lane
Wembley
Middlesex HA9 7RW
Tel: 020 8937 3000
Fax: 020 8937 3023
Website: www.brent.gov.uk
Director: John Christie
Head of Service: Sue Hasty

London Borough of Bromley

Adult and Community Services
Civic Centre
Stockwell Close
Bromley
Kent BR1 3UH
Tel: 020 8464 3333
Fax: 020 8313 4620
Website: www.bromley.gov.uk
Director of Adult and Community Services:
Terry Rich
Assistant Director, Libraries and Lifelong
Learning: Linda Simpson

London Borough of Camden

Children, Schools and Families Directorate
Crowndale Centre
218 Eversholt Street
London NW1 1BD
Tel: 020 7974 2148
Fax: 020 7974 1536
Website: www.camden.gov.uk
Director of Children, Schools and Families
Directorate: Ann Baxter
Head of Adult and Community Learning:
Brian Mitchell

London Borough of Croydon

Department for Children, Young People and
Learners
Taberner House
Park Lane
Croydon
Surrey CR9 1TP
Tel: 020 8686 4433
Fax: 020 8760 5447
Website: www.croydon.gov.uk
Website: www.cets.co.uk
Director for Children, Young People and
Learners: Dave Hill
Head of Adult Learning and Training:
Rosemary Sloman

London Borough of Ealing

Adult Education Department
4th Floor, Perceval House
14–16 Uxbridge Road
Ealing
London W5 2HL
Tel: 020 8825 5577
Fax: 020 8579 5453
Email: adultlearning@ealing.gov.uk
Website: www.ealing.gov.uk
Interim Head of Adult Learning:
Emma Peglar-Willis

London Borough of Enfield

Education, Children's Services and Leisure
PO Box 56
Civic Centre
Silver Street
Enfield
Middlesex EN1 3XQ
Tel: 020 8379 3201
Fax: 020 8379 3243
Director of Education, Children's Services
and Leisure: Peter Lewis
Head of Lifelong and Community Learning:
Dr Ben Charles

London Borough of Greenwich
Adult and Community Learning
Regeneration and Enterprise Skills
Directorate
Peggy Middleton House
50 Woolwich New Road
London SE18 6HQ
Tel: 020 8921 6834
Fax: 020 8921 6283
Website: www.greenwich.gov.uk
Director of Regeneration and Enterprise
Skills: John Comber
Head of Adult and Community Learning:
Katie Clarricoates
Email: katie.clarricoates@greenwich.gov.uk

London Borough of Hackney
The Learning Trust
Hackney Technology and Learning Centre
1 Reading Lane
London E8 1GQ
Tel: 020 8820 7339
Fax: 020 8820 7174
Email: adult.egsa@learningtrust.co.uk
Website: www.learningtrust.co.uk
Chief Executive of the Learning Trust:
Alan Wood
Head of Adult Learning Services:
Trish Smith

London Borough of Hammersmith and Fulham
Adult Education
Macbeth Centre
Macbeth Street
London W6 9JJ
Website: www.lbhf.gov.uk
Director of Community Services:
James Reilly
Head of Learning and Skills: Robert Raven

London Borough of Haringey
Adults, Culture and Community Services
40 Cumberland Road
London N22 7SG
Tel: 020 8489 0000
Fax: 020 8489 3864
Website: www.haringey.gov.uk
Director of the Adults, Culture and
Community Services: Mun Thong Phung
Deputy Director for Culture, Libraries and
Learning: Diana Edmonds
Head of Service: Pat Duffy

London Borough of Harrow
Community and Cultural Services
Civic Centre
Harrow
Middlesex HA1 2UL
Tel: 020 8424 3805
Website: www.learninharrow.org.uk
Director of Community and Cultural
Services: Javed Khan
Service Manager for Adult and Community
Learning: Dr Geoff Trodd

London Borough of Havering
Adult Education, Learning and Achievement
Whitworth Centre
Noak Hill Road
Noak Hill
Romford RM3 7YA
Tel: 01708 433790
Email:
enquiries-adultcollege@havering.gov.uk
Website: www.havering.gov.uk
Group Director: Andrew Ireland
Lifelong Learning Manager: Jeffrey Hooton
Email: jeff.hooton@havering.gov.uk

London Borough of Hillingdon
Hillingdon Adult Education
86 Long Lane
Ickenham
Uxbridge
Middlesex UB10 8SX
Tel: 01895 676690
Fax: 01895 673089
Email: hae@hillingdongrid.org
Website: www.hae-acl.ac.uk
Corporate Director Planning and
Community Services: Jean Palmer
Head of Adult Education: Tricia Collis
Programme Manager, Skills for Life:
Terry Stothard

London Borough of Hounslow
Children's Services and Lifelong Learning
Civic Centre
Lampton Road
Hounslow
Middlesex TW3 4DN
Tel: 020 8583 6000
Fax: 020 8583 2751
Website: www.hounslowlea.org.uk
Director of Children's Services and Lifelong
Learning: Judith Pettersen
Acting Principal: Liz Meagher

London Borough of Islington
Adult and Community Learning Service
Room 202
159 Upper Street
London N1 1RE
Tel: 020 7527 5782
Fax: 020 7527 5033
Email: acl@islington.gov.uk
Website: www.islington.gov.uk
Head of Adult and Community Learning:
Liz Armstrong

London Borough of Lambeth
Regeneration and Enterprise
Hambrook House
Porden Road
London SW2 5RW
Tel: 020 7926 1000
Fax: 020 7926 9778
Website: www.lambeth.gov.uk
Divisional Director of Regeneration and
Enterprise: Jo Negrini
Head of Employment, Learning and Skills:
Bernard Corless

London Borough of Lewisham
Community Services
Town Hall
Lewisham
London SE6 4RU
Tel: 020 8314 6000
Fax: 020 8314 3023
Website: www.lewisham.gov.uk
Executive Director of Community Services:
Aileen Buckton
Head of Strategy, Performance and
Partnership: Sarah Wainer
Head of Service: Lesley Robinson

Community Education HQ:
Tel 020 8314 3300
Fax: 020 8314 3254
Minicom: 020 8314 3268
Email:
community.education@lewisham.gov.uk

London Borough of Merton
Community and Housing
Merton Adult Education
Whatley Avenue
London SW20 9NS
Tel: 020 8543 9292
Fax: 020 8544 1421
Email: info@merton-adult-college.ac.uk
Website:
www.merton.gov.uk/adulteducation
Head of Service: Yvonne Tomlin

London Borough of Newham
NEWCEYS (Newham Community
Education and Youth Service)
The Web
49 The Broadway
Stratford
London E15 4BQ
Tel: 020 8430 4057
Fax: 020 8227 1001
Website: www.newham.gov.uk
Executive Director, Children and Young
People's Services: Kim Bromley-Derry
Principal Manager for Young People and
Lifelong Learning: Steve Cameron
Adult Learning Manager: Robert Murphy

London Borough of Redbridge

Culture, Sport and Community Learning
8th Floor, Lynton House
255–259 High Road
Ilford
Essex IG1 1NN
Tel: 020 8708 3100
Fax: 020 8708 3109
Email: pat.reynolds@redbridge.gov.uk
Website: www.redbridge.gov.uk
Director of Housing and Community
Services: John Drew
Director of Children's Services: Pat Reynolds
Chief Culture and Community Services
Officer: Iain Varah

London Borough of Richmond upon Thames

Adult and Community Services
42 York Street
Twickenham TW1 3BW
Tel: 020 8891 7600
Fax: 020 8831 6252
Email: education@richmond.gov.uk
Website: www.richmond.gov.uk
Director of Adult and Community Services:
Jeff Jerome
Principal Manager, Community Services:
Grahame Freeland-Bright

London Borough of Southwark

Southwark Adult Learning Service
Thomas Caxton Centre
Alpha Street
London SE15 4NX
Tel: 020 7358 2100
Fax: 020 7525 5200
Manager Adult Learning Services:
Dolly Naeem

London Borough of Sutton

c/o SCOLA (Sutton College of Learning for
Adults)
St Nicholas Way
Sutton
Surrey SM1 1EA
Tel: 020 8770 6901
Email: reception@scola.ac.uk
Website: www.sutton.gov.uk
Strategic Director of Children, Young People
and Learning Services: Dr I Birnbaum
Executive Head, Service Management:
Stephen Ingram
Principal: Christine Jones

London Borough of Tower Hamlets

Lifelong Learning, Children's Services
The Shadwell Centre
455 The Highway
London E1W 3HP
Tel: 020 7364 5673
Fax: 020 7364 5712
Email: info.lls@towerhamlets.gov.uk
Website: www.towerhamlets.gov.uk
Corporate Director, Children's Services:
Kevan Collins
Head of Adult and Community Learning:
Fiona Paterson

London Borough of Waltham Forest

Waltham Forest Community Learning and
Skills Service (CLaSS)
Chesnuts House
398 Hoe Street
London E17 9AA
Tel: 020 8521 4311
Fax: 020 8521 1329
Website: www.lbwf.gov.uk
Head of Service: Anne Perez
Skills for Life Manager: Jill Ross
Administration Manager: Veronica Shaw

London Borough of Wandsworth
Children's Services
Town Hall
Wandsworth High Street
London SW18 2PU
Tel: 020 8871 7890
Fax: 020 8871 6609
Website: www.wandsworth.gov.uk
Director of Children's Services:
Paul Robinson
Head of Lifelong Learning and 14–19
Development: Santino Fragola

**Royal Borough of Kensington
and Chelsea**
Town Hall
Hornton Street
London W8 7NX
Tel: 020 7361 3000
Fax: 020 7938 1445
Website: www.rbkc.gov.uk
Executive Director for Family and Children's
Services: Anne-Marie Carrie
Director of Community Learning:
Karen Tyerman
Head of Adult and Family Learning:
Don McBean

**Royal Borough of Kingston
upon Thames**
Kingston Adult Education
North Kingston Centre
Richmond Road
Kingston upon Thames
Surrey KT2 5PE
Tel: 020 8547 6700
Fax: 020 8547 6747
Email: adult.education@rbk.kingston.gov.uk
Website:
www.kingston.gov.uk/education/
adulteducation
Strategic Director of Learning and Children's
Services: Patrick Leeson
Principal: Barrie Selwyn
Tel: 020 8547 6702
Deputy Principal: Katherine Fisher

Westminster City Council
Adults Services
Westminster City Hall
PO Box 240
Victoria Street
London SW1E 6QP
Tel: 020 7641 6000
Fax: 020 7641 3404
Website: www.westminster.gov.uk
Director of Adults Services:
Marian Harrington
Head of Service: Barbara Holm

Isle of Man

Isle of Man Government
Department of Education
St George's Court
Upper Church Street
Douglas
Isle of Man IM1 2SG
Tel: 01624 685820
Fax: 01624 685834
Email: enquiries@doe.gov.im
Website: www.gov.im
Director of Education: John Cain
Acting Deputy Director of Education:
Stuart Dobson

Channel Islands

States of Guernsey
States Education Department
PO Box 32
Grange Road
St Peter Port
Guernsey
Channel Islands GY1 3AU
Tel: 01481 710821
Fax: 01481 714475
Email: awilliams@education.gov.gg
Website: www.careers.gg
Director of Education: D T Neale
Lifelong Learning Manager: Alun Williams

States of Jersey
Department for Education, Sport and
Culture
PO Box 142
Jersey
Channel Islands JE4 8QJ
Tel: 01534 445504
Fax: 01534 449400
Email: esc@gov.je
Website: www.esc.gov.je
Director of Education, Sport and Culture:
Mario Lundy
Assistant Director of Education (Lifelong
Learning): David Greenwood

Further Education – England

National and Regional Further Education Agencies

Association for College Management
35 The Point
Market Harborough
Leicestershire LE16 7QU
Tel: 01858 461110
Fax: 01858 461366
Email: administration@acm.uk.com
Website: www.acm.uk.com
General Secretary/Chief Executive:
Peter Pendle
Head of Policy: Nadine Cartner
Head of Employment Relations:
David Green
Head of Corporate Services: Sara Shaw

The Association for College Management is a TUC affiliated trade union and professional association which represents managers of post-16 education and training.

Association of Colleges
2–5 Stedham Place
London WC1A 1HU
Tel: 020 7034 9900
Fax: 020 7034 9950
Email: enquiries@aoc.co.uk
Website: www.aoc.co.uk
Chief Executive: Martin Doel

The Association of College's (AOC's) role is to provide leadership within the new culture of lifelong learning. It lobbies for the resources its learners and colleges need.

Association of Colleges in the Eastern Region (ACER)
Suite 1, Lancaster House
Meadow Lane
St Ives
Huntingdon
Cambridgeshire PE27 4LG
Tel: 01480 468198
Fax: 01480 468601
Email: general@acer.ac.uk
Website: www.acer.ac.uk
Chief Executive: Veronica Windmill

ACER is based in the East of England and its main purpose is to serve the needs of its member colleges (general FE, specialist colleges and sixth-form colleges) and other providers in the learning and skills sector. ACER provides a range of services including regional networks and forums, management development, training, conferences and consultancy. They also manage a number of projects often with member colleges as partners. ACER's provision is open to all and many participants are from outside the region. ACER is the regional office for the Association of Colleges (AoC) and represents the FE system in the region. Much of ACER's work is carried out in collaboration with key regional partners and stakeholders.

Association of South East Colleges (AOSEC)
Building 11
University of Reading
London Road
Reading
Berkshire RG1 5AQ
Tel: 0118 378 6325
Fax: 0118 378 6324
Email: enquiries@aosec.org.uk
Website: www.aosec.org.uk
Chief Executive: Janet Eldrich
Chair: Barry Hicks

British Accreditation Council for Independent Further and Higher Education (BAC)

44 Bedford Row
London WC1R 4LL
Tel: 020 7447 2584
Fax: 020 7447 2585
Email: info@the-bac.org
Website: www.the-bac.org
Chief Executive: Dr Stephen Vickers

CENTRA (Education and Training Services) Ltd

Duxbury Park
Duxbury Hall Road
Chorley
Lancashire PR7 4AT
Tel: 01257 241428
Fax: 01257 260357
Email: enquiries@centra.org.uk
Website: www.centra.org.uk
Chief Executive: Mike Frain

EMFEC (East Midlands Further Education Council)

Robins Wood House
Robins Wood Road
Aspley
Nottingham NG8 3NH
Tel: 0115 854 1616
Fax: 0115 854 1617
Email: enquiries@emfec.co.uk
Website: www.emfec.co.uk
Chief Executive: Jennie Gardiner

EMFEC is an independent, not-for-profit company limited by guarantee with charitable status which delivers high quality support services to providers of vocational education and training in the post-14 sector.

FENC

Hamlin Way
Hardwick Narrows
King's Lynn
Norfolk PE30 4NG
Tel: 01553 776909
Fax: 01553 764824
Email: support@fenc.org.uk
Website: www.fenc.org.uk
Chief Executive: David Holland

Further Education Research Association

Lifelong Learning Office
University of Worcester
Henwick Grove
Worcester WR2 6AJ
Tel: 01905 855145
Fax: 01905 855132
Email: g.elliott@worc.ac.uk
Website: www.fera.uk.net
Chairperson: Prof. Geoffrey Elliott

The Further Education Research Association sponsors the *Journal of Research in Post-Compulsory Education*, and through conferences, sponsors research and information, dissemination on current issues and developments in further education. Chairperson is Geoffrey Elliott, University College Worcester.

Learning and Skills Network (LSN)

5th Floor
120 Holborn
London EC1N 2AD
Tel: 020 7297 9000
Fax: 020 7297 9001
Email: enquiries@lsneducation.org.uk
Website: www.lsneducation.org.uk
Chief Executive: John Stone

The Learning and Skills Network (LSN) is an independent not-for-profit organisation committed to making a difference to learning and skills. LSN aims to do this by delivering quality improvement and staff development programmes that support specific government initiatives, through research, training and consultancy; and by supplying services directly to schools, colleges and training organisations. Its support is practical and is delivered by skilled staff with a close appreciation and understanding of its sector. LSN is one of the two successor organisations of the Learning and Skills Development Agency (LSDA). Find out more about LSN by visiting the website www.lsneducation.org.uk

Learning South West
Bishops Hull House
Bishops Hull Road
Taunton
Somerset TA1 5EP
Tel: 01823 335 491
Fax: 01823 323 388
Email: enquiries@learning-southwest.org.uk
Website: www.learning-southwest.org.uk
Chief Executive: Tim Boyes-Watson

Learning South West is a membership
organisation working to support the
learning and skills and youth work sectors
across the region.

Mature Students Union
6 Salisbury Road
Harrow
Middlesex HA1 1NY
Website: www.msu.org.uk
National Secretary: Barry Donovan

NCFE
Citygate
St James Boulevard
Newcastle upon Tyne NE1 4JE
Tel: 0191 239 8000
Fax: 0191 239 8001
Email: info@ncfe.org.uk
Website www.ncfe.org.uk
Chief Executive: David Grailey

Principals' Professional Council
1 Heath Square
Boltro Road
Haywards Heath
West Sussex RH16 1BL
Tel: 01444 472499
Fax: 01444 472493
Email: ppc@naht.org.uk
General Secretary: Dr Michael Thrower

Further Education Institutions

North East

Bishop Auckland College
Woodhouse Lane
Bishop Auckland
Durham DL14 6JZ
Tel: 01388 443000
Fax: 01388 609294
Email: enquiries@bacoll.ac.uk
Website: www.bacoll.ac.uk
Principal and Chief Executive: Joanna Tait
Community Learning Manager:
Dawn Fairlamb
Head of Faculty: Louise Kemp

City of Sunderland College
Bede Centre
Durham Road
Sunderland SR3 4AH
Tel: 0191 511 6000
Fax: 0191 511 6380
Website: www.citysun.ac.uk
Principal: Angela O'Donohue
Director of Skills for Life: Julie Raine

Cleveland College of Art and Design
Green Lane
Linthorpe
Middlesbrough TS5 7RJ
Tel: 01642 288000
Fax: 01642 288828
Email: shortcourses@ccad.ac.uk
Website: www.ccad.ac.uk
Principal: Martin Raby
Continuing Education Manager:
Amanda Smith

Darlington College
Central Park
Haughton Road
Darlington
County Durham DL1 1DR
Tel: 01325 503050
Fax: 01325 503000
Email: enquire@darlington.ac.uk
Website: www.darlington.ac.uk
Principal and Chief Executive:
Sarah Robinson

Derwentside College
Front Street
Consett
County Durham DH8 5EE
Tel: 01207 585900
Fax: 01207 585996
Website: www.derwentside.ac.uk
Principal: Albert Croney
Director of Finance and Resources:
Richard Oliver
Director of Business Development:
Susan Errington
Director of Curriculum and Quality:
Susan Welsh

East Durham College
Willerby Grove
Peterlee
Durham SR8 2AN
Tel: 0191 518 2000
Fax: 0191 586 7125
Email: enquiry@edhcc.ac.uk
Website: www.eastdurham.ac.uk
Principal and Chief Executive:
Ian W Prescott
Curriculum Manager: Carina Tomlinson
Student Services Manager: Nora Gregory

Gateshead College
Baltic Campus
Quarryfield Road
Baltic Business Quarter
Gateshead
Tyne and Wear NE8 8BE
Tel: 0191 490 2246
Website: www.gateshead.ac.uk
Principal: Richard Thorold
PA to Principal: Linda Hough
Secretary to Deputy Principals:
Debra Murphy

**Hartlepool College of
Further Education**
Stockton Street
Hartlepool TS24 7NT
Tel: 01429 295111
Fax: 01429 292999
Email: enquiries@hartlepoolfe.ac.uk
Website: www.hartlepoolfe.ac.uk
Principal and Chief Executive:
David Waddington

Vice-Principal and Deputy Chief Executive:
Michael Bretherick

Hartlepool Sixth Form College
Brinkburn
Hartlepool TS25 5PF
Tel: 01429 294444
Fax: 01429 294455
Email: hsfc@hpoolsfc.ac.uk
Principal: Rick Wells
Assistant Principal: Carole Horseman

Middlesbrough College
Dock Street
Middlesbrough
Cleveland TS2 1AD
Tel: 01642 333 333
Fax: 01642 333 310
Website: www.mbro.ac.uk
Principal and Chief Executive: John Hogg
Assistant Principal, Student Services:
Karen Joyce

Newcastle College
Rye Hill Campus
Scotswood Road
Newcastle upon Tyne NE4 7SA
Tel: 0191 200 4000
Fax: 0191 200 4517
Email: enquiries@ncl-coll.ac.uk
Website: www.ncl-coll.ac.uk
Principal: Jackie Fisher

New College Durham
Framwellgate Moor Campus
Durham DH1 5ES
Tel: 0191 375 4000
Fax: 0191 375 4222
Email: information@newdur.ac.uk
Website: www.newdur.ac.uk
Principal and Chief Executive:
John Widdowson
Deputy Principal and Director of
Curriculum and Quality: Lindsey Whiterod

Northumberland College
College Road
Ashington
Northumberland NE63 9RG
Tel: 01670 841200
Fax: 01670 841201
Email: advice.centre@northland.ac.uk

Website: www.northland.ac.uk
Principal: Rachel Ellis-Jones

Prior Pursglove College
Church Walk
Guisborough
Redcar and Cleveland TS14 6BU
Tel: 01287 280800
Fax: 01287 280280
Website: www.pursglove.ac.uk
Principal: Stephen G Whitehead
Director of Community Learning and
Leisure: Asma Shaffi

Queen Elizabeth Sixth Form College
Vane Terrace
Darlington
County Durham DL3 7AU
Tel: 01325 461315
Fax: 01325 361705
Email: enquiry@qeliz.ac.uk
Website: www.qeliz.ac.uk
Principal: Tim Fisher
Assistant Principal: Laurence Job

Redcar and Cleveland College
Corporation Road
Redcar TS10 1EZ
Tel: 01642 473132
Fax: 01642 490856
Website: www.cleveland.ac.uk
Principal: Gary Groom
Higher Education Development Manager:
Tom Kinneavy

South Tyneside College
St Georges Avenue
South Shields
Tyne and Wear NE34 6ET
Tel: 0191 427 3500
Fax: 0191 427 3653
Email: info@stc.ac.uk
Website: www.stc.ac.uk
Principal: Jim Bennett

Stockton Riverside College
Harvard Avenue
Thornaby
Stockton on Tees TS17 6FB
Tel: 01642 865400
Fax: 01642 865404
Website: www.stockton.ac.uk
Principal and Chief Executive:
Sujinder Sangha
Deputy Principal, Learning, Skills and
Development: Robert Winter
Deputy Principal, Head of Sixth Form:
Miriam Stanton
Deputy Principal, Finance, Planning and
Resources: Alan Pilkington
Assistant Principal, Curriculum and
Standards: Sandra Morton

Stockton Sixth Form College
Bishopton Road West
Stockton on Tees TS19 0QD
Tel: 01642 612611
Fax: 01642 618225
Email: admin@stocktonsfc.ac.uk
Website: www.stocktonsfc.ac.uk
Principal: Martin T Clinton
Vice-Principal: Susan Knox

Tyne Metropolitan College
Embleton Avenue
Wallsend
Tyne and Wear NE28 9NJ
Tel: 0191 229 5000
Fax: 0191 229 5301
Email: enquiries@tynemet.ac.uk
Website: www.tynemet.ac.uk
Principal: Phil Green
Deputy Principal, Curriculum and Learning:
Paula McNeany
Deputy Principal, Corporate Development:
Anne-Marie Crozier

North West

Accrington and Rossendale College
Broad Oak Campus
Broad Oak Road
Accrington
Lancashire BB5 2AW
Tel: 01254 389933
Fax: 01254 354001
Website: www.accross.ac.uk
Principal: Stephen Carlisle

Aquinas College
Adult Centre
Nangreave Road
Stockport
Cheshire SK2 6TH
Tel: 0161 419 9163
Fax: 0161 487 4072
Email: sheila@aquinas.ac.uk
Website: www.aquinas.ac.uk
Principal: Dr Ambrose Smith
Assistant Principal: Mark Sutherland

Ashton-under-Lyne Sixth Form College
Darnton Road
Ashton-under-Lyne
Lancashire OL6 9RL
Tel: 0161 330 2330
Fax: 0161 339 1772
Email: info@asfc.ac.uk
Website: www.asfc.ac.uk
Principal: Janet Nevin
Lifelong Learning Manager:
Jo Fletcher-Saxon

Barrow in Furness Sixth Form College
Rating Lane
Barrow in Furness
Cumbria LA13 9LE
Tel: 01229 828377
Fax: 01229 836874
Email: principal@barrow6fc.ac.uk
Website: www.barrow6fc.ac.uk
Principal: Dave Kelly

Birkenhead Sixth Form College
Park Road West
Prenton
Birkenhead CH43 8SQ
Tel: 0151 652 5575
Fax: 0151 653 4419
Website: www.bsfc.ac.uk
Principal: Kathryn Podmore
Assistant Principal: Ted Behan
Director of Adult and Community
Education: Peter Howarth
Adult Community Training Co-ordinator:
Terry Ford

Blackburn College
Feilden Street
Blackburn
Lancashire BB2 1LH
Tel: 01254 292929
Fax: 01254 682700
Email: studentservices@blackburn.ac.uk
Website: www.blackburn.ac.uk
Principal: Ian Clinton
Essential Studies Manager: Wendy Simms

Blackpool and the Fylde College
Ashfield Road
Bispham
Blackpool
Lancashire FY2 0HB
Tel: 01253 352352
Fax: 01253 356127
Website: www.blackpool.ac.uk
Principal: Pauline Waterhouse
Head of Access and Continuing Education:
Jackie Wooding
Curriculum Manager Adult Community
Learning: Rona Blanchard

Bolton Community College
Manchester Road Centre
Manchester Road
Bolton BL2 1ER
Tel: 01204 907200
Fax: 01204 907472
Website:
www.bolton-community-college.ac.uk
Principal: Carol Bannerman

Bolton Sixth Form College
North Campus
Smithills Dean Road
Bolton
Lancashire BL1 6JT
Tel: 01204 846215
Email: enquiries@bolton-sfc.ac.uk
Website: www.bolton-sfc.ac.uk
Principal: Steve Wetton
Deputy Principal: Joan E Leavy

Burnley College
Ormerod Road
Burnley
Lancashire BB11 2RX
Tel: 01282 711200
Fax: 01282 415063
Email: student.services@burnley.ac.uk
Website: www.burnley.ac.uk
Principal: John T Smith
Assistant Principal, Adult and Higher
Education: John D Clarke

Bury College
Woodbury Centre
Market Street
Bury
Lancashire BL9 0BG
Tel: 0161 280 8280
Fax: 0161 280 8228
Email: information@burycollege.ac.uk
Website: www.burycollege.ac.uk
Principal: Lauran Chatburn
Director of Curriculum: Glyn Whitworth
Deputy Principal: Andrew Patience
Community and Adult IT Programme
Manager: Sandra Newton

Cardinal Newman College
Larkhill Road
Preston PR1 4HD
Tel: 01772 460 181
Fax: 01772 204 671
Email: adults@cnc.hope.ac.uk
Website: www.cardinalnewman.ac.uk
Deputy Principal: Lynne Caddick

Carlisle College
Victoria Place
Carlisle
Cumbria CA1 1HS
Tel: 01228 822700
Fax: 01228 827710
Email: marketing@carlisle.ac.uk
Website: www.carlisle.ac.uk
Principal: Moira Tattersall

Cheadle and Marple Sixth Form College
Cheadle Campus, Cheadle Road
Cheadle Hulme
Cheadle
Cheshire SK8 5HA
Tel: 0161 486 4600
Fax: 0161 482 8129
Email: info@camsfc.ac.uk
Website: www.camsfc.ac.uk
Principal: Christina Cassidy
Adult Learning Co-ordinator: Hilary
Margaret Fidler
Tel: 0161 486 4615

Co-operative College Trust
Holyoake House
Hanover Street
Manchester M60 0AS
Tel: 0161 246 2926
Fax: 0161 246 2946
Email: enquiries@co-op.ac.uk
Website: www.co-op.ac.uk
Chief Executive and Principal:
Mervyn Wilson

Eccles College
Chatsworth Road
Eccles
Manchester M30 9FJ
Tel: 0161 789 5876
Fax: 0161 789 1123
Email: admin@ecclescollege.ac.uk
Website: www.ecclescollege.ac.uk
Principal: Stuart Wattam
Deputy Principal: Richard Nelson

Furness College
Channelside
Barrow-in-Furness
Cumbria LA14 2PJ
Tel: 01229 825017
Fax: 01229 870964
Website: www.furness.ac.uk
Principal and Chief Executive:
Anne Attwood

Holy Cross Sixth Form College
Manchester Road
Bury
Lancashire BL9 9BB
Tel: 0161 762 4500
Fax: 0161 762 4501
Email: information@holycross.ac.uk
Website: www.holycross.ac.uk
Principal: David Frost
Director (University Centre): John Barton

Hopwood Hall College
Middleton Campus
Rochdale Road
Middleton
Manchester M24 6XH
Tel: 0161 643 7560
Fax: 0161 643 2114
Email: enquiries@hopwood.ac.uk
Website: www.hopwood.ac.uk
Principal: Derek O'Toole

Hugh Baird College
Balliol Road
Bootle
Merseyside L20 7EW
Tel: 0151 353 4444
Fax: 0151 353 4469
Email: info@hughbaird.ac.uk
Website: www.hughbaird.ac.uk
Principal: Dr Jette Burford
Head of School of Health, Social and Child
Care: Liz Rowland

Kendal College
Milnthorpe Road
Kendal
Cumbria LA9 5AY
Tel: 01539 814700
Fax: 01539 814701
Email: enquiries@kendal.ac.uk
Website: www.kendal.ac.uk
Principal: Graham Wilkinson
Vice-Principal and Head of Curriculum:
Anne Isherwood
Head of Personnel: Louise Shrapnel
Head of Quality: Brenda Brew

King George V College
Scarisbrick New Road
Southport
Merseyside PR8 6LR
Tel: 01704 500065
Fax: 01704 548656
Email: adulted@kgv.ac.uk
Website: www.kgv.ac.uk
Principal: Hilary Anslow OBE
Adult Education Co-ordinator:
Alison Rothwell

Knowsley Community College
Roby Campus
Rupert Road
Roby
Merseyside L36 9TD
Tel: 0151 477 5700
Fax: 0151 477 5703
Website: www.knowsleycollege.ac.uk
Principal: Frank Gill
Vice-Principal: Lyn Eaton

Lakes College
Hallwood Road
Lillyhall Business Park
Workington
Cumbria CA14 4JN
Tel: 01946 839300
Fax: 01946 839302
Email: student.services@lcwc.ac.uk
Principal: Cath Richardson
Assistant Principal, Curriculum and Quality:
Jo Lomax
Assistant Principal, External Relations:
Cyril Wheat

Lancaster and Morecambe College
Morecambe Road
Lancaster LA1 2TY
Tel: 01524 66215
Fax: 01524 843078
Website: www.lmc.ac.uk
Principal: David Wood
Deputy Principal: Anne Purvis

Liverpool Community College
Clarence Street Centre
Clarence Street
Liverpool L3 5TP
Tel: 0151 252 1515
Email: lcc@liv-coll.ac.uk
Website: www.liv-coll.ac.uk
Principal: Maureen Mellor MBE
Email: maureen.mellor@liv-coll.ac.uk
Vice-Principal Curriculum:
Marie Allen MBE

Loreto Sixth Form College
Chichester Road South
Manchester M15 5PB
Tel: 0161 226 5156
Fax: 0161 227 9174
Email: enquiries@loreto.ac.uk
Website: www.loreto.ac.uk
Principal: Ann Clynch

Macclesfield College
Park Lane
Macclesfield
Cheshire SK11 8LF
Tel: 01625 410000
Fax: 01625 410001
Email: info@macclesfield.ac.uk
Website: www.macclesfield.ac.uk
Principal: Wendy Wright

The Manchester College
Openshaw Campus
Whitworth House
Ashton Old Road
Openshaw
Manchester M11 2WH
Tel: 0161 953 5995
Fax: 0161 953 3909
Email:
enquiries@themanchestercollege.co.uk
Website: www.themanchestercollege.co.uk
Principal: Peter Tavernor

Mid Cheshire College
Hartford Campus
Chester Road
Northwich
Cheshire CW8 1LJ
Tel: 01606 74444
Fax: 01606 720700
Principal: John Reilly
Team Leader: Noelle Bracewell

Myerscough College
Myerscough Hall
St Michael's Road
Bilsborrow
Preston
Lancashire PR3 0RY
Tel: 01995 642222
Fax: 01995 642333
Email: mailbox@myerscough.ac.uk
Website: www.myerscough.ac.uk
Principal and Chief Executive:
Ann Turner FCMA
Assistant Director, Skills: Peter Cavey

Nelson and Colne College
Scotland Road
Nelson
Lancashire BB9 7YT
Tel: 01282 440200
Fax: 01282 440274
Email: reception@nelson.ac.uk
Website:www.nelson.ac.uk
Principal and Chief Executive: Lyn Surgeon
Deputy Principal: John Farrington
Director of Curriculum (19+) and Support:
Judith Watson
Director of Curriculum (14–19) and
Quality: Mike Smith
Director of Finance and Information
Services: David Rothwell

The Oldham College
Rochdale Road
Oldham
Lancashire OL9 6AA
Tel: 0161 624 5214
Fax: 0161 785 4234
Email: info@oldham.ac.uk
Website: www.oldham.ac.uk
Principal: Kath Thomas
Adult and Community Education Manager:
Carl Morrison

Pendleton College
Dronfield Road
Salford
Greater Manchester M6 7FR
Tel: 0161 736 5074
Fax: 0161 737 4103
Email: admin@pendcoll.ac.uk
Website: www.pendcoll.ac.uk
Principal: Peter Crompton
Assistant Principal (Adult Education):
Jackie Moores
Deputy Principal: Martin Sim
Adult Programme Manager: Mick Bowden
Community Programme Manager:
Pauline Howarth

Preston College
Fulwood Campus
St Vincents Road
Preston
Lancashire PR2 8UR
Tel: 01772 225000
Fax: 01772 225002
Email: wmills@preston.ac.uk
Website: www.preston.ac.uk
Principal: Willie Mills

Priestley College
Loushers Lane
Warrington
Cheshire WA4 6RD
Tel: 01925 633591
Fax: 01925 413887
Email: enquiries@priestley.ac.uk
Website: www.priestley.ac.uk
Principal: Michael Southworth
Adult Curriculum Manager: Glennis Hassall

Reaseheath College
Reaseheath
Nantwich
Cheshire CW5 6DF
Tel: 01270 625131
Fax: 01270 625665
Website: www.reaseheath.ac.uk
Principal: T E M David
Learning Resources and Support Manager:
Karen Myatt
Curriculum Leader IT and Business:
Hazel Shimmin

Riverside College Halton
Kingsway
Widnes
Cheshire WA8 7QQ
Tel: 0151 257 2020
Fax: 0151 420 2408
Website: www.riversidecollegehalton.ac.uk
Principal: Pat Grunwell
Head of Lifelong Learning: Janet Stanley
Email: jan.stanley@riversidecollege.ac.uk

Runshaw College
Langdale Road
Leyland
Lancashire PR25 3DQ
Tel: 01772 622677
Fax: 01772 642009
Website: www.runshaw.ac.uk
Principal: Kathy Passant
Assistant Principal: Claire Foreman
Adult Marketing and Admissions Manager:
Leslie Hudson

Salford College
Worsley Campus
Walkden Road
Worsley
Manchester M28 7QD
Tel: 0161 702 8272
Fax: 0161 211 5020
Email: centad@salford-col.ac.uk
Website: www.salford-col.ac.uk
Principal and Chief Executive: Tony Craven
Deputy Principal: Tom Webb

Sir John Deane's College
Northwich
Cheshire CW9 8AF
Tel: 01606 46011
Fax: 01606 47170
Email: chuter_p@sjd.ac.uk
Website: www.sjd.ac.uk
Principal: Andrew Jones
Adult Education Manager: Patsy Chuter

Skelmersdale and Ormskirk Colleges
Westbank Campus
Yewdale
Skelmersdale
Lancashire WN8 6JA
Tel: 01695 52300
Fax: 01695 721682
Email: admissions@skelmersdale.ac.uk
Website: www.skelmersdale.ac.uk
Principal and Chief Executive:
Beverley Robinson

South Cheshire College
Dane Bank Avenue
Crewe
Cheshire CW2 8AB
Tel: 01270 654654
Fax: 01270 651515
Email: info@s-cheshire.ac.uk
Website: www.s-cheshire.ac.uk
Principal: Dr David J Collins

South Trafford College
Manchester Road
West Timperley
Altrincham
Cheshire WA14 5PQ
Tel: 0161 952 4600
Fax: 0161 952 4672
Email: enquiries@stcoll.ac.uk
Website: www.stcoll.ac.uk
Principal: Bill Moorcroft
Head of Guidance and Counselling:
Amanda Melton
Adult and Community Learning Manager:
Jill Quigley
Email: jquigley@stcoll.ac.uk

Southport College
Mornington Road
Southport
Merseyside PR9 0TT
Tel: 01704 500606
Fax: 01704 392794
Website: www.southport-college.ac.uk
Principal: Brian Mitchell
Assistant Principal (Curriculum):
Gillian Kitchen

St Helens College
Water Street
St. Helens
Merseyside WA10 1PP
Tel: 01744 733766
Fax: 01744 623400
Website: www.sthelens.ac.uk
Principal: Pat Bacon
Adult Learning Manager: Jan Higgins

St John Rigby Sixth Form College
Gathurst Road
Orrell
Wigan WN5 0LJ
Tel: 01942 214797
Fax: 01942 216514
Website: www.sjr.ac.uk
Principal: John Crowley
Deputy Principal: Alex Fau-Goodwin

St Mary's College
Shear Brow
Blackburn
Lancashire BB1 8DX
Tel: 01254 580464
Fax: 01254 665991
Email: s.cash@stmarysblackburn.ac.uk
Website: www.stmarysblackburn.ac.uk
Principal: Kevin McMahon
Director of Development: Sarah Flanagan

Stockport College
Town Centre Campus
Wellington Road South
Stockport
Cheshire SK1 3UQ
Tel: 0161 958 3266
Fax: 0161 958 3407
Email: stockcoll@stockport.ac.uk
Website: www.stockport.ac.uk
Principal: Peter Roberts
Continuing and Community Education
Manager: Karen Moss

Tameside College
Beaufort Road
Ashton-under-Lyne
Tameside
Greater Manchester OL6 6NX
Tel: 0161 908 6600
Fax: 0161 908 6611
Email: info@tameside.ac.uk
Website: www.tameside.ac.uk
Principal and Chief Executive: John Carroll

Trafford College
Talbot Road Centre
Stretford
Manchester M32 0XH
Tel: 0161 886 7070/7000
Fax: 0161 872 7921
Email: enquiries@trafford.ac.uk
Website: www.trafford.co.uk
Principal: W Moorcroft

Warrington Collegiate
Winwick Road Campus
Winwick Road
Warrington
Cheshire WA2 8QA
Tel: 01925 494494
Fax: 01925 418328
Website: www.warrington.ac.uk
Principal/Chief Executive: Paul Hafren

West Cheshire College
Eaton Road
Hanbridge
Chester CH4 7ER
Tel: 01244 677677
Fax: 01244 670676
Website: www.west-cheshire.ac.uk
Principal: Sara Mogel
Area Manager for Learning Services:
Julie McGinn
j.mcginn@west-cheshire.ac.uk

Chester Campus
Eaton Road
Handbridge
Chester CH4 7ER

Ellesmere Port Campus
Off Sutton Way
Ellesmere Port
Cheshire CH65 7BF

Wigan and Leigh College
PO Box 53
Parsons Walk
Wigan WN1 1RS
Tel: 01942 761600
Fax: 01942 761553
Website: www.wigan-leigh.ac.uk
Principal: Cath Hurst
College in the Community Manager:
Phil Varley

Wirral Metropolitan College
Carlett Park Campus
Eastham
Wirral
Merseyside CH62 0AY
Tel: 0151 551 7777
Fax: 0151 551 7701
Email: enquiries@wmc.ac.uk
Website: www.wmc.ac.uk
Principal: Michael Potter CBE
Community Network Manager:
Faith Everest

Xaverian College
Lower Park Road
Manchester M14 5RB
Tel: 0161 224 1781
Fax: 0161 248 9039
Website: www.xaverian.ac.uk
Principal: Mary Hunter

Yorkshire and Humberside

Askham Bryan College
Askham Bryan
York
North Yorkshire YO23 3FR
Tel: 01904 772277
Fax: 01904 772288
Email: enquiries@askham-bryan.ac.uk
Website: www.askham-bryan.ac.uk
Principal: Liz Philip
Section Leader, Skills for Work and Life:
Jeanette Macnaught
Adult Education and Lifelong Learning:
Anne Dale

Barnsley College
PO Box 266
Church Street
Barnsley
South Yorkshire S70 2YW
Tel: 01226 216216
Fax: 01226 216615
Website: www.barnsley.ac.uk
Assistant Principal: Dave Harding
Head of Department: Mark Doyle

Bishop Burton College
Bishop Burton
Beverley
East Yorkshire HU17 8QG
Tel: 01964 553000
Fax: 01964 553101
Email: enquiries@bishopburton.ac.uk
Website: www.bishopburton.ac.uk
Principal: Jeanette Dawson
Deputy Principal – Academic:
Graham Towse

Bradford College
Great Horton Road
Bradford
West Yorkshire BD7 1AY
Tel: 01274 433004
Fax: 01274 741060
Email: info@bradfordcollege.ac.uk
Website: www.bradfordcollege.ac.uk
Principal: Michele Sutton
Assistant Director: Julie Hinchliffe

Calderdale College
Francis Street
Halifax
West Yorkshire HX1 3UZ
Tel: 01422 357357
Fax: 01422 399320
Email: enquiries@calderdale.ac.uk
Website: www.calderdale.ac.uk
Chief Executive and Principal: Chris Jones
Head of Faculty (Cross-College
Curriculum): John Bullock

Craven College
High Street
Skipton
North Yorkshire BD23 1JY
Tel: 01756 791411
Fax: 01756 794872
Email: enquiries@craven-college.ac.uk
Website: www.craven-college.ac.uk
Principal: Alan Blackwell
Student Services Manager: Lauren Ingram
Student Services Manager: Sue Cullen

Dearne Valley College
Manvers Park
Wath upon Dearne
Rotherham S63 7EW
Tel: 01709 513333
Fax: 01709 513110
Website: www.dearne-coll.ac.uk
Principal: Sue Ransom
Head of Student Support Services:
Alison Marquand

Doncaster College
The Hub
Chappell Drive
Doncaster
South Yorkshire DN1 2RF
Tel: 01302 553553
Fax: 01302 553559
Website: www.don.ac.uk
Principal and Chief Executive:
Rowland Foote
Assistant Principal, Learner Services and
Inclusion: Diane Bailey

East Riding College
Gallows Lane
Beverley
East Yorkshire HU17 7DT
Tel: 0845 120 0037
Fax: 01482 306 675
Email: reception@eastridingcollege.ac.uk
Website: www.eastridingcollege.ac.uk
Principal: Derek Branton
Vice-Principal: Sue Tuckey

Also at: St Marys Walk
Bridlington
East Yorkshire YO16 7JW

Franklin College
Chelmsford Avenue
Grimsby
North East Lincolnshire DN34 5BY
Tel: 01472 875000/875012
Fax: 01472 875019
Email: college@franklin.ac.uk
Website: www.franklin.ac.uk
Principal: Peter Newcome
Director of Adult Learning and Learning
Skills: Sarah Gillingham
Email: alt@franklin.ac.uk

**Grimsby Institute of Further and
Higher Education**
Nuns Corner
Grimsby
North East Lincolnshire DN34 5BQ
Tel: 01472 311222
Fax: 01472 879924
Email: khand@grimsby.ac.uk
Website: www.grimsby.ac.uk
Principal and Chief Executive:
Prof. Daniel Khan OBE
Executive Director of Communications and
Marketing: Hugh Callaway

Harrogate College
Hornbeam Park
Hookstone Road
Harrogate
North Yorkshire HG2 8QT
Tel: 01423 879466
Fax: 01423 879829
Email: j.davidson@leedsmet.ac.uk
Website: www.harrogate.ac.uk
Principal: Dr Geoff Hitchins
Adult Education Contact: Julia Davidson

Huddersfield New College
New Hey Road
Huddersfield
West Yorkshire HD3 4GL
Tel: 01484 652341
Fax: 01484 649923
Email: info@huddnewcoll.ac.uk
Website: www.huddnewcoll.ac.uk
Principal: Angela Williams
Lifelong Learning Manager: Neville Phillips

Hull College
Maxwell Bird Building
Queen's Gardens
Wilberforce Drive
Hull HU1 3DG
Tel: 01482 329943
Fax: 01482 598733
Email: emcmahon@hull-college.ac.uk
Website: www.hull-college.ac.uk
Principal and Chief Executive:
Elaine McMahon
Deputy Principal: Gary Warke

John Leggott College
West Common Lane
Scunthorpe
North Lincolnshire DN17 1DS
Tel: 01724 407100
Fax: 01724 407018
Website: www.leggott.ac.uk
Principal: Nicholas Dakin
Adult Learning Co-ordinator: Cheryl Riley

Joseph Priestley College
Beeston Campus
Burton Avenue
Beeston
Leeds
West Yorkshire LS11 5ER
Tel: 0113 307 6002
Fax: 0113 271 3546
Website: www.joseph-priestley.ac.uk
Principal: Carolyn Wright

Kirklees College
Dewsbury Campus
Halifax Road
Dewsbury
West Yorkshire WF13 2AS
Tel: 01924 465916
Fax: 01924 457047
Email: info@dewsbury.ac.uk
Website: www.dewsbury.ac.uk
Principal and Chief Executive: Chris Sadler

Also at: Huddersfield Centre
New North Road
Huddersfield
West Yorkshire HD1 5NN
Tel: 01484 437000
Email: info@huddcoll.ac.uk

Leeds College of Art and Design
Blenheim Walk
Leeds
West Yorkshire LS2 9AQ
Tel: 0113 202 8000
Fax: 0113 202 8001
Email: info@leeds-art.ac.uk
Website: www.leeds-art.ac.uk
Principal: Edmund Wigan
Co-ordinator: Garry Barker

Leeds College of Building
North Street
Leeds
West Yorkshire LS2 7QT
Tel: 0113 222 6000
Fax: 0113 222 6001
Website: www.lcb.ac.uk
Principal: Ian Billyard
Student Services Manager: Julie Theakston

Leeds College of Music
3 Quarry Hill
Leeds
West Yorkshire LS2 7PD
Tel: 0113 222 3400
Fax: 0113 243 8798
Email: enquiries@lcm.ac.uk
Website: www.lcm.ac.uk
Principal: Philip Meaden
Head of Community Education: Lis Parry

Leeds College of Technology
Cookridge Street
Leeds
West Yorkshire LS2 8BL
Tel: 0113 297 6300
Fax: 0113 297 6301
Email: info@lct.ac.uk
Website: www.lct.ac.uk
Principal: Peter Ryder

Leeds Thomas Danby
Roundhay Road
Sheepscar
Leeds
West Yorkshire LS7 3BG
Tel: 0113 249 4912
Fax: 0113 240 1967
Email: info@thomasdanby.ac.uk
Website: www.leedsthomasdanby.ac.uk
Principal: Roy Thorpe
Director, Learner and Enrichment Services:
Howard Browes

New College
Park Lane
Pontefract
West Yorkshire WF8 4QR
Tel: 01977 702139
Fax: 01977 600708
Email: reception@newcollpont.ac.uk
Website: www.newcollpont.ac.uk
Principal: Peter Hillman

North Lindsey College
Kingsway
Scunthorpe
North Lincolnshire DN17 1AJ
Tel: 01724 281111
Fax: 01724 294020
Email: info@northlindsey.ac.uk
Website: www.northlindsey.ac.uk
Principal: Prof. Roger Bennett

Northern College
Lowe Lane
Stainborough
Barnsley
South Yorkshire S75 3ET
Tel: 01226 776000
Fax: 01226 776025
Website: www.northern.ac.uk
Principal: Jill Westerman

Notre Dame Catholic Sixth Form College
St Mark's Avenue
Leeds
West Yorkshire LS2 9BL
Tel: 0113 294 6644
Fax: 0113 294 6006
Email: admin@notredamecoll.ac.uk
Website: www.notredamecoll.ac.uk
Principal: Dr Anthony Adlard
Vice-Principal: Terry Coen

Park Lane College Leeds
Park Lane
Leeds
West Yorkshire LS3 1AA
Tel: 0845 045 7275
Fax: 0113 216 2020
Email: course.enquiries@parklanecoll.ac.uk
Website: www.parklanecoll.ac.uk
Principal: Maxine Room
Director, Adult and Community Education:
Ann Buckley

Rotherham College of Arts and Technology
Eastwood Lane
Rotherham
South Yorkshire S65 1EG
Tel: 01709 362111
Fax: 01709 373053
Website: www.rotherham.ac.uk
Principal and Chief Executive: George Trow
Director of Curriculum and Strategy:
Elaine Woodhams
Email: ewoodhams@rotherham.ac.uk

Scarborough Sixth Form College
Sandybed Lane
Scarborough
North Yorkshire YO12 5LF
Tel: 01723 365032
Fax: 01723 367049
Email: general@scarb-6-form.ac.uk
Website: www.scarb-6-form.ac.uk
Principal: Tom Potter
Mature Student Co-ordinator:
Rowan Johnson
Lifelong Learning Centre Manager:
Joyce Nash

Selby College
Abbots Road
Selby
North Yorkshire YO8 8AT
Tel: 01757 211000
Fax: 01757 213137
Email: watsona@selby.ac.uk
Website: www.selbycollege.co.uk
Principal: Allan Stewart
Director of Curriculum and Quality:
Alan Watson

Sheffield College
PO Box 345
Sheffield
South Yorkshire S2 2YY
Tel: 0114 260 2600
Fax: 0114 260 2601
Website: www.sheffcol.ac.uk
Principal and Chief Executive:
Heather McDonald

Shipley College
Exhibition Road
Saltaire
Shipley
West Yorkshire BD18 3JW
Tel: 01274 327 222
Fax: 01274 327 219
Email: enquiries@shipley.ac.uk
Website: www.shipley.ac.uk
Principal: Jean McAllister

Thomas Rotherham College
Moorgate Road
Rotherham
South Yorkshire S60 2BE
Tel: 01709 300671
Fax: 01709 300601
Email: enquiries@thomroth.ac.uk
Website: www.thomroth.ac.uk
Principal: Richard Williams
Director of Community Development:
John Garrett

Wakefield College
Margaret Street
Wakefield
West Yorkshire WF1 2DH
Tel: 01924 789789
Fax: 01924 789340
Website: www.wakefield.ac.uk
Interim Principal: Sue Griffiths
Vice-Principal – Teaching and Learning:
Kaye Fisher

Wilberforce College
Saltshouse Road
Hull HU8 9HD
Tel: 01482 711688
Fax: 01482 798991
Email: college@wilberforce.ac.uk
Website: www.wilberforce.ac.uk
Principal: Stephan Jungnitz
Vice-Principal: Sue Firth
Vice-Principal: David Cooper

Wyke College
Grammar School Road
Hull HU5 4NX
Tel: 01482 346347
Fax: 01482 473336
Email: office@wyke.ac.uk
Website: www.wyke.ac.uk
Principal: Dr Richard Smith
Adult Education Manager: David Green
Vice-Principal: Ian Taylor
Vice-Principal: Mike Rogerson
Assistant Principal: Mark Rothery

York College
Sim Balk Lane
York YO23 2BB
Tel: 01904 770200
Fax: 01904 770499
Email: customer-services@yorkcollege.ac.uk
Website: www.yorkcollege.ac.uk
Principal: Dr Alison Birkinshaw
Assistant Principal: Bob Saynor

Yorkshire Coast College
Lady Edith's Drive
Scarborough
North Yorkshire YO12 5RN
Tel: 01723 372105
Fax: 01723 501918
Website: www.ycoastco.ac.uk
Interim Principal and Chief Executive:
Carol Kitching
Director of Resources: Felix Adenaike

West Midlands

Bournville College of Further Education
Bristol Road South
Northfield
Birmingham B31 2AJ
Tel: 0121 483 1000
Fax: 0121 411 2231
Email: info@bournville.ac.uk
Website: www.bournville.ac.uk
Principal: Norman Cave
Assistant Principal: Christine Horton

Burton College
Lichfield Street
Burton upon Trent
Staffordshire DE14 3RL
Tel: 01283 494400
Fax: 01283 494800
Email: enquiries@burton-college.ac.uk
Website: www.burton-college.ac.uk
Principal and Chief Executive: Keith Norris
Head of Sixth Form and Skills for Life:
Hilary Morgan

Cadbury College
Downland Close
Kings Norton
Birmingham B38 8QT
Tel: 0121 458 3898
Fax: 0121 433 2619
Email: enquiry@cadcol.ac.uk
Website: www.cadcol.ac.uk
Principal: David J Igoe

Cannock Chase Technical College
The Green
Cannock
Staffordshire WS11 1UE
Tel: 01543 462200
Fax: 01543 574223
Email: enquiries@cannock.ac.uk
Website: www.cannock.ac.uk
Principal: Graham Morley

City College Birmingham
Garretts Green Lane
Garretts Green
Birmingham B33 0TS
Tel: 0121 204 0000
Fax: 0121 204 0150
Email: enquiries@citycol.ac.uk
Website: www.citycol.ac.uk
Interim Principal: David Gibson
Vice-Principal, Curriculum Development:
Everton Burke
Vice-Principal, Curriculum Delivery:
Stuart Cutforth
Director of Planning and Information:
Anthony Gribben

City College Coventry
Butts Centre
Butts
Coventry CV1 3GD
Tel: 024 7679 1000
Fax: 024 7679 1670
Email: info@covcollege.ac.uk
Website: www.covcollege.ac.uk
Principal: Paul Taylor
Email: p.taylor@staff.covcollege.ac.uk
Vice-Principal, Quality and Curriculum:
Christina Fowers

City of Wolverhampton College
Paget Road Campus
Wolverhampton
West Midlands WV6 0DU
Tel: 01902 836000
Fax: 01902 423070
Email: mail@wolverhamptoncollege.ac.uk
Website: www.wolverhamptoncollege.ac.uk
Principal and Chief Executive: Ian Millard

Dudley College of Technology
The Broadway
Dudley
West Midlands DY1 4AS
Tel: 01384 363000
Fax: 01384 363311
Website: www.dudleycol.ac.uk
Principal: Lowell Williams
Deputy Principal: John Scott
Head of Division of Community and Adult
Education: Santokh Singh Uppal

Evesham and Malvern Hills College
Davies Road
Evesham
Worcestershire WR11 1LP
Tel: 01386 712600
Fax: 01386 712640
Website: www.evesham.ac.uk
Principal: David Blades
Lifelong Learning Officer: Jane Dunn

Fircroft College
1018 Bristol Road
Selly Oak
Birmingham B29 6LH
Tel: 0121 472 0116
Fax: 0121 471 1503
Website: www.fircroft.ac.uk
Principal: Fiona Larden
Head of Staff and Student Support:
Alex Miles

Halesowen College
Whittingham Road
Halesowen
West Midlands B63 3NA
Tel: 0121 602 7777
Fax: 0121 585 0369
Email: info@halesowen.ac.uk
Website: www.halesowen.ac.uk
Principal: Keith Bate

Henley College Coventry
Henley Green
Coventry
West Midlands CV2 1ED
Tel: 024 7662 6300
Fax: 024 7661 1837
Email: info@henley-cov.ac.uk
Website: www.henley-cov.ac.uk
Principal: Ray Goy
Head of Department: David Pryke
Email: dpryke@henley-cov.ac.uk

Hereford College of Art
Folly Lane
Hereford HR1 1LT
Tel: 01432 273359
Fax: 01432 341099
Email: enquiries@hca.ac.uk
Website: www.hca.ac.uk
Principal: Richard Heatly

Herefordshire College of Technology
Folly Lane
Hereford HR1 1LS
Tel: 01432 352235
Fax: 01432 353449
Email: enquiries@hct.ac.uk
Website: www.hct.ac.uk
Principal and Chief Executive: Ian Peake
Assistant Principal, Faculty of Community
Studies: Ruth Johnson

Hereford Sixth Form College
Folly Lane
Hereford HR1 1LU
Tel: 01432 355166
Fax: 01432 346901
Email: sixth-form@hereford.ac.uk
Website: www.hereford.ac.uk
Principal: Dr Jonathan Godfrey
Deputy Principal (Curriculum and Quality):
Peter Cooper
Deputy Principal (Staff and Students):
Dr Ruth Brinton

Hereward College
Bramston Crescent
Tile Hill Lane
Coventry CV4 9SW
Tel: 024 7646 1231
Fax: 024 7669 4305
Email: enquiries@hereward.ac.uk
Website: www.hereward.ac.uk
Principal: Janis Firminger

Joseph Chamberlain Sixth Form College
1 Belgrave Road
Highgate
Birmingham B12 9FF
Tel: 0121 446 2223
Email: info@jcc.ac.uk
Website: www.jcc.ac.uk
Principal: Lynne Morris
Assistant Community Principal:
Andrea Quigley

Kidderminster College
Market Street
Kidderminster
Worcestershire DY10 1LX
Tel: 01562 820811
Fax: 01562 512006
Website: www.kidderminster.ac.uk
Principal and Chief Executive:
Andrew Miller
Email: amiller@kidderminster.ac.uk

King Edward VI College
King Edward Road
Nuneaton
Warwickshire CV11 4BE
Tel: 024 7632 8231
Fax: 024 7632 6686
Email: enquiries@kinged6nun.ac.uk
Website: www.kinged6nun.ac.uk
Principal: Esther Maughan

King Edward VI College
Lower High Street
Stourbridge DY8 1TD
Tel: 01384 398100
Fax: 01384 398123
Email: office@kedst.ac.uk
Website: www.kedst.ac.uk
Principal: Sharon Phillips

Leek College of Further Education and School of Art
Stockwell Street
Leek
Staffordshire ST13 6DP
Tel: 01538 398866
Fax: 01538 399506
Email: admissions@leek.ac.uk
Website: www.leek.ac.uk
Principal: Rob Morrey
Curriculum Director: Peter Turpie

Ludlow College
Castle Square
Ludlow
Shropshire SY8 1GD
Tel: 01584 872846
Fax: 01584 876012
Email: info@ludlow-college.ac.uk
Website: www.ludlow-college.ac.uk
Principal: Chris Conoley
Deputy Principal: Jennie Cole

Matthew Boulton College of Further and Higher Education
4 Jennens Road
Birmingham B4 7PS
Tel: 0121 446 4545
Email: ask@mbc.ac.uk
Website: www.mbc.ac.uk
Principal and Chief Executive:
Christine Braddock
Director of Finance and Corporate Affairs:
Bob Battini

Newcastle-under-Lyme College
Liverpool Road
Newcastle-under-Lyme
Staffordshire ST5 2DF
Tel: 01782 715111
Fax: 01782 717396
Email: info@nulc.ac.uk
Website: www.nulc.ac.uk
Principal and Chief Executive:
Karen Dobson
Head of Lifelong Learning: Janet Scrivens

New College Telford
King Street
Wellington
Telford
Shropshire TF1 1NY
Tel: 01952 641892
Fax: 01952 243564
Email: info@nct.ac.uk
Website: www.newcollegetelford.ac.uk
Principal: Graham Clark
Vice-Principal – Resources: Beverley Tyley

North East Worcestershire College
Redditch Campus
Peakman Street
Redditch
Worcestershire B98 8DW
Tel: 01527 570020
Fax: 01527 572901
Email: info@ne-worcs.ac.uk
Website: www.ne-worcs.ac.uk
Principal: Neil Bromley

**North Warwickshire and
Hinckley College**
Hinckley Road
Nuneaton
Warwickshire CV11 6BH
Tel: 024 7624 3100
Fax: 024 7624 3500
Email: the.college@nwhc.ac.uk
Website: www.nwhc.ac.uk
Principal and Chief Executive: Marion Plant

Rodbaston College
Rodbaston
Penkridge
Stafford ST19 5PH
Tel: 01785 712209
Fax: 01785 715701
Website: www.rodbaston.ac.uk
Principal: Dr Ralph Alcock
Email: ralph.alcock@rodbaston.ac.uk
Business Development Manager:
Judith Mills

Sandwell College
Oldbury Campus
Pound Road
Oldbury
West Midlands B68 8NA
Tel: 0121 556 6000
Fax: 0121 253 6836
Email: enquiries@sandwell.ac.uk
Website: www.sandwell.ac.uk
Principal: Val Bailey

**Shrewsbury College of Arts
and Technology**
Main Campus
London Road
Shrewsbury
Shropshire SY2 6PR
Tel: 01743 342342
Fax: 01743 342343
Email: prospects@shrewsbury.ac.uk
Website: www.shrewsbury.ac.uk
Principal and Chief Executive: Greg Molan

The Sixth Form College, Solihull
Widney Manor Road
Solihull
West Midlands B91 3WR
Tel: 0121 704 2581
Fax: 0121 711 1598
Email: enquiries@solihullsfc.ac.uk
Website: www.solihullsfc.ac.uk
Principal: Colleen Charter
Vice-Principal: Elizabeth Linker
Vice-Principal: Adele Wills

Solihull College

Blossomfield Road
Solihull
West Midlands B91 1SB
Tel: 0121 678 7000
Fax: 0121 678 7200
Email: enquiries@solihull.ac.uk
Website: www.solihull.ac.uk
Principal: Brenda Sheils
Senior Director of Community Education –
Skills for Life: Gill Hutchings

South Birmingham College

High Street
Deritend
Digbeth
Birmingham B5 5SU
Tel: 0121 694 5000
Fax: 0121 694 6330
Website: www.sbc.ac.uk
Principal: Mike Hopkins
Deputy Principal: Phyllis Warde
Vice-Principal: Sardul Dhesi
Vice-Principal: Glynis Nicholson
Senior Management: Alan Howey,
Naz Khan, Paul Morris

Stafford College

Earl Street
Stafford ST16 2QR
Tel: 01785 223800
Fax: 01785 259953
Website: www.staffordcoll.ac.uk
Principal: Stephen Willis
Skills and Support: Janice Gormley

Stoke-on-Trent College

Cauldon Campus
Stoke Road
Shelton
Stoke-on-Trent ST4 2DG
Tel: 01782 208208
Fax: 01782 603504
Email: info@stokecoll.ac.uk
Website: www.stokecoll.ac.uk
Principal and Chief Executive:
Graham Moore

Stoke-on-Trent Sixth Form College

Victoria Road
Fenton
Stoke-on-Trent ST4 2RR
Tel: 01782 848736
Fax: 01782 747456
Email: admissions@stokesfc.ac.uk
Website: www.stokesfc.ac.uk
Principal: Helen Pegg
Deputy Principal: Paul Mangnall
Director of Curriculum: Mike Casey
Director of Student Guidance and Support:
Nigel Mansfield
Director of Finance and Resources:
Steve Murfin

Stourbridge College

Hagley Road
Stourbridge
West Midlands DY8 1QU
Tel: 01384 344344
Fax: 01384 344345
Email: info@stourbridge.ac.uk
Website: www.stourbridge.ac.uk
Principal: Lynette Cutting
Vice-Principal, Curriculum and Quality:
Kevin Smith

Stratford upon Avon College

The Willows North
Alcester Road
Stratford upon Avon
Warwickshire CV37 9QR
Tel: 01789 266245
Fax: 01789 267524
Email: college@stratford.ac.uk
Website: www.stratford.ac.uk
Principal: Martin Penny
Deputy Principal: Charles Anderson
Vice-Principal, Resources: David Jackson
Vice-Principal, Finance:
Norman MacDonald
Vice-Principal, Corporate Development:
Kay Taylor
Head of Skills Development: Simon Rouch

Sutton Coldfield College
Lichfield Road
Sutton Coldfield
West Midlands B74 2NW
Tel: 0121 355 5671
Fax: 0121 355 0799
Email: infoc@sutcol.ac.uk
Website: www.sutcol.ac.uk
Principal: Christine Braddock
Faculty Director, Access, Early Years, Health
and Social Care: Anna Green
Executive Director, Higher Education and
International: Roger Minett
Executive Director, Adult: Hilary Rimmer

Tamworth and Lichfield College
Croft Street
Upper Gungate
Tamworth
Staffordshire B79 8AE
Tel: 01827 310202
Fax: 01827 59437
Email: enquiries@tamworth.ac.uk
Website: www.tlc.ac.uk
Principal: A Neville
Community Education Manager:
Christine Summerton

Telford College of Arts and Technology
Haybridge Road
Wellington
Telford TF1 2NP
Tel: 01952 642200
Fax: 01952 642263
Website: www.tcat.ac.uk
Principal: Doug Boynton
Email: doug.boynton@tcat.ac.uk
Director of Community Education and
Essential Skills: David Gill
Email: dave.gill@tcat.ac.uk

University College Birmingham
Summer Row
Birmingham B3 1JB
Tel: 0121 604 1000
Fax: 0121 604 1101
Website: www.ucb.ac.uk
Principal: Ray Linforth
Equal Opportunities Co-ordinator:
Godfrey Henry

Walford and North Shropshire College
Oswestry Campus
Shrewsbury Road
Oswestry
Shropshire SY11 4QB
Tel: 01691 688000
Fax: 01691 688001
Email: enquiries@wnsc.ac.uk
Website: www.wnsc.ac.uk
Principal: Andrew Tyley
Head of School, Continuing Education:
Cheryl Greaves

Walsall College
PO Box 4203
St Pauls Street
Walsall WS1 1WY
Tel: 01922 657000
Fax: 01922 657083
Email: info@walsallcollege.ac.uk
Website: www.walsallcollege.ac.uk
Principal and Chief Executive: Amarjit Basi
Student Services Manager: June Morrow

Walsall College of Continuing Education
Hawbush Road (Beeches Road Entrance)
Forest Estate
Walsall
West Midlands WS3 1AG
Tel: 01922 654510
Fax: 01922 400569
Email: bellt@walsall.gov.uk
Principal, College of Continuing Education:
Terry Bell

Warwickshire College
Main Campus
Warwick New Road
Royal Leamington Spa
Warwickshire CV32 5JE
Tel: 01926 318000
Fax: 01926 318111
Email: enquiries@warkscol.ac.uk
Website: www.warkscol.ac.uk
Principal: Ioan Morgan
Vice-Principal/Dean of Faculty:
Sarah Wright
Director of Studies: Jean Feely

Worcester College of Technology
Deansway
Worcester WR1 2JF
Tel: 01905 743 480
Fax: 01905 721 001
Email: enrol@wortech.ac.uk
Website: www.wortech.ac.uk
Principal: Chris Morecroft
Head of Faculty of Care, Community and
Foundation Learning: Chris Harrison

Worcester Sixth Form College
Spetchley Road
Worcester WR5 2LU
Tel: 01905 362600
Fax: 01905 362633
Email: enquiries@wsfc.ac.uk
Website: www.wsfc.ac.uk
Principal: Michael Kitcatt
Adult and Community Education
Co-ordinator: Steve Ryding
Admin Assistant: Hayley Ashby

East Midlands

Bilborough Sixth Form College
Bilborough Road
College Way
Nottingham NG8 4DQ
Tel: 0115 851 5000
Fax: 0115 942 5561
Email: enquiries@bilborough.ac.uk
Website: www.bilborough.ac.uk
Principal: Chris Bradford

Boston College
Rochford Campus
Skirbeck Road
Boston
Lincolnshire PE21 6JF
Tel: 01205 365701
Fax: 01205 310847
Email: info@boston.ac.uk
Website: www.boston.ac.uk
Principal: Sue Daley
Director of Business Development:
Paul Collins
Community Learning Manager:
Dr Josie Pedersen

Brooksby Melton College
Brooksby
Melton Mowbray
Leicestershire LE14 2LJ
Tel: 01664 850850
Fax: 01664 855355
Email:
course.enquiries@brooksbymelton.ac.uk
Website: www.brooksbymelton.ac.uk
Principal: James Horrocks OBE

Castle College Nottingham
Maid Marian Way
Nottingham NG1 6AB
Tel: 0845 845 0500
Email: learn@castlecollege.ac.uk
Website: www.castlecollege.ac.uk
Principal and Chief Executive: Nick Lewis
Director of Faculty for Community
Education: Arnie Hattersley

Chesterfield College
Infirmary Road
Chesterfield
Derbyshire S41 7NG
Tel: 01246 500500
Fax: 01246 500587
Email: advice@chesterfield.ac.uk
Website: www.chesterfield.ac.uk
Acting Principal: J McArthur
Learner Support Manager: Heather Boylan

Derby College
Prince Charles Avenue
Mackworth
Derby DE22 4LR
Tel: 01332 520200
Fax: 01332 510548
Email: enquiries@derby-college.ac.uk
Website: www.derby-college.ac.uk
Principal and Chief Executive: David Croll
Freephone 0800 028 0289

Gateway College
The Newarke
Leicester LE2 7BY
Tel: 0116 258 0700
Fax: 0116 258 0701
Email: admin@gateway.ac.uk
Website: www.gateway.ac.uk
Principal: Nick Goffin
Deputy Principal (Adults): Nigel Proctor

Grantham College
Stonebridge Road
Grantham
Lincolnshire NG31 9AP
Tel: 01476 400200
Fax: 01476 400291
Email: enquiry@grantham.ac.uk
Website: www.grantham.ac.uk
Principal: M D Saville

Leicester College
Freemen's Park Campus
Aylestone Road
Leicester LE2 7LW
Tel: 0116 224 2000
Fax: 0116 224 2190
Email: info@leicestercollege.ac.uk
Website: www.leicestercollege.ac.uk
Principal: Maggie Galliers
Director of Curriculm: Keith Whittaker

Lincoln College
Monks Road
Lincoln LN2 5HQ
Tel: 01522 876000
Fax: 01522 876200
Website: www.lincolncollege.ac.uk
Principal: John S Allen
Community Development Manager:
Janet Cannon
Lincoln College has merged with -:

Gainsborough College
Acland Street
Gainsborough DN21 2SU
Tel: 01427 617471
Fax: 01522 876200

Newark College
Friary Road
Newark NG24 1PB
Tel: 01636 680680
Fax: 01636 680681

Loughborough College
Radmoor Road
Loughborough
Leicestershire LE11 3BT
Tel: 01509 215831
Fax: 01509 618109
Email: info@loucoll.ac.uk
Website: www.loucoll.ac.uk
Principal: James Mutton
Careers Advisor: Mike Gordon

Moulton College
West Street
Moulton
Northampton NN3 7RR
Tel: 01604 491131
Fax: 01604 491127
Email: enquiries@moulton.ac.uk
Website: www.moulton.ac.uk
Principal: Chris Moody

New College Nottingham
1 Broadway
Nottingham NG1 1PR
Tel: 0115 910 0100
Email: enquiries@ncn.ac.uk
Website: www.ncn.ac.uk
Chief Executive: Geoff Hall

New College Stamford
Drift Road
Stamford
Lincolnshire PE9 1XA
Tel: 01780 484300
Fax: 01780 484301
Email: enquiries@stamford.ac.uk
Website: www.stamford.ac.uk
Principal: M Dibsdall

Northampton College
Booth Lane
Northampton NN3 3RF
Tel: 01604 734567
Fax: 01604 734207
Email: enquiries@northamptoncollege.ac.uk
Website: www.northamptoncollege.ac.uk
Principal: Len Closs
Vice-Principal, Planning and Business
Development: Ray Starkey
Director of Learning: John Bexson

North Nottinghamshire College
Carlton Road
Worksop
Nottinghamshire S81 7HP
Tel: 01909 504504
Fax: 01909 504505
Email: contact@nnc.ac.uk
Website: www.nnc.ac.uk
Principal and Chief Executive:
John Connolly

Regent College
Regent Road
Leicester LE1 7LW
Tel: 0116 255 4629
Fax: 0116 254 5680
Email: support@regent-college.ac.uk
Website: www.regent-college.ac.uk
Principal: Paul Wilson
Vice-Principal: Peter Bignold
Head of Adult Community Provision:
Elaine Nixon
Head of ESOL: Elisabeth Merrion-Lancaster
Head of Careers: Dan Gurr

South Leicestershire College
Station Road
Wigston
Leicestershire LE18 2DW
Tel: 0116 288 5051
Fax: 0116 288 0823
Email: lgs@slcollege.ac.uk
Website: www.slcollege.ac.uk
Careers Officer: Andrew Spencer
Admissions Manager: Heather Draper
External Projects Manager: Jan Meredith

South Nottingham College
West Bridgford Centre
Greythorn Drive
West Bridgford
Nottingham NG2 7GA
Tel: 0115 914 6400
Fax: 0115 914 6444
Email: enquiries@snc.ac.uk
Website: www.snc.ac.uk
Principal: Malcolm Cowgill
Head of School, Lifelong Learning:
Dave Buckley

Stephenson College
Thornborough Road
Coalville
Leicestershire LE67 3TN
Tel: 01530 836136
Fax: 01530 814253
Email: services@stephensoncoll.ac.uk
Website: www.stephensoncoll.ac.uk
Principal and Chief Executive: Nigel Leigh

Tresham Institute of Further and Higher Education
Windmill Avenue
Kettering
Northamptonshire NN15 6ER
Tel: 01536 413000
Fax: 01536 522500
Email: info@tresham.ac.uk
Website: www.tresham.ac.uk
Principal: Mark Silverman

West Nottinghamshire College
Derby Road
Mansfield
Nottinghamshire NG18 5BH
Tel: 01623 627191
Fax: 01623 623063
Email: info@westnotts.ac.uk
Website: www.westnotts.ac.uk
Principal: Asha Khemka

Wyggeston and Queen Elizabeth I College
University Road
Leicester LE1 7RJ
Tel: 0116 223 1900
Fax: 0116 223 1999
Email: enquiries@wqeic.ac.uk
Website: www.wqeic.ac.uk
Principal: Ian Wilson
Vice-Principal, Support and Guidance:
Sue Ashwin
Vice-Principal, Curriculum and Quality:
Tim Cullinan
Vice-Principal, Estates and Services:
John Thawley

Eastern

Barnfield College
York Street
Luton LU2 0EZ
Tel: 01582 569850
Fax: 01582 569821
Website: www.barnfield.ac.uk
Principal: Peter Birkett
Campus Director: Meryl Harris

Bedford College
Cauldwell Street
Bedford MK42 9AH
Tel: 01234 291 000
Fax: 01234 342 674
Email: info@bedford.ac.uk
Website: www.bedford.ac.uk
Chief Executive: Ian Pryce
Director of Foundation and Community
Learning: Christine Inglis

Braintree College
Church Lane
Braintree
Essex CM7 5SN
Tel: 01376 321711
Fax: 01376 340799
Website: www.braintree.ac.uk
Acting Principal: David Mason
Deputy Principal, Teaching and Learning:
Christopher Hudson

Cambridge Regional College
Kings Hedges Road
Cambridge CB4 2QT
Tel: 01223 418200
Fax: 01223 426425
Email: enquiry@camre.ac.uk
Website: www.camre.ac.uk
Principal/Chief Executive: Rick Dearing
Skills for Life and Outreach Manager:
Kathy Bowles

Chelmsford College
Moulsham Street
Chelmsford
Essex CM2 0JQ
Tel: 01245 265611
Fax: 01245 266908
Email:
information@chelmsford-college.ac.uk
Website: www.chelmsford-college.ac.uk
Principal: David Law
Adult Education Organiser:
Francoise Mortimer

City College Norwich
Norwich Building
Ipswich Road
Norwich
Norfolk NR2 2LJ
Tel: 01603 773773
Fax: 01603 773301
Email: information@ccn.ac.uk
Principal: Dick Palmer
IAG Services Manager: Helen Richardson
Head of Adult Provision: Tina Neil

Colchester Institute
Sheepen Road
Colchester
Essex CO3 3LL
Tel: 01206 712000
Fax: 01206 763041
Email: info@colchester.ac.uk
Website: www.colchester.ac.uk
Principal and Chief Executive:
Danny Clough

College of West Anglia
Tennyson Avenue
Kings Lynn
Norfolk PE30 2QW
Tel: 01553 761144
Fax: 01553 815555
Email: enquiries@col-westanglia.ac.uk
Website: www.col-westanglia.ac.uk
Principal: David Pomfret
Executive Director: Jill Francis

Dunstable College
Kingsway
Dunstable
Bedfordshire LU5 4HG
Tel: 01582 477776
Fax: 01582 478801
Email: enquiries@dunstable.ac.uk
Website: www.dunstable.ac.uk
Student Welfare Co-ordinator: Natasha Ray
Head of Learner Services: Eamonn Egan

East Norfolk Sixth Form College
Church Lane
Gorleston
Great Yarmouth
Norfolk NR31 7BQ
Tel: 01493 662234
Fax: 01493 441405
Email: enquiries@enorf.ac.uk
Website: www.enorf.ac.uk
Principal: Laurie Poulson

Easton College
Easton
Norwich
Norfolk NR9 5DX
Tel: 01603 731200
Fax: 01603 741438
Email: info@easton-college.ac.uk
Website: www.easton.ac.uk
Principal: David C Lawrence
Head of Department for Foundation
Learning: Marie Pacey

Epping Forest College
Borders Lane
Loughton
Essex IG10 3SA
Tel: 020 8508 8311
Fax: 020 8502 0186
Website: www.efc.ac.uk
Principal: David Butler BA MSc
Head of Partnership Services: Quentin Buller

Great Yarmouth College
Southtown
Great Yarmouth
Norfolk NR31 0ED
Tel: 01493 655261
Fax: 01493 653423
Email: info@gyc.ac.uk
Website: www.gyc.ac.uk
Principal: Robin Parkinson
Vice-Principal: Daphne King

Harlow College
Velizy Avenue
Town Centre
Harlow
Essex CM20 3LH
Tel: 01279 868000
Fax: 01279 868260
Email: learninglink@harlow-college.ac.uk
Website: www.harlow-college.ac.uk
Principal: Colin Hindmarch

Hertford Regional College
Ware Centre
Scotts Road
Ware
Hertfordshire SG12 9JF
Tel: 01992 411400
Fax: 01992 411885
Email: info@hrc.ac.uk
Website: www.hrc.ac.uk
Principal: Paul Harvey
Head of Department: Joan Bowen

Hills Road Sixth Form College
Hills Road
Cambridge CB2 8PE
Tel: 01223 247251
Fax: 01223 416979
Email: adulted@hillsroad.ac.uk
Website: www.hillsroad.ac.uk
Principal: Linda Sinclair

Huntingdonshire Regional College
California Road
Huntingdon
Cambridgeshire PE29 1BL
Tel: 01480 379100
Fax: 01480 379127
Email: college@huntingdon.ac.uk
Website: www.huntingdon.ac.uk
Principal: Anne Constantine
Quality and Community Learning Manager:
Steve Rogers
Information Advisor: Julia Young

Lowestoft College
St Peters Street
Lowestoft
Suffolk NR32 2NB
Tel: 01502 583521
Fax: 01502 500031
Email: info@lowestoft.ac.uk
Website: www.lowestoft.ac.uk
Principal: Gwen Parsons

North Hertfordshire College

Monkswood Way
Stevenage
Hertfordshire SG1 1LA
Tel: 01462 424242
Fax: 01462 443054
Website: www.nhc.ac.uk
Principal: Fintan Donohue
Head of Academy, Community and Health
Services: David Pitcher

Oaklands College

St Albans Smallford Campus
Hatfield Road
St Albans
Hertfordshire AL4 0JA
Tel: 01727 737000
Website: www.oaklands.ac.uk
Principal: Mark Dawe

Otley College

Charity Lane
Otley
Ipswich
Suffolk IP6 9EY
Tel: 01473 785543
Fax: 01473 785353
Email: info@otleycollege.ac.uk
Website: www.otleycollege.ac.uk
Principal: Philip Winfield
Vice-Principal, Curriculum: Jenny Milsom
Vice-Principal, Business and Corporate
Services: Rosanne Wijnberg

Paston College

Grammar School Road
North Walsham
Norfolk NR28 9JL
Tel: 01692 402334
Fax: 01692 500630
Website: www.paston.ac.uk
Principal: Peter Mayne

Peterborough Regional College

Park Crescent
Peterborough PE1 4DZ
Tel: 0845 8728722
Fax: 01733 767986
Email: info@peterborough.ac.uk
Website: www.peterborough.ac.uk
Principal: Don Lawson
Teacher Qualifications Framework
Manager: Angela Joyce
Vice-Principal (Finance, Audit and MIS):
Peter Walker
Vice-Principal (Planning and Resources):
Brian Redshaw

SEEVIC College

Runnymede Chase
Benfleet
Essex SS7 1TW
Tel: 01268 756111
Fax: 01268 565515
Email: info@seevic-college.ac.uk
Website: www.seevic-college.ac.uk
Principal: Geoff P Arnott
Admissions Officer: Vivien Allen

Sixth Form College Colchester

North Hill
Colchester
Essex CO1 1SN
Tel: 01206 500700
Fax: 01206 500770
Email: enquiries@colchsfc.ac.uk
Website: www.colchsfc.ac.uk
Principal: Ian MacNaughton

South East Essex College

Luker Road
Southend-on-Sea SS1 1ND
Tel: 01702 220400
Fax: 01702 432320
Email: marketing@southend.ac.uk
Website: www.southend.ac.uk
Principal and Chief Executive: Jan Hodges
Director of Student and Community
Services: Sue Coole
Director of Business Development:
Carol Anson-Higgs

Suffolk New College
Rope Walk
Ipswich
Suffolk IP4 1LT
Tel: 01473 255885
Fax: 01473 230054
Email: info@suffolk.ac.uk
Website: www.suffolk.ac.uk
Principal: Prof. Dave Muller
Deputy Principal: Marilyn Watsham

Thurrock and Basildon College
Woodview Campus
Woodview
Grays
Essex RM16 2YR
Tel: 01375 391199
Fax: 01375 373356
Email: info@tab.ac.uk
Principal: Denise Fielding
Vice-Principal, Curriculum and Business
Development: Julia Spearman

West Hertfordshire College
Watford Campus
Hempstead Road
Watford
Hertfordshire WD17 3EZ
Tel: 01923 812000
Fax: 01923 812556
Email: louise.thurston@westherts.ac.uk
Website: www.westherts.ac.uk
Principal and Chief Executive:
Elizabeth Rushton
Head of Adult, Community and Family
Learning: Louise Thurston

West Suffolk College
Out Risbygate
Bury St Edmunds
Suffolk IP33 3RL
Tel: 01284 701301
Fax: 01284 750561
Email: info@westsuffolk.ac.uk
Website: www.westsuffolk.ac.uk
Principal: Dr Ann Williams
Head of Adult Education: Mary Taylor

South West

Bicton College
East Budleigh
Budleigh Salterton
Devon EX9 7BY
Tel: 01395 562300
Fax: 01395 567502
Email: enquiries@bicton.ac.uk
Website: www.bicton.ac.uk
Principal: LouiseTwigg
Assistant Principal, Learner Responsive:
Jane Townsend
Head of Essential Skills: Graham Cook

Bournemouth and Poole College
North Road
Poole
Dorset BH14 0LS
Tel: 01202 205205
Fax: 01202 205719
Email: enquiries@thecollege.co.uk
Website: www.thecollege.co.uk
Principal and Chief Executive:
Lawrence Vincent

Bridgwater College
Bath Road
Bridgwater
Somerset TA6 4PZ
Tel: 01278 441234
Fax: 01278 444363
Email: information@bridgwater.ac.uk
Website: www.bridgwater.ac.uk
Principal: Fiona McMillan OBE
Adult Marketing Manager: Lisa Flahant

Cirencester College
Fosse Way Campus
Stroud Road
Cirencester
Gloucestershire GL7 1XA
Tel: 01285 640994
Fax: 01285 644171
Email: adult.guidance@cirencester.ac.uk
Website: www.cirencester.ac.uk
Principal: Nigel Robbins OBE
Email: principal@cirencester.ac.uk

City College Plymouth
Kings Road
Devonport
Plymouth
Devon PL1 5QG
Tel: 01752 305300
Fax: 01752 305343
Email: reception@cityplym.ac.uk
Website: www.cityplym.ac.uk
Principal: Viv Gillespie
Deputy Principal, Corporate Development
and Students: Phil Davies
Vice-Principal, Skills and HR: Sam Parrett
Deputy Principal, Finance and Resources:
Nicola Cove
Vice-Principal, Planning: Matthew Orford

City of Bath College
1 Avon Street
Bath BA1 1UP
Tel: 01225 312191
Fax: 01225 444213
Email: enquiries@citybathcoll.ac.uk
Website: www.citybathcoll.ac.uk
Principal: Matt Atkinson

City of Bristol College
LRC College Green
St Georges Road
Bristol BS1 5UA
Tel: 0117 312 5000
Fax: 0117 312 5053
Email: enquiries@cityofbristol.ac.uk
Website: www.cityofbristol.ac.uk
Principal: Keith Elliott
Vice-Principal, Curriculum and Students:
Judith Stradling
Vice-Principal, Skills and Partnerships:
Christine Bullock
Head of Faculty, Skills for Life: Jan Bovill

Cornwall College Corporation
John Keay House
Tregonissey Road
St. Austell
Cornwall PL25 4DJ
Tel: 01726 226526
Email: ccho@cornwall.ac.uk
Website: www.cornwall.ac.uk
Chief Executive: John Latham

East Devon College
Bolham Road
Tiverton
Devon EX16 6SH
Tel: 01884 235200
Fax: 01884 235262
Email: enquiries@admin.eastdevon.ac.uk
Website: www.edc.ac.uk
Principal: David Dodd
Vice-Principal: Mike O'Brien
Deputy Principal, Curriculum: John Laramy

Exeter College
Hele Road
Exeter EX4 4JS
Tel: 01392 205222
Fax: 01392 205225
Email: reception@exe-coll.ac.uk
Website: www.exe-coll.ac.uk
Principal: Richard Atkins
Director of Business and Marketing:
Chris Lorimer
Assistant Principal (Access and Support):
Malcolm Walsh
Head of Skills for Life and Learning:
Caroline Romijn

Filton College
Filton Avenue
Filton
Bristol BS34 7AT
Tel: 0117 931 2121
Fax: 0117 931 2233
Email: info@filton.ac.uk
Website: www.filton.ac.uk
Principal: Kevin Hamblin

Gloucestershire College of Arts and Technology
Cheltenham Campus
Princess Elizabeth Way
Cheltenham
Gloucestershire GL51 7SJ
Tel: 01242 532000
Fax: 01242 532196
Email: info@gloscat.ac.uk
Website: www.gloscat.ac.uk
Principal: Greg Smith
Email: smithg@gloscat.ac.uk
Vice-Principal, Corporate Development
Services: Annette Cast
Director of Adult and Community Learning:
Richard Hewlett

Hartpury College
Hartpury House
Hartpury
Gloucestershire GL19 3BE
Tel: 01452 700283
Fax: 01452 700629
Email: enquire@hartpury.ac.uk
Website: www.hartpury.ac.uk
Principal: Malcolm Wharton
Vice-Principal: Graham Ledden

Kingston Maurward College
Kingston Maurward
Dorchester
Dorset DT2 8PY
Tel: 01305 215000
Fax: 01305 215001
Email: administration@kmc.ac.uk
Website: www.kmc.ac.uk
Principal: David Henley
Deputy Principal: Clare Davison
Director of Finance and Corporate Services:
Giles Pugh
Director of Commercial Development:
Ivan Smith

New College Swindon
New College Drive
Swindon SN3 1AH
Tel: 01793 611470
Fax: 01793 436437
Email: webmaster@newcollege.ac.uk
Website: www.newcollege.ac.uk
Principal and Chief Executive:
Graham Taylor
Email: graham.taylor@newcollege.ac.uk
Community Education Manager:
Paula Kimmel
Email: paula.kimmel@newcollege.ac.uk

North Devon College
Old Sticklepath Hill
Barnstaple
Devon EX31 2BQ
Tel: 01271 345291
Fax: 01271 338121
Email: postbox@ndevon.ac.uk
Website: www.ndevon.ac.uk
Principal: David Dodd
Vice-Principal, Director of Studies:
Michael O'Brien
Vice-Principal, Director of Resources:
Karen Trigger

Norton Radstock College
South Hill Park
Radstock
Bath BA3 3RW
Tel: 01761 433161
Fax: 01761 436173
Website: www.nortcoll.ac.uk
Principal: Shirley Arayan
Email: sarayan@nortcoll.ac.uk
Senior Manager, Student Support Services:
Penny Routledge
Senior Manager, College Information
Services: David Grant

Penwith and Truro College
St Clare Street
Penzance
Cornwall TR18 2SA
Tel: 01736 335000
Fax: 01736 335100
Website: www.penwith.ac.uk
Principal and Chief Executive:
Jonathan Burnett
Director of Services: Jonathan Jones

Plymouth College of Art and Design
Tavistock Place
Plymouth
Devon PL4 8AT
Tel: 01752 203434
Fax: 01752 203444
Email: enquiries@pcad.ac.uk
Website: www.pcad.ac.uk
Principal: Lynne Staley-Brookes

Richard Huish College
South Road
Taunton
Somerset TA1 3DZ
Tel: 01823 320800
Fax: 01823 320801
Website: www.richuish.ac.uk
Principal: Peter Avery
Email: petera@richuish.ac.uk

Royal Forest of Dean College
Five Acres Campus
Berry Hill
Coleford
Gloucestershire GL16 7JT
Tel: 01594 833416
Fax: 01594 837497
Website: www.rfdc.ac.uk
Principal: Dawn Ward
Head of Learner Services: Sandy Lang

Salisbury College
Southampton Road
Salisbury
Wiltshire SP1 2LW
Tel: 01722 344344
Fax: 01722 344345
Email: enquiries@salisbury.ac.uk
Website: www.salisbury.ac.uk
Principal: Gill Thompson
PA to Principal: Debi Lisseman-Edge
Head of Learning Resources:
Nick Beauchamp

**Somerset College of Arts
and Technology**
Wellington Road
Taunton
Somerset TA1 5AX
Tel: 01823 366366
Fax: 01823 366418
Email: enquiries@somerset.ac.uk
Website: www.somerset.ac.uk
Principal and Chief Executive:
Rachel Davies
Head of Division, Employer Services:
Neil Higginson

South Devon College
Vantage Point
Long Road
Paignton
Devon TQ4 7EJ
Tel: 01803 540540
Fax: 01803 540541
Email: enquiries@southdevon.ac.uk
Website: www.southdevon.ac.uk
Principal: Heather Maxwell
Adult and Community Learning Manager:
John Demeger

St Brendan's Sixth Form College
Broomhill Road
Brislington
Bristol BS4 5RQ
Tel: 0117 977 7766
Fax: 0117 972 3351
Email: info@stbrn.ac.uk
Website: www.stbrn.ac.uk
Principal: Derek Bodey

Strode College
Church Road
Street
Somerset BA16 0AB
Tel: 01458 844400
Fax: 01458 844411
Website: www.strode-college.ac.uk
Principal: Ian Bennett
Head of Continuing Education Team:
Deborah Cummings

Stroud College in Gloucestershire
Stratford Road
Stroud
Gloucestershire GL5 4AH
Tel: 01453 763 424
Fax: 01453 753 543
Email: enquire@stroudcol.ac.uk
Website: www.stroud.ac.uk
Principal: Beri Hare
Adult and Community Learning
Co-ordinator: Emma Clark

Swindon College
North Star Avenue
Swindon SN2 1DY
Tel: 01793 491591
Fax: 01793 430503
Email: advice@swindon-college.ac.uk
Acting Principal: Nick Letchett
Operational Manager for Adult and
Community Education: Julia Hoskins

Truro and Penwith College
College Road
Truro
Cornwall TR1 3XX
Tel: 01872 267000
Fax: 01872 267100
Email: enquiry@trurocollege.ac.uk
Website: www.trurocollege.ac.uk
Principal: Jonathan Burnett OBE

Weston College
Knightstone Road
Weston-super-Mare
Somerset BS23 2AL
Tel: 01934 411411
Fax: 01934 411410
Email: enquiries@weston.ac.uk
Website: www.weston.ac.uk
Principal and Chief Executive:
Dr Paul Phillips
Head of Skills for Life: Jacqui Ford

Weymouth College
Cranford Avenue
Weymouth
Dorset DT4 7LQ
Tel: 01305 761100
Fax: 01305 208892
Email: igs@weymouth.ac.uk
Website: www.weymouth.ac.uk
Principal and Chief Executive: Susan Moore

Wiltshire College
Cocklebury Road
Chippenham
Wiltshire SN15 3QD
Tel: 01249 464644
Fax: 01249 705206
Email: info@wiltscoll.ac.uk
Website: www.wiltscoll.ac.uk
Principal: Di Dale

Yeovil College
Mudford Road
Yeovil
Somerset BA21 4DR
Tel: 01935 423921
Fax: 01935 429962
Email: info@yeovil.ac.uk
Website: www.yeovil.ac.uk
Principal: James Hampton
Access to Higher Education Co-ordinator:
Melanie Sherbourne
Employer Engagement: Shaun Hindle
Adult Guidance Manager: Angela Coward
HE Advice and Guidance: Richard Foyle

South East

Abingdon and Witney College
Wootton Road
Abingdon
Oxfordshire OX14 1GG
Tel: 01235 555585
Fax: 01235 553168
Email: enquiry@abingdon-witney.ac.uk
Website: www.abingdon-witney.ac.uk
Principal: Teresa Kelly

Alton College
Old Odiham Road
Alton
Hampshire GU34 2LX
Tel: 01420 592200
Fax: 01420 592253
Email: enquiries@altoncollege.ac.uk
Website: www.altoncollege.ac.uk
Principal: Jane Machell
Vice-Principal, Student Services and Business
Development: Steve MacCormack
Vice-Principal, Curriculum and
Organisational Development: David Vasse
Head of Faculty for Social, Business and
Adult Studies: John Stratford

Amersham and Wycombe College
Lycrome Road
Chesham
Buckinghamshire HP5 3LA
Tel: 01494 585555
Fax: 01494 585566
Email: info@amersham.ac.uk
Website: www.amersham.ac.uk
Principal and Chief Executive: Gill Clipson
Vice-Principal, Curriculum and Quality:
John Spencer

Andover College
A Campus of Sparsholt College
Charlton Road
Andover
Hampshire SP10 1EJ
Tel: 01264 360000
Fax: 01264 360010
Email: info@andover.ac.uk
Website: www.andover.ac.uk
Vice-Principal: Martin Simmonds

Aylesbury College
Oxford Road
Aylesbury
Buckinghamshire HP21 8PD
Tel: 01296 588588
Fax: 01296 588589
Email: customerservices@aylesbury.ac.uk
Website: www.aylesbury.ac.uk
Principal: Pauline Odulinski

Barton Peveril College
Chestnut Avenue
Eastleigh
Hampshire SO50 5ZA
Tel: 023 8036 7225
Fax: 023 8036 7228
Email: enquiries@barton.ac.uk
Website: www.barton-peveril.ac.uk
Principal: Godfrey Glyn
Curriculum Director, Adult Learning:
Christine Archdeacon
Basic Skills Co-ordinator: Elizabeth Caush

Basingstoke College of Technology
Worting Road
Basingstoke
Hampshire RG21 8TN
Tel: 01256 354141
Fax: 01256 306444
Email: information@bcot.ac.uk
Website: www.bcot.ac.uk
Principal: Judith Armstrong
Deputy Principal, Curriculum and Quality:
Peter Phillips

Berkshire College of Agriculture (BCA)
Hall Place
Burchetts Green
Maidenhead
Berkshire SL6 6QR
Tel: 01628 824444
Fax: 01628 824695
Email: enquiries@bca.ac.uk
Website: www.bca.ac.uk
Principal: Peter Thorn
Vice-Principal: Julie Walsh

Bexhill College
Penland Road
Bexhill-on-Sea
East Sussex TN40 2JG
Tel: 01424 214545
Fax: 01424 215050
Website: www.bexhillcollege.ac.uk
Principal: Karen Hucker
Adult Learning Co-ordinator: Judith Hattam

Bracknell and Wokingham College
Church Road
Bracknell
Berkshire RG12 1DJ
Tel: 01344 460200
Fax: 01344 460360
Email: study@bracknell.ac.uk
Website: www.bracknell.ac.uk
Principal and Chief Executive:
Howard O'Keeffe
Head of Adult and Community Education:
Jan Sellwood

Brighton, Hove and Sussex Sixth Form College
205 Dyke Road
Hove
East Sussex BN3 6EG
Tel: 01273 552200
Fax: 01273 563139
Website: www.bhasvic.ac.uk
Principal: Chris Thomson
Vice-Principal: Anne Fielding Smith

Brockenhurst College
Lyndhurst Road
Brockenhurst
Hampshire SO42 7ZE
Tel: 01590 625555
Fax: 01590 625526
Email: enquiries@brock.ac.uk
Website: www.brock.ac.uk
Principal: Di Roberts
Lifelong Learning Manager: Mark Howarth

Brooklands College
Heath Road
Weybridge
Surrey KT13 8TT
Tel: 01932 797700
Fax: 01932 797800
Principal: Colin B Staff
Deputy Principal: Andy Bendix

Brooklands College (Ashford Campus)
Church Road
Ashford
Middlesex TW15 2XD
Tel: 01784 248666
Fax: 01784 254132

Canterbury College
New Dover Road
Canterbury
Kent CT1 3AJ
Tel: 01227 811111
Fax: 01227 811101
Email: courseenquiries@cant-col.ac.uk
Website: www.cant-col.ac.uk
Principal and Executive Director:
Alison Clarke

Central Sussex College
College Road
Crawley
West Sussex RH10 1NR
Tel: 01293 442200
Fax: 01293 442399
Email: info@centralsussex.ac.uk
Website: www.centralsussex.ac.uk
Principal: Dr Russell Strutt
Head of Adult and Community Learning:
Clare Wallace

Chichester College
Westgate Fields
Chichester
West Sussex PO19 1SB
Tel: 01243 786321
Fax: 01243 539481
Email: info@chichester.ac.uk
Website: www.chichester.ac.uk
Principal: Dr Richard Parker
Email: richard.parker@chichester.ac.uk
Director of International Operations:
Peter Brown

City College Brighton and Hove
Pelham Street
Brighton
East Sussex BN1 4FA
Tel: 01273 667788
Fax: 01273 667703
Email: info@ccb.ac.uk
Website: www.ccb.ac.uk
Principal: Phil Friar
Head of Adult Learning and Higher
Education: Steve Lewis
Adult Centre Manager: Heather Shaw

College of Richard Collyer
Hurst Road
Horsham
West Sussex RH12 2EJ
Tel: 01403 210822
Fax: 01403 211915
Email: admin@collyers.ac.uk
Website: www.collyers.ac.uk
Principal: Dr Jackie Johnston
Adult Programme Manager: Paul Clarke

East Berkshire College
Station Road
Langley
Slough
Berkshire SL3 8BY
Tel: 01753 793000
Fax: 01753 793316
Email: info@eastberks.ac.uk
Website: www.eastberks.ac.uk
Principal: Jean Robertson
Vice-Principal, Curriculum and Quality:
Kate Webb

Eastleigh College
Chestnut Avenue
Eastleigh
Hampshire SO50 5FS
Tel: 023 8091 1000
Fax: 023 8032 2131
Email: goplaces@eastleigh.ac.uk
Website: www.eastleigh.ac.uk
Chief Executive: Anthony Lau-Walker

East Surrey College
Gatton Point
London Road
Redhill
Surrey RH1 2JT
Tel: 01737 772611
Fax: 01737 768641
Website: www.esc.ac.uk
Principal and CEO: Frances Wadsworth
Deputy Principal: Jayne Dickinson

Fareham College
Bishopsfield Road
Fareham
Hampshire PO14 1NH
Tel: 01329 815200
Fax: 01329 822483
Website: www.fareham.ac.uk
Principal: Carl Groves
Director of Faculty, General Studies:
Simon Neale

Farnborough College of Technology
Boundary Road
Farnborough
Hampshire GU14 6SB
Tel: 01252 405555
Fax: 01252 407041
Email: info@farn-ct.ac.uk
Website: www.farn-ct.ac.uk
Principal: Christine Davis
Deputy Principal, Curriculum: Phelim Brady
Vice-Principal, Quality: Iain Wolloff

Farnham College
Morley Road
Farnham
Surrey GU9 8LU
Tel: 01252 716988
Fax: 01252 723969
Email: enquiries@farnham.ac.uk
Website: www.farnham.ac.uk
Principal: Clive Cooke
Adult Education Programme Manager:
Vicky Owen

Godalming College
Tuesley Lane
Godalming
Surrey GU7 1RS
Tel: 01483 423526
Fax: 01483 417079
Email: college@godalming.ac.uk
Website: www.godalming.ac.uk
Principal and Chief Executive:
David Adelman BA
Director, Business Training Services:
Daniel Power

Business Training Services
Godalming College
The Chestnut Suite
Guardian House
Borough Road
Goldalming
Surrey GU7 2AE
Tel: 01483 423292
Fax: 01483 425164
Email: bts@godalming.ac.uk

Guildford College of Further and Higher Education
Stoke Park
Guildford
Surrey GU1 1EZ
Tel: 01483 448585
Fax: 01483 448600
Email: info@guildford.ac.uk
Website: www.guildford.ac.uk
Principal: Clive Cooke

Hadlow College
Hadlow
Tonbridge
Kent TN11 0AL
Tel: 01732 850551
Fax: 01732 853207
Email: enquiries@hadlow.ac.uk
Website: www.hadlow.ac.uk
Principal and Chief Executive: Paul Hannan

Hastings College of Arts and Technology

Archery Road
St Leonards-on-Sea
East Sussex TN38 0HX
Tel: 01424 458310
Fax: 01424 718834
Email: principalspa@hastings.ac.uk
Website: www.hastings.ac.uk
Principal: Sue Middlehurst

Havant College

New Road
Havant
Hampshire PO9 1QL
Tel: 023 9248 3856
Fax: 023 9247 0621
Website: www.havant.ac.uk
Principal: John McDougall
Adult Learning Co-ordinator: Karen Willis

Henley College

Deanfield Avenue
Henley on Thames
Oxfordshire RG9 1UH
Tel: 01491 579988
Fax: 01491 410099
Email: info@henleycol.ac.uk
Website: www.henleycol.ac.uk
Principal: Tom Espley
Director of Student Services: Peter Allen

Highbury College, Portsmouth

Cosham
Portsmouth
Hampshire PO6 2SA
Tel: 023 9238 3131
Fax: 023 9232 5551
Website: www.highbury.ac.uk
Principal and Chief Executive: Stella
Mbubaegbu CBE
Email: principal@highbury.ac.uk
Head of Community Development:
Teresa Dowie

Isle of Wight College

Medina Way
Newport
Isle of Wight PO30 5TA
Tel: 01983 526631
Fax: 01983 521707
Email: info@iwcollege.ac.uk
Website: www.iwcollege.ac.uk
Principal: Debbie Lavin
Assistant Principal: Roland White

Itchen College

Middle Road
Bitterne
Southampton SO19 7TB
Tel: 023 8043 5636
Fax: 023 8042 1911
Email: acet@itchen.ac.uk
Website: www.itchen.ac.uk
Principal: Barry Hicks
Head of Adult Education: Victor Scott

Mid-Kent College of Further and Higher Education

Horsted Centre
Maidstone Road
Chatham
Kent ME5 9UQ
Tel: 01634 830633
Fax: 01634 830224
Email: course.enquiries@midkent.ac.uk
Website: www.midkent.ac.uk
Principal: Stephen Grix
Vice-Principal, Curriculum: Sue McLeod

Milton Keynes College

Chaffron Way Campus
Woughton Campus West
Leadenhall
Milton Keynes MK6 5LP
Tel: 01908 684444
Fax: 01908 684399
Email: info@mkcollege.ac.uk
Website: www.mkcollege.ac.uk
Principal: Rob Badcock

Newbury College
Monks Lane
Newbury
Berkshire RG14 7TD
Tel: 01635 845000
Fax: 01635 845312
Email: r-gill@newbury-college.ac.uk
Website: www.newbury-college.ac.uk
Principal: Dr Anne Murdoch
Learner Services and Information Manager:
Rosie Gill
Section Manager – Adult and Community
Learning: Gemma Baker

North East Surrey College of Technology (NESCOT)
Reigate Road
Ewell
Surrey KT17 3DS
Tel: 020 8394 1731
Fax: 020 8394 3030
Email: info@nescot.ac.uk
Website: www.nescot.ac.uk
Principal and Chief Executive:
Sunaina Mann
Vice-Principal, Further Education:
Rosalind Le Quesne
Director of Higher Education: Mark Foster

Northbrook College Sussex
Littlehampton Road
Goring by Sea
Worthing
West Sussex BN12 6NU
Tel: 0845 155 6060
Fax: 01903 606007
Email: enquiries@nbcol.ac.uk
Website: www.northbrook.ac.uk
Principal: David Percival
Vice-Principal: Karimah Butcher

Oxford and Cherwell Valley College
Oxford Campus
Oxpens Road
Oxford OX1 1SA
Tel: 01865 550550
Fax: 01865 248871
Email: enquiries@ocvc.ac.uk
Website: www.ocvc.ac.uk
Principal and Chief Executive: Sally Dicketts

Peter Symonds College
Owens Road
Winchester
Hampshire SO22 6RX
Tel: 01962 857500
Fax: 01962 857501
Email: ace@psc.ac.uk
Website: www.psc.ac.uk/ace
Principal: Neil Hopkins
Head of Adult Education Division:
Alexandra Day

Adult Education delivered at:
Adult Continuing Education Centre
Stoney Lane
Weeke
Winchester
Hampshire SO22 6DR
Tel: 01962 886166
Fax: 01962 889540

Plumpton College
Ditchling Road
Plumpton
Lewes
East Sussex BN7 3AE
Tel: 01273 890454
Fax: 01273 890071
Email: enquiries@plumpton.ac.uk
Website: www.plumpton.ac.uk
Principal: Des Lambert

Portsmouth College
Tangier Road
Portsmouth
Hampshire PO3 6PZ
Tel: 023 9266 7521
Fax: 023 9234 4363
Email: registry@portsmouth-college.ac.uk
Website: www.portsmouth-college.ac.uk
Principal: Steve Frampton
Head of Business Development and
Continuing Education: Karen Hills

Queen Mary's College
Cliddesden Road
Basingstoke
Hampshire RG21 3HF
Tel: 01256 417500
Fax: 01256 417501
Email: admissions@qmc.ac.uk
Website: www.qmc.ac.uk
Principal: Stephen Sheedy
Deputy Principal: Alan Heap

Reigate College
Castlefield Road
Reigate
Surrey RH2 0SD
Tel: 01737 221118
Fax: 01737 222657
Email: enquiries@reigate.ac.uk
Website: www.reigate.ac.uk
Principal: Dr Paul Rispoli
Deputy Principal, Operations, Marketing
and Resources: Ian Tapp
Deputy Principal, Teaching, Learning and
Student Support: Steve Oxlade

Ruskin College
Walton Street
Oxford OX1 2HE
Tel: 01865 554331
Fax: 01865 554372
Email: enquiries@ruskin.ac.uk
Website: www.ruskin.ac.uk
Principal: Prof. Audrey Mullender
General Secretary: Dr Chris Wilkes

Southampton City College
St Mary Street
Southampton
Hampshire SO14 1AR
Tel: 023 8057 7400
Fax: 023 8057 7473
Email: information@southampton-city.ac.uk
Website: www.southampton-city.ac.uk
Principal: Lindsey Noble
Executive Director of Teaching, Learning
and Curriculum: Ivan Gregory

South Downs College
College Road
Waterlooville
Hampshire PO7 8AA
Tel: 023 9279 7979
Fax: 023 9279 7940
Email: college@southdowns.ac.uk
Website: www.southdowns.ac.uk
Principal: Michael Oakes
Head of Faculty: Elizabeth Norland
Minicom 023 9278 2214

South Kent College
Shorncliffe Road
Folkestone
Kent CT20 2TZ
Tel: 08457 207 8220
Website: www.southkent.ac.uk
Interim Principal: Monica Box

Sparsholt College Hampshire
Sparsholt
Winchester
Hampshire SO21 2NF
Tel: 01962 776441
Fax: 01962 776587
Email: enquiries@sparsholt.ac.uk
Website: www.sparsholt.ac.uk
Principal: T D Jackson

St Vincent College
Mill Lane
Gosport
Hampshire PO12 4QA
Tel: 023 9258 8311
Fax: 023 9251 1186
Email: info@stvincent.ac.uk
Website: www.stvincent.ac.uk
Principal: Stephen Wain

Strode's College
High Street
Egham
Surrey TW20 9DR
Tel: 01784 437506
Fax: 01784 471794
Email: adulteducation@strodes.ac.uk
Website: www.strodes.ac.uk
Principal: Dr Frank Botham
Director of Continuing Education:
Tony Woodward

Sussex Downs College
Eastbourne Campus
Cross Levels Way
Eastbourne
East Sussex BN21 2UF
Tel: 01323 637637
Fax: 01323 637472
Email: info@sussexdowns.ac.uk
Website: www.sussexdowns.ac.uk
Principal and Chief Executive:
Dr John D Blake
Executive Director Skills: Gill Short

Taunton's College
Hill Lane
Southampton
Hampshire SO15 5RL
Tel: 023 8051 1811
Fax: 023 8051 1991
Email: email@tauntons.ac.uk
Website: www.tauntons.ac.uk
Principal: Alice Wrighton
Director of Adult Education: Matt Atkinson

Thames Valley University
St Mary's Road
Ealing
London W5 5RF
Tel: 020 8579 5000
Fax: 020 8566 1353
Website: www.tvu.ac.uk
Vice-Chancellor: Prof. Peter John
Pro-Vice-Chancellor: Lee Nicholls

Thanet College
Ramsgate Road
Broadstairs
Kent CT10 1PN
Tel: 01843 605040
Fax: 01843 605013
Website: www.thanet.ac.uk
Principal: Sue Buss
Deputy Principal: Anne Leese
Section Leader, International and
Community Education: Lucy McLeod

Totton College
Calmore Road
Totton
Southampton
Hampshire SO40 3ZX
Tel: 023 8087 4874
Fax: 023 8087 4879
Email: info@totton.ac.uk
Website: www.totton.ac.uk
Principal: Mark Bramwell
Head of Projects and Participation:
Diana Kossler-Smith

Varndean College
Surrenden Road
Brighton
East Sussex BN1 6WQ
Tel: 01273 508011
Fax: 01273 542950
Email: info@varndean.ac.uk
Website: www.varndean.ac.uk
Principal: Dr Philip Harland
Adult Education Co-ordinator:
Angela Pamely
Adult Education Direct Line
Tel: 01273 546602
Adult Education email:
Commed@varndean.ac.uk

West Dean College
West Dean
Chichester
West Sussex PO18 0QZ
Tel: 01243 811301
Fax: 01243 811343
Email: short.courses@westdean.org.uk
Website: www.westdean.org.uk
Principal: Robert Pulley
Head of Short Courses and Conferences:
Alison Baxter

West Kent College
Brook Street
Tonbridge
Kent TN9 2PW
Tel: 01732 358101
Fax: 01732 771415
Website: www.wkc.ac.uk
Principal and Chief Executive: Bill Fearon

Woking College
Rydens Way
Woking
Surrey GU22 9DL
Tel: 01483 761036
Fax: 01483 728144
Email: adult@woking.ac.uk
Website: www.woking.ac.uk
Principal: Martin Ingram
Vice-Principal: Brett Freeman

Worthing College
Bolsover Road
Worthing
West Sussex BN13 1NS
Tel: 01903 243389
Fax: 01903 243390
Website: www.worthing.ac.uk
Principal: Peter Corrigan
Adult Administrator: Debbie Robinson

London

Barking College
Dagenham Road
Romford
Essex RM7 0XU
Tel: 01708 770000
Fax: 01708 770007
Website: www.barkingcollege.ac.uk
Principal: Kathy Walsh

Barnet College
Grahame Park Way
London NW9 5RA
Tel: 020 8200 8300
Fax: 020 8205 7177
Email: info@barnet.ac.uk
Website: www.barnet.ac.uk
Principal: Marilyn Hawkins

Bexley College
Tower Road
Belvedere
Kent DA17 6JA
Tel: 01322 442331
Fax: 01322 448403
Email: courses@bexley.ac.uk
Website: www.bexley.ac.uk
Interim Principal: David Gleed

Bromley College of Further and Higher Education
Rookery Lane
Bromley
Kent BR2 8HE
Tel: 020 8295 7000
Fax: 020 8295 7099
Email: info@bromley.ac.uk
Website: www.bromley.ac.uk
Principal: Peter Jones
Vice-Principal, Curriculum and
Partnerships: Valerie West

Capel Manor College
Main Campus
Bullsmoor Lane
Enfield
Middlesex EN1 4RQ
Tel: 08456 122122
Fax: 01992 717544
Email: enquiries@capel.ac.uk
Website: www.capel.ac.uk
Chief Executive: Dr Steven Dowbiggin
Head of College: Madeline Hall MA

Also campuses across London, including
Gunnersbury Park, Regent's Park,
Crystal Palace and Castle Green

Carshalton College
Nightingale Road
Carshalton
Surrey SM5 2EJ
Tel: 020 8544 4444
Fax: 020 8544 4440
Email: helpline@carshalton.ac.uk
Website: www.carshalton.ac.uk
Principal: Dr David Watkins

City and Islington College
Centre for Lifelong Learning
28–42 Blackstock Road
Finsbury Park
London N4 2DG
Tel: 020 7700 9333
Fax: 020 7700 9222
Website: www.candi.ac.uk
Principal: Frank McLoughlin
Director of Centre for Lifelong Learning:
Mila Caley

City Lit
1–10 Keeley Street
Covent Garden
London WC2B 4BA
Tel: 020 7492 2600
Fax: 020 7492 2736
Email: infoline@citylit.ac.uk
Website: www.citylit.ac.uk
Principal/Chief Executive:
Peter Davies CB CBE

City of Westminster College
North Wharf Road
London W2 1LF
Tel: 020 7723 8826
Fax: 020 7258 2700
Email: customer.services@cwc.ac.uk
Website: www.cwc.ac.uk
Principal: Robin Shreeve
Vice-Principal, Innovation and Business
Development: Suzanne Overton-Edwards

College of North East London
Tottenham Centre
High Road
London N15 4RU
Tel: 020 8802 3111
Fax: 020 8442 3085
Email: admissions@staff.conel.ac.uk
Website: www.conel.ac.uk
Principal and Chief Executive: Paul Head
Vice-Principal: Cathy Walsh

The College of North West London
Dudden Hill Lane
London NW10 2XD
Tel: 020 8208 5050
Fax: 020 8208 5151
Email: cic@cnwl.ac.uk
Website: www.cnwl.ac.uk
Principal: Vicki Fagg
Textphone: 020 8208 5163

Coulsdon College
Placehouse Lane
Coulsdon
Surrey CR5 1YA
Tel: 01737 551176
Fax: 01737 551282
Email: gen.enquiries@coulsdon.ac.uk
Website: www.coulsdon.ac.uk
Principal: David Goodlet
Deputy Principal: Yolanda Botham

Croydon College
Fairfield
College Road
Croydon
Surrey CR9 1DX
Tel: 020 8686 5700
Fax: 020 8760 5880
Email: info@croydon.ac.uk
Website: www.croydon.ac.uk
Principal: Mariane Cavalli

Ealing, Hammersmith and West London College
Gliddon Road
Barons Court
London W14 9BL
Tel: 020 8741 1688
Fax: 020 8741 2491
Email: cic@wlc.ac.uk
Website: www.wlc.ac.uk
Principal: Paula Whittle

Enfield College
73 Hertford Road
Ponders End
Enfield
Middlesex EN3 5HA
Tel: 020 8443 3434
Fax: 020 8804 7028
Email: courseinformation@enfield.ac.uk
Website: www.enfield.ac.uk
Principal and Chief Executive: Jean Carter
Director of Curriculum:
Bernadette McAnespie

Esher College
Weston Green Road
Thames Ditton
Surrey KT7 0JB
Tel: 020 8398 0291
Fax: 020 8339 0207
Email: eshercollege@esher.ac.uk
Website: www.esher.ac.uk
Principal: Keith Blackwell
Adult and Leisure Activities Manager:
Jo Hampton

Greenwich Community College
95 Plumstead Road
London SE18 7DZ
Tel: 020 8488 4800
Fax: 020 8488 4899
Email: info@gcc.ac.uk
Website: www.gcc.ac.uk
Principal: Geoff Pine
Vice-Principal: Ian Mitton
Director of Adult and Community Learning:
Kim Miller
Head of Community Development:
Barbara Smith

Hackney Community College
Learning Resources Centre
Shoreditch Campus
Falkirk Street
London N1 6HQ
Tel: 020 7613 9000
Fax: 020 7613 9003
Website: www.tcch.ac.uk
Principal: Ian Ashman
Head of Community Education:
Adebisi Mohammed

Harrow College
Lifelong Learning Centre
Harrow-on-the-Hill Campus
Lowlands Road
Harrow
Middlesex HA1 3AQ
Tel: 020 8909 6400
Fax: 020 8909 6050
Email: enquiries@harrow.ac.uk
Website: www.harrow.ac.uk
Principal: Tony Medhurst
Vice-Principal: Susan Harrison
Head of Arts and Computing: Sue Wilson
Adult Community Learning Manager:
Chris Spellen

Havering College of Further and Higher Education
Ardleigh Green Road
Hornchurch
Essex RM11 2LL
Tel: 01708 455011
Fax: 01708 462788
Email: information@havering-college.ac.uk
Website: www.havering-college.ac.uk
Principal and Chief Executive: Noel Otley
Email: notley@havering-college.ac.uk
Deputy Principal: Maria Thompson

Hillcroft College
South Bank
Surbiton
Surrey KT6 6DF
Tel: 020 8399 2688
Fax: 020 8390 9171
Email: enquiry@hillcroft.ac.uk
Website: www.hillcroft.ac.uk
Principal: June Ireton

John Ruskin College
Selsdon Park Road
South Croydon
Surrey CR2 8JJ
Tel: 020 8651 1131
Fax: 020 8651 4011
Email: info@johnruskin.ac.uk
Website: www.johnruskin.ac.uk
Principal: Jennifer Sims
Vice-Principal, Curriculum and Quality:
Barbara Prior
Vice-Principal, Support Services:
Malcolm Staton

Kensington and Chelsea College
Sloane Building
Hortensia Road
Chelsea
London SW10 0QS
Tel: 020 7573 3600
Fax: 020 7351 0956
Website: www.kcc.ac.uk
Principal: Mike Jutsum
Vice-Principal, Curriculum and Quality:
Dr Amanda Hayes

Kingston College
Kingston Hall Road
Kingston upon Thames
Surrey KT1 2AQ
Tel: 020 8546 2151
Fax: 020 8268 2900
Email: info@kingston-college.ac.uk
Website: www.kingston-college.ac.uk
Principal: Dr N G Sinnamon
Dean of Faculty – Business and Professional
Studies: Jo Monk

Lambeth College
Clapham Centre
45 Clapham Common South Side
London SW4 9BL
Tel: 020 7501 5010
Fax: 020 7501 5084
Email: courses@lambethcollege.ac.uk
Website: www.lambethcollege.ac.uk
Principal: Richard Chambers

Lewisham College
Lewisham Way
London SE4 1UT
Tel: 020 8692 0353
Fax: 020 8694 9163
Website: www.lewisham.ac.uk
Principal: Ruth Silver DBE
Deputy Principal: Tim Potter
Vice-Principal, Quality and Curriculum
Development: Peter Mayhew-Smith

Leyton Sixth Form College
Essex Road
Leyton
London E10 6EQ
Tel: 020 8928 9000
Fax: 020 8928 9200
Website: www.leyton.ac.uk
Principal and Chief Executive: Sue Lakeman

The Marine Society and Sea Cadets
202 Lambeth Road
London SE1 7JW
Tel: 020 7654 7051
Fax: 020 7928 8914
Email: education@ms-sc.org
Website: www.mscos.ac.uk
Director, Education and Adult Learning:
Brian Thomas BA(Hons) PGCE

Mary Ward Centre
42–43 Queen Square
London WC1N 3AQ
Tel: 020 7269 6000
Fax: 020 7269 6002
Email: info@marywardcentre.ac.uk
Website: www.marywardcentre.ac.uk
Principal: Ceri Williams
Vice-Principal – Curriculum and Quality:
Suzanna Jackson
Vice-Principal – Finance and Resources:
Clive Hutton

Merton College
Morden Park
London Road
Morden
Surrey SM4 5QX
Tel: 020 8408 6500
Fax: 020 8408 6666
Email: info@merton.ac.uk
Principal: Sally McEnhill
Head of Human Resources: Mary Segovia

Morley College
61 Westminster Bridge Road
London SE1 7HT
Tel: 020 7928 8501
Fax: 020 7928 4074
Email: enquiries@morleycollege.ac.uk
Website: www.morleycollege.ac.uk
Principal: Ela Piotrowska

Newham College of Further Education
East Ham Campus
High Street South
London E6 6ER
Tel: 020 8257 4000
Fax: 020 8257 4325
Email: on-line.enquiries@newham.ac.uk
Website: www.newham.ac.uk
Principal and Chief Executive:
Martin Tolhurst
Deputy Principal: Denise Brown-Sackey

Newham Sixth Form College
Prince Regent Lane
London E13 8SG
Tel: 020 7473 4110
Fax: 020 7511 9463
Email: info@newvic.ac.uk
Website: www.newvic.ac.uk
Principal: Eddie Playfair
Centre Manager: Alan Kunna

North West Kent College
Oakfield Lane
Dartford DA1 2JT
Tel: 01322 629400
Fax: 01322 629468
Website: www.nwkcollege.ac.uk
Principal: Malcolm Bell
Director of Faculty: Ian Goodwin
Director of Faculty: Jane Freeman
Director of Faculty: Lesley Caldwell

Orpington College of Further Education
The Learning Shop
Ground Floor
42 The Walnuts
Orpington
Kent BR6 0TW
Tel: 01689 885359
Fax: 01689 877949
Email: learningshop@orpington.ac.uk
Website: www.orpington.ac.uk
Principal: Simon Norton
Community Education Manager: Janis Kent

Redbridge College
Little Heath, Barley Lane
Romford
Essex RM6 4XT
Tel: 020 8548 7400
Fax: 020 8599 8224
Email: info@redbridge-college.ac.uk
Website: www.redbridge-college.ac.uk
Principal and Chief Executive:
Theresa Drowley

Richmond Adult Community College
Parkshot Centre
Parkshot
Richmond
Surrey TW9 2RE
Tel: 020 8891 5907
Fax: 020 8332 6560
Website: www.racc.ac.uk
Principal and Chief Executive:
Christina Conroy OBE

Richmond upon Thames College
Egerton Road
Twickenham
Middlesex TW2 7SJ
Tel: 020 8607 8000
Fax: 020 8744 9738
Website: www.rutc.ac.uk
Principal and Chief Executive: Kevin Watson
Vice-Principal, Student and Staff Services:
Gillian Fogg
Vice-Principal, Curriculum and Quality:
Michael Rennie

Sir George Monoux College
190 Chingford Road
Walthamstow
London E17 5AA
Tel: 020 8523 3544
Fax: 020 8498 2443
Email: info@george-monoux.ac.uk
Website: www.george-monoux.ac.uk
Principal: Kim Clifford
Director of Curriculum Services: Elaine Hare

Southgate College
High Street
Southgate
London N14 6BS
Tel: 020 8886 6521/020 8982 5050
Fax: 020 8982 5051
Email: admiss@southgate.ac.uk
Website: www.southgate.ac.uk
Principal and Chief Executive:
Michael Blagden
Vice-Principal and Director of Curriculum:
Angelique Gainza

South Thames College
Wandsworth High Street
Wandsworth
London SW18 2PP
Tel: 020 8918 7000
Fax: 020 8918 7140
Website: www.south-thames.ac.uk
Principal: Sue Rimmer
Deputy Principal: Mike Burridge
Vice-Principal, Lesley DeCourcy
Course Enquiries: Tel: 020 89187777

Southwark College
Bermondsey Centre
Keetons Road
London SE16 4EE
Tel: 020 7815 1500
Fax: 020 7815 1525
Email: info@southwark.ac.uk
Website: www.southwark.ac.uk
Principal: Dorothy Jones

St Dominic's Sixth Form College
Mount Park Avenue
Harrow on the Hill
Middlesex HA1 3HX
Tel: 020 8422 8084
Fax: 020 8422 3759
Email: stdoms@stdoms.ac.uk
Website: www.stdoms.ac.uk
Principal: Patrick Harty

St Francis Xavier College
Broadoak Training Centre
Malwood Road
London SW12 8EN
Tel: 020 8772 6060
Fax: 020 8772 6098
Email: broadoak@sfx.ac.uk
Website: www.sfx.ac.uk
Principal: Bernie Borland
Head of Community Education:
Eleanor Lewis

Stanmore College
Elm Park
Stanmore
Middlesex HA7 4BQ
Tel: 020 8420 7700
Fax: 020 8420 6502
Email: enquiry@stanmore.ac.uk
Website: www.stanmore.ac.uk
Principal: Jacqui Mace
Vice-Principal (Curriculum): Archie Foulds

Sutton College of Learning for Adults
St Nicholas Way
Sutton
Surrey SM1 1EA
Tel: 020 8770 6901
Fax: 020 8770 6933
Email: reception@scola.ac.uk
Website: www.scola.ac.uk
Principal: Christine Jones
Director: Jenny Sims
Director: Sonja Compton
Director: Margaret White
Director: Cherry Yates

Tower Hamlets College
Poplar Centre
112 Poplar High Street
London E14 0AF
Tel: 020 7510 7510
Fax: 020 7538 9153
Email: advice@tower.ac.uk
Website: www.tower.ac.uk
Principal: Joanna Gaukroger

Uxbridge College
Park Road
Uxbridge
Middlesex UB8 1NQ
Tel: 01895 853333
Fax: 01895 853377
Email: enquiries@uxbridgecollege.ac.uk
Website: www.uxbridgecollege.ac.uk
Principal: Laraine Smith
Vice-Principal – Curriculum and Standards:
Darrell De Souza
Vice-Principal of Partnership and Planning:
Michael Farley

Waltham Forest College
707 Forest Road
Walthamstow
London E17 4JB
Tel: 020 8501 8000
Fax: 020 8501 8001
Website: www.waltham.ac.uk
Principal and Chief Executive:
Linnia Khemdoudi
Deputy Principal: Robin Jones
Vice-Principal, Curriculum.: Peter Glasgow

Westminster Kingsway College
Victoria Centre
76 Vincent Square
London SW1P 2PD
Tel: 020 7802 8984
Fax: 020 7802 8929
Website: www.westking.ac.uk
Principal: Andy Wilson
Head of Department: Rochelle Scholar

West Thames College
London Road
Isleworth
Middlesex TW7 4HS
Tel: 020 8326 2000
Fax: 020 8326 2001
Email: info@west-thames.ac.uk
Website: www.west-thames.ac.uk
Principal: Marjorie Semple
Learning Support /Basic Skills Co-ordinator:
Julie Search-Whittaker

Working Men's College
44 Crowndale Road
London NW1 1TR
Tel: 020 7255 4700
Fax: 020 7383 5561
Email: info@wmcollege.ac.uk
Website: www.wmcollege.ac.uk
Principal: Satnam Gill
Deputy Principal: Theresa Hoenig
Vice-Principal, Resources: Stewart Cross
Assistant Director: Sarah Kiernan
Assistant Director, Quality: Ilgun Yusuf
Assistant Director, Skills for Life:
Kanwal Pattar
Head of Student Services: Andrea Lewis

Isle of Man

Isle of Man College
Homefield Road
Douglas
Isle of Man IM2 6RB
Tel: 01624 648200
Fax: 01624 648201
Email: enquiries@iomcollege.ac.im
Website: www.iomcollege.ac.im
Principal: Dr Ian R Killip
Programme Manager – Adult Community
Education: Paul Wilkinson

Channel Islands

Guernsey College of Further Education
Route des Coutanchez
St Peter Port
Guernsey GY1 2TT
Tel: 01481 737500
Fax: 01481 746730
Email: college@cfe.edu.gg
Website: www.cfe.edu.gg
Principal: Trevor Wakefield
Head of Adult Education: Jane Walden

Highlands College
PO Box 1000
St Saviour
Jersey
Channel Islands JE4 9QA
Tel: 01534 608608
Fax: 01534 608600
Email: lynda.battersby@highlands.ac.uk
Website: www.highlands.ac.uk
Principal: Dr E Sallis
Adult Education Programme Manager:
Laura Goldstein

Higher Education – England

Higher Education Councils and Committees

British Accreditation Council for Independent Further and Higher Education (BAC)
44 Bedford Row
London WC1R 4LL
Tel: 020 7447 2584
Fax: 020 7447 2585
Email: info@the-bac.org
Website: www.the-bac.org
Chief Executive: Dr Stephen Vickers

Forum for Access and Continuing Education (FACE)
University of East London
Docklands Campus
4–6 University Way
London E16 2RD
Tel: 020 8223 4936
Fax: 020 8223 3394
Website: www.f-a-c-e.org.uk
Chair: John Storan
Partnership Support Officer: Jackie Leach

The Forum for Access and Continuing Education (FACE) is a charitable organisation established to support, promote and further develop continuing education opportunities. As an inclusive body, FACE members are to be found in higher education, further education, employer organisations, funding councils and many other related bodies. Members' benefits include a quarterly bulletin, conference and seminars, compendium of research/consultancy contacts, representation of members' interest on national policy development, access to FACE development funds and website.

Higher Education Funding Council for England (HEFCE)
Northavon House
Coldharbour Lane
Bristol BS16 1QD
Tel: 0117 931 7317
Fax: 0117 931 7203
Email: hefce@hefce.ac.uk
Website: www.hefce.ac.uk
Chairman: Tim Melville-Ross CBE
Chief Executive: Prof. David Eastwood
Director, Education and Participation: Dr John Selby

The Quality Assurance Agency for Higher Education
Southgate House
Southgate Street
Gloucester GL1 1UB
Tel: 01452 557000
Fax: 01452 557070
Email: comms@qaa.ac.uk
Website: www.qaa.ac.uk
Chairman: Sam Younger
Chief Executive: Peter Williams

The Quality Assurance Agency for Higher Education's (QAA's) mission is to safeguard the public interest in sound standards of higher education qualifications and to inform and encourage continuous improvement in the management of the quality of higher education. Established in 1997 to provide an integrated quality assurance service for UK higher education, QAA is an independent body funded by subscriptions from universities and colleges of higher education, and through contracts with the main funding bodies. QAA's core business is to review the quality and standards of higher education in universities and colleges of higher education. It does this by auditing institutional arrangements for managing quality and standards, including arrangements for collaboration with overseas partners, and by reviewing the quality and standards of higher education programmes offered in further education colleges. These activities result in reports that are available to the public on QAA's website. Other work carried out involves advising government on the applications for degree awarding powers and university title; and licensing the agencies that validate Access to Higher Education provision in England, Wales and Northern Ireland, and reviewing their assurance mechanisms.

Universities Association for Lifelong Learning

21 De Montfort Street
Leicester LE1 7GE
Tel: 0116 285 9702
Email: admin@uall.ac.uk
Website: www.uall.ac.uk
Chair: Prof. Peter Scott
Administrator: Lucy Bate
Secretary: Prof. Katherine Leni Oglesby

UALL (formerly UACE) is an association which represents the lifelong learning interests of the higher education sector. UALL plays a leading role in national and international policy formulation, advocacy, research and practice in lifelong learning and continuing education. It has well-established links with all major agencies in lifelong learning and higher education, including Funding Councils, UK Government Education and Lifelong Learning Departments, University and College Associations, Quality Assurance Bodies, as well as with other national and international organisations. Membership of UALL is open to all institutions providing higher education opportunities in the field of adult and continuing education. Membership is open to international as well as UK institutions and to individual members. The Association is affiliated to its USA sister body, UCEA. Activities include the annual conference, other conferences, events and workshops. The Assocation publishes papers and represents the sector to policy-making bodies.

Universities UK

Woburn House
20 Tavistock Square
London WC1H 9HQ
Tel: 020 7419 4111
Fax: 020 7388 8649
Email: info@universitiesuk.ac.uk
Website: www.universitiesuk.ac.uk
President: Prof. Rick Trainor
Chief Executive: Baroness Diana Warwick
Information Officer: Susan Bradley

Universities UK is the essential voice of UK universities, promoting their interests and supporting their work. It represents all UK universities and some higher education institutions. Its members are the executive heads of these institutions. Universities UK was formerly known as the Committee of Vice-Chancellors and Principals (CVCP).

National Higher Education Agencies

Association of University Administrators

University of Manchester
Oxford Road
Manchester M13 9PL
Tel: 0161 275 2063
Fax: 0161 275 2036
Email: aua@manchester.ac.uk
Website: www.aua.ac.uk
Executive Director: Alison Robinson

GuildHE

Woburn House
20 Tavistock Square
London WC1H 9HB
Tel: 020 7387 7711
Fax: 020 7387 7712
Email: info@guildhe.ac.uk
Website: www.guildhe.ac.uk
Chief Executive: Alice Hynes

GuildHE is a recognised representative organisation within the higher education sector. Its members comprise higher education colleges, specialist institutions and some universities.

The Higher Education Academy
Innovation Way
York Science Park
Heslington
York YO10 5BR
Tel: 01904 717500
Fax: 01904 717505
Email: enquiries@heacademy.ac.uk
Website: www.heacademy.ac.uk
Chief Executive: Paul Ramsden

Mature Students Union
6 Salisbury Road
Harrow
Middlesex HA1 1NY
Website: www.msu.org.uk
National Secretary: Barry Donovan

Office for Fair Access
Northavon House
Coldharbour Lane
Bristol BS16 1QD
Tel: 0117 931 7171
Fax: 0117 931 7479
Email: enquiries@offa.org.uk
Website: www.offa.org.uk
Director: Sir Martin Harris
Assistant Director: David Barrett
Operations and Research Manager:
Jean Arnold

The Office for Fair Access (OFFA) is an
independent, non-departmental public body
which aims to promote and safeguard fair
access to higher education for
under-represented groups in light of the
introduction of variable tuition fees in
2006–07.

Society for Research into Higher Education
76 Portland Place
London W1B 1NT
Tel: 020 7637 2766
Fax: 020 7637 2781
Email: srheoffice@srhe.ac.uk
Website: www.srhe.ac.uk
Chair: Prof. George Gordon

Staff and Educational Development Association
Woburn House
20–24 Tavistock Square
London WC1H 9HF
Tel: 020 7380 6767
Fax: 020 7387 2655
Email: office@seda.ac.uk
Website: www.seda.ac.uk
Co-Chair: Liz Shrives
Co-Chair: Lawrie Phipps

Standing Conference on University Teaching and Research in the Education of Adults (SCUTREA)
Centre for Continuing Education
Essex House
University of Sussex
Falmer
Brighton BN1 9RH
Tel: 01273 872 534
Fax: 01273 877 534
Website: www.scutrea.ac.uk
Secretary: Linda Morrice
Senior Lecturer: Dr Rob Mark
Treasurer: Anne-Marie Houghton

The object of SCUTREA is to enable those in
higher education who engage in the teaching
of, and research into the teaching of, adults
to express and share their academic
concerns. Membership is open to individuals
in the UK and overseas, whether or not they
are members of universities who are
accepted as making contributions to the
study of, or research into, the education of
adults. SCUTREA also welcomes into
membership institutions which are accepted
on the grounds that they are furthering the
study of, or research into, the education of
adults. Publications: *SCUTREA Papers*;
regular newsletter.

UCAS
Rosehill
New Barn Lane
Cheltenham
Gloucestershire GL52 3LZ
Tel: 01242 222444
Fax: 01242 544959
Email: info@ucas.ac.uk
Website: www.ucas.com
Chief Executive: Anthony McClaran

Regional Higher Education Agencies

East Midlands Universities Association (EMUA)
Unit 3, Technology Centre
Epinal Way
Loughborough
Leicestershire LE11 3GE
Tel: 01509 217797
Email: j.l.kenning@lboro.ac.uk
Website: www.emua.ac.uk
Director of Operations: Jenny Kenning

HERDA-SW
6 Barnfield Crescent
Exeter EX1 1RF
Email: info@herda-sw.ac.uk
Website: www.herda-sw.ac.uk
Executive Director: Rachel Cowie

Higher Education South East
London Square, Cross Lanes
Guildford
Surrey GU1 1UN
Tel: 01483 484257
Fax: 01483 484291
Email: enquiries@hese.ac.uk
Website: www.hese.ac.uk
Chief Executive: John Weston

London Higher
Senate House
Malet Street
London WC1E 7HU
Tel: 020 7664 4843
Fax: 020 7664 4850
Email: enquiry@londonhigher.ac.uk
Website: www.londonhigher.ac.uk
Chair: Prof. David Latchman
Director: Jane Glanville

London Higher is a membership organisation that promotes and acts as an advocate for London's higher education. It is an 'umbrella' body representing over 40 publicly funded universities and colleges.

North West Universities Association
4th Floor, Albert House
17 Bloom Street
Manchester M1 3HZ
Tel: 0161 234 8880
Fax: 0161 236 8467
Website: www.nwua.ac.uk
Executive Director: Keith Burnley

Universities for the North East
1 Hylton Park
Wessington Way
Sunderland SR5 3HD
Tel: 0191 516 4403
Fax: 0191 516 4401
Email: a.sanderson@unis4ne.ac.uk
Website: www.unis4ne.ac.uk
Director of Operations: Alan Sanderson

West Midlands Higher Education Association
c/o University of Wolverhampton
Executive Suite, Room SH101
Priorslee Hall
Telford
Shropshire TF2 9NP
Tel: 01902 321666
Fax: 01902 323945
Email: helen.brown@wlv.ac.uk
Website: www.wmhea.ac.uk
Director: Dr Helen Brown

Yorkshire Universities
University House
Cromer Terrace
Leeds
West Yorkshire LS2 9JT
Tel: 0113 343 1582
Fax: 0113 343 1583
Email: enquiries@yorkshireuniversities.ac.uk
Website: www.yorkshireuniversities.ac.uk
Chief Executive Officer: Michael Noble

Open University

The Open University
Walton Hall
Milton Keynes MK7 6AA
Tel: 01908 274066
Fax: 01908 653744
Website: www.open.ac.uk
Chancellor: The Lord Puttnam of
Queensgate CBE
Pro-Chancellor and Chairman of Council:
Baron Haskins of Skidby
Treasurer: Richard Delbridge
Vice-Chancellor: Prof. Brenda Gourley
University Secretary: Fraser Woodburn
Pro-Vice-Chancellors:
Prof. Brigid Heywood;
Prof. Denise Kirkpatrick; Prof. Alan Tait;
Prof. David Vincent
Director, Students: Will Swann
Director, Centre for Widening Participation:
Dr Christine Wise

The Open University was founded by Royal Charter in 1969 with the aim of providing educational opportunities for adults to study part-time in their own homes and in their own time. It operates throughout the whole of the UK and across parts of Europe by sending its educational material to people in their own homes or places of work. To give local assistance to students it has 13 regional centres. The University uses 'multimedia techniques' – that is, its courses and study packs may include not only textbooks and other printed matter but television programmes or video/DVDs, radio broadcasts or audio CDs/cassettes, home-computing, other audio-visual aids and equipment for practical work and experiments. Students have their own tutors and meet them and fellow students at the study centres or on some courses at one-week or weekend residential schools.

The wide range of subjects available stretches from everyday concerns like personal and career development to traditional university disciplines such as history, chemistry, IT or physics. The University also offers many training and updating courses for people in industry, commerce and the professions who want to improve their skills, gain better qualifications or prepare for a new career. Courses vary in length from those that involve a few hours of work for a few weeks to those that take nine months at the rate of fifteen or more hours each week. No educational qualifications are necessary, but students must have a UK or EC address where course materials can be sent. The only exception to this 'open entry' rule is postgraduate study for which a good honours degree is the normal starting point.

The Open University, like all other British universities with a Royal Charter, is empowered to award qualifications to students who successfully complete a programme of study. These are:

- certificates or course credits for successful completion of a number of designated courses;
- diplomas and advanced diplomas for successful completion of designated courses;
- degree (BA/BSc) for successful completion of a programme of study over a period of years; and an honours degree (BA/BSc with Honours) for study at advanced level;
- higher degrees (MA, MBA, MSc, EdD, MPhil, PhD) for postgraduate study, either taught or by research.

The cost of study varies from course to course. Over £35 million per annum allows the University to defray fees for over 33,000 students who are either unemployed or on a low income. In 2006–07 over 200,000 students and customers studied with the University. Some were preparing to join the 279,000 BA/BSc and BA/BSc (Hons) graduates, while others were studying single courses and study packs in the University's programme of continuing education.

For further details contact the Student Registration and Enquiry Service on 0845 300 6090. Alternatively, details of all University courses and advice about studying with The Open University are available on its extensive website at www.open.ac.uk/study

Open University Students' Association
PO Box 397
Walton Hall
Milton Keynes MK7 6BE
Tel: 01908 652026
Fax: 01908 654326
Email: ousa@student.open.ac.uk
Website: www.ousa.org.uk
General Manager: Trudi de Haney

Regional Offices

The Open University in the East of England
Cintra House
12 Hills Road
Cambridge CB2 1PF
Tel: 01223 364721
Fax: 01223 355207
Email: east-of-england@open.ac.uk
Website: www.open.ac.uk
Regional Director: Helen Wildman

The Open University in the East Midlands
Clarendon Park
Clumber Avenue
Sherwood Rise
Nottingham NG5 1AH
Tel: 0115 962 5451
Fax: 0115 971 5575
Email: eastmidlands@open.ac.uk
Website: www.open.ac.uk
Regional Director: Gordon Lammie

The Open University in London
1–11 Hawley Crescent
Camden Town
London NW1 8NP
Tel: 020 7485 6597
Fax: 020 7556 6196
Email: london@open.ac.uk
Website: www.open.ac.uk
Regional Director: Rosemary Mayes

The Open University in the North
Eldon House
Regent Centre
Gosforth
Newcastle upon Tyne NE3 3PW
Tel: 0191 284 1611
Fax: 0191 284 6592
Email: north@open.ac.uk
Website: www.open.ac.uk/north
Regional Director: Dr David Knight

The Open University in the North West
351 Altrincham Road
Sharston
Manchester M22 4UN
Tel: 0161 998 7272
Fax: 0161 945 3356
Email: north-west@open.ac.uk
Website: www.open.ac.uk
Regional Director: Lynda Brady
Courses and Enrolment Advisor:
Angela Naylor

The Open University in the South
Foxcombe Hall
Boars Hill
Oxford OX1 5HR
Tel: 01865 327000
Fax: 01865 736288
Email: south@open.ac.uk
Website: www.open.ac.uk
Regional Director: Celia Cohen

The Open University in the South East
St James's House
150 London Road
East Grinstead
West Sussex RH19 1HG
Tel: 01342 327821
Fax: 01342 317411
Email: south-east@open.ac.uk
Website: www.open.ac.uk
Regional Director: Liz Gray
Assistant Director: Hilary Caminer

The Open University in the South West
4 Portwall Lane
Bristol BS1 6ND
Tel: 0117 929 9641
Fax: 0117 925 5215
Email: south-west@open.ac.uk
Website: www.open.ac.uk
Regional Director: Linda Brightman

The Open University in the West Midlands
66 High Street
Harborne
Birmingham B17 9NB
Tel: 0121 426 1661
Fax: 0121 427 9484
Email: west-midlands@open.ac.uk
Website: www.open.ac.uk
Regional Director: Mike Rookes

The Open University in Yorkshire
2 Trevelyan Square
Boar Lane
Leeds
West Yorkshire LS1 6ED
Tel: 0113 244 4431
Fax: 0113 234 1862
Email: yorkshire@open.ac.uk
Website: www.open.ac.uk
Regional Director: Nicholas W Berry

Universities and University Colleges

Anglia Ruskin University
Bishop Hall Lane
Chelmsford
Essex CM1 1SQ
Tel: 0845 271 3333
Email: answers@anglia.ac.uk
Website: www.anglia.ac.uk
Vice-Chancellor: Prof. Michael Thorne

Aston University
Aston Triangle
Birmingham B4 7ET
Tel: 0121 359 3611
Fax: 0121 333 5774
Website: www.aston.ac.uk
Vice-Chancellor: Julia King
Director, Business Partnership Unit:
John Bailey
Email: j.r.bailey@aston.ac.uk

University of Bath
Claverton Down
Bath BA2 7AY
Tel: 01225 388388
Fax: 01225 386849
Website: www.bath.ac.uk/lifelong-learning
Vice-Chancellor: Prof. Glynis Breakwell
Director, Division for Lifelong Learning:
Dr Faith Butt
Lifelong Learning Administrator:
Alice Reeves
Tel: 01225 388703

Bath Spa University
Newton Park
Newton St Loe
Bath BA2 9BN
Tel: 01225 875875
Fax: 01225 875444
Website: www.bathspa.ac.uk
Vice-Chancellor: Prof. Frank Morgan
Marketing: Tessa Alton

University of Bedfordshire
Park Square
Luton
Bedfordshire LU1 3JU
Tel: 01234 400400
Fax: 01582 743400
Email: admission@beds.ac.uk
Website: www.beds.ac.uk
Vice-Chancellor: Prof. Les Ebdon
Email: vc@beds.ac.uk
Director of Student Recruitment and
Admissions: Dr Moira Hampson

Birkbeck College, University of London
Faculty of Lifelong Learning
26 Russell Square
London WC1B 5DQ
Tel: 020 7631 6000
Fax: 020 7631 6688
Email: info@bbk.ac.uk
Website: www.bbk.ac.uk
Vice-Master: Philip Dewe
Prof. Citizenship and Lifelong Learning:
John Annette

University College Birmingham
Summer Row
Birmingham B3 1JB
Tel: 0121 604 1000
Fax: 0121 604 1101
Website: www.ucb.ac.uk
Principal: Ray Linforth
Equal Opportunities Co-ordinator:
Godfrey Henry

University of Birmingham
Edgbaston
Birmingham B15 2TT
Tel: 0121 414 3344
Fax: 0121 414 3971
Email: education@bham.ac.uk
Website: www.bham.ac.uk
Vice-Chancellor and Principal:
Prof. Michael Sterling

Birmingham City University
Franchise Street
Perry Barr
Birmingham B42 2SU
Tel: 0121 331 5595
Fax: 0121 331 7994
Email: choices@bcu.ac.uk
Website: www.bcu.ac.uk
Assistant Director, Marketing:
Kim Langford
Short Course Co-ordinator: Dawn
Meaden-Johnson
Tel: 0121 248 4584 (Monday to Thursday
9am–3pm)

Bishop Grosseteste University College Lincoln
Newport
Lincoln LN1 3DY
Tel: 01522 527347
Fax: 01522 530243
Email: info@bishopg.ac.uk
Website: www.bishopg.ac.uk
Principal: Prof. Muriel Robinson

The University of Bolton
Deane Road
Bolton
Lancashire BL3 5AB
Tel: 01204 900600
Fax: 01204 399074
Email: enquiries@bolton.ac.uk
Website: www.bolton.ac.uk
Vice-Chancellor: Dr George E Holmes
Head of Marketing and Recruitment:
Phil Lloyd

Bournemouth University
Talbot Campus
Fern Barrow
Poole
Dorset BH12 5BB
Tel: 01202 524111
Fax: 01202 965069
Website: www.bournemouth.ac.uk
Vice-Chancellor: Prof. Paul Curran
Director of Partnerships and Widening
Access: Jacky Mack

University of Bradford
Richmond Road
Bradford
West Yorkshire BD7 1DP
Tel: 01274 233210
Fax: 01274 235915
Email: learning@bradford.ac.uk
Website: www.bradford.ac.uk
Vice-Chancellor and Principal:
Prof. Mark Cleary
Dean, School of Lifelong Learning and
Development: Nadira Mirza

University of Brighton
Mithras House
Lewes Road
Brighton BN2 4AT
Tel: 01273 600900
Fax: 01273 642010
Email: admissions@brighton.ac.uk
Website: www.brighton.ac.uk
Vice-Chancellor: Prof. Julian Crampton
Widening Participation Manager:
Sarah Cullen

University of Bristol
Senate House
Tyndall Avenue
Clifton
Bristol BS8 1TH
Tel: 0117 928 9000
Fax: 0117 929 2396
Website: www.bris.ac.uk/esu
Vice-Chancellor: Prof. Eric Thomas

Brunel University
Uxbridge
Middlesex UB8 3PH
Tel: 01895 265189
Fax: 01895 273545
Website: www.brunel.ac.uk
Vice-Chancellor: Prof. Chris Jenks

Buckinghamshire New University
Queen Alexandra Road
High Wycombe
Buckinghamshire HP11 2JZ
Tel: 01494 522141
Fax: 01494 524392
Website: www.bucks.ac.uk
Vice-Chancellor and Chief Executive:
Dr Ruth Farwell

University of Cambridge
The Old Schools
Trinity Lane
Cambridge CB2 1TN
Tel: 01223 337733
Fax: 01223 332277
Website: www.cam.ac.uk
Vice-Chancellor: Prof. Alison Richard
Director of Continuing Education and
Lifelong Learning: Prof. Richard Taylor

Institute of Continuting Education
University of Cambridge
Madingley Hall
Cambridge CB3 8AQ
Tel: 01954 280280
Email: susan.rawlings@cont-ed.cam.ac.uk
Website: www.cont-ed.cam.ac.uk

Canterbury Christ Church University
North Holmes Road
Canterbury
Kent CT1 1QU
Tel: 01227 767700
Fax: 01227 470442
Website: www.canterbury.ac.uk
Vice-Chancellor: Prof. Michael Wright

University of Central Lancashire
Preston
Lancashire PR1 2HE
Tel: 01772 201201
Fax: 01772 892911
Website: www.uclan.ac.uk
Vice-Chancellor: Dr Malcolm McVicar
Lifelong Learning contact: Harold Potts
Email: hpotts@uclan.ac.uk

**The Central School of Speech
and Drama**
Embassy Theatre
Eton Avenue
London NW3 3HY
Tel: 020 7722 8183
Fax: 020 7722 4132
Website: www.cssd.ac.uk
Principal: Prof. Gavin Henderson CBE

University of Chester
Chester Campus
1 Parkgate Road
Chester CH1 4BJ
Tel: 01244 511000
Fax: 01244 511300
Email: enquiries@chester.ac.uk
Website: www.chester.ac.uk
Vice-Chancellor: Prof. Timothy Wheeler
Business & Communities Manager:
Connie Hancock

University of Chichester
College Lane
Chichester
West Sussex PO19 6PE
Tel: 01243 816000
Fax: 01243 816080
Website: www.chi.ac.uk
Pro-Vice-Chancellor: Prof. Sandra Jowett
Widening Participation Manager:
Janet Johnston

City University, London
Northampton Square
London EC1V 0HB
Tel: 020 7040 5060
Fax: 020 7040 8256
Website: www.city.ac.uk
Vice-Chancellor: Prof. Malcolm Gillies
Head of Department: Laurence Solkin

Coventry University
Priory Street
Coventry
West Midlands CV1 5FB
Tel: 024 7688 7688
Fax: 024 7688 8793
Website: www.coventry.ac.uk
Vice-Chancellor: Prof. Madeleine Atkins

Cranfield University
Cranfield
Bedfordshire MK43 0AL
Tel: 01234 750111
Fax: 01234 750875
Website: www.cranfield.ac.uk
Vice-Chancellor: Prof. Sir John O'Reilly

University for the Creative Arts
Falkner Road
Farnham
Surrey GU9 7DS
Tel: 01252 722441
Fax: 01252 892616
Email: info@ucreative.ac.uk
Website: www.ucreative.ac.uk
Vice-Chancellor: Prof Elaine Thomas
Deputy Vice-Chancellor: Prof Mark Hunt

University of Cumbria
Fusehill Street
Carlisle CA1 2HH
Tel: 01228 616234
Fax: 01228 616235
Website: www.cumbria.ac.uk
Vice-Chancellor and Chief Executive:
Prof. C J Carr
Admissions: Alison Bolton

De Montfort University
The Gateway
Leicester LE1 9BH
Tel: 0116 255 1551
Fax: 0116 255 0307
Website: www.dmu.ac.uk
Chief Executive and Vice-Chancellor:
Prof. Philip Tasker

University of Derby
Kedleston Road
Derby DE22 1GB
Tel: 01332 590 500
Website: www.derby.ac.uk
Vice-Chancellor: Prof. John Coyne
Director: Prof. David Gray

University of Durham
University Office
Old Elvet
Durham DH1 3HP
Tel: 0191 334 2000
Fax: 0191 374 3740
Website: www.dur.ac.uk
Vice-Chancellor and Warden:
Prof. Chris Higgins
Course Director in Foundation Programme:
Catherine Hyde-Wesson

University of East Anglia
University Plain
Norwich NR4 7TJ
Tel: 01603 456161
Fax: 01603 458553
Website: www.uea.ac.uk
Vice-Chancellor: Prof. Bill MacMillan
Director of Lifelong Learning: Erica Towner
Email: e.towner@uea.ac.uk

University of East London
UEL Docklands Campus
4–6 University Way
London E16 2RD
Tel: 020 8223 4001
Fax: 020 8223 4100
Website: www.uel.ac.uk
Acting Vice-Chancellor: Prof. Susan Price
Director, External and Strategic
Development Services: Selina Bolingbroke
Director and Regional Adviser for the South
West: Prof. John Storan

Edge Hill University
St Helens Road
Ormskirk
Lancashire L39 4QP
Tel: 01695 575171
Fax: 01695 579997
Email: enquiries@edgehill.ac.uk
Website: www.edgehill.ac.uk
Vice-Chancellor: Dr John Cater

University of Essex
Wivenhoe Park
Colchester
Essex CO4 3SQ
Tel: 01206 873 333
Fax: 01206 873 598
Email: eds@essex.ac.uk
Website: www.essex.ac.uk
Vice-Chancellor: Prof. Colin Riordan
Director of Educational Development
Services: Stella Heath
Email: heaths@essex.ac.uk

University of Exeter
Northcote House
The Queen's Drive
Exeter
Devon EX4 4QJ
Tel: 01392 661000
Fax: 01392 263108
Website: www.ex.ac.uk
Vice-Chancellor: Prof. Steve Smith
Director of Masters Programme Department
of Lifelong Learning: Dr John Blewitt

University College Falmouth
(Incorporating Dartington College of Arts)
Woodlane
Falmouth
Cornwall TR11 4RH
Tel: 01326 211077
Fax: 01326 318971
Email: admissions@falmouth.ac.uk
Website: www.falmouth.ac.uk
Rector: Prof. Alan Livingston

University of Gloucestershire
The Park
Cheltenham
Gloucestershire GL50 2RH
Tel: 01242 714169
Fax: 01242 714489
Website: www.glos.ac.uk
Vice-Chancellor: Prof. Patricia
Broadfoot CBE

Goldsmiths College
University of London
New Cross
London SE14 6NW
Tel: 020 7919 7766
Fax: 020 7717 2240
Email: admissions@gold.ac.uk
Website: www.goldsmiths.ac.uk
Warden: Prof. Geoffrey Crossick
Widening Participation Co-ordinator:
Annette Hayton

University of Greenwich
Greenwich Campus
Old Royal Naval College
Park Row
Greenwich
London SE10 9LS
Tel: 020 8331 8000
Fax: 020 8331 8145
Email: info@gre.ac.uk
Website: www.gre.ac.uk
Vice-Chancellor: Baroness Tessa Blackstone

University of Hertfordshire
Room C210A
College Lane
Hatfield
Hertfordshire AL10 9AB
Tel: 01707 284000
Fax: 01707 284115
Website: www.herts.ac.uk
Vice-Chancellor: Prof. Tim Wilson
Head of School of Continuing Education
and Partnerships: Steve Culliford

University of Huddersfield
Queensgate
Huddersfield
West Yorkshire HD1 3DH
Tel: 01484 422288
Fax: 01484 516151
Website: www.hud.ac.uk
Vice-Chancellor: Prof. Bob Cryan
Email: b.cryan@hud.ac.uk
Deputy Vice-Chancellor: Prof. Mike Page
Email: m.i.page@hud.ac.uk

University of Hull
Cottingham Road
Hull HU6 7RX
Tel: 01482 346311
Fax: 01482 465977
Email: cll@hull.ac.uk
Website: www.hull.ac.uk
Vice-Chancellor: Prof. David Drewry
Head of Centre for Lifelong Learning:
Dina Lewis
Email: d.lewis@hull.ac.uk

Imperial College London
Centre for Professional Development
Sherfield Building
South Kensington Campus
Exhibition Road
London SW7 2AZ
Tel: 0207 594 6885
Fax: 0207 594 6883
Email: cpd@imperial.ac.uk
Website: www.imperial.ac.uk/cpd
Director of Centre for Professional
Development: Dr Mervyn E Jones

Institute of Education
University of London
20 Bedford Way
London WC1H 0AL
Tel: 020 7612 6000
Fax: 020 7312 6126
Website: www.ioe.ac.uk
Director: Prof. Geoff Whitty

Keele University
Keele
Staffordshire ST5 5BG
Tel: 01782 621111
Fax: 01782 584181
Website: www.keele.ac.uk
Vice-Chancellor: Professor Janet Finch
Head of Continuing and Professional
Education: Dr Marian Whittaker
Email: m.whittaker@acad.keele.ac.uk

University of Kent
The Registry
Canterbury
Kent CT2 7NZ
Tel: 01227 764000
Fax: 01227 452196
Email: postmaster@kent.ac.uk
Website: www.kent.ac.uk
Vice-Chancellor: Prof. Julia Goodfellow
Head of Partnership Development Office:
Jennifer Wyatt

Kingston University
River House
53–57 High Street
Kingston upon Thames
Surrey KT1 1LQ
Tel: 020 8547 2000
Fax: 020 8547 7093
Website: www.kingston.ac.uk
Vice-Chancellor: Peter Scott
Academic Head, Academic Development:
Michael Hill

Lancaster University
University House
Bailrigg
Lancaster LA1 4YW
Tel: 01524 65201
Fax: 01524 592448
Email: conted@lancaster.ac.uk
Website: www.lancs.ac.uk/depts/conted
Vice-Chancellor: Prof. Paul Wellings
Director, Continuing Education Department:
Prof. Keith Percy
Email: conted@lancaster.ac.uk

University of Leeds
Cromer Terrace
University House
Woodhouse Lane
Leeds LS2 9JT
Tel: 0113 343 3000
Fax: 0113 343 4122
Email: j.pharoah@adm.leeds.ac.uk
Vice-Chancellor: Prof. Michael Arthur
Director: Dr Stella Cottrell

Lifelong Learning Centre
The University of Leeds
Leeds LS2 9JT

Leeds Metropolitan University
F402, Civic Quarter Campus
Calverley Street
Leeds LS1 3HE
Tel: 0113 283 2600
Email: vc@leedsmet.ac.uk
Website: www.leedsmet.ac.uk
Vice-Chancellor: Prof. Simon Lee

University of Leicester
Fielding Johnson Building
University Road
Leicester LE1 7RH
Tel: 0116 252 2522
Fax: 0116 252 2200
Website: www.leicester.ac.uk
Vice-Chancellor: Prof. Bob Burgess

University of Lincoln
Brayford Pool
Lincoln LN6 7TS
Tel: 01522 882000
Email: enquiries@lincoln.ac.uk
Website: www.lincoln.ac.uk
Vice-Chancellor: Prof. David Chiddick

University of Liverpool
Centre for Lifelong Learning
126 Mount Pleasant
Liverpool L69 3GR
Tel: 0151 794 6900
Fax: 0151 794 2544
Email: conted@liverpool.ac.uk
Website: www.liverpool.ac.uk/conted/
Vice-Chancellor: Prof. Drummond Bone
Director of Lifelong Learning:
Dr Anne Merry

Liverpool Hope University
Hope Park
Liverpool L16 9JD
Tel: 0151 291 3000
Fax: 0151 291 3100
Website: www.hope.ac.uk
Vice-Chancellor and Rector: Gerald J Pillay
Dean of Arts and Humanities:
Dr Terry Phillips
Director of Marketing, Recruitment and
External Relations: John McCarthy
Admissions: Catherine Harvey

Liverpool John Moores University
Egerton Court
2 Rodney Street
Liverpool L3 5UX
Tel: 0151 231 2121
Fax: 0151 708 8607
Website: www.ljmu.ac.uk
Vice-Chancellor and Chief Executive:
Prof. Michael Brown CBE DL

University of the Arts, London
65 Davies Street
London W1K 5DA
Tel: 020 7514 6000
Fax: 020 7514 6175
Website: www.arts.ac.uk
Rector: Nigel Carrington

University of London
Senate House
Malet Street
London WC1E 7HU
Tel: 020 7862 8000
Fax: 020 7862 8358
Email: enquiries@lon.ac.uk
Website: www.lon.ac.uk
Vice-Chancellor: Sir Graeme Davies

London Metropolitan University
166–220 Holloway Road
London N7 6PP
Tel: 020 7423 0000
Website: www.londonmet.ac.uk
Vice-Chancellor and Chief Executive:
Brian Roper
Head of Access Development:
Harinder Lawley

London South Bank University
103 Borough Road
London SE1 0AA
Tel: 020 7815 6004
Fax: 020 7815 6099
Website: www.lsbu.ac.uk
Vice-Chancellor: Deian Hopkin
Director of Student Recruitment:
Gary Davies
Course Enquiries Tel: 020 7815 7815

Loughborough University
Ashby Road
Loughborough
Leicestershire LE11 3TU
Tel: 01509 263171
Fax: 01509 223927
Website: www.lboro.ac.uk
Vice-Chancellor: Prof. Shirley Pearce CBE
Tel: 01509 222001
Fax: 01509 223900

University of Manchester
Oxford Road
Manchester M13 9PL
Tel: 0161 306 6010
Fax: 0161 306 6011
Website: www.manchester.ac.uk
President and Vice-Chancellor:
Prof. Alan Gilbert
Head of Teaching and Learning Support
Office: Louise Walmsley

Manchester Metropolitan University
All Saints Building
Oxford Road
Manchester M15 6BH
Tel: 0161 247 2000
Fax: 0161 247 6551
Website: www.mmu.ac.uk/
Vice-Chancellor: Prof. John Brooks
Head of Learning and Teaching:
Robert Ready
Collaborative Partnerships Co-ordinator:
Dr Liz Marr

Middlesex University
North London Business Park
Oakleigh Road South
London N11 1QS
Tel: 020 8411 5555
Fax: 020 8411 5649
Email: admissions@mdx.ac.uk
Website: www.mdx.ac.uk
Vice-Chancellor: Prof. Michael Driscoll

University of Newcastle upon Tyne
6 Kensington Terrace
Newcastle upon Tyne NE1 7RU
Tel: 0191 222 6000
Website: www.ncl.ac.uk

Newman University College
Genners Lane
Bartley Green
Birmingham B32 3NT
Tel: 0121 476 1181
Fax: 0121 476 1196
Website: www.newman.ac.uk
Principal: Pamela Taylor
Head of School of Community and
Professional Development: Prof. Stan Tucker
Head of School of Education: Sally Yates
Head of School of Social Sciences and
Humanities: Dr Stephen Bulman

University of Northampton
Park Campus
Boughton Green Road
Northampton NN2 7AL
Tel: 01604 735500
Fax: 01604 720636
Email: study@northampton.ac.uk
Website: www.northampton.ac.uk
Vice-Chancellor: Ann Tate
Pro-Vice-Chancellor (Academic):
Prof. Peter Bush
Director of Educational Partnerships and
Lifelong Learning: Dr Maxine Rhodes
Director of Office of Learning and Teaching:
Dr Caroline Stainton
Head of Centre for Continuing Professional
Development in Professional Education:
Ken Bland

Northumbria University
Lifelong Learning, Academic Registry
Ellison Terrace
Newcastle upon Tyne NE1 8ST
Tel: 0191 232 6002
Website: www.unn.ac.uk
Vice-Chancellor: Prof. Andrew Wathey
Head of Lifelong Learning: Nick Hall

Norwich University College of the Arts
Francis House
3–7 Redwell Street
Norwich NR2 4SN
Tel: 01603 610561
Fax: 01603 615728
Email: info@nuca.ac.uk
Website: www.nuca.ac.uk
Principal: Susan Tuckett

University of Nottingham
Centre for Continuing Education
The Dearing Building
Jubilee Campus
Wollaton Road
Nottingham NG8 1BB
Tel: 0115 846 6466
Fax: 0115 846 6600
Website: www.nottingham.ac.uk/education
Vice-Chancellor: Prof. Sir Colin Campbell
Head of School of Education:
Prof. Carol Hall
Director, Centre for Continuing Education:
Dr Sarah Speight

Nottingham Trent University
Newton Building
Burton Street
Nottingham NG1 4BU
Tel: 0115 941 8418
Fax: 0115 848 6747
Website: www.ntu.ac.uk
Vice-Chancellor: Prof. Neil Gorman
Dean, School of Education: Gill Scott

University of Oxford
Department for Continuing Education
Rewley House
1 Wellington Square
Oxford OX1 2JA
Tel: 01865 270360
Fax: 01865 270309
Email: enquiries@conted.ox.ac.uk
Website: www.conted.ox.ac.uk
Director: Prof. Jonathan Michie
Deputy Director (Director of Public
Programmes): Philip Healy

Oxford Brookes University
Gipsy Lane Campus
Headington
Oxford OX3 0BP
Tel: 01865 741111
Fax: 01865 483073
Website: www.brookes.ac.uk
Vice-Chancellor: Prof. Janet Beer
Head of Student Learning Experience:
Clive Robertson

**University College Plymouth St Mark
and St John**
Derriford Road
Plymouth
Devon PL6 8BH
Tel: 01752 636890
Fax: 01752 636820
Email: admissions@marjon.ac.uk
Website: www.ucmarjon.ac.uk
Principal: Dr David Baker

University of Plymouth
Drake Circus
Plymouth
Devon PL4 8AA
Tel: 01752 600600
Website: www.plymouth.ac.uk
Vice-Chancellor: Prof. Wendy Purcell
Director of Research and Innovation:
Julian Beer

University of Portsmouth
University House
Winston Churchill Avenue
Portsmouth PO1 2UP
Tel: 023 9284 8484
Fax: 023 9284 5365
Email: info.centre@port.ac.uk
Website: www.port.ac.uk
Vice-Chancellor: Prof. John Craven
Head of School of Education and
Continuing Studies: Mike Coeshott
Access Co-ordinator: Kevin White

Queen Mary, University of London
Mile End Road
London E1 4NS
Tel: 020 7882 5555
Website: www.qmul.ac.uk
Principal: Prof. Adrian Smith
Director of Corporate Affairs: Nigel Relph

University of Reading
Whiteknights
PO Box 217
Reading
Berkshire RG6 6AH
Tel: 0118 987 5123
Fax: 0118 931 4404
Website: www.reading.ac.uk
Vice-Chancellor: Prof. Gordon Marshall
Head of School of Continuing Education:
Dr Brian O'Callaghan

Roehampton University
Roehampton Lane
London SW15 5PH
Tel: 020 8392 3000
Fax: 020 8392 3029
Email: enquiries@roehampton.ac.uk
Website: www.roehampton.ac.uk
Vice-Chancellor: Prof. Paul O'Prey
Email: paul.oprey@roehampton.ac.uk

St Mary's University College
Waldegrave Road
Strawberry Hill
Twickenham
Middlesex TW1 4SX
Tel: 020 8240 4000
Fax: 020 8240 4255
Website: www.smuc.ac.uk
Principal: Dr Arthur Naylor
Marketing Manager, Recruitment UK and
Widening Participation: Kevin Germaine

University of Salford
The Crescent
Salford M5 4WT
Tel: 0161 295 5000
Fax: 0161 295 5999
Website: www.salford.ac.uk
Vice-Chancellor: Prof. Michael Harloe
Enterprise Development Manager:
Claire MacLean

Sheffield Hallam University
City Campus
Howard Street
Sheffield
South Yorkshire S1 1WB
Tel: 0114 225 5555
Minicom: 0114 225 3582
Website: www.shu.ac.uk
Vice-Chancellor: Prof. Philip Jones
Director, Student and Academic Services:
Clive Macdonald
Email: c.macdonald@shu.ac.uk

University of Sheffield
Western Bank
Sheffield
South Yorkshire S10 2TN
Tel: 0114 222 2000
Website: www.shef.ac.uk
Vice-Chancellor: Prof. Keith Burnett
Director of the Institute for Lifelong
Learning: Prof. Sue Webb
Tel: 0114 222 7000
Fax: 0114 222 7001
Email: s.webb@sheffield.ac.uk

University of Southampton
Highfield
Southampton
Hampshire SO17 1BJ
Tel: 023 8059 5000
Fax: 023 8059 3939
Website: www.soton.ac.uk
Vice-Chancellor: Prof. William Wakeham

Southampton Solent University
East Park Terrace
Southampton SO14 0YN
Tel: 023 8031 9000
Fax: 023 8033 2259
Email: enquiries@solent.ac.uk
Website: www.solent.ac.uk
Vice-Chancellor: Prof. Van Gore
Senior Study Assistance Tutor: John Craig

Staffordshire University
Blackheath Lane
Stafford ST18 0AD
Tel: 01782 294000
Fax: 01782 295723
Website: www.staffs.ac.uk/
Vice-Chancellor and Chief Executive:
Prof. Christine King
Email: c.e.king@staffs.ac.uk
Director of Education Partnerships:
David Jenkins
Higher Education Shop Manager:
Lynne Tolley
Widening Participation and Lifelong
Learning Co-ordinator: Peter Jones
Tel: 01782 294941

University of Sunderland
School of Education and Society
Foster Building
Chester Road
Sunderland
Tyne and Wear SR1 3SD
Tel: 0191 515 3192
Fax: 0191 515 2628
Website: www.sunderland.ac.uk
Vice-Chancellor: Prof. Peter Fidler
Dean of Faculty of Education and Society:
Prof. Gary Holmes
Head of Department of Culture:
Dr Felicity Breet
Head of Continuing Education: Tim Crocker

Centre for Lifelong Learning
Bedson Building
Kings Road
Newcastle NE1 7RU
Tel: 0191 515 2841
Email: tim.crocker@sunderland.ac.uk

University of Surrey
Senate House
Guildford
Surrey GU2 7XH
Tel: 01483 300800
Fax: 01483 300803
Website: www.surrey.ac.uk
Vice-Chancellor: Prof. Chris Snowden
Head of Department of Culture, Media, and
Communication: Dr Margaret Rogers

University of Sussex
Centre for Continuing Education
School of Community Engagement
Essex House
Falmer
Brighton BN1 9QQ
Tel: 01273 606755
Fax: 01273 877534
Email: cce@sussex.ac.uk
Website: www.sussex.ac.uk/cce
Vice-Chancellor: Prof. Michael Farthing
Director – Centre for Continuing Education:
Pam Coare

University of Teesside
Borough Road
Middlesbrough TS1 3BA
Tel: 01642 218121
Fax: 01642 342067
Email: lifelong@tees.ac.uk
Website: www.tees.ac.uk
Vice-Chancellor: Prof. G Henderson
Director of Educational Partnerships:
Lynn Parker

Thames Valley University
St Mary's Road
Ealing
London W5 5RF
Tel: 020 8579 5000
Fax: 020 8566 1353
Website: www.tvu.ac.uk
Vice-Chancellor: Prof. Peter John
Pro-Vice-Chancellor: Lee Nicholls

University of Warwick
Coventry
Warwickshire CV4 7AL
Tel: 024 7652 4617
Fax: 024 7652 4223
Email: cll@warwick.ac.uk
Website: www.warwick.ac.uk/cll
Vice-Chancellor: Prof. Nigel Thrift
Director – Centre for Lifelong Learning:
Dr Russell Moseley

University of the West of England
Outreach Centre
Frenchay Campus
Coldharbour Lane
Bristol BS16 1QY
Tel: 0117 328 2262
Fax: 0117 328 2412
Email: enquiries@uwe.ac.uk
Website: www.uwe.ac.uk
Vice-Chancellor: Prof. Stephen West
Director of Outreach Centre:
Chris Croudace
Co-ordinator Widening Participation and
Community Action: Diane Stone

University of Westminster
309 Regent Street
London W1B 2UW
Tel: 020 7911 5115
Fax: 020 7911 5103
Website: www.wmin.ac.uk
Vice-Chancellor and Rector:
Prof. Geoffrey Petts
Head of Educational Initiative Centre:
Dr Ann Rumpus

The University of Winchester
Winchester
Hampshire SO22 4NR
Tel: 01962 841515
Fax: 01962 842280
Email: course.enquiries@winchester.ac.uk
Website: www.winchester.ac.uk
Vice-Chancellor: Prof. Joy Carter

University of Wolverhampton
Wulfruna Street
Wolverhampton WV1 1SB
Tel: 01902 321000
Fax: 01902 322680
Email: enquiries@wlv.ac.uk
Website: www.wlv.ac.uk
Vice-Chancellor: Prof. Caroline Gipps
Education Partnerships: Ian Hart
Tel: 01902 518945
Fax: 01902 824418

University of Worcester
Henwick Grove
Worcester WR2 6AJ
Tel: 01905 855000
Fax: 01905 855132
Website: www.worc.ac.uk
Vice-Chancellor: Prof. David Green

University of York
Centre for Lifelong Learning
Heslington
York YO10 5DD
Tel: 01904 434620
Fax: 01904 434621
Email: lifelonglearning@york.ac.uk
Website: www.york.ac.uk/inst/cce
Vice-Chancellor: Prof. Brian Cantor
Head of Lifelong Learning: Lesley Booth

York St John University
Lord Mayor's Walk
York
North Yorkshire YO31 7EX
Tel: 01904 624624
Fax: 01904 612512
Website: www.yorksj.ac.uk
Vice-Chancellor: Prof. Dianne Willcocks
Pro-Vice-Chancellor: Prof. Stuart Billingham

Colleges and Institutes of Higher Education

Arts Institute at Bournemouth
Wallisdown
Poole
Dorset BH12 5HH
Tel: 01202 533011
Fax: 01202 537729
Email: general@aib.ac.uk
Website: www.aib.ac.uk
Principal and Chief Executive:
Prof. Stuart Bartholomew

Harper Adams University College
Edgmond
Newport
Shropshire TF10 8NB
Tel: 01952 820280
Fax: 01952 814783
Email: admissions@harper-adams.ac.uk
Website: www.harper-adams.ac.uk
Principal: Prof. E Wynne Jones

Leeds Trinity and All Saints
Brownberrie Lane
Horsforth
Leeds
West Yorkshire LS18 5HD
Tel: 0113 283 7100
Fax: 0113 283 7200
Email: admissions@leedstrinity.ac.uk
Website: www.leedstrinity.ac.uk
Principal: Dr Freda Bridge

Northern School of Contemporary Dance
98 Chapeltown Road
Leeds
West Yorkshire LS7 4BH
Tel: 0113 219 3000
Fax: 0113 219 3030
Email: info@nscd.ac.uk
Website: www.nscd.ac.uk

Ravensbourne College of Design and Communication
Walden Road
Chislehurst
Kent BR7 5SN
Tel: 020 8289 4900
Fax: 020 8325 8320
Email: info@rave.ac.uk
Website: www.ravensbourne.co.uk

Rose Bruford College
Theatre and Related Arts
Lamorbey Park
Burnt Oak Lane
Sidcup
Kent
DA15 9DF
Tel: 020 8308 2600
Fax: 020 8308 0542
Email: enquiries@bruford.ac.uk
Website: www.bruford.ac.uk
Acting Principal: David Cunningham

Royal Academy of Music
Marylebone Road
London NW1 5HT
Tel: 020 7873 7373
Fax: 020 7873 7374
Email: registry@ram.ac.uk
Website: www.ram.ac.uk
Principal: Prof. Jonathan Freeman-Attwood

Royal College of Art
Kensington Gore
London SW7 2EU
Tel: 020 7590 4444
Fax: 020 7590 4500
Website: www.rca.ac.uk
Rector: Prof. Sir Christopher Frayling

Royal College of Music
Prince Consort Road
London SW7 2BS
Tel: 020 7589 3643
Fax: 020 7589 7740
Email: info@rcm.ac.uk
Website: www.rcm.ac.uk
Director: Dr Colin Lawson

Royal Northern College of Music
124 Oxford Road
Manchester M13 9RD
Tel: 0161 907 5200
Fax: 0161 273 7611
Email: info@rncm.ac.uk
Website: www.rncm.ac.uk
Principal: Prof. Jonty Stockdale

Trinity Laban Conservatoire of Music and Dance
King Charles Court
Old Royal Naval College
Greenwich
London SE10 9JF
Tel: 020 8305 4444
Fax: 020 8305 9444
Website: www.tcm.ac.uk
Joint Principal: Derek Aviss
Joint Principal: Anthony Bowne
Deputy Principal: John Heighway
Deputy Principal and Dean of Studies:
Mirella Bartrip
Creative Futures Director:
Dr Claire Mera Nelson

Writtle College
Lordship Road
Chelmsford
Essex CM1 3RR
Tel: 01245 424200
Fax: 01245 420456
Email: info@writtle.ac.uk
Website: www.writtle.ac.uk
Principal: Prof. David Butcher
Head of Higher Education:
Dr Jeremy Strong
Head of Registry: Brenda Jordt

Residential Adult Education – England

National Organisations

Adult Residential Colleges Association (ARCA)
6 Bath Road
Felixstowe
Suffolk IP11 7JW
Tel: 01394 278161
Fax: 01394 271083
Email: arcasec@aol.com
Website: www.arca.uk.net
Secretary: Janet Dann
Chair of ARCA: Lisa Railton

ARCA is a well-established association of Residential Colleges for Adult Education. Its members provide a wide range of short-stay courses for the general public. All share a professional approach to education in a residential setting and are wholeheartedly committed to the principle of 'lifelong learning'; learning for personal satisfaction and enjoyment.

Residential Colleges Committee
Ruskin College
Walton Street
Oxford OX1 2HE
Tel: 01865 517824
Fax: 01865 554372
Email: enquiries@ruskin.ac.uk
Secretary: Chris Wilkes

The Residential Colleges Committee includes the six long-term residential colleges providing courses for adult students. The member colleges are Coleg Harlech, Hillcroft College (women), Fircroft College, the Northern College, Ruskin College and Newbattle Abbey College. Students on one-year full-time courses are eligible for grants under an Adult Education Bursaries Scheme. The colleges also accept a proportion of overseas students who may be awarded scholarships through voluntary organisations.

Long-term Colleges

Fircroft College
1018 Bristol Road
Selly Oak
Birmingham B29 6LH
Tel: 0121 472 0116
Fax: 0121 471 1503
Website: www.fircroft.ac.uk
Principal: Fiona Larden
Head of Staff and Student Support:
Alex Miles

Fircroft College of Adult Education offers resident and non-resident places on a one-year full-time General Access to Higher Education (HE) Course. Organised around four stages, each building on the previous, learners begin by developing effective study skills in literacy, numeracy and information technology. Alongside this, the academic areas of studying society, history and literature are introduced, and with information, advice and guidance learners make informed choices from the full curriculum.

Successful completion would include GCSE English Language Equivalence for all learners. While all learners take some maths, a full GCSE Maths Equivalence is an optional element. There are opportunities for learners to undertake a research project or engage in a community placement; both are fully supported by tutors.

At the end of the Access course, learners will have developed a range of skills and knowledge and will be equipped to move on to Higher Education. The residential environment provides open access to well equipped learning resource centres: the residential experience has proven to make a real difference in promoting independent learners.

The college also runs a variety of short courses (two days to one week) aimed at personal, professional and political development. Some draw on the same subject expertise as the Access course above. Many are designed around the needs of the voluntary and community sector. There are specific courses for those wanting to explore future options in learning and work. There is a ten-week residential study programme for adults aged 55+ who wish to research a topic of interest to them. Fircroft is open to all over the age of 19 with no upper age limit. No previous qualifications are required for entry. For people on low income, courses are free or at reduced cost and grants are available for full-time students.

Hillcroft College
South Bank
Surbiton
Surrey KT6 6DF
Tel: 020 8399 2688
Fax: 020 8390 9171
Email: enquiry@hillcroft.ac.uk
Website: www.hillcroft.ac.uk
Principal: June Ireton

Hillcroft is a vibrant and innovative residential college for adult women. It specialises in working with women who may not yet have had the opportunity to achieve their full potential. There are no formal entrance requirements and grants are available to cover accommodation and tuition costs for most women who enrol. Learners are aged from 19 to 70+.

The college offers courses from Entry Level to Level 3 across four main programme areas: Ways into Learning (short courses for women returning to learning or work which allow them to explore their educational needs and longer term goals; creative writing; health; confidence building and decision-making); Skills for Life (short and modular courses covering literacy, ESOL, numeracy; IT and digital skills); Further and Higher Education (a one-term 'Gateway' Certificate or Diploma course to consolidate skills at Level 2 and a two/three term Access to Higher Education Diploma); Employability (a range of courses appropriate for women who are working or volunteering and which develop skills in

coaching, team leading and management, including a modular ILM Certificate in First Line Management at Level 3).

As well as the courses listed, older learners can attend a 'Ransackers' programme which is a supported independent study opportunity over one term. Courses vary in length from one day, one weekend, one week, one month right through to three terms full time. Courses run in school holidays and at weekends and women can be accompanied by children under 12 who are looked after in class times in college childcare facilities. Residential students have 24-hour access to computer facilities and the internet, as well as a well-equipped Learning Resources Centre.

Hillcroft enrols learners from all over England as it is conveniently situated for public transport access (21 minutes from Waterloo) on the outskirts of London. Feedback from women who have attended Hillcroft is very positive and comments on the personalised support offered to individual learners and the progression opportunities at the college.

Northern College
Lowe Lane
Stainborough
Barnsley
South Yorkshire S75 3ET
Tel: 01226 776000
Fax: 01226 776025
Website: www.northern.ac.uk
Principal: Jill Westerman

The Northern College for Residential Adult Education offers a varied programme of long and short courses. The one-year full-time course leads to the award of the Access to HE Diploma; places are also available for part-time students. No formal entry qualifications are required, although applicants will be expected to demonstrate commitment to study and the readiness to benefit from and engage with the course. Residential and non-residential places are available and bursaries are available for full-time students. A number of trade unions provide additional bursaries. The college also offers an extensive range of short courses, ranging from three days to a week, aimed at adults returning to education, as well as courses for those working with parents or in the voluntary and community sector and for trade unionists. There are foundation degrees in Community Regeneration and teacher training programmes for Level 2 to Level 4. The college provides childcare in its children's centre for children from six months up to 14 years (primary school age for full-time students).

Ruskin College
Walton Street
Oxford OX1 2HE
Tel: 01865 554331
Fax: 01865 554372
Email: enquiries@ruskin.ac.uk
Website: www.ruskin.ac.uk
Principal: Prof. Audrey Mullender
General Secretary: Dr Chris Wilkes

Choice of courses to suit the needs of adult students include: Certificate of Higher Education with a variety of pathways, available full-time or part-time (grants covering fees and some living expenses are available for full-time students); degree in Social Work, a professional qualification for people wishing to become social workers; degree in Youth and Community Work for those who want to train as youth workers; degrees in Social Science, English Studies: Creative Writing and Critical Practice, and International Labour and Trade Union Studies aimed at those who have completed a CertHE or equivalent (120 CATS points); return to learn and changing direction part-time courses; short courses for individuals and voluntary organisations, trade unions and community groups. MAs in Women's Studies, Public History and International Labour and Trade Union Studies. Enquiries are welcomed at any time of the year.

Urban Theology Unit (UTU)
210 Abbeyfield Road
Sheffield
South Yorkshire S4 7AZ
Tel: 0114 243 5342
Fax: 0114 243 5356
Email: office@utusheffield.org.uk
Website: www.utusheffield.org.uk
Director: Rev Christine Jones
Administrator: Kate Thompson

Founded in 1969 to develop new insights of theology derived from life in the city, to create a community of clergy and laity looking to discover relevant forms of ministry and action in urban areas and to help people discover their vocation in response to gospel calls. It conducts courses at all levels from Diploma to Doctorate, as well as ministerial training. Membership of UTU gives access to libraries and resource materials. Books are published on urban issues.

Woodbrooke Quaker Study Centre
1046 Bristol Road
Selly Oak
Birmingham B29 6LJ
Tel: 0121 472 5171
Fax: 0121 472 5173
Email: enquiries@woodbrooke.org.uk
Website: www.woodbrooke.org.uk
Director: Jennifer Barraclough
Head of Education: Helen Rowlands
Marketing Manager: Heather Child

Woodbrooke offers study and reflection on a range of issues from personal spirituality to issues of faith and social justice. Set in Birmingham's largest organically managed garden, it offers a year-round programme of short courses. There are also opportunities to undertake longer periods of study with the support of a tutor. Conference and residential facilities are available for hire. As the only Quaker training college in Europe, it also hosts adult students from many countries around the world.

Short-term Colleges

Alston Hall College
Alston Lane
Longridge
Preston
Lancashire PR3 3BP
Tel: 01772 784661
Fax: 01772 785835
Email: alston.hall@ed.lancscc.gov.uk
Website: www.alstonhall.com
Manager: Anne Sturzaker

This former Victorian mansion is located in an attractive, peaceful setting in the beautiful Ribble Valley. Both day and short residential courses are available in a wide range of subjects, including practical crafts and visual arts, natural history and the countryside, music and dance, health and fitness, history and architecture, personal development, literature and creative writing, and cookery. There are also courses in astronomy, gardening and antiques. Outside organisations can book the facilities for conference and training work. Most bedrooms have full en-suite facilities. Excellent home-made food and a friendly ambience are the college hallmarks.

Arvon Foundation
Lumb Bank
The Ted Hughes Arvon Centre
Heptonstall
Hebden Bridge
West Yorkshire HX7 6DF
Tel: 01422 843714
Fax: 01422 843714
Email: l-bank@arvonfoundation.org
Website: www.arvonfoundation.org
Centre Director: Caron May
Centre Director: Stephen May
Administrator: Ilona Jones

Residential writing centre. Five-day courses in the company of two established writers.

Belstead House Education and Conference Centre
Belstead House
Sprites Lane
Ipswich
Suffolk IP8 3NA
Tel: 01473 686321
Fax: 01473 686664
Email:
belstead.house@educ.suffolkcc.gov.uk
Conference and Courses Manager:
Louise Peck

Belstead House Education and Conference Centre offers a full programme of short residential adult education courses run throughout the year. These are mainly leisure learning subjects. The House is available as a venue for education and training, residential and day conferences and workshops.

Benslow Music Trust
Little Benslow Hills
Ibberson Way
Hitchin
Hertfordshire SG4 9RB
Tel: 01462 459446
Fax: 01462 440171
Email: info@benslow.org
Website: www.benslow.org
Chief Executive: Lisa Railton Jones
Development Co-ordinator: Clare Talbot

A unique centre for music making, offering over 100 mid-week, weekend and summer school courses each year, for adult amateur musicians of all ages and standards. Courses include string and wind, chamber music, orchestras, big bands, piano, recorder, early music, jazz, choral and voice and conducting.The Benslow Musical Instrument Loan Scheme lends good quality instruments to promising young musicians. Instruments are either donated or loaned to the Scheme. Concerts are given each year by top British artists and the beautiful buildings and grounds are available for hire by individuals or groups.

Burton Manor College

The Village
Burton
Neston
Cheshire CH64 5SJ
Tel: 0151 336 5172
Fax: 0151 336 6586
Email: enquiry@burtonmanor.com
Website: www.burtonmanor.com
Principal: Keith Chandler

Day, residential and weekend courses are
available in a wide range of subject areas,
including languages, music, art, history,
literature, computers, crafts, gardening,
natural history, china painting, philosophy,
aromatherapy and complementary health.
Management and community development
training and accredited programmes are also
offered. It is also available for hire as a
training venue.

Burwell House Residential Centre

44 North Street
Burwell
Cambridge CB5 0BA
Tel: 01638 741256
Fax: 01638 741256
Email:
burwell.house@cambridgeshire.gov.uk
Website: www.burwellhouse.com
Warden: James Scarborough

A county-run residential study centre,
available for booking throughout the year by
any group, delivering courses with an
educational focus.

Denman College

Marcham
Abingdon
Oxfordshire OX13 6NW
Tel: 01865 391 991
Fax: 01865 391 966
Email: info@denman.org.uk
Website:
www.womens-institute.org.uk/college
Principal: Stephen Hackett

Denman College, opened in 1948, is the
Women's Institute (WI)'s adult residential
college near Oxford and has a proud
heritage as a provider of informal learning
for women. Over 6,000 students visit the
college each year, participating in a
programme of 500+ short residential courses
(two to four nights and weekends), day
schools and other events. Denman College is
open to all, members and non-members
alike. Subjects provided include arts and
crafts, social history, gardening, performing
arts and literature, and the college is home to
the WI Cookery School. The college
occupies a magnificent Georgian House,
along with purpose-built residential and
teaching facilities, set in 17 acres of gardens.
A new 120-seat conference room was added
in 2008, and from Easter 2009 all 70
bedrooms will have en-suite facilities.
Denman College offers a number of
accredited courses in association with other
providers: opportunities for collaboration
and partnership with like-minded
organisations are welcomed. The college's
facilities are also available for organisations
and groups to hire.

Dillington House

Ilminster
Somerset TA19 9DT
Tel: 01460 52427
Fax: 01460 52433
Email: dillington@somerset.gov.uk
Website: www.dillington.com
General Manager: Wayne Bennett
Programme Manager: Lesley Wood

Dillington House offers a wide range of
residential and non-residential courses for
adults throughout the year, including the
arts, history, music, archaeology,
photography, painting and crafts. The house
is one of the finest in Somerset and is set in
beautiful grounds and parkland. In addition,
there are superb facilities for conferences,
seminars and other events. Dillington is a
service provided by Somerset County
Council.

Earnley Concourse

Earnley Place
Earnley
Chichester
West Sussex PO20 7JN
Tel: 01243 670392
Fax: 01243 670832
Email: info@earnley.co.uk
Website: www.earnley.co.uk
Chief Executive: Owain Roberts

The Concourse is administered by the
Earnley Trust Ltd, a non-profit-making independent charity. It offers weekend, mid-week
or week-long courses in a variety of subjects.

Grafham Water Centre

Perry
Huntingdon
Cambridgeshire PE28 0BX
Tel: 01480 810521
Fax: 01480 813850
Email:
grafham.water@cambridgeshire.gov.uk
Website: www.grafham-water-centre.co.uk
Head of Centre: Ian Downing

Residential courses include jazz music for
players, yoga and relaxation, wood carving
and painting. The Centre is also used for
outdoor education trips for schools and
youth groups, water sports courses, young
people's activity holidays, management
training and conferences.

Higham Hall College

Bassenthwaite Lake
Cockermouth
Cumbria CA13 9SH
Tel: 01768 776276
Fax: 01768 776013
Email: admin@highamhall.com
Website: www.highamhall.com
Principal: Alex Alexandre

This is the Lake District's residential college
for adult education, now an independent
charitable trust. Short courses open to all
include arts and crafts, languages, music,
history and music and dance. The college is
available to local authorities, organisations,
private groups and industry for training
courses.

Horncastle College

Mareham Road
Horncastle
Lincolnshire LN9 6BW
Tel: 01507 522449
Fax: 01507 524382
Email:
horncastle.college@lincolnshire.gov.uk

Daytime, evening and weekend residential
courses are offered in a friendly and
welcoming environment, on the edge of the
Lincolnshire Wolds, an area of outstanding
natural beauty.

Knuston Hall

Irchester
Wellingborough
Northamptonshire NN29 7EU
Tel: 01933 312104
Fax: 01933 357596
Email: enquiries@knustonhall.org.uk
Website: www.knustonhall.org.uk

Knuston Hall offers residential courses,
conferences and training events, ranging
from one day to two weeks. Subjects covered
are those of general interest to the public.
Training and seminar facilities are available
for public and commercial bodies.

Lancashire College

Southport Road
Chorley
Lancashire PR7 1NB
Tel: 01257 276719
Fax: 01257 241370
Email: insight@ed.lancscc.gov.uk
Website: www.lancashirecollege.com
Principal: Steve Hailstone

Lancashire College is a purpose-built adult,
residential college offering a wide range of
weekend, evening and day courses, together
with customised training for people in
business, industry and the public sector. It
has an ICT learning centre providing flexible
online learning. Community learning is
offered for adults in over 200 venues in
Chorley, West Lancashire, South Ribble and
Preston. Main specialisms include Business
Language Training, Skills for Life, IT and

courses for unpaid carers and deaf and visually impaired adults. It is an ideal venue for conferences, seminars and training courses.

Losehill Hall
Peak District National Park Centre for Environmental Learning
Castleton
Hope Valley
Derbyshire S33 8WB
Tel: 01433 620373
Fax: 01433 620346
Email: training.losehill@peakdistrict.gov.uk
Website: www.peakdistrict.gov.uk
Bookings Administrator: Sue Field

Losehill Hall is the Peak District National Park Authority's Learning and Environmental Conference Centre, situated in 27 acres of countryside in the heart of the Peak District National Park. Each year it organises an extensive programme of week long and short-break residential training courses, including countryside management, communication and interpretation, surveying and navigation skills. Losehill Hall offers great food, a friendly atmosphere and comfortable en-suite accommodation, as well as tuition by expert tutors. Small groups ensure personal needs are catered for.

Missenden Abbey
Great Missenden
Buckinghamshire HP16 0BD
Tel: 01296 383582
Fax: 01753 783756
Email: dcevreham@buckscc.gov.uk
Website: www.adultlearningbcc.ac.uk
Curriculum Manager: Rosa Maria Welsh

Missenden Abbey hosts Summer and Easter schools, as well as weekday and weekend courses. Students from 16 to 90+ study a wide selection of writing, crafts, music, languages, drama, history, literature, art, photography, tai chi, and many City & Guilds courses in various types of embroidery, patchwork, felt making, wood carving, bead needle weaving, stumpwork, creative computing, floristry and jewellery making.

Pendrell Hall College of Residential Adult Education
Codsall Wood Road
Codsall Wood
Wolverhampton WV8 1QP
Tel: 01902 434112
Fax: 01902 434113
Email: pendrell.college@staffordshire.gov.uk
Website: www.pendrell-hall.org.uk
Principal: David George Evans

The college is situated in ten acres of landscaped private grounds in rural Staffordshire. It is easily accessed from the M6 (junction 12) and M54 (both a distance of six miles away). It provides a wide range of weekend and week courses held in a friendly and relaxed atmosphere, with excellent food and a licensed bar. It is available for use as a venue for conferences, staff training courses and seminars. It has 28 en-suite rooms. The college is fully accessible for those who have mobility concerns. There are ramped entrances to the buildings, automatic doors and lifts to the first floor of the main hall and dining room. Some toilets have been adapted for wheelchair users. All seminar rooms are equipped with hearing induction loops, as is the reception desk. 'Fire alarm pagers' are available for those who require them. The college endeavours to provide all who use it with equality of opportunity.

Pyke House Education and Training Centre
Upper Lake
Battle
East Sussex TN33 0AN
Tel: 01424 772495
Fax: 01424 775041
Email: pykehouse@hastings.ac.uk
Website: www.hastings.ac.uk/pykehouse

This is Hastings College's education and training centre, providing adult education courses, residential adult leisure and management training. Pyke House will be closed for refurbishment from August 2008 until June 2009.

Urchfont Manor College

Urchfont Manor
Urchfont
Nr. Devizes
Wiltshire SN10 4RG
Tel: 01380 840495
Fax: 01380 840005
Email: urchfontmanor@wiltshire.gov.uk
Principal: Jim Ross

Urchfont Manor College is a 17th century
Manor House set in ten acres of beautiful
parkland in the heart of the Wiltshire
countryside. The College offers a wide
selection of short study and leisure breaks
throughout the year: days, weekends and
weeks, in a range of subjects, including art,
crafts, history and archaeology, literature
and the arts, music, science and natural
history, writing and personal development. It
is also a delightful venue for small
conferences, seminars and training events.

Wensum Lodge Centre for Adult and Continuing Education

169 King Street
Norwich
Norfolk NR1 1QW
Tel: 01603 306606
Fax: 01603 765633
Email: wensum.adult.edu@norfolk.gov.uk
Website: www.norfolk.gov.uk
Assistant Head of Service: Denise Saadvandi

Wensum Lodge Centre is a former Victorian
brewery site near Norwich city centre, beside
the river Wensum, and includes a 12th
century historic house, accommodating
activities of the Norfolk Adult Education
Service. Facilities include teaching rooms,
arts, crafts and a sports centre with squash
courts and a licensed bar. Accommodation is
used for day and evening activity.

West Dean College

West Dean
Chichester
West Sussex PO18 0QZ
Tel: 01243 811301
Fax: 01243 811343
Email: short.courses@westdean.org.uk
Website: www.westdean.org.uk
Principal: Robert Pulley
Head of Short Courses and Conferences:
Alison Baxter

A renowned centre for specialist study, West
Dean College offers an inspiring, year-round
programme of residential short courses in
the visual arts, crafts, music, creative writing
and gardening. Courses are conducted in
exceptionally well-designed and equipped
workshops, and the tutors are rare
practitioners (working artists, craftspeople,
photographers, musicians, lecturers,
gardeners or garden designers) who cater for
all levels of ability. West Dean House itself
and the outstanding landscaped gardens and
parkland surrounding the college provide
further stimulus. In addition, West Dean
College offers graduate, postgraduate and
professional development programmes in
conservation, the visual arts, tapestry and
textiles and the making of stringed musical
instruments. It is also home to the West
Dean Tapestry Studio, Sussex Barn Gallery
and West Dean Gardens.

Voluntary and Community Sector Organisations – England

Workers' Educational Association

70 Clifton Street
London EC2A 4HB
Tel: 020 7426 3450
Fax: 020 7426 3451
Email: national@wea.org.uk
Website: www.wea.org.uk
General Secretary: Richard Bolsin

The Workers' Educational Association (WEA) is the largest voluntary sector provider of adult education in Britain and provides learning opportunities for over 80,000 people each year. It operates in all nine English regions and in Scotland, and employs over 3,000 part-time tutors. The WEA creates and delivers courses in response to local need, often in partnership with community groups, local charities and other organisations. The WEA believes that education is life-long and should continue beyond school, college and university in order to help people develop their full human potential in society.

The WEA has always been committed to democratic practice in its teaching and learning, planning and governance. It values the experience and interests of its learners and sees its historic commitment to an educated democracy as very relevant to modern British society, communities and individuals.

Workers' Educational Association Regions

WEA East Midlands Region
39 Mapperley Road
Mapperley
Nottingham NG3 5AQ
Tel: 0115 962 8400
Fax: 0115 962 8402
Email: eastmidlands@wea.org.uk
Website: www.wea.org.uk
Regional Director: Michael Attwell

WEA Eastern Region
Cintra House
12 Hills Road
Cambridge CB2 1JP
Tel: 01223 350978
Fax: 01223 300911
Email: eastern@wea.org.uk
Website: www.wea.org.uk
Regional Director: Carolyn Daines

WEA London Region
4 Luke Street
London EC2A 4XW
Tel: 020 7426 1950
Fax: 020 7729 9821
Email: london@wea.org.uk
Website: www.london.wea.org.uk
Regional Director: Soraya Patrick

WEA North East Region
21 Portland Terrace
Newcastle upon Tyne NE2 1QQ
Tel: 0191 212 6100
Fax: 0191 212 6101
Email: northeast@wea.org.uk
Website: www.wea.org.uk
Regional Secretary: Nigel Todd

WEA North West Region
Suite 405
Old Hall Street
Liverpool L3 9JR
Tel: 0151 243 5340
Fax: 0151 243 5359
Email: northwest@wea.org.uk
Website: www.nw.wea.org.uk
Regional Director: Greg Coyne

WEA South West Region
Bradninch Court
Castle Street
Exeter EX4 3PL
Tel: 01392 490970
Fax: 01392 474330
Email: sw-regionaloffice@wea.org.uk
Website: www.wea.org.uk
Regional Secretary: Steve Martin

WEA Southern Region
Unit 57, Riverside 2
Sir Thomas Longley Road
Rochester
Kent ME2 4DP
Tel: 01634 298 600
Fax: 01634 298 601
Email: southern@wea.org.uk
Website: www.wea.org.uk
Regional Secretary: John Williams

WEA West Midlands Region
4th Floor, Lancaster House
67 Newhall Street
Birmingham B3 1NQ
Tel: 0121 237 8120
Fax: 0121 237 8121
Email: westmidlands@wea.org.uk
Website: www.westmidlands.wea.org.uk
Regional Director: Pete Caldwell

WEA Yorkshire and Humber Region
6 Woodhouse Square
Leeds
West Yorkshire LS3 1AD
Tel: 0113 245 3304
Fax: 0113 245 0883
Email: yorkshumber@wea.org.uk
Website: www.wea.org.uk/yh
Regional Director: Ann Walker

National Organisations

Age Concern England
Astral House
268 London Road
Norbury
London SW16 4ER
Tel: 020 8765 7200
Fax: 020 8765 7211
Email: ace@ace.org.uk
Website: www.ageconcern.org.uk
Policy Manager: Andrea Baron

Age Concern promotes the development of learning and leisure opportunities for older people. A fact sheet on leisure and learning and other relevant materials are available: Tel: 0800 009966. Publications covering health education and active volunteering are also available from the Active Age Unit, at the address above, and from Age Concern Books, Units 5 & 6, Industrial Estate, Brecon, Powys LD3 8LA.
Tel: 0870 4422 120.

Association for Research in the Voluntary and Community Sector (ARVAC)
c/o School of Business and Social Sciences
Roehampton University
Southlands College
80 Roehampton Lane
London SW15 5SL
Email: s.howlett@roehampton.ac.uk
Website: www.arvac.org.uk
Vice-Chair: Steven Howlett

Better Government for Older People
25–31 Ironmonger Row
London EC1V 3QP
Tel: 0207 553 6530
Fax: 0207 553 6531
Email: information@bgop.org.uk
Website: www.bgop.org.uk
Director: Dr Mervyn Eastman

Ransackers
25–31 Ironmonger Row
London EC1V 3QP
Tel: 0207 553 6500
Fax: 0207 553 6501

Black Training and Enterprise Group (BTEG)
31–33 Islington High Street
London N1 9LH
Tel: 020 7843 6110
Fax: 020 7833 1723
Email: info@bteg.co.uk
Website: www.bteg.co.uk
Director: Jeremy Crook

British Deaf Association Midlands
10th Floor, Coventry Point
Market Way
Coventry CV1 1EA
Tel: 02476 550936
Fax: 02476 221541
Email: midlands@bda.org.uk
Website: www.bda.org.uk
Acting Chief Executive Director:
Francis P Murphy
Textphone: 02476 550393
Videophone: IP: 84.12.97.143

British Institute of Learning Disabilities

Campion House
Green Street
Kidderminster
Worcestershire DY10 1JL
Tel: 01562 723010
Fax: 01562 723029
Email: enquiries@bild.org.uk
Website: www.bild.org.uk
Information Administrator: Josie Edwards

CACDP

Durham University Science Park
Block 4
Stockton Road
Durham DH1 3UZ
Tel: 0191 383 1155
Fax: 0191 383 7914
Email: durham@cacdp.org.uk
Website: www.cacdp.org.uk
Chief Executive: Jim Edwards

Centre for Sustainable Energy

3 St Peter's Court
Bedminster Parade
Bristol BS3 4AQ
Tel: 0117 934 1400
Website: www.cse.org.uk
Chief Executive: Simon Roberts
Head of Advice, Education and Community
Initiatives: Sarah Davies

Citizens Advice

Central Office for England and Wales
Myddleton House
115–123 Pentonville Road
London N1 9LZ
Tel: 020 7833 2181
Fax: 020 7833 4371
Website: www.citizensadvice.org.uk
Chief Executive: David Harker

The Citizens Advice Service helps people
resolve their legal, money, consumer and
other problems by providing free
information and advice and by influencing
policymakers. Every Citizens Advice Bureau
(CAB) is a registered charity. For online
advice go to: www.adviceguide.org.uk

Community Matters

12–20 Baron Street
London N1 9LL
Tel: 020 7837 7887
Fax: 020 7278 9253
Email:
communitymatters@communitymatters.org.uk
Website: www.communitymatters.org.uk
Chair: Lesley Michie
National Director: David Tyler

Community Matters is the nationwide
federation of community associations and
similar organisations. It works with
community groups who are concerned with
the well-being of their community in its
educational, recreational and social needs.
Community Matters has a particular interest
in helping community organisations who
run community buildings.

ContinYou

Unit C1, Grovelands Court
Grovelands Estate
Longford Road
Exhall
Coventry CV7 9NE
Tel: 024 7658 8440
Fax: 024 7658 8441
Email: info.coventry@continyou.org.uk
Website: www.continyou.org.uk
Chief Executive Officer: Laurence Blackhall
Senior Administrator: Sharon Barker

ContinYou believes in the power of learning
as a means of achieving social justice.
ContinYou uses learning to tackle inequality
and build social inclusion. It creates learning
programmes and services that offer fresh
opportunities to people who have gained
least from formal education and training.
ContinYou is one of the UK's leading
community learning organisations.

DEA

CAN Mezzanine
32–36 Loman Street
London SE1 0EH
Tel: 020 7922 7930
Fax: 020 7922 7929
Email: info@dea.org.uk
Website: www.dea.org.uk
Director: Hetan Shah

DEA is an education charity that promotes global learning.

It has a national network of member organisations and supporters that share a conviction that the role of education today is crucial in shaping a better tomorrow.

For learners and society to flourish in a world which faces issues such as global poverty, climate change and racial and religious tensions, DEA believes that education should put learning in a global context, fostering critical thinking and creative thinking, self-awareness and open-mindedness towards difference; understanding of global issues and power relationships, and optimism and action for a better world.

It works to change both what people learn and how they learn by influencing policy and improving educator's practice. Its primary focus is on schools and teacher training, and global youth work.

Dyslexia Action

Park House
Wick Road
Englefield Green
Egham
Surrey TW20 0HR
Tel: 01784 222300
Email: info@dyslexiaaction.org.uk
Website: www.dyslexiaaction.org.uk
Chief Executive: Shirley Cramer
National Adult Dyslexia Co-ordinator:
Jenny Lee
National Outreach Co-ordinator:
Margaret Jackson

Dyslexia Action (formerly the Dyslexia Institute) is a national registered charity and is the UK's leading provider of specialist services for dyslexia. It works to ensure that individuals with dyslexia have access to specialist advice, assessment and tuition which is of consistently high quality. It undertakes research into dyslexia, as well as lobbying and campaigning at a national and regional level. It offers specialist teacher training courses, for both pre-and post-16 sectors and it is the largest supplier of specialist training in this field. It also develops and distributes teaching materials. As well as specialist, individualised teaching programmes for dyslexic adults, it also offers workplace consultations to help employers comply with the DDA, and dyslexic employees reach their potential. Dyslexia Action has a high-quality, thriving and dynamic service for dyslexic adults in all of its 26 centres and 160 teaching locations throughout the country. It works in partnership with Learning and Skills Councils, education authorities, colleges, local and national employers, and other providers from the voluntary sector to ensure an integrated and balanced service.

Educational Centres Association (ECA)

21 Ebbisham Drive
Norwich NR4 6HQ
Tel: 08442 495594
Fax: 01603 469292
Email: info@e-c-a.ac.uk
Website: www.e-c-a.ac.uk
Chief Executive: Bernard Godding
President:
Prof. Emeritus Brian Groombridge
Regional Contact, North: Walt Crowson
Email: walt.crowson@ntlworld.com
Regional Contact, West: Paul Olver
Email: paulolver@hotmail.com

The ECA is a practice-based, membership organisation representing a wide range of learners and providers in adult education. It is involved in citizenship education, widening participation, intergenerational learning, sustainability, staff development and social inclusion, and is the voice of adult learning in the Community Sector Coalition. Students, teachers, managers and governors from across the sector are active in responding to consultations and organising regional and national conferences, some sponsored by DIUS. The ECA is a UK-wide organisation with strong links to Europe. It was founded in 1920 and current projects include 'Every Action Counts', promoting environmental sustainability, and its acclaimed Grundtvig projects are 'Teach' active citizenship training and 'Teddy Bear' linking reminiscence by older people with activities in the primary school.

Family Education Development Trust
4 Barnfield Hill
Exeter EX1 1SR
Tel: 01392 499994
Fax: 01392 499994
Email: fedt@fedt.co.uk
Website: www.fedt.co.uk
Company Secretary: Pat Colling

Federation for Community Development Learning
3rd Floor, The Circle
33 Rockingham Lane
Sheffield S1 4FW
Tel: 0114 253 6770
Fax: 0114 253 6771
Email: info@fcdl.org.uk
Website: www.fcdl.org.uk
Head of Agency: Janice Marks

Foyer Federation
3rd Floor
5–9 Hatton Wall
London EC1N 8HX
Tel: 020 7430 2212
Fax: 020 7430 2213
Email: federation@foyer.net
Website: www.foyer.net
Chief Executive: Jane Slowey
Policy and Research Manager:
Steve Hillman
Give us a Chance Campaign website:
www.giveusachance.net
Give us a Voice Campaign website:
www.giveusavoice.net

Hearing Concern LINK
19 Hartfield Road
Eastbourne
East Sussex BN21
Tel: 01323 638230
Fax: 01323 64296
Email: info@hearningconcernlink.org
Website: www.hearingconcernlink.org
Chief Executive: Dr Lorraine Gailey

Hearing Concern LINK is the UK's leading charity for adults with acquired hearing loss, active in rehabilitation and training, campaigning and lobbying, research and community development.
Text: 01323 739998, Minicom: 01323 739998

Help the Aged
York House
207–221 Pentonville Road
London N1 9UZ
Tel: 020 7278 1114
Fax: 020 7278 1116
Email: info@helptheaged.org.uk
Website: www.helptheaged.org.uk
Director General: Michael Lake CBE

Joseph Rowntree Foundation
The Homestead
40 Water End
York YO30 6WP
Tel: 01904 629241
Fax: 01904 620072
Email: info@jrf.org.uk
Website: www.jrf.org.uk
Director: Julia Unwin CBE

Media Trust
2nd Floor, Riverwalk House
157–161 Millbank
London SW1P 4RR
Tel: 020 7217 3717
Fax: 020 7217 3716
Website: www.mediatrust.org
Chief Executive: Caroline Diehl

Media Trust harnesses the skills, resources and creativity of the media industry to help voluntary organisations and charities make a difference to people's lives.

Mencap
123 Golden Lane
London EC1Y 0RT
Tel: 020 7454 0454
Fax: 020 7608 3254
Email: information@mencap.org.uk
Website: www.mencap.org.uk
Chief Executive: Dame Jo Williams

Migrants Resource Centre
24 Churton Street
London SW1V 2LP
Tel: 020 7834 6650
Fax: 020 7931 8187
Email: info@migrants.org.uk
Website: www.migrantresourcecentre.org.uk

The Migrants Resource Centre work with,
and for, migrants and refugees to enable
them to improve the quality of their lives and
to raise awareness of issues affecting migrant
and refugee communities:
www.thenewlondoners.co.uk

Mind
15–19 Broadway
London E15 4BQ
Tel: 020 8519 2122
Fax: 020 8522 1725
Email: contact@mind.org.uk
Website: www.mind.org.uk
Administrator to Fundraising
Communication Director: Kellie Field
Mind*info*Line: 0845 766 0163

Nacro
Park Place
10–12 Lawn Lane
London SW8 1UD
Tel: 020 7840 7200
Fax: 020 7840 7240
Email: communications@nacro.org.uk
Website: www.nacro.org.uk
Head of Communications: Melior Whitear

Nacro runs education and employment
projects in over 30 areas in England and
Wales, specialising in working with
ex-offenders, those at risk of offending and
other socially excluded people. Services
include work-based learning for adults and
young people, basic skills training,

vocational guidance and other education,
training and employment programmes.
Nacro works in partnership with the
National Probation Service, the Prison
Service, Learning and Skills Councils,
education authorities, local and national
employers, and other local and national
organisations, to increase opportunities for
disadvantaged people.

NATECLA
South Birmingham College
Room HB110
Hall Green Campus
Cole Bank Road
Hall Green
Birmingham B28 8ES
Tel: 0121 688 8121
Fax: 0121 694 5062
Email: co-ordinator@natecla.fsnet.co.uk
Website: www.natecla.org.uk
Co-Chair: Irene Austin
Co-chair: Anne McKeown

NATECLA (the National Association for
Teaching English and other Community
Languages to Adults) is the national forum
for English and community language issues.
NATECLA campaigns for: educational
opportunities for adults from ethnic
minorities and for anti-racist education and
training; educational rights and
opportunities for refugees and asylum
seekers; and evaluation and recognition of
overseas qualifications. NATECLA
represents members through a variety of
consultative bodies and is consulted by
national organisations and decision makers
on the needs of ESOL learners.

**National Association for Voluntary and
Community Action (NAVCA)**
The Tower
2 Furnival Square
Sheffield
South Yorkshire S1 4QL
Tel: 0114 278 6636
Fax: 0114 278 7004
Email: navca@navca.org.uk
Website: www.navca.org.uk
Chief Executive: Kevin Curley
Interim Learning and Development
Manager: Shaun Masterman

NAVCA is the national voice of local voluntary and community sector infrastructure in England. Its 360 members work with 160,000 local community groups and voluntary organisations which provide services, regenerate neighbourhoods, increase volunteering and tackle discrimination, in partnership with local public bodies.

National Association of Women's Clubs
5 Vernon Rise
Kings Cross Road
London WC1X 9EP
Tel: 020 7837 1434
Fax: 020 7713 0727
Website: www.nawc.org.uk

The National Association of Women's Clubs co-ordinates non-political, non-sectarian, autonomous women's clubs throughout Great Britain, and is open to all women over 18.

National Council for Voluntary Organisations (NCVO)
Regents Wharf
8 All Saints Street
London N1 9RL
Tel: 020 7713 6161
Fax: 020 7713 6300
Email: ncvo@ncvo-vol.org.uk
Website: www.ncvo-vol.org.uk
Chief Executive: Stuart Etherington

Established in 1919 as the representative body for the voluntary sector in England, NCVO has over 3,750 members involved in all areas of voluntary and social action on a national, regional and local basis. It is also in daily contact with thousands of other voluntary bodies and groups, as well as government departments, local authorities and the business sector. NCVO believes that the voluntary sector enriches society and needs to be promoted and supported. NCVO champions the cause of the sector to government and policy makers to improve its effectiveness and provides services to support the organisations within it.

Publications include a wide range of guides and good practice material, plus *Engage* magazine.

National Federation of Women's Institutes (NFWI)
104 New Kings Road
London SW6 4LY
Tel: 020 7371 9300
Fax: 020 7736 3652
Email: hq@nfwi.org.uk
Website: www.thewi.org.uk
General Secretary: Jana Osborne
Principal: Stephen Hackett

The NFWI is a non-party political, non-sectarian voluntary organisation with around 210,000 members. It provides a democratically controlled educational and social organisation for women with rural interests, giving members the opportunity of working and learning together to improve the quality of rural life and develop their own skills and talents. Educational activities include talks and demonstrations at monthly meetings, as well as more informal learning opportunities at and in between meetings. The NFWI owns its adult residential college in Oxfordshire, Denman College, which runs over 500 short courses to develop new skills and knowledge.

The National Trust
Learning Department
Heelis
Kemble Drive
Swindon SN2 2NA
Tel: 01793 817646
Fax: 01793 817575
Email: learning@nationaltrust.org.uk
Website: www.nationaltrust.org.uk/main
Head of Learning: Ann Nicol

Pre-School Learning Alliance
The Fitzpatrick Building
188 York Way
London N7 9AD
Tel: 020 7697 2500
Fax: 020 7700 0319
Email: information@pre-school.org.uk
Website: www.pre-school.org.uk
Chief Executive: Steve Alexander

Prisoners' Education Trust

Ground Floor, Wandle House
Riverside Drive
Mitcham
Surrey CR4 4BU
Tel: 020 8648 7760
Fax: 020 8648 7762
Email: info@prisonerseducation.org.uk
Website: www.prisonerseducation.org.uk
Chairman: John Samuels QC
Director: Pat Jones

RNID

19–23 Featherstone Street
London EC1Y 8SL
Tel: 0808 808 0123/0808 808 9000 (text)
Fax: 020 7296 8199
Email: informationline@rnid.org.uk
Website: www.rnid.org.uk

RNID (the Royal National Institute for Deaf
People) is the largest charity representing 9
million deaf and hard of hearing people in
the UK. It offers a range of services for deaf
and hard of hearing people, and provides
information and support on all aspects of
deafness, hearing loss and tinnitus. As a
membership charity, it aims to achieve a
radically better quality of life for deaf and
hard of hearing people. Its work involves
campaigning and lobbying, providing
services, training products and equipment,
and undertaking medical and technical
research. It works throughout the UK.

Royal National Institute of Blind People (RNIB)

105 Judd Street
London WC1H 9NE
Tel: 020 7388 1266
Fax: 020 7388 2034
Website: www.rnib.org.uk
National Post Compulsory Education and
Training Development Officer:
Anne Rehahn

The RNIB is working to ensure that blind
and partially sighted people have equal
access to education, training, employment
and leisure. The www.rnib.org.uk/pcet
section of its website supports staff in the
lifelong learning sector working with blind
and partially sighted learners.

RNIB College Loughborough
Radmoor Road
Loughborough
Leicestershire LE11 3BS
Tel: 01509 611077
Fax: 01509 232013
Email: enquiries@rnibvocoll.ac.uk
Website: www.rnibvocoll.ac.uk
Principal: Tony Warren

TAEN – The Age and Employment Network

207–221 Pentonville Road
London N1 9UZ
Tel: 020 7843 1590
Fax: 020 7843 1599
Email: info@taen.org.uk
Website: www.taen.org.uk
Chief Executive: Chris Ball

Tavistock Institute

30 Tabernacle Street
London EC2A 4UE
Tel: 020 7417 0407
Fax: 020 7417 0566
Email: central.admin@tavinstitute.org
Website: www.tavistockinstitute.org
Operations Manager: Coreene Archer

Third Age Trust

The Old Municipal Buildings
19 East Street
Bromley BR1 1QE
Tel: 020 8466 6139
Email: national.office@u3a.org.uk
Website: www.u3a.org.uk
Chair: Jean Goodeve
Company Secretary: Lin Jonas

Townswomen's Guilds

Tomlinson House
329 Tyburn Road
Birmingham B24 8HJ
Tel: 0121 326 0400
Fax: 0121 326 1976
Email: tghq@townswomen.org.uk
Website: www.townswomen.org.uk
National Chairman: Sue Smith

Townswomen's Guilds are groups of women
who meet regularly, regardless of politics,
race, age, religion or circumstance to

exchange ideas, develop new skills and interests, get involved with various issues and, above all, have fun. Britain's leading women's organisation has 40,000 members in 900 Guilds grouped in 90 Federations across England, Scotland, Wales, Northern Ireland and the Isle of Man. Periodical: *Townswoman*.

UK Workforce Hub
Regents Wharf
8 All Saints Street
London N1 9RL
Tel: 020 7520 2490
Fax: 020 7713 6300
Email:
workforcehub@ukworkforcehub.org.uk
Website: www.ukworkforcehub.org.uk
Head of Workforce Hub in England:
Janet Fleming

The UK Workforce Hub works to promote skills development and good employment practice. It represents the interests of the third sector on these issues to government and other key stakeholders in the learning and skills arena.

Voluntary Arts England
PO Box 1056
Newcastle upon Tyne NE99 1UE
Tel: 0191 230 4464
Email: info@vaengland.org.uk
Website: www.vaengland.org.uk
England Co-ordinator: Reemer Bailey

Voluntary Arts England promotes participation in arts and crafts activities for the well-being of individuals and communities as a whole. It provides information and advice to help voluntary arts groups thrive, and works across all art forms, from drama and dance to weaving and visual arts. It lobbies government for greater recognition of the value of participation and aims to improve the environment for everyone who volunteers in the arts and crafts. Voluntary Arts England believes that the skills learned through creative participation are transferable to all aspects of life.

Volunteering England
Regents Wharf
8 All Saints Street
London N1 9RL
Tel: 0845 305 6979
Fax: 020 7520 8910
Email:
volunteering@volunteeringengland.org
Website: www.volunteering.org.uk
Head of Policy and Information: Susan Lee

Regional and Sub-regional Networks

North East

BECON
182 Portland Road
Shieldfield
Newcastle upon Tyne NE2 1DJ
Tel: 0191 209 4747
Email: information@becon.org.uk
Website: www.becon.org.uk
Executive Director: Abdul Khan

Voluntary Organisations Network North East (VONNE)
9th Floor, Cale Cross
156 Pilgrim Street
Newcastle upon Tyne NE1 6SU
Tel: 0191 233 2000
Fax: 0191 222 1998
Email: vonne@vonne.co.uk
Website: www.vonne.co.uk
Chief Executive: Jo Curry

North West

Cumbria CVS
27 Spencer Street
Carlisle CA1 1BE
Tel: 01228 512513
Email: kittybc@cumbriacvs.org.uk
Manager: Kitty Booth-Clibborn

Lancashire Wide Network for Minority Ethnic Women

Spring Hill Community Centre
Exchange Street
Accrington
Lancashire BB5 0JD
Tel: 01254 392974
Fax: 01254 381349
Email: alison@lancashire-bme-pact.org.uk
Website: www.lwnmew.fsnet.co.uk
Project Co-ordination Officer: Jabien Kauser

The aim of the project is to help to build the capacity of minority ethnic women working in the voluntary sector to participate effectively in the social, economic and political life of the community in which they live.

Voluntary Sector North West

St Thomas Centre
Ardwick Green North
Manchester M12 6FZ
Tel: 0161 276 9300
Fax: 0161 276 9301
Email: info@vsnw.org.uk
Website: www.vsnw.org.uk
Chief Executive: Richard Caulfield

Yorkshire and Humberside

Assessment Centre for Voluntary Organisations (ACVO)

Tower Court
Oakdale Road
Clifton Moor
York YO30 4XL
Tel: 01904 557605
Email: enquiries@acvo.co.uk
Website: www.acvo.co.uk
Chief Executive: Stuart Plant
Email: stuart.plant@acvo.co.uk

Humberside Learning Consortium

Goodwin Centre
Icehouse Road
Hull HU3 2HQ
Tel: 01482 327438
Fax: 01482 212227
Email: office@hlc-vol.org
Chief Executive Officer: Helen Groves

VC TRAIN (South Yorkshire Voluntary and Community Sector Training Consortium)

Thornfield
Cross Street
Bramley
Rotherham
South Yorkshire S66 2SA
Tel: 01709 518 800
Fax: 01709 533 555
Email: contact@vctrain.org
Website: www.vctrain.org
Executive Director: Andrew Coulthard

West Yorkshire Learning Consortium

Suite 12, The Basement
Oxford Place Centre
Oxford Place
Leeds LS1 3AX
Tel: 0113 245 3111
Fax: 0113 245 2969
Email: info@wylc.org.uk
Website: www.wylc.org.uk
Project Director: David Wears

Yorkshire and the Humber Regional Forum

Suite D10, Joseph's Well
Hanover Walk
Leeds LS3 1AB
Tel: 0113 394 2300
Fax: 0113 394 2301
Email: office@regionalforum.org.uk
Website: www.regionalforum.org.uk
Director: Judy Robinson

West Midlands

Community First

Malvern View
Willow End Park
Blackmore Park Road
Malvern
Worcestershire WR13 6NN
Tel: 01684 312730
Fax: 01684 311278
Email: markh@comfirst.org.uk
Website: www.comfirst.org.uk
Development Manager, Performance and Learning: Mark Herriott

EMBRACE West Midlands
Elite House
70 Warwick Street
Birmingham B12 0NL
Tel: 0121 766 0810
Fax: 0121 766 3090
Email: info@embrace.org.uk
Website: www.embrace.org.uk
Chief Officer: Gerald Nembhard

Herefordshire Voluntary Action
Berrows Business Centre
Bath Street
Hereford HR1 2HE
Tel: 01432 343932
Email: enquiries@herefordshireva.org
Website: www.herefordshireva.org
Chief Executive: Will Lindesay

Regional Action West Midlands
Ground Floor, Waterlinks House
Richard Street
Birmingham B7 4AA
Tel: 0121 359 9100
Fax: 0121 359 9101
Email: rawm@rawm.co.uk
Website: www.rawm.org.uk
Acting Network Director: Sharon Palmer

East Midlands

CEFET
114 Mansfield Road
Nottingham NG1 3HL
Tel: 0115 911 0419
Fax: 0115 911 0418
Email: info@cefet.org.uk
Website: www.cefet.org.uk
Chief Executive: Laurie Moran

CVS Northamptonshire
32–36 Hazelwood Road
Northampton NN1 1LN
Tel: 01604 624121
Fax: 01604 627618
Email: cvs@cvsnorthamptonshire.org.uk

Derbyshire Learning and Development Consortium
32 Charnwood Street
Derby DE1 2GU
Tel: 01332 265 960
Fax: 01332 267 954
Email: info@consortium.org.uk
Website: www.consortium.org.uk
Chief Executive: William Allen

Enable
Nottingham and Notts Voluntary &
Community Sector Learning & Skills
Consortium
Voluntary Action Centre
7 Mansfield Road
Nottingham NG1 3FB
Tel: 0115 934 9543
Fax: 0115 934 8440
Website: www.enable.uk.net
Chief Executive: Don Hayes

One East Midlands
7 Mansfield Road
Nottingham NG1 3FB
Tel: 0115 934 8471
Fax: 0115 934 8498
Email: office@one-em.org.uk
Website: www.oneeastmidlands.org.uk
Chief Executive: Wynne Garnett

VOCOLLS
c/o CVS Community Partnership
Beaumont Enterprise Centre
Boston Road
Leicester LE4 1HB
Tel: 0116 229 3051
Fax: 0116 235 1844
Email: mick@ccp.org.uk
Website: www.ccp.org.uk
CCP Learning and Skills Manager:
Mick O'Hara

Voluntary and Community Sector
Opportunities for Learning in Leicestershire

Voice East Midlands
66 Carlton Road
Nottingham NG3 2AP
Tel: 0115 950 8820
Fax: 0115 950 9232
Email: admin@voice-em.org.uk
Website: www.voice-em.org.uk
Chief Executive: Shahid Sharif

Voluntary Action Leicester
Leicester Active Community Centre
9 Newarke Street
Leicester LE1 5SN
Tel: 0116 258 0666
Fax: 0116 257 5059
Email: info@voluntaryactionleicester.org.uk
Website:
www.voluntaryactionleicester.org.uk
Administrator: Heather Jallands

Eastern

**Community and Voluntary Forum for
the Eastern Region (COVER)**
Eagle Stile
Rectory Farm Barns
Walden Road
Little Chesterford
Saffron Walden
Essex CB10 1UD
Tel: 01799 532880
Fax: 01799 532899
Email: office@cover-east.org
Website: www.cover-east.org
Chief Executive: Andrew Cogan

**Community Development Agency
for Hertfordshire**
Birchwood Avenue
Hatfield
Hertfordshire AL10 0PS
Tel: 01707 695500
Fax: 01707 695525
Email: kath.sexton@cdaforherts.org.uk
Website: www.cdaforherts.org.uk
Chief Executive: Kate Belinis

**MENTER (East of England Black and
Minority Ethnic Network)**
62–64 Victoria Road
Cambridge CB4 3DU
Tel: 01223 355034
Fax: 01223 359047
Email: office@menter.org.uk
Website: www.menter.org.uk
Head of Infrastructure: Liesbeth ten Ham

Voluntary Norfolk
83–87 Pottergate
Norwich NR2 1DZ
Tel: 01603 883819
Fax: 01603 764109
Email:
sue.beswick@voluntarynorfolk.org.uk
Website: www.norfolkportfolio.org.uk
Workforce Development Officer:
Sue Beswick

South West

Black South West Network
5 Russell Town Avenue
Redfield
Bristol BS5 9LT
Tel: 0117 939 6648
Fax: 0117 939 6647
Email: bswn@bswn.org.uk
Website: www.bswn.org.uk
Regional Programme Director:
Rupert Daniel

Learning Curve
Unit 2
Challeymead Business Park
Melksham
Wiltshire SN12 8BU
Tel: 01225 792500
Fax: 01225 792501
Email: enquiries@learningcurve.org.uk
Website: www.learningcurve.org.uk
Chief Executive: Tim Ward

Learning Plus
6 River Court
Kingsmill Road
Tamar View Industrial Estate
Saltash
Cornwall PL12 6LE
Tel: 01752 208352
Fax: 01752 208354
Website: www.learningplus.org.uk
Chief Executive: David Carter

South West Forum

Unit 6, Cranmere Court
Lustleigh Close
Matford Business Park
Exeter EX2 8PW
Tel: 01392 823758
Fax: 01392 823033
Email: admin@southwestforum.org.uk
Website: www.southwestforum.org.uk
Chief Executive: Stephen Woollett

South East

Ladder4Learning

Ladder4Learning Project
Unit 2, Challeymead Business Park
Bradford Road
Melksham
Wiltshire SN12 8BU
Tel: 01225 792505
Email:
ladder4learning@learningcurve.org.uk
Website: www.ladder4learning.org.uk
Project Manager: Jaclyn Cross

Regional Action and Involvement South East (RAISE)

Bridge House
1 Walnut Tree Close
Guildford
Surrey GU1 4UA
Tel: 01483 885266
Fax: 01483 301269
Email: email@raise-networks.org.uk
Website: www.raise-networks.org.uk
Chief Executive Officer: Catherine Johnstone

London

London Voluntary Sector Training Consortium

Bromley Hall
43 Gillender Street
London E14 6RN
Tel: 0845 262 2006
Fax: 0845 262 2005
Email: info@lvstc.org.uk
Website: www.lvstc.org.uk
Director: Ray Phillips

Second Tier Advisors Network (STAN)

London Voluntary Service Council
356 Holloway Road
London N7 6PA
Tel: 020 7700 8219
Fax: 020 7700 8108
Website: www.lvsc.org.uk/stan
Second Tier Advisors Network
Co-ordinator: Gemma Cossins
Email: gemma@lvsc.org.uk

Third Sector Alliance (3SA)

London Voluntary Service Council
356 Holloway Road
London N7 6PA
Tel: 020 7700 8107
Fax: 020 7700 8108
Email: info@lvsc.org.uk
3SA Regional Development Officer: Jane Tanner

Adult and Community Education Organisations – England

National and Regional Organisations

Educational Centres Association (ECA)
21 Ebbisham Drive
Norwich NR4 6HQ
Tel: 08442 495594
Fax: 01603 469292
Email: info@e-c-a.ac.uk
Website: www.e-c-a.ac.uk
Chief Executive: Bernard Godding
President:
Prof. Emeritus Brian Groombridge
Regional Contact, North: Walt Crowson
Email: walt.crowson@ntlworld.com
Regional Contact, West: Paul Olver
Email: paulolver@hotmail.com

The ECA is a practice-based, membership organisation representing a wide range of learners and providers in adult education. It is involved in citizenship education, widening participation, intergenerational learning, sustainability, staff development and social inclusion, and is the voice of adult learning in the Community Sector Coalition. Students, teachers, managers and governors from across the sector are active in responding to consultations and organising regional and national conferences, some sponsored by DIUS. The ECA is a UK-wide organisation with strong links to Europe. It was founded in 1920 and current projects include 'Every Action Counts', promoting environmental sustainability, and its acclaimed Grundtvig projects are 'Teach' active citizenship training and 'Teddy Bear' linking reminiscence by older people with activities in the primary school.

Learning Communities Network (LCN)
Secretariat Office
111 Grantham Road
Bingham
Nottingham NG13 8DF
Tel: 01949 878118
Fax: 01949 831171
Email: lc-network@ntlworld.com
Website: www.lc-network.com
Network Manager: Karen Shepperson

LCN – founded in 1995 – is the world's largest network of learning communities, towns, cities and regions. Its aim is to support learning communities by creating a voice that raises local profile, uses local and regional expertise and encourages effectiveness through networking and the sharing of good practice. Membership is open to all partnerships working in the field of lifelong learning, representing learning communities, towns, cities and regions. LCN, a company limited by guarantee and a charity, is run by its members through a Board of Directors which annually elects a Chair and Deputy Chair.

Workers' Educational Association
70 Clifton Street
London EC2A 4HB
Tel: 020 7426 3450
Fax: 020 7426 3451
Email: national@wea.org.uk
Website: www.wea.org.uk
General Secretary: Richard Bolsin

The Workers' Educational Association (WEA) is the largest voluntary sector provider of adult education in Britain and provides learning opportunities for over 80,000 people each year. It operates in all nine English regions and in Scotland and employs over three thousand part-time tutors.

The WEA creates and delivers courses in response to local need, often in partnership with community groups, local charities and other organisations. The WEA believes that education is life-long and should continue beyond school, college and university in order to help people develop their full human potential in society.

The WEA has always been committed to democratic practice in its teaching and learning, planning and governance. It values the experience and interests of its learners and sees its historic commitment to an educated democracy as very relevant to modern British society, communities and individuals.

Adult and Community Education Providers

Independent Organisations

Alpha Grove Community Centre
Alpha Grove
Isle of Dogs
London E14 8LH
Tel: 020 7538 1714
Fax: 020 7093 4131
Email: postmaster@alphagrove.org
Website: www.alphagrove.org
Centre Manager: Rhys Johnson

Aston-Mansfield
Durning Hall
Earlham Grove
London E7 9AB
Tel: 020 8536 3800
Fax: 020 8519 5472
Email: ceo@aston-mansfield.org.uk
Website: www.aston-mansfield.org.uk
Company Secretary: Geoffrey Wheeler

BEC Ltd
1st Floor, Rotherhithe Library
Albion Street
London SE16 7BS
Tel: 020 7394 6836
Fax: 020 7064 0578
Email: admin@bedeeducation.co.uk
Website: www.bedeeducation.co.uk
Centre Manager: Tony Luxford

Birmingham Settlement
Reynolds House Annexe
Newbury Road
Newtown
Birmingham B19 2RH
Tel: 0121 250 3000
Fax: 0121 250 3050
Website: www.birminghamsettlement.org.uk

Bishop Creighton House
378 Lillie Road
Fulham
London SW6 7PH
Tel: 020 7385 9689
Fax: 020 7386 9149
Email: info@creightonhouse.org
Website: www.creightonhouse.org
Director: Rory Gillert
Administrator: Stuart Moon

Blackfriars Settlement
1–5 Rushworth Street
London SE1 0RB
Tel: 020 7928 9521
Fax: 020 7620 1409
Email: info@blackfriars-settlement.org.uk
Website: www.blackfriars-settlement.org.uk
Skills for Life Manager: Cliff Docherty

Copleston Centre
Copleston Road
Peckham
London SE15 4AN
Tel: 020 7732 3435
Fax: 020 7635 9522
Email: office@coplesoncentre.org.uk

Dukeries College
Adult and Community Learning
Whinney Lane
New Ollerton
Nottinghamshire NG22 9TD
Tel: 01623 860304
Fax: 01623 836082
Email: adulted@dukeries.notts.sch.uk
Website: www.dukeries.notts.sch.uk
Director of Adult and Community Learning:
David Staples

Friends Centre
23 Vine Street
Brighton BN1 4AG
Tel: 01273 689265
Fax: 01273 689276
Email: info@friendscentre.org
Website: www.friendscentre.org
Principal: Dr Juliet Mary Merrifield

John Kitto Community College
Brunell Centre
Honicknowle Lane
Plymouth
Devon PL5 3NE
Tel: 01752 208 380
Email: nwacl@plymouth.gov.uk
Website: www.plymouthoncourse.com
Learning Development Manager:
John Shanahan

Katherine Low Settlement
108 Battersea High Street
London SW11 3HP
Tel: 020 7223 2845
Fax: 020 7223 6471
Email: sarah@klsettlement.org.uk
Community Development Worker:
Sarah Rackham

Lady Margaret Hall Settlement
The Co-op Centre
11 Mowll Street
London SW9 6BG
Tel: 020 7793 1110
Fax: 020 7793 0426
Email: lmhs@lmhs.org.uk
Website: www.lmhs.org.uk
Director: Jeffe Jeffers

Learning Links (Southern) Ltd
1st Floor, 2a The Hard
Portsmouth PO1 3PU
Tel: 023 9229 6460
Fax: 023 9288 2938
Email: admin@learninglinks.co.uk
Website: www.learninglinks.co.uk
Chief Executive Officer: Janet de Bathe

Letchworth Settlement
Nevells Road
Letchworth Garden City
Hertfordshire SG6 4UB
Tel: 01462 682828
Website: www.letchworthsettlement.org.uk
Manager: Amanda West

Manchester Settlement
31 Bosworth Street
Beswick
Manchester M11 3AP
Tel: 0161 231 1114
Fax: 0161 231 1115
Email: info@manchestersettlement.org.uk
Website: www.manchestersettlement.org.uk
General Manager: Maria Gardiner

Opportunities and Activities Voluntary Initiative in Adult Education
Union Chapel
Wellington Road
Fallowfield
Manchester M14 6EQ
Tel: 0161 225 4226
Website: www.unionchapelmanchester.co.uk
ECA Secretary: Eileen Land

Oxford House
Derbyshire Street
Bethnal Green
London E2 6HG
Tel: 020 7739 9001
Fax: 020 7729 0435
Email: info@oxfordhouse.org.uk
Website: www.oxfordhouse.org.uk
Education Co-ordinator: Liezel Contreras

Peckham Settlement
Goldsmith Road
Peckham
London SE15 5TF
Tel: 020 7639 1823
Fax: 020 7635 9830
Email: admin@peckhamsettlement.org.uk
Director: William Thomas

Percival Guildhouse
St Matthews Street
Rugby
Warwickshire CV21 3BY
Tel: 01788 542467
Fax: 01788 535249
Email: percival-guildhouse@tiscali.co.uk
Website: www.percival-guildhouse.co.uk
Centre Manager: Elaine Faller

St Margaret's House Settlement
21 Old Ford Road
Bethnal Green
London E2 9PL
Tel: 020 8980 2092
Fax: 020 8981 9944
Director: Tony Hardie

Toynbee Hall
28 Commercial Street
London E1 6LS
Tel: 020 7247 6943
Fax: 020 7377 5964
Email: info@toynbeehall.org.uk
Website: www.toynbeehall.org.uk

The Workshop at Barton Hill Settlement
43 Ducie Road
Barton Hill
Bristol BS5 0AX
Tel: 0117 955 6971
Email: admin@bartonhillsettlement.org.uk
Website: www.bartonhillsettlement.org.uk
Senior Manager: Joanna Holmes
Adult Learning Manager: Gary Blake

Adult and Community Education Providers

This section lists adult and community education providers who are corporate members of NIACE.

Accounting for Safety Ltd
Phoenix Business Centre
Unit 8, Phoenix Road
Barrow-in-Furness
Cumbria LA14 2UA
Tel: 01229 840 243
Fax: 01229 840 241
Email: jim@accounting4safety.co.uk
Website: www.accounting4safety.co.uk
Director: Jim Tongue

ACE Adult Community Education (Wigan) Ltd
2nd Floor, Queen's Hall
Market Street
Wigan
Lancashire WN1 1HX
Tel: 01942 829321
Fax: 01942 829321
Wesite: www.ace-wigan.co.uk
Joint Project Manager: Olive Halliwell
Email: ohalliwell@ace-wigan.co.uk

Also at:
3rd Floor, Magnum House
Lord Street
Leigh
Greater Manchester WN7 1DT
Tel: 01942 261220
Fax: 01942 261220
Joint Project Manager: Pauline Wake
Email: pwake@ace-wigan.co.uk

Adult College of Barking and Dagenham
Fanshawe Crescent
Dagenham
Essex RM9 5QA
Tel: 020 8270 4722
Fax: 020 8270 4733
Email: adult-collegeenquiries@lbbd.gov.uk
Website:
www.adult-college.bardaglea.org.uk
Head of College: Patricia Cooney

Adult College Lancaster
White Cross Education Centre
Quarry Road
Lancaster LA1 3SE
Tel: 01524 581217
Fax: 01524 849458
Website: www.theadultcollege.org
Principal: John Wright

Art Shape
26 Station Road
Gloucester GL1 1EW
Tel: 01452 307684
Fax: 01452 541145
Email: info@artshape.co.uk
Website: www.artshape.co.uk
Managing Director: Lucy Sharp

Birmingham and Solihull Mental Health Trust

Social Inclusion Team
Uffculme Annexe
52–80 Queensbridge Road
Moseley
Birmingham B13 8QY
Tel: 0121 678 2700
Fax: 0121 678 2701
Website: www.bsmht.nhs.uk

Bromley Adult Education College

London Borough of Bromley
Widmore Centre
Nightingale Lane
Bromley
Kent BR1 2SQ
Tel: 020 8460 0020
Fax: 020 8466 7299
Website: www.bromleyadulteducation.ac.uk
Principal: Michael Wheeler

Centrepoint

25 Camperdown Street
London E1 8DZ
Tel: 0845 466 3400
Fax: 0845 466 3500
Website: www.centrepoint.org.uk

Comberton Village College

West Street
Comberton
Cambridge CB23 7DU
Tel: 01223 264721
Fax: 01223 264548
Email: commed@comberton.cambs.sch.uk
Deputy Principal, Community Education:
Diana Cook

The Connection at St Martins

12 Adelaide Street
London WC2N 4HW
Tel: 020 7766 5547
Fax: 020 7839 6277
Email: denise.henson@cstm.org.uk
Website:
www.connection-at-stmartins.org.uk
Manager, Employment, Training and
Education Services: Bill Williams

County Durham Learning

Bishop Auckland College
Woodhouse Lane
Bishop Auckland
Durham DL14 6JZ
Tel: 01388 443 078
Fax: 01388 609 294
Project Manager: Charmian Walter

Crewe and Nantwich Lifelong Learning Partnership

Part of Crewe and Nantwich Local Strategic
Partnership
4th Floor, Delamere House
Delamere Street
Crewe CW1 2JZ
Tel: 01270 537510
Fax: 01270 537265
Website: www.cnlsp.org.uk
Lifelong Learning Partnership Co-ordinator:
Helen Costello

DC Accountancy Services Ltd

Waltham Forest Business Centre
Unit 11, 2nd Floor
5 Blackhorse Lane
London E17 6DS

The Disabled People's Electronic Village Hall

The Walsh Building
Town Hall Way
Dewsbury
West Yorkshire WF12 8EE
Tel: 01924 453502
Fax: 01924 461084
Website: www.electroville.org.uk

E-mpirical Ltd

Science and Technology Centre
University of Reading
Earley Gate
Whiteknights Road
Reading RG6 6BZ
Tel: 0118 935 7370
Fax: 0118 926 7917
Website: www.e-mpirical.com
Managing Director: Tony Worsdall

The Elthorne Learning Centre
7 Elthorne Road
London N19 4AJ
Tel: 020 7272 8960
Fax: 020 7561 0084
Website: www.elthornelearningcentre.co.uk
Director: Rebecca Brown

Foleshill Women's Training
70–72 Elmsdale Avenue
Coventry CV6 6ES
Tel: 02476 637 693
Fax: 02476 662 854
Email: office@fwt.org.uk
Website: www.fwt.org.uk
Centre Manager: Christine McNaught

Granada Learning
414 Chiswick High Street
London W4 5TF
Tel: 020 8996 3362
Fax: 020 8742 8390
Website: www.granada-learning.com

Hampstead Garden Suburb Institute
11 High Road
East Finchley
London N2 8LL
Tel: 020 8829 4141
Fax: 020 8829 4131
Email: office@hgsi.ac.uk
Website: www.hgsi.ac.uk
Principal and Chief Executive: Fay Naylor

Joint Society of Business Practitioners and Managing and Marketing Association
New House
Warmingham Road
Warmingham
Sandbach
Cheshire CW11 3QP
Tel: 01270 526339
Fax: 01270 526339
Email: info@mamsasbp.com

Kalyx Services
HMP Peterborough
Saville Road
Westwood
Peterborough PE3 7PD

Kent Adult Education Service
College Road
Sittingbourne
Kent ME10 1LF
Tel: 01795 415900
Email: contactcentre.adulteducation@kent.gov.uk
Website: www.kent.gov.uk/adulted
Assistant to Head of Adult Education Service: Cheryl Melloy
Head of Service: Ian Forward

Kenton College
Drayton Road
Newcastle upon Tyne NE3 3RU
Tel: 0191 271 4222
Fax: 0191 271 6777
Email: kcce@kenton.newcastle.sch.uk
Area Manager: Caroline Miller

Learning Skills Wales – Dysgu'r Ddawn Cymru
Community Learning Centre
The Old Stables
Tydden-Y-Waen
Llanfechell
Amlwch
Isle of Anglesey LL68 0UF
Tel: 01407 711599
Email: learningskillswales@btinternet.com
Website: www.learning-skills-wales.com

Lifeline Community Projects
Lifeline Family Training Centre
Lifeline House
Neville Road
Dagenham
Essex RM8 3QL
Tel: 020 8597 2900
Fax: 020 8597 1990
Website: www.lifelineprojects.co.uk

Linkage Community Trust
Toynton Campus
Main Road
Toynton All Saints
Spilsby
Lincolnshire PE23 5AE
Tel: 01970 752499
Fax: 01970 754058
Email: college@linkage.org.uk
Website: www.linkage.org.uk

MacIntyre
602 South Seventh Street
Milton Keynes MK9 2JA
Tel: 01908 230100
Fax: 01908 695643
Website: www.macintyrecharity.org
Lifelong Learning Director: Brenda Mullen

McKenley-Simpson Ltd
Woodlands
New Road
Churchill
North Somerset BS25 5NR
Tel: 01934 853 739
Email: mckenley-simpson@btconnect.com
Website: www.mckenley-simpson.co.uk
Director: Dr Jan McKenley
Email: mckenley-simpson@btconnect.com

Medway Adult Learning Service
Green Street
Gillingham
Kent ME7 5TJ
Tel: 01634 338 400
Fax: 01634 338 401
Website:
www.medway.gov.uk/learning/adults
Acting Adult Learning Manager: Sue
Hopkins

Merton Adult Education
Whatley Avenue
London SW20 9NS
Tel: 020 8543 9292
Fax: 020 8544 1421
Email: info@merton-adult-education.ac.uk
Website:
www.merton.gov.uk/adulteducation
Head of Service: Yvonne Tomlin

**Open Doors International
Language School**
28 Woodland Terrace Lane
Plymouth
Devon PL4 8QL
Tel: 01752 258771
Website: www.odils.com
Chief Executive Officer: Cassie Roberts

**Orchard Hill College of
Further Education**
Old Town Hall
Woodcote Road
Wallington
Surrey SM6 0NB
Tel: 020 8254 7820
Fax: 020 8254 9800
Email: orchardhill@suttonlea.org
Website: www.orchardhill.ac.uk
Vice-Principal: Simon Vines

Peabody Trust
45 Westminster Bridge Road
London SE1 7JB
Tel: 020 7021 4254
Fax: 020 7021 4006
Website: www.peabody.org.uk
Community Services Director:
Stephen Burns

Preston DISC
103 Church Street
Preston PR1 3BS
Tel: 01772 558 863
Website: www.prestondisc.org.uk
Manager: Melanie Close

**Preston Road Neighbourhood
Development Company**
Preston Road Regeneration Centre
Flinton Grove
Hull HU9 5SN
Tel: 01482 789 680
Fax: 01482 710 011
Email: lee.west@kuhregen.org
Website: www.prndc.com

Redbridge Institute of Adult Education
Gaysham Avenue, Gants Hill
Ilford
Essex IG2 6TD
Tel: 020 8550 2398
Fax: 020 8551 7584
Email: info@redbridge-iae.ac.uk
Website: www.redbridge-iae.ac.uk
Head of Adult and Community Learning:
Joni Cunningham

South Craven Community Action
Community Office
Holme Lane
Cross Hills
Keighley
West Yorkshire BD20 7RL
Tel: 01535 639 040
Website: www.sccaco.com
Chief Executive: Milton Pearson

Southend Adult Community College
Southchurch Centre
Ambleside Drive
Southend on Sea
Essex SS1 2UP
Tel: 01702 445700
Fax: 01702 445739
Email: sacc@southend-adult.ac.uk
Website: www.southend-adult.ac.uk
Principal: Ali Hadawi

SOVA Head Office
1st Floor, Chichester House
37 Brixton Road
London SW9 6DZ
Tel: 020 7793 0404
Fax: 020 7735 4410
Website: www.sova.org.uk/about.htm
Director of Learning and Quality:
Susan Cooper

Thurrock Adult Community College
Richmond Road
Grays
Essex RM17 6DN
Tel: 01375 372476
Fax: 01375 394104
Email: s.walsh@tacc.ac.uk
Website: www.thurrock.gov.uk/adultcollege
Principal: Sharon Walsh

Tribal Learning and Publishing
Forsyth House
Alpha Business Park
Monks Cross Drive
Huntington
York YO32 9WN
Tel: 01904 550110
Fax: 01904 640703
Website: www.network-publishing.co.uk
Business Development Manager:
Sandra Furby

Voice of the Listener & Viewer
101 King's Drive
Gravesend
Kent DA12 5BQ
Tel: 01474 352835
Fax: 01474 351112
Email: info@vlv.org.uk
Website: www.vlv.org.uk

Waterford Institute of Technology
Cork Road
Waterford
Ireland
Email: info@wit.ie
Website: www.wit.ie

Westminster Adult Education Service
Amberley Road Centre
Amberley Road
Maida Vale
London W9 2JJ
Tel: 020 7641 8182
Website: www.waes.ac.uk
Head of Service: Barbara Holm

Westwood and Ravensthorpe Development Trust
33 Hampton Court
Westwood
Peterborough PE3 7JB
Tel: 01733 268106
Fax: 01733 333044
Deputy Trust Manager: David Spark

Workplace-led Learning – England

UK Commission for Employment and Skills (UKCES)
3 Callflex Business Park
Golden Smithies Lane
Wath-upon-Dearne
Rotherham
South Yorkshire S63 7ER
Tel: 01709 774800
Fax: 01709 774801
Email: info@ukces.org.uk
Website: www.ukces.org.uk
Chief Executive: Chris Humphries

The Commission aims to raise UK prosperity and opportunity by improving employment and skills.

Its ambition is to benefit employers, individuals and government by advising how improved employment and skills systems can help the UK become a world-class leader in productivity, in employment and in having a fair and inclusive society: all this in the context of a fast-changing global economy. Because employers, whether in private business or the public sector, have prime responsibility for the achievement of greater productivity, the UK Commission will strengthen the employer voice and provide greater employer influence over the employment and skills systems.

Having developed a view of what's needed, the UK Commission will provide independent advice to the highest levels in the four UK governments to help achieve those improvements through strategic policy development, evidence-based analysis and the exchange of good practice.

Sector Skills Councils

Asset Skills
2 The Courtyard
48 New North Road
Exeter EX4 4EP
Tel: 01392 423399
Fax: 01392 423373

Email: enquiries@assetskills.org
Website: www.assetskills.org
Chief Executive: Richard Beamish

Also at:
Northampton Office
Sol House
29 St. Katherine's Street
Northampton NN1 2QZ
Tel: 01604 233336
Fax: 01604 233573
Website: www.assetskills.org
Director of Research & Development:
Chris James

Automotive Skills
Fanshaws
Brickendon
Hertford SG13 8PQ
Tel: 01992 511521
Fax: 01992 511548
Email: imi@motor.org.uk
Website: www.motor.org.uk
Chief Executive: Sarah Sillars
Head of Skills Development: Steve Schofield

Cogent SSC Ltd
Unit 5, Mandarin Court
Centre Park
Warrington WA1 1GG
Tel: 01925 515200
Fax: 01925 515240
Email: info@cogent-ssc.com
Website: www.cogent-ssc.com

The Sector Skills Council for chemicals, pharmaceuticals, nuclear, oil and gas, petroleum and polymers.

Also at:
Minerva House
Bruntland Road
Portlethen
Aberdeen AB12 4QL
Tel: 01224 787800
Fax: 01224 787830

ConstructionSkills
Bircham Newton
Kings Lynn
Norfolk PE31 6RH
Tel: 01485 557557
Fax: 01485 577793
Email: call.centre@cskills.org
Website: www.constructionskills.net

Creative and Cultural Skills
Lafone House
The Leathermarket
Weston Street
London SE1 3HN
Tel: 020 7015 1800
Fax: 020 7015 1847
Email: info@ccskills.org.uk
Website: www.ccskills.org.uk
Chief Executive: Tom Bewick

e-skills UK
1 Castle Lane
London SW1E 6DR
Tel: 020 7963 8920
Fax: 020 7592 9138
Email: info@e-skills.com
Website: www.e-skills.com
Chief Executive Officer: Karen Price

Energy and Utility Skills
Friars Gate
1011 Stratford Road
Shirley
Solihull
West Midlands B90 4BN
Tel: 0845 077 9922
Fax: 0845 077 9933
Email: enquiries@euskills.co.uk
Website: www.euskills.co.uk
Chief Executive: Tim Balcon

Financial Services Skills Council
51 Gresham Street
London EC2V 7HQ
Tel: 0845 257 3772
Fax: 0845 257 3770
Email: info@fssc.org.uk
Website: www.fssc.org.uk
Chief Executive: Teresa Sayers
Communications and PR Officer:
Sue Martin

GoSkills
Concorde House
Trinity Park
Solihull
Birmingham B37 7UQ
Tel: 0121 635 5520
Fax: 0121 635 5521
Email: info@goskills.org
Website: www.goskills.org
Chief Executive: Peter Huntington

The Sector Skills Council for passenger
transport.

Government Skills
c/o DIUS
1st Floor, Kingsgate House
66–74 Victoria Street
London SW1E 6SW
Tel: 020 7276 1338
Email: info@government-skills.gsi.gov.uk
Website: www.government-skills.gov.uk
Head of Professional Skills for Government:
David Weaver

Improve Ltd – The Food and Drink Sector Skills Council
Ground Floor, Providence House
2 Innovation Close
Heslington
York YO10 5ZF
Tel: 0845 644 0448
Fax: 0845 644 0449
Email: info@improveltd.co.uk
Website: www.improveltd.co.uk
Company Secretary: Stephen Chambers
Chief Executive Officer: Jack Matthews

Lantra
Lantra House
Stoneleigh Park
Kenilworth
Coventry
Warwickshire CV8 2LG
Tel: 0845 707 8007
Fax: 024 769 6732
Email: connect@lantra.co.uk
Website: www.lantra.co.uk
Interim Head of Marketing:
Christopher Hobbs

The Sector Skills Council for the
environmental and land-based sector
(including farming, agriculture, forestry and
rural development).

Lifelong Learning UK
5th Floor, St Andrew's House
18–20 St. Andrew Street
London EC4A 3AY
Tel: 0870 757 7890
Fax: 0870 757 7889
Email: enquiries@lluk.org
Website: www.lluk.org
Chief Executive: David Hunter

Lifelong Learning UK is responsible for the
professional development of all those
working in libraries, archives and
information services, work-based learning,
higher education, further education and
community learning and development.

People First
2nd Floor, Armstrong House
38 Market Square
Uxbridge
Middlesex UB8 1LH
Tel: 0870 060 2550
Fax: 0870 060 2551
Email: info@people1st.co.uk
Website: www.people1st.co.uk
Director of Research and Policy:
Martin-Christian Kent

Proskills
Centurion Court
85b Milton Park
Abingdon
Oxfordshire OX14 4RY
Tel: 01235 432032
Fax: 01235 833733
Email: info@proskills.co.uk
Website: www.proskills.co.uk
Chief Executive: Terry Watts

Sector Skills Council for Science, Engineering and Manufacturing Technologies
14 Upton Road
Watford
Hertfordshire WD18 0JT
Tel: 01923 238441
Fax: 01923 256086
Website: www.semta.org.uk

SEMTA – Science, Engineering and
Manufacturing Technologies Alliance

Skillfast-UK
Richmond House
Lawnswood Business Park
Redvers Close
Leeds LS16 6RD
Tel: 0113 239 9600
Fax: 0113 239 9601
Email: enquiries@skillfast-uk.org
Website: www.skillfast-uk.org
Chief Executive: Linda Florance

The Sector Skills Council for Fashion and
Textiles.

Skills Active
Castlewood House
77–91 New Oxford Street
London WC1A 1PX
Tel: 020 7632 2000
Fax: 020 7632 2001
Website: www.skillsactive.com
Chief Executive: Stephen Studd

Skills for Care and Development
2nd Floor, City Exchange
11 Albion Street
Leeds LS1 5ER
Tel: 0113 390 7666
Email:
sscinfo@skillsforcareanddevelopment.org.uk

Skills for Health
1st Floor, Goldsmiths House
Broad Plain
Bristol BS2 0JP
Tel: 0117 922 1155
Fax: 0117 925 1800
Email: office@skillsforhealth.org.uk
Website: www.skillsforhealth.org.uk
Chief Executive: John Rogers

Skills for Justice
Centre Court
Atlas Way
Sheffield S4 7QQ
Tel: 0114 261 1499
Email: info@skillsforjustice.com
Website: www.skillsforjustice.com
Chief Executive: Alan Woods

Skills for Logistics
12 Warren Yard
Warren Farm Office Village
Stratford Road
Milton Keynes
Buckinghamshire MK12 5NW
Tel: 01908 313360
Fax: 01908 313006
Email: info@skillsforlogistics.org
Website: www.skillsforlogistics.org
Interim Chief Executive: Dr Mick Jackson

Skillset
Focus Point
21 Caledonian Road
London N1 9GB
Tel: 020 7713 9800
Email: info@skillset.org
Website: www.skillset.org
Chief Executive: Dinah Caine

The Sector Skills Council for the creative
media industries.

Skillsmart Retail Ltd
4th Floor
93 Newman Street
London W1T 3DT
Tel: 020 7462 5060
Fax: 020 7462 5061
Email: contactus@skillsmartretail.com
Website: www.skillsmartretail.com
Chief Executive Officer: Anne Seaman
Standards and Qualifications Manager:
Beverley Paddey
Skills Co-ordinator (Literacy, Numeracy,
ESOL and ICT): Jayne Norman

Summitskills
Vega House
Opal Court
Opal Drive
Fox Milne
Milton Keynes MK15 0DF
Tel: 01908 303960
Fax: 01908 303989
Email: enquiries@summitskills.org.uk
Website: www.summitskills.org.uk
Chief Executive: Keith Marshall

National and Regional Organisations

Association of Learning Providers
Colenso House
46 Bath Hill
Keynsham
Bristol BS31 1HG
Tel: 0117 986 5389
Fax: 0117 986 6196
Website: www.learningproviders.org
Chairman: Martin Dunford
Chief Executive: Graham Hoyle

Representing providers of quality
work-based and other vocational learning,
working with government and others, to
develop and implement effective workforce
development policies.

Business in the Community
137 Shepherdess Walk
London N1 7RQ
Tel: 020 7566 8650
Fax: 020 7253 1877
Email: information@bitc.org.uk
Website: www.bitc.org.uk
Education Director: Nick Chambers

Chartered Institute of Personnel and Development
151 The Broadway
London SW19 1JQ
Tel: 020 8612 6200
Email: cipd@cipd.co.uk
Website: www.cipd.co.uk
Chief Executive Officer: Jackie Orme

The Chartered Institute of Personnel and
Development is the pre-eminent professional
body in the field of people management and
development with over 130,000 members.
The Institute was formed from the Institute
of Personnel Management and the Institute
of Training and Development, which were
united on 1 July 1994. It received its Royal
Charter in July 2000. The CIPD offers a
wide range of services, including over 130
training events, various levels of
membership, a professional education
scheme, books, consultancy and a full
library and information service.

College of Estate Management

Whiteknights
Reading
Berkshire RG6 6AW
Tel: 0800 019 9697
Fax: 0118 921 4620
Email: courses@cem.ac.uk
Website: www.cem.ac.uk

Ford EDAP

40–107 Trafford House
Station Way
Basildon
Essex SS16 5XX
Tel: 01268 702268
Fax: 01268 702145
EDAP National Co-ordinator: Rob Brittle
EDAP National Co-ordinator: John Scarola
EDAP National Co-ordinator: Des Marples

GMB Learning Partnerships
London Region

38–40 Bethel Street
Norwich NR2 1NR
Tel: 01603 625260
Fax: 01603 766516
Email: jenny.webber@gmb.org.uk
Website: www.gmbunion-eastlearning.org
Project Worker (Suffolk and Norfolk):
Lillian Dobbs
Project Worker (London): Sean Ellis
Project Worker (Migrant Workers):
Adriano Guedes
Training and Development Officer:
Jenny Webber

Hertsmere Worknet

The Old Post Office
23 Shenley Road
Borehamwood
Hertfordshire WD6 1AU
Tel: 020 8236 7600
Fax: 020 8236 7609
Email: admin@worknet.org.uk
Website: www.worknet.org.uk
Business Manager: Allison Overington

Investors in People UK

7–10 Chandos Street
London W1G 9DQ
Tel: 020 7467 1900
Fax: 020 7636 2386
Website: www.investorsinpeople.co.uk
Chief Executive: Simon Jones

The National Council for Work Experience (NCWE)

Prospects House
Booth Street East
Manchester M13 9EP
Tel: 0845 601 5510
Fax: 0161 277 5220
Website: www.work-experience.org
Director: Heather Collier

UK Skills

5 Portland Place
London W1B 1PW
Tel: 020 7580 1011
Fax: 020 7612 9277
Email: ukskills@ukskills.org.uk
Website: www.ukskills.org.uk
Chief Executive: Kevin Bartley CBE

The Work Foundation

21 Palmer Street
London SW1H 0AD
Tel: 020 7976 3500
Fax: 020 7976 3600
Website: www.theworkfoundation.com
Executive Vice-Chair: Will Hutton

Other Workplace-led Learning Organisations

Association for Ceramic Training and Development

Unit 1, Riverside 2
Campbell Road
Stoke-on-Trent ST4 4RJ
Tel: 01782 747828
Fax: 01782 846450
Email: actd@actd.co.uk
Website: www.actd.co.uk
Director: Keith Marsh

Association of the British Pharmaceutical Industry (ABPI)
12 Whitehall
London SW1A 2DY
Tel: 020 7930 3477
Fax: 020 7747 1411
Website: www.abpi.org.uk
Chief Executive: Ian Irving

BPEC Services Ltd
2 Mallard Way
Pride Park
Derby DE24 8GX
Tel: 0845 121 6558
Fax: 0845 121 1931
Email: info@bpec.org.uk
Website: www.bpec.org.uk
Business Development Manager: Paul Cullen

British Coatings Federation
James House
Bridge Street
Leatherhead
Surrey KT22 7EP
Tel: 01372 360660
Fax: 01372 376069
Email: carol.walsh@bcf.co.uk
Website: www.careersincoatings.org.uk

Confederation of Paper Industries
1 Rivenhall Road
Swindon
Wiltshire SN5 7BD
Tel: 01793 889600
Fax: 01793 878700
Email: cpi@paper.org.uk
Website: www.paper.org.uk
Company Secretary: Des Fogerty

Council for Administration (CfA)
6 Graphite Square
Vauxhall Walk
London SE11 5EE
Tel: 020 7091 9620
Fax: 020 7091 7340
Email: info@cfa.uk.com
Website: www.cfa.uk.com
Chief Executive Officer: Jenny Hewell

The Council for Administration is the leading authority for Business and Administration Skills in the UK.

ECITB (Engineering Construction Industry Training Board)
Blue Court
Church Lane
Kings Langley
Hertfordshire WD4 8JP
Tel: 01923 260000
Fax: 01923 270969
Email: ecitb@ecitb.org.uk
Website: www.ecitb.org.uk

ENTO
Kimberley House
47 Vaughan Way
Leicester LE1 4SG
Tel: 0116 251 7979
Fax: 0116 251 1464
Email: info@ento.co.uk
Website: www.ento.co.uk
Managing Director: Tony Green
Director of Sales and Marketing: David Morgan

ENTO is the guardian of standards responsible for representing people who work in learning and development, personnel, health and safety, trade unions and advice, guidance and counselling. This includes responsibility for developing the National Occupational Standards that form the basis of S/NVQs in these areas.

EPIC Training and Consulting Services Limited
Alban Row
27–31 Verulan Road
St Albans
Hertfordshire AL3 4DG
Tel: 01727 869008
Fax: 01727 843318
Email: info@epicltd.co.uk
Website: www.epicltd.com
Financial and Systems Manager: Lynda McKill
Senior Training Advisor: Graham Crawshaw

FFINTO
67 Wollaton Road
Beeston
Nottingham NG9 2NG
Tel: 0115 922 1200
Fax: 0115 922 3833
Website: www.proskills.co.uk
Chief Executive: Julie Svimberska

Glass Training Limited
Suite 28, The Quadrant
99 Parkway Avenue
Sheffield S9 4WG
Tel: 0114 227 0070
Fax: 0114 227 0073
Email: info@glass-training.co.uk
Website: www.glass-training.co.uk
Training and Development Manager:
Denise Noble

Habia
Oxford House
Sixth Avenue
Sky Business Park
Robin Hood Airport
Doncaster
South Yorkshire DN9 3GG
Tel: 08452 306080
Fax: 01302 774949
Email: info@habia.org
Website: www.habia.org
PR and Communications Manager:
Mark Phillips

Habia is the government recognised
standards setting body for hair, beauty, nails
and spa therapy.

Institute of Customer Service
2 Castle Court
St Peters Street
Colchester
Essex CO1 1EW
Tel: 01206 571716
Fax: 01206 546688
Email: enquiries@icsmail.co.uk
Website:
www.instituteofcustomerservice.com
Standards and Qualifications Manager:
Beverly Dann

**Leadership Foundation for
Higher Education**
88 Kingsway
London WC2B 6AA
Tel: 020 7841 2804
Fax: 020 7681 6219
Email: tricia.wombell@lfhe.ac.uk
Website: www.lfhe.ac.uk
Director of Marketing and
Communications: Tricia Wombell

The Leadership Foundation for Higher
Education provides a dedicated service of
support and advice on leadership,
governance and management for all the UK's
Universities and Higher Education Colleges.

Meat Training Council
PO Box 141
Winterhill House
Snowdon Drive
Milton Keynes MK6 1YY
Tel: 01908 231062
Fax: 01908 231063
Email: info@meattraining.org.uk
Website: www.fdq.org.uk
Chief Executive: Bill Jermey
Awarding Body Manager: Angela Long

Merchant Navy Training Board
Carthusian Court
12 Carthusian Street
London EC1M 6EZ
Tel: 0800 085 0973
Email: enquiry@careersatsea.org
Website: www.careersatsea.org
Head of Education, Training and Careers:
Glenys Jackson

MetSkill (part of the Semta Group)
5–6 Meadowcourt
Amos Road
Sheffield
South Yorkshire S9 1BX
Tel: 0114 244 6833
Fax: 0114 256 2855
Email: enquiries@metskill.co.uk
Website: www.metskill.co.uk
Executive Director: Neil Smith

Port Skills and Safety
4th Floor, Carthusian Court
12 Carthusian Street
Tel: 020 7260 1790
London EC1M 6EZ
Email: info@portskillsandsafety.co.uk
Website: www.portskillsandsafety.co.uk

Sea Fish Industry Authority
Training and Accreditation Department
Humber Seafood Institute
1 Origin Way
Europarc
Grimsby
South Humberside DN37 9TZ
Tel: 01472 252300
Fax: 01472 268792
Email: training@seafish.co.uk
Website: www.seafish.org
Training Manager: Simon Potten

The Sea Fish Industry Authority develops, delivers and promotes training to people working in all aspects of the seafood industry from fishing to fish and chips. It is a partner in IMPROVE (The Sector Skills Council for Food and Drink) and a founder member of the Maritime Skills Alliance.

Skills for Security
Security House
Barbourne Road
Worcester WR1 1RS
Tel: 0845 0750111
Fax: 01905 724949
Email: info@skillsforsecurity.org.uk
Website: www.skillsforsecurity.org.uk
Chief Executive: David Greer

UK Workforce Hub
Regents Wharf
8 All Saints Street
London N1 9RL
Tel: 020 7520 2490
Fax: 020 7713 6300
Email: workforcehub@ukworkforcehub.org.uk
Website: www.ukworkforcehub.org.uk
Head of Workforce Hub in England:
Janet Fleming

The UK Workforce Hub works to promote skills development and good employment practice, and represents the interests of the third sector on these issues to government and other key stakeholders in the learning and skills arena.

Trade Union Education

Unionlearn
Congress House
23–28 Great Russell Street
London WC1B 3LS
Tel: 020 7467 1264
Fax: 020 7467 1265
Email: imurray@tuc.org.uk
Website: www.tuc.org.uk
Senior Policy Officer (Learning and Skills):
Iain Murray

In April 2006 the delivery of the TUC's union learning and education services was transferred to a new body called unionlearn, which also has its national headquarters at Congress House in London. However, the TUC retains responsibility for policy development on education, learning and skills. Unionlearn provides a range of support services for building union learning across the trade union movement and in particular by building the capacity of union learning reps and Union Learning Fund projects. It also provides support and advice to unions on negotiating with employers for education and training, and works with national, sectoral and local bodies on training policy and practice. Unionlearn also provides a programme of accredited courses for stewards, safety representatives, union learning reps, pension scheme trustees and other trade union representatives. Courses are provided on a day release from work basis and online, and access is free to representatives of affiliated trade unions.
Contact Liz Smith, Director:
Tel: 020 7079 6920
Email: lsmith@tuc.org.uk
Liz Rees, Trade Union Education Manager:
Tel: 020 7079 6922
Email: lrees@tuc.org.uk

Associated Society of Locomotive Engineers and Firemen

9 Arkwright Road
Hampstead
London NW3 6AB
Tel: 020 7317 8600
Fax: 020 7794 6406
Email: info@aslef.org.uk
Website: www.aslef.org.uk
National Organiser: Andy Reed

Association for College Management

35 The Point
Market Harborough
Leicestershire LE16 7QU
Tel: 01858 461110
Fax: 01858 461366
Email: administration@acm.uk.com
Website: www.acm.uk.com
General Secretary/Chief Executive:
Peter Pendle
Head of Policy: Nadine Cartner
Head of Employment Relations:
David Green
Head of Corporate Services: Sara Shaw

The Association for College Management is
a TUC affiliated trade union and
professional association which represents
managers of post-16 education and training.

Association of Teachers and Lecturers

7 Northumberland Street
London WC2N 5RD
Tel: 020 7930 6441
Fax: 020 7930 1359
Email: info@atl.org.uk
Website: www.atl.org.uk
General Secretary: Dr Mary Bousted

Bakers, Food and Allied Workers Union

Stanborough House
Great North Road
Stanborough
Welwyn Garden City
Hertfordshire AL8 7TA
Tel: 01707 260150
Fax: 01707 261570
Website: www.bfawu.org
General Secretary: Joe Marino

Broadcasting, Entertainment, Cinematograph and Theatre Union

373–377 Clapham Road
London SW9 9BT
Tel: 020 7346 0900
Fax: 020 7346 0901
Email: learn@bectu.org.uk
Website: www.bectu.org.uk/training
Training Officer: Brian Kelly

Communication Workers Union

150 The Broadway
Wimbledon
London SW19 1RX
Tel: 020 8971 7340
Fax: 020 8971 7300
Email: tlavelle@cwu.org
Website: www.cwueducation.org
Head of Education and Training:
Trish Lavelle
Policy Adviser: Patrick Styles
Learning Projects: Paul Dovey

Community

Swinton House
324 Gray's Inn Road
London WC1X 8DD
Tel: 020 7239 1200
Fax: 020 7278 8378
Email: info@community-tu.org
Website: www.community-tu.org
Chief Executive Officer: Michael Leahy

Community and Youth Workers' Union (CYWU)

CYWU/Unite
Transport House
211 Broad Street
Birmingham B15 1AY
Tel: 0121 643 6221
Email: kerry.jenkins@unitetheunion.com
Website: www.cywu.org.uk
National Secretary: Doug Nicholls
Section Operations Officer: Kerry Jenkins

Connect

30 St George's Road
Wimbledon
London SW19 4BD
Tel: 020 8971 6000
Fax: 020 8971 6002
Email: union@connectuk.org
Website: www.connectuk.org

Fire Brigades Union
Bradley House
68 Coombe Road
Kingston upon Thames
Surrey KT2 7AE
Tel: 020 8541 1765
Fax: 020 8546 5187
Email: office@fbu.org.uk
Website: www.fbu.org.uk
National Officer: Dean Mills

GMB
National Office
22–24 Worple Road
London SW19 4DD
Tel: 020 8947 3131
Fax: 020 8944 6552
Email: info@gmb.org.uk
Website: www.gmb.org.uk

National Association of Schoolmasters Union of Women Teachers (NASUWT)
Hillscourt Education Centre
Rose Hill
Rednal
Birmingham B45 8RS
Tel: 0121 453 6150
Fax: 0121 457 6208
Email: nasuwt@mail.nasuwt.org.uk
Website: www.teachersunion.org.uk
General Secretary: Chris Keates

National Union of Journalists
Headland House
308 Gray's Inn Road
London WC1X 8DP
Tel: 020 7278 7916
Fax: 020 7837 8143
Email: info@nuj.org.uk
General Secretary: Jeremy Dear

National Union of Mineworkers
Miners' Offices
2 Huddersfield Road
Barnsley
South Yorkshire S70 2LS
Tel: 01226 215555
Fax: 01226 215561
Website: www.num.org.uk
NUM President: Ian Lavery

National Union of Rail, Maritime and Transport Workers
39 Chalton Street
London NW1 1JD
Tel: 020 7387 4771
Fax: 020 7529 8808
Email: info@rmt.org.uk
Website: www.rmt.org.uk
Education Officer: Ray Spry-Shute
Email: r.spryshute@rmt.org.uk

National Union of Teachers
Membership and Communications
Department
Hamilton House
Mabledon Place
London WC1H 9BD
Tel: 020 7388 6191
Fax: 020 7387 8458
Website: www.teachers.org.uk
Principal Officer, Recruitment and Training:
Ruth Blunt

Prospect
New Prospect House
8 Leake Street
London SE1 7NN
Tel: 020 7902 6600
Fax: 020 7902 6667
Email: enquiries@prospect.org.uk
Website: www.prospect.org.uk
Education and Development Officer:
Paul Casey
Education and Development Officer:
Rachel Bennett

Public and Commercial Services Union
Organising and Learning Services
Department
160 Falcon Road
London SW11 2LN
Tel: 020 7924 2727
Fax: 020 7801 2630
Email: learningservices@pcs.org.uk
Website: www.pcs.org.uk/learning
Director of Organising and Learning
Services: Kim Burridge

Society of Radiographers
207 Providence Square
Mill Street
London SE1 2EW
Tel: 020 7740 7200
Fax: 020 7740 7204
Email: info@sor.org
Website: www.sor.org
Research Officer: Claire Dumbleton

Transport Salaried Staffs' Association
Walkden House
10 Melton Street
London NW1 2EJ
Tel: 020 7387 2101
Fax: 020 7383 0656
Email: enquiries@tssa.org.uk
Website: www.tssa.org.uk
Education Officer: Jon Clark

Union of Construction, Allied Trades and Technicians
UCATT House
177 Abbeville Road
London SW4 9RL
Tel: 020 7622 2442
Fax: 020 7720 4081
Website: www.ucatt.org.uk
National Education Training Co-ordinator:
Jeffrey Hopewell
Email: jhopewell@ucatt.org.uk

Union of Shop, Distributive and Allied Workers
188 Wilmslow Road
Fallowfield
Manchester M14 6LJ
Tel: 0161 224 2804
Fax: 0161 257 2566
Email: enquiries@usdaw.org.uk
Website: www.usdaw.org.uk
Head of Education and Training: James Rees
Email: james.rees@usdaw.org.uk

UNISON
1 Mabledon Place
London WC1H 9AJ
Tel: 0845 355 0845
Fax: 0207 551 1758
Email:
learning&organisingenquiries@unison.co.uk
Website: www.unison.org.uk
Head of Learning and Organising Services:
Pamela Johnson

Unite the Union
Education and International Department
128 Theobalds Road
London WC1X 8TN
Tel: 020 7611 2628
Website: www.unitetheunion.org.uk
Director of Education: Jim Mowatt
Email: jim.mowatt@unitetheunion.com

Lifelong Learning
Hayes Court
West Common Road
Hayes
Bromley
Kent BR2 7AU
Tel: 020 8462 7755
Fax: 020 8315 8234
Email: tom.beattie@unitetheunion.com
Website: www.unitetheunion.org.uk
Head of Lifelong Learning: Tom Beattie

Unity
Hillcrest House
Garth Street
Hanley
Stoke-on-Trent ST1 2AB
Tel: 01782 272 755
Fax: 01782 284 902
Email: all@unitytheunion.org.uk
Website: www.unitytheunion.org.uk
General Secretary: Geoff Bagnall
Education Officer: Garry Oakes

UCU University and College Union
27 Britannia Street
London WC1X 9JP
Tel: 020 7837 3636
Fax: 020 7837 4403
Email: hq@ucu.org.uk
Website: www.ucu.org.uk
General Secretary: Sally Hunt
Senior National Official: Dan Taubman
Tel: 020 7520 3230
Email: dtaubman@natfhe.org.uk

The largest trade union and professional association for lecturers, trainers, researchers and managers working in adult, further and higher education throughout England, Wales, Scotland and Northern Ireland.

Education-related and Other Organisations

Action for Blind People
14–16 Verney Road
London SE16 3DZ
Tel: 020 7635 4800
Fax: 020 7635 4900
Email: info@actionforblindpeople.org
Website: www.actionforblindpeople.org.uk
Head of Services: Miriam Martin
Head of Service Development:
Colin Whitbourn
Information and Advice Service National
Helpline: 0800 915 4666

Action with Communities in Rural England (ACRE)
Somerford Court
Somerford Road
Cirencester
Gloucestershire GL7 1TW
Tel: 01285 653477
Fax: 01285 654537
Email: acre@acre.org.uk
Website: www.acre.org.uk
Head of Corporate Development:
Julie Soutter

ADSET
The Business Exchange
Rockingham Road
Kettering
Northamptonshire NN16 8JX
Tel: 0779 627 3792
Email: info@adset.org.uk
Website: www.adset.org.uk
General Manager: Hazel Edmunds

An Viet Foundation
12–14 Englefield Road
London N1 4LS
Tel: 020 7275 7780
Fax: 020 7275 8510
Email: anviet@anvietuk.org
Website: www.anvietuk.org
Director: Vu Khanth Thanh

Arts Council England
14 Great Peter Street
London SW1P 3NQ
Tel: 0845 300 6200
Fax: 020 7973 6833
Email: enquiries@artscouncil.org.uk
Website: www.artscouncil.org.uk
Director of Learning and Skills: Laura
Gander-Howe

The Arts Council has nine regional offices
covering the whole of England. Information
about the offices can be found at
www.artscouncil.org.uk

Arts Council England, East
Eden House
48–49 Bateman Street
Cambridge CB2 1LR
Tel: 01223 454400
Fax: 0870 242 1271
Website: www.artscouncil.org.uk
Head of Development: Paul Russ
Textphone: 01223 306893

Arts Council England, East Midlands
St Nicholas Court
25–27 Castle Gate
Nottingham NG1 7AR
Tel: 0845 300 6200
Fax: 0115 989 2467
Email: enquiries@artscouncil.org.uk
Website: www.artscouncil.org.uk
Head of Development: Rebecca Blackman

Arts Council England, London
2 Pear Tree Court
London EC1R 0DS
Tel: 0845 300 6200
Fax: 020 7608 4100
Email: london@artscouncil.org.uk
Website: www.artscouncil.org.uk
Head of Development, Education and
Learning: Abigail Moss
Textphone: 020 608 6158

Arts Council England, North East

Central Square
Forth Street
Newcastle upon Tyne NE1 3PJ
Tel: 0845 300 6200
Fax: 0191 230 1020
Email: northeast@artscouncil.org.uk
Website: www.artscouncil.org.uk
Education and Learning Officer:
Clare Edwards
Textphone: 0191 255 8500

Arts Council England, North West

Manchester House
22 Bridge Street
Manchester M3 3AB
Tel: 0845 300 6200
Fax: 0161 834 6969
Email: northwest@artscouncil.org.uk
Website: www.artscouncil.org.uk
Education and Learning Officer:
Claire Eddleston-Rose
Textphone: 0161 827 9215

Arts Council England, South East

Sovereign House
Church Street
Brighton BN1 1RA
Tel: 0870 300 6200
Fax: 0870 242 1257
Email: southeast@artscouncil.org.uk
Website: www.artscouncil.org.uk
Head of Development: Marina Norris
Development Officer – Education and
Learning: Rose Kigwana
Textphone: 01273 710659

Arts Council England, South West

Senate Court
Southernhay Gardens
Exeter EX1 1UG
Tel: 0845 300 6200
Fax: 01392 229229
Email: enquiries@artscouncil.org.uk
Website: www.artscouncil.org.uk
Head of Learning: Rachael Sutton
Head of Development: Simon Sutton
Textphone: 01392 433503

Arts Council England, West Midlands

82 Granville Street
Birmingham B1 2LH
Tel: 0845 300 6200
Fax: 0121 643 7239
Email: westmidlands@artscouncil.org.uk
Website: www.artscouncil.org.uk
Officer, Learning and Education:
Emma Watson
Textphone: 0121 643 2815

Arts Council England, Yorkshire

21 Bond Street
Dewsbury
West Yorkshire WF13 1AX
Tel: 0845 300 6200
Fax: 01924 466522
Email: stephanie.simm@artscouncil.org.uk
Website: www.artscouncil.org.uk
Education and Learning Officer:
Stephanie Simm
Textphone: 01924 438585

ASET

International House
Siskin Parkway East
Middlemarch Business Park
Coventry CV3 4PE
Tel: 08707 202 909
Fax: 02476 516 505
Email: enquiries@ediplc.com
Website: www.aset.ac.uk
Chief Executive: Chris Daniel

Asian Advisory Service

26 Pear Tree Road
Derby DE23 6PY
Tel: 01332 224 106
Fax: 01332 297796
Email: asianadvisory@hotmail.com
Manager: Saima Ayaz

The Asian Advisory Service Derby is a
registered charity which exists to relieve
poverty, advance education, preserve and
protect the health of the ethnic minority
communities in the inner city of Derby by
provision of advice and information through
its drop-in centre.

Association For Education and Ageing
132 Dawes Road
London SW6 7EF
Tel: 020 7385 4641
Fax: 020 7385 4641
Email: aeasecretary@googlemail.com
Secretary: Carol Allen

The Association came into existence in 1985 and seeks to promote learning in later life. It includes within its international membership adult educators, policy makers, researchers and practitioners in various disciplines relevant to an ageing society and older people themselves.

Association for Language Learning
c/o University of Leicester
University Road
Leicester LE1 7RH
Tel: 0116 229 7453
Email: info@all-languages.org.uk
Website: www.all-languages.org.uk
Director: Linda Parker

The Association encourages membership of part-time teachers by offering a reduced subscription to those working less than eight hours per week. Its short in-service training courses cater for specific languages, language teaching in general, and for specific groups such as adult education tutors and trainees. There is always a programme for adult education language teachers at its annual conference and exhibition, Language World.

Association for Learning Technology (ALT)
Gipsy Lane
Headington
Oxford OX3 0BP
Tel: 01865 484125
Fax: 01865 484165
Email: admin@alt.ac.uk
Website: www.alt.ac.uk
Chief Executive: Seb Schmoller
Director of Development: Mark van Harmelen
Director of Operations: Marion Samler

ALT provides a website with contacts in UK universities, FE colleges and commercial and government organisations who are working on the application of technology in teaching and learning. It organises conferences and training events, responds to policy consultations and publishes a quarterly web and print-based newsletter, a tri-annual peer-reviewed journal and books. ALT-C 2009 will take place in Manchester.

Association for Science Education
College Lane
Hatfield
Hertfordshire AL10 9AA
Tel: 01707 283000
Fax: 01707 266532
Email: info@ase.org.uk
Website: www.ase.org.uk
Chief Executive: Prof. Derek Bell

Association of British Correspondence Colleges (ABCC)
PO Box 17926
London SW19 3WB
Tel: 020 8544 9559
Fax: 020 8540 7657
Email: info@homestudy.org.uk
Website: www.homestudy.org.uk
Secretary: Heather Owen

The Association represents the major private correspondence colleges in the UK. Its aims are to provide information and advice on correspondence education in Britain; to ensure that its members provide a high standard of tuition and efficient service; to safeguard the interests of students taking correspondence courses; to co-operate with ODLQC and other bodies concerned with further education; and to enhance the prestige of correspondence education.

Association of Continuing Education Librarians
South Wales Miners' Library
Swansea University
Hendrefoelan Campus
Swansea SA2 7NB
Tel: 0179 251 8693
Fax: 0179 251 8694
Email: s.f.williams@swansea.ac.uk
Librarian: Sian Williams

Association of National Specialist Colleges (NATSPEC)
27 Surrey Road
Bishopston
Bristol BS7 9DJ
Tel: 0117 923 2830
Email: chiefexecutive@natspec.org.uk
Website: www.natspec.org.uk
Chief Executive: Alison Boulton

Association of School and College Leaders
130 Regent Road
Leicester LE1 7PG
Tel: 0116 299 1122
Fax: 0116 299 1123
Email: info@ascl.org.uk
Website: www.ascl.org.uk
General Secretary: Dr John Dunford

Association of Teachers and Lecturers
7 Northumberland Street
London WC2N 5RD
Tel: 020 7930 6441
Fax: 020 7930 1359
Email: info@atl.org.uk
Website: www.atl.org.uk
General Secretary: Dr Mary Bousted

Association of Teachers of Lipreading to Adults
Westwood Park
London Road
Great Horkesley
Colchester CO6 4BS
Email: atla@lipreading.org.uk
Website: www.lipreading.org.uk
Chairperson: Bert Smale
Honorary Secretary: Mary Bayntun

BBC Learning
White City
201 Wood Lane
London W12 7TS
Tel: 020 8752 5252
Email: learning@bbc.co.uk
Website: www.bbc.co.uk/learning
Controller: Liz Cleaver
Head of Interactive Learning:
Myles Runham
Head of Learning Campaigns:
Elizabeth McKay
Head of Policy and Public Affairs:
Wendy Jones

Birmingham Royal Ballet
Thorp Street
Birmingham
West Midlands B5 4AU
Tel: 0121 245 3500
Fax: 0121 245 3570
Website: www.brb.org.uk
Human Resources Director: Lynn Colledge
Director for Learning: Pearl Chesterman

British Association for Literacy in Development (BALID)
36 Causton Street
London SW1P 4AU
Tel: 020 7426 5849
Fax: 020 7251 1314
Email: admin@balid.org.uk
Website: www.balid.org.uk
Chair: Brian Street
Administrator: Sarah Snow

BALID seeks to promote adult literacy as an integral part of the development process through professional networking and by sharing experience among practitioners and institutions in Britain and developing countries.

British Association for the Advancement of Science
Welcome Wolfson Building
165 Queen's Gate
London SW7 5HD
Tel: 020 7019 4930
Email: info@the-ba.net
Website: www.the-ba.net
Chief Executive: Sir Roland Jackson
Email: roland.jackson@the-ba.net

British Association of Settlements and Social Action Centres (bassac)
33 Corsham Street
London N1 6DR
Tel: 08452 410375
Fax: 08452 410376
Email: info@bassac.org.uk
Website: www.bassac.org.uk
Chief Executive: Ben Hughes
Head of Operations and Resources:
Kelly Essery

Bassac is a membership body for a network of organisations. It harnesses the power of its members' knowledge and experience by promoting collaborative partnerships, lobbying for change and sharing learning. Its members are 'multipurpose' organisations, providing an impressive range of high-quality services and facilities tailored to the needs of local people.

The British Council

10 Spring Gardens
London SW1A 2BN
Tel: 0161 957 7755 (general enquiries)
Fax: 0161 9577762
Email: general.enquiries@britishcouncil.org
Website: www.britishcouncil.org/learning

British Dyslexia Association

Unit 8, Bracknell Beeches
Old Bracknell Lane
Bracknell
Berkshire RG12 7BW
Tel: 0845 251 9003
Fax: 0845 251 9005
Email: admin@bdadyslexia.org.uk
Website: www.bdadyslexia.org.uk
Chief Executive: Judi Stewart
Helpline: 0845 251 9002
Email: helpline@bdadyslexia.org.uk

The British Institute for Learning and Development

Trym Lodge
1 Henbury Road
Westbury-on-Crym
Bristol BS39 3HQ
Tel: 0117 959 6517
Fax: 0117 959 6518
Email: info@thebild.org
Website: www.thebild.org
Business Manager: Sarah Wills

The New British Institute for Learning and Development builds on the success of the British Learning Association and will address the needs and raise the status of all those involved in learning and development (both organisations and individuals). With a focus on professionalism and performance improvement, it will provide coherence to a sector that embraces corporate, work-based and lifelong learning and vocational training.

British Interactive Media Association (BIMA)

Briarlea House
Southend Road
Billericay
Essex CM11 2PR
Tel: 0127 765 8107
Fax: 0870 051 7842
Email: info@bima.co.uk
Website: www.bima.co.uk
Administrator: Janice Cable

BIMA is the UK trade association for the interactive media industries. The BIMA Awards, which are presented annually, is the oldest established and most prestigious awards event in the interactive media calendar and celebrate the best in interactive media design and aptitude. The BIMA website also carries job vacancies and a discussion page for posting questions, answers, comments and criticisms.

British Library

96 Euston Road
London NW1 2DB
Tel: 0870 444 1500
Website: www.bl.uk
Chief Executive: Lynne Brindley
Head of Learning: Roger Walshe

The British Library is the UK's national library. The library has one of the largest collections anywhere in the world, spanning all subjects, and a huge range of formats – from manuscripts to maps, books to newspapers, sound to philatelic collections. The Library provides comprehensive reference, lending, document supply and bibliographic services on a national scale. Through its reading rooms it offers on-site access to our collections, with reference teams and search interfaces to help users find what they need. It also offers customised research services, specialising in intellectual property, science, medicine, business information and legislation. It runs the world's largest document supply service offering 24-hour access to collections – predominantly at article level. This service covers all disciplines across traditionally published material, as well as conferences, reports and theses, and provides a range of delivery options to suit customers, including electronic delivery. It aims to make the widest possible audience aware of its resources. Its public programme includes exhibitions, displays and events within the framework of faith, cultural, literary and science topics, all designed to inspire and stimulate, as well as encouraging people to consider further learning. Treasures from the national collections are on permanent display in the Library galleries, and digitised versions of a selection are also available online. Via the website users also have digital access to thousands of maps, prints and sound recordings and can access current and past exhibitions. The Library plays a crucial role in supporting education across the whole spectrum from primary schools to developing future researchers and participants in Higher Education. It has an active programme involving extensive use of the web, as well as on-site activities for learning groups. Further details can be found at www.bl.uk/learning.

British Refugee Council
240–250 Ferndale Road
London SW9 8BB
Tel: 020 7346 6700
Fax: 020 7737 3306
Website: www.refugeecouncil.org.uk
Director of Policy and Development:
Jonathan Ellis
Policy Adviser, Employment and Training:
James Lee

Campaign for Drawing
7 Gentleman's Row
Enfield
Middlesex EN2 6PT
Tel: 020 8351 1719
Fax: 020 8351 1719
Email: info@campaignfordrawing.org
Website: www.campaignfordrawing.org
Director: Sue Grayson Ford

Campaign for Learning
19 Buckingham Street
London WC2N 6EF
Tel: 020 7930 1111
Fax: 020 7930 1551
Email: info@cflearning.org.uk
Website: www.campaign-for-learning.org.uk
Chair: Simon Fuchs
Chief Executive: Tricia Hartley

The Campaign for Learning is working for a society where:

- everyone has the right to learn
- everyone understands and values learning
- everyone has chances to learn throughout their lives.

It has existed since 1996, helping to stimulate learning which excites, supports, develops and involves people all through their lives.

Campaign for Learning through Museums and Galleries
Gooseham Mill
Gooseham
Bude
Cornwall EX23 9PQ
Tel: 01288 331615
Email: directorsoffice@clmg.org.uk
Website: www.clmg.org.uk
Executive Director: Nicola Nuttall

Cathedrals as Partners in Adult Learning
c/o Gillian Aird – CPAL Secretary
NIACE
21 De Montfort Street
Leicester LE1 7GE
CPAL Secretary: Gillian Aird

Central Council of Physical Recreation (CCPR)
4th Floor, Burwood House
14–16 Caxton Street
London SW1H 0QT
Tel: 020 7976 3900
Fax: 020 7976 3901
Email: admin@ccpr.org.uk
Website: www.ccpr.org.uk
Chief Executive: Tim Lamb

The CCPR is the national umbrella association for governing bodies of sport and physical recreation.

Centre for Policy on Ageing
25–31 Ironmonger Row
London EC1V 3QP
Tel: 020 7553 6500
Fax: 020 7553 6501
Email: cpa@cpa.org.uk
Website: www.cpa.org.uk
Director: Gillian Crosby

Centre for Research into the Older Workforce (CROW)
21 De Montfort Street
Leicester LE1 7GE
Website: www.niace.org.uk/crow
Associate Director for Older Learners:
Prof. Stephen McNair

The Centre for Research into the Older Workforce exists to study the behaviour of the workforce after the age of 50. This includes the motivation of older people and their attitudes to work and retirement, the management and training of older workers and age discrimination law and practice. The Centre, created in 2003 as a research centre of the University of Surrey, became part of NIACE in August 2006.

The Centre for Research on the Wider Benefits of Learning
Institute of Education
20 Bedford Way
London WC1H 0AL
Tel: 020 7612 6291
Fax: 020 7612 6880
Email: info@learningbenefits.net
Website: www.learningbenefits.net
Director: Dr John Vorhaus

Centre for Studies on Inclusive Education
New Redland Building
Coldharbour Lane
Frenchay
Bristol BS16 1QU
Tel: 0117 328 4007
Fax: 0117 328 4005
Website: www.csie.org.uk
Director: Dr Artemi Sakellariadis

Chartered Institute of Library and Information Professionals (CILIP)
7 Ridgmount Street
London WC1E 7AE
Tel: 020 7255 0500
Fax: 020 7255 0501
Email: info@cilip.org.uk
Website: www.cilip.org.uk
Chief Executive: Dr Bob McKee
Managing Director, Enterprises:
John Woolley

The Chartered Institute of Library and Information Professionals is the professional body that represents 22,000 librarians and information workers in the UK. The Institute advises government, employers and others on all aspects of library and information provision and, through its lifelong learning policy, promotes the entitlement of people to learning opportunities and their right to have access to the learning resources necessary to maximise the benefits from their learning experiences. The focus of CILIP is on the needs of the learner, the skills of the library staff and partnership and access issues. It campaigns within its own membership to promote this role, as well as within the learning community as a whole. It also seeks to influence those creating new learning networks, both courseware and content, and those who design human spaces for learning.

Church of England Education Division
The Archbishops' Council
Church House
Great Smith Street
London SW1P 3AZ
Tel: 020 7898 1511
Fax: 020 7898 1520
Website: www.cofe.anglican.org
Adult Education Adviser: Joanna Cox
Further Education Adviser:
Revd. Dr John Breadon

The Adult Education Adviser of the Church of England services various networks of adult educators and trainers working in 44 dioceses. Their briefs are diverse, and include theological and biblical enquiry; consultancies to local groups; relationship skills; lay and ministerial training; learning methodologies and experiential learning. The Further Education Adviser covers policy on colleges and LSC provision for both adults and young people, and also services a network of chaplains in FE colleges, many of which are multi-faith. The Church's concern is "full development of persons in society, their intellectual, emotional and social growth in the light of the Christian faith, and working out the implications of this faith in practical activity in the world".

CILT, The National Centre for Languages
3rd Floor, 111 Westminster Bridge Road
London SE1 7HR
Tel: 020 7379 5101
Fax: 020 7379 5082
Email: info@cilt.org.uk
Website: www.cilt.org.uk
Chief Executive: Kathryn Board
Head of Communications and Marketing: Tamzin Caffrey

CILT, the National Centre for Languages seeks to promote a greater national capability in languages, supporting and developing multilingualism and intercultural competence in all sectors of society. CILT offers an extensive range of conference and in-service training (including the annual Adult Education Show), a full and authoritative catalogue of publications and a resource library housing an extensive collection of language teaching materials. Adult Education and Further Education tutors will be interested in Netword, an interactive network providing local support for language for teachers in further and higher education. Comprising a national network of local groups, online forum and website (www.cilt.org.uk/adulteducation), Netword aims to promote the teaching of language to adults and raise the status of AE tutors. CILT and its Regional Language Networks support the work of NIACE and its campaigns, including activity surrounding Adult Learners' Week.

Citizenship Foundation
63 Gee Street
London EC1V 3RS
Tel: 020 566 4141
Fax: 020 566 4131
Email: info@citizenshipfoundation.org.uk
Website: www.citizenshipfoundation.org.uk
Chief Executive: Tony Breslin

City & Guilds
1 Giltspur Street
London EC1A 9DD
Tel: 020 7294 2800
Fax: 020 7294 2400
Email: learnersupport@cityandguilds.com
Website: www.cityandguilds.com
Director General: Chris Jones

Communitas
1st Floor, Carpet Weavers Hall
Callows Lane
Kidderminster
Worcestershire DY10 2JG
Tel: 01562 749170
Fax: 01562 749171
Website: www.communitas.org.uk
Learning Centre Tutor: Paul White

Communiweb Ltd
19 Normandy Street
Alton
Hampshire GU34 1DD
Tel: 01420 549385
Email: alan@communiweb.com
Website: www.communiweb.co.uk
Director: Alan Smith

Confederation of British Industry
Centre Point
103 New Oxford Street
London WC1A 1DU
Tel: 020 7379 7400
Fax: 020 7240 1578
Website: www.cbi.org.uk
Director, Education and Skills Policy: Susan Anderson

Conservation Foundation

1 Kensington Gore
London SW7 2AR
Tel: 020 7591 3111
Fax: 020 7591 3110
Email: info@conservationfoundation.co.uk
Website:
www.conservationfoundation.co.uk
Executive Director: David Shreeve

Co-operative College Trust

Holyoake House
Hanover Street
Manchester M60 0AS
Tel: 0161 246 2926
Fax: 0161 246 2946
Email: enquiries@co-op.ac.uk
Website: www.co-op.ac.uk
Chief Executive and Principal:
Mervyn Wilson

The Co-operative College specialises in
providing education, training, research and
consultancy for the co-operative, Mutual
and Social Enterprise Sector in the UK and
internationally. The College is active in four
key areas:

- developing members and managers –
  delivering accredited programmes for
  directors, members and staff for a wide
  range of co-operatives and mutuals
- working with co-operatives globally –
  working in partnership in over 20
  countries to support the co-operative
  movement and help build capacity,
  especially in Africa
- learning from our heritage – managing
  and developing the National
  Co-operative Archive and the Rochdale
  Pioneers Museum
- working with schools and young people
  – developing co-operative resources for
  the curriculum, managing the Young
  Co-operative Network and promoting
  innovative co-operative models for
  schools.

The Crafts Council

44a Pentonville Road
London N1 9BY
Tel: 020 7278 7700
Fax: 020 7837 6891
Email: reference@craftscouncil.org.uk
Website: www.craftscouncil.org.uk
Director: Rosy Greenlees

Demos

3rd Floor, Magdalen House
136 Tooley Street
London SE1 2TU
Tel: 0845 458 5949
Fax: 020 7367 6326
Email: hello@demos.co.uk
Website: www.demos.co.uk
Director: Richard Reeves

Design Council

34 Bow Street
London WC2E 7DL
Tel: 020 7420 5200
Fax: 020 7420 5300
Email: info@designcouncil.org.uk
Website: www.designcouncil.org.uk
Chief Executive: David Kester

Digital Unite Ltd

PO Box 1271
Woking
Surrey GU22 2FP
Email: du@digitalunite.net
Website: www.digitalunite.net
Manager/Founder-Director: Emma Solomon

Digital Unite Ltd (DU) is a national
organisation devoted to Digital Inclusion
and in particular for older people. It recruits,
trains and monitors specialist home-visit
tutors nationwide. DU devised the Silver
Surfers' Day campaign in 2001 with the help
of NIACE and now manages it, yearly
increasing the number of free or nearly free
IT taster events that are offered by a huge
variety of organisations every year on the
Friday of Adult Learners' Week. DU also
delivers the UK Silver Surfer of the Year
Awards annually in October at Westminster.
DU helps disadvantaged communities
address and solve their need for IT literacy
through the medium of Digital Unite

Community Programmes. It is an independent social enterprise. Founded in 1996, it tackles digital exclusion head-on by engaging people with technology through the issues that affect them, such as personal and civic well-being, individual and communal heritage, participation in, and benefit from, society. Digital Unite's success in promoting take-up of technology is rooted in its primary focus on engagement and motivation issues rather than on technology per se.

Directory of Social Change
24 Stephenson Way
London NW1 2DP
Tel: 08450 777707
Fax: 020 7391 4808
Email: info@dsc.org.uk
Website: www.dsc.org.uk
Chief Executive: Debra Allcock Tyler

The Directory of Social Change is a registered educational charity which undertakes research and provides information and training to the voluntary sector. Publications include *The Educational Grants Directory* on charitable grants for students in need, and a range of handbooks on fundraising and management. It also runs training courses and events for voluntary and community organisations. A full booklist and courses brochure are available on request.

Dyslexia Action
Park House, Wick Road
Englefield Green
Egham
Surrey TW20 0HR
Tel: 01784 222300
Email: info@dyslexiaaction.org.uk
Website: www.dyslexiaaction.org.uk
Chief Executive: Shirley Cramer
National Adult Dyslexia Co-ordinator:
Jenny Lee
National Outreach Co-ordinator:
Margaret Jackson

Dyslexia Action (formerly the Dyslexia Institute) is a national registered charity and is the UK's leading provider of specialist services for dyslexia. It works to ensure that individuals with dyslexia have access to specialist advice, assessment and tuition which is of consistently high quality. It undertakes research into dyslexia as well as lobbying and campaigning at a national and regional level. Dyslexia Action offers specialist teacher training courses, for both pre-and post-16 sectors and is the largest supplier of specialist training in this field. It also develops and distributes teaching materials. As well as its specialist, individualised teaching programmes for dyslexic adults, it also offers workplace consultations to help employers comply with the DDA, and dyslexic employees reach their potential. Dyslexia Action has a high-quality, thriving and dynamic service for dyslexic adults in all of its 26 centres and 160 teaching locations throughout the country. It works in partnership with Learning and Skills Councils, education authorities, colleges, local and national employers and other providers from the voluntary sector to ensure an integrated and balanced service.

East London Advanced Technology Training (ELATT)
260–264 Kingsland Road
London E8 4DG
Tel: 020 7275 6750
Fax: 020 7275 6775
Email: enquiries@elatt.org.uk
Website: www.elatt.org.uk
Training Manager/Director:
Anthony Harmer

Economic and Social Research Council
Polaris House
North Star Avenue
Swindon
Wiltshire SN2 1UJ
Tel: 01793 413000
Fax: 01793 413056
Website: www.esrcsocietytoday.ac.uk
Chief Executive: Prof. Ian Diamond

For more information on studentships email PTD enquiries@esrc.ac.uk
For more information on Research Funding email RTD enquiries@esrc.ac.uk
Any further information call 01793 413122
– ask for Danielle Moore.

Edge

10 Golden Square
London W1F 9JA
Tel: 020 7734 6414
Fax: 020 7734 8328
Email: centre@edge.co.uk
Website: www.edge.co.uk
Chair: Garry Hawkes CBE
Chief Executive: Andy Powell

Edge is an educational foundation dedicated
to making practical and vocational learning
a route to success for young people. It
primarily targets young people between 14
and 24 years old and wants them to learn
through practical training and experience
how to succeed at a vast range of jobs – from
building work to business by doing work
experience, apprenticeships and training
schemes. For more information on the range
of projects Edge funds please visit the
website: www.edge.co.uk

Education Action International

3 Dufferin Street
London EC1Y 8NA
Tel: 020 7426 5800
Fax: 020 7251 1314
Email: info@education-action.org
Website: www.education-action.org

Educational Grants Advisory
Service (EGAS)

Family Action
501–505 Kingsland Road
London E8 4AU
Tel: 020 7254 6251 (2pm–4pm Tuesday,
Wednesday and Thursday)
Fax: 020 7249 5443
Email: egas.enquiry@family-action.org.uk
Website: www.family-action.org.uk
Chief Executive: Helen Dent

The Educational Grants Advisory Service
(EGAS) offers a range of services providing
information on funding for those studying in
post-16 education in the UK.

EGAS specialises in funding from
charitable trusts and maintains a database of
trusts and charities that assist students. As
part of Family Action it also administers
over 30 educational trusts, giving small

grants to students who study at institutions
that are affiliated to its service.

Students trying to identify charitable
funding for education or training to which
they may be eligible can use the online
Educational Grants Search which is
available via the Family Action website at
www.family-action.org.uk.

If a student in unable to access the
Educational Grants Search online, it will run
the search for them on receipt of a written
Educational Grants Search Form.
A copy of the Educational Grants Search
form can be printed off from the Family
Action website at www.family-action.org.uk
or by sending a stamped, self-addressed
envelope, marked 'Educational Grants
Search' to the address above.

EGAS's online Guide to Student Funding
provides written information on the sources
of funding available for education and
training in England and Wales. The Guide to
Student Funding is available via the Family
Action website.

The Education Network

5a The Court Yard
707 Warwick Road
Solihull
West Midlands B91 3DA
Tel: 0121 7127832
Fax: 0808 1444645
Email: westmidlands@t-e-n.co.uk
Website: www.t-e-n.co.uk/
Director: Elis Jones

EMIE at NFER

The Mere
Upton Park
Slough
Berkshire SL1 2DQ
Tel: 01753 523156
Fax: 01753 531458
Email: emie@nfer.ac.uk
Website: www.nfer.ac.uk/emie
Head of Service: Geoff Gee

EMIE provides an information service and
exchange for staff in local authority
education and children's services
departments in England, Wales, Scotland
and Northern Ireland. Registered users can

access a wide range of information, including instant links to resources and themes; an online database of downloadable local authority documents; publications, such as current awareness bulletins, reports on topical issues, and research briefings, again all downloadable; email discussion forums; a customised enquiry service, links to a selection of councils' plans, policies, reviews and inspection reports; and a daily updated news service.

Employers' Forum on Age
Floor 3, Downstream
1 London Bridge
London SE1 9BG
Tel: 0845 456 2495
Fax: 020 7785 6536
Email: efa@efa.org.uk
Website: www.efa.org.uk
Director: Catherine Pusey
Head of Employer Relations:
Karen Constantine

Engineering and Physical Sciences Research Council
Polaris House
North Star Avenue
Swindon
Wiltshire SN2 1ET
Tel: 01793 444000
Fax: 01793 444005
Website: www.epsrc.ac.uk
Head of Public Engagement: Rachel Bishop
Email: rachel.bishop@epsrc.ac.uk

English Speaking Board (International) Ltd
26a Princes Street
Southport PR8 1EQ
Tel: 01704 501730
Fax: 01704 539637
Email: admin@esbuk.org
Website: www.esbuk.org
Company Secretary: Veronica Swift

ENGLISH UK
219 St. John Street
London EC1V 4LY
Tel: 0207 608 7960
Fax: 0207 608 7961
Email: info@englishuk.com
Website: www.englishuk.com
Chair: Sue Edwards
Chief Executive: Tony Millns

Publications: *English in the UK*.

Field Studies Council (FSC)
Preston Montford
Montford Bridge
Shrewsbury
Shropshire SY4 1HW
Tel: 01743 852100
Fax: 01743 852101
Email:
fsc.headoffice@field-studies-council.org
Website: www.field-studies-council.org
Chief Executive: Anthony David Thomas

The FSC is a pioneering educational charity which was set up in 1943 to help people of all ages and background to discover, explore, understand and be inspired by the natural environment. The organisation works through a network of 17 residential and day centres throughout the UK providing courses for schools and colleges at all levels. A programme of leisure learning and professional development courses is offered in the UK giving the opportunity for individuals of all ages to study various aspects of the environment under expert guidance. Courses vary from one day to a week in duration and weekend courses are also available. The subjects are varied and range from general natural history, painting and drawing, walking, to more specific plant and animal identification courses which can be accredited for continuing personal development. The FSC also provides outreach education, training and consultancy and publishes many titles to support its work, including the popular fold-out identification charts.

Forum for Access and Continuing Education (FACE)
University of East London
Docklands Campus
4–6 University Way
London E16 2RD
Tel: 020 8223 4936
Fax: 020 8223 3394
Website: www.f-a-c-e.org.uk
Chair: John Storan
Partnership Support Officer: Jackie Leach

FACE is a charitable organisation established to support, promote and further develop continuing education opportunities. As an inclusive body, FACE members are to be found in higher education, further education, employer organisations, funding councils and many other related bodies. Members' benefits include a quarterly bulletin, conferences and seminars, a compendium of research/consultancy contacts, representation of members' interest on national policy development, and access to FACE development funds and website.

Foundation for Community Dance
LCB Depot
31 Rutland Street
Leicester LE1 1RE
Tel: 0116 253 3453
Fax: 0116 261 6801
Email: info@communitydance.org.uk
Website: www.communitydance.org.uk
Creative Director: Ken Bartlett

Groundwork UK
Lockside
5 Scotland Street
Birmingham B1 2RR
Tel: 0121 236 8565
Fax: 0121 236 7356
Email: info@groundwork.org.uk
Website: www.groundwork.org.uk
Development Co-ordinator:
Chris Southwood

Improvement and Development Agency for Local Government (IdeA)
Layden House
76–86 Turnmill Street
London EC1M 5LG
Tel: 020 7296 6600
Fax: 020 7296 6666
Email: ihelp@idea.gov.uk
Website: www.idea-knowledge.gov.uk
Executive Director: Lucy de Groot

Indian Muslim Welfare Society
Al-Hikmah Centre
28 Track Road
Batley
West Yorkshire WF17 7AA
Tel: 01924 500555
Fax: 01924 500556
Email: info@imws.org.uk
Website: www.imws.org.uk
Centre Manager: M Kazi

Institute for Employment Studies
Mantell Building
University of Sussex
Falmer
Brighton
East Sussex BN1 9RF
Tel: 01273 686751
Fax: 01273 690430
Email:
directors.office@employment-studies.co.uk
Website: www.employment-studies.co.uk
Director: Nigel Meager

Institute for Public Policy Research
30–32 Southampton Street
London WC2E 7RA
Tel: 020 7470 6100
Fax: 020 7470 6111
Email: info@ippr.org
Website: www.ippr.org
Co-Directors: Lisa Harker, Carey Oppenheim

Investors in People UK
7–10 Chandos Street
London W1G 9DQ
Tel: 020 7467 1900
Fax: 020 7636 2386
Website: www.investorsinpeople.co.uk
Chief Executive: Simon Jones

Kesslers International Limited
Rick Roberts Way
London E15 2NF
Tel: 020 8522 3000
Fax: 020 8522 3129
Email: kesslerg@kesslers.com
Website: www.kesslers.com
Deputy Chairman: George Kessler CBE

Lancashire Wide Network for Minority Ethnic Women
Spring Hill Community Centre
Exchange Street
Accrington
Lancashire BB5 0JD
Tel: 01254 392974
Fax: 01254 381349
Email: alison@lancashire-bme-pact.org.uk
Website: www.lwnmew.fsnet.co.uk
Project Co-ordination Officer: Jabien Kauser

The aim of the project is to help to build the capacity of minority ethnic women working in the voluntary sector to participate effectively in the social, economic and political life of the community in which they live.

Lancaster Literacy Research Centre
Institute for Advanced Studies
Lancaster University
Bailrigg
Lancaster LA1 4YT
Tel: 01524 510853
Fax: 01524 510855
Website: www.literacy.lancs.ac.uk
Research Co-ordinator: Jessica Abrahams

Learning from Experience Trust
Goldsmiths College
Deptford Town Hall
New Cross Road
London SE14 6AE
Tel: 020 7919 7739
Fax: 020 7919 7762
Email: let@gold.ac.uk
Website: www.learningexperience.org.uk
Director: Dr Michael Field

Life Academy
9 Chesham Road
Guildford
Surrey GU1 3LS
Tel: 01483 301170
Fax: 01483 300981
Email: info@life-academy.co.uk
Website: www.life-academy.co.uk
Chairman: Alan Pickering
Chief Executive: Stuart Royston
Head of Education and Training:
Anthony Chiva

Life Academy is an educational charity and an Associated Institute of the University of Surrey. Its mission is to help people cope with the changes they face through life. It provides the national focus on life planning and pre-retirement education. Its interests also include demographic changes, age diversity, the older workforce and basic financial education. Life Academy runs post-graduate and Foundation programmes in life planning, and short pre-retirement courses. It has a generic financial education programme, 'Learn about Money', and is involved in consultancy and research. The publication list includes the reference book *Your Retirement* that covers the basic issues and information in retirement planning.

Local Government Association (LGA)
Local Government House
Smith Square
London SW1P 3HZ
Tel: 020 7664 3000
Fax: 020 7664 3030
Website: www.lga.gov.uk
Chief Executive: Sir Brian Briscoe
Elected Member: Cllr. Graham Lane

The LGA represents local councils in England and Wales, and is the single voice for local government in representing views to government, the media and other organisations. It serves the interests of those elected to represent local communities as well as the officials who work to provide the services to residents, voluntary organisations and businesses on which they rely. The LGA promotes better local government and advocates the provision of high-quality educational services in the cities, towns and rural areas of the UK, stressing the importance in a civilised society of lifelong learning opportunities that can enhance the quality of life for citizens of all ages.

The Marine Society and Sea Cadets
202 Lambeth Road
London SE1 7JW
Tel: 020 7654 7051
Fax: 020 7928 8914
Email: education@ms-sc.org
Website: www.mscos.ac.uk
Director, Education and Adult Learning:
Brian Thomas BA (Hons) PGCE

Founded in 1756, The Marine Society incorporates Seafarers Libraries and College of the Sea. Functions are to provide seafarers with general educational facilities by distance learning (College of the Sea); to provide a first-class library service for merchant ships and offshore platforms (Seafarers Libraries). In 2004, The Marine Society merged with the Sea Cadet Association to form 'The Marine Society and Sea Cadets' – the nation's largest maritime charity. Periodical: *Seafarer*, thrice yearly and occasional publications.

Mentoring and Befriending Foundation
1st Floor, Charles House
Albert Street
Eccles
Manchester M30 0PW
Tel: 0161 787 8600
Fax: 0161 787 8100
Email: info@mandbf.org.uk
Website: www.mandbf.org.uk
Information and Research Officer:
Jeanette Boyd

Ming-Ai (London) Institute
1 Cline Road
London N11 2LX
Tel: 020 8361 7161
Fax: 020 8361 4207
Email: enquiry@ming-ai.org.uk
Website: www.ming-ai.org.uk
Director: Dr Therese W H Shak
Dean: Chungwen Li

Museums, Libraries and Archives Council
Welcome Wolfson Building
165 Queen's Gate
London SW7 5HD
Tel: 020 7273 1444
Fax: 020 7273 1404
Website: www.mla.gov.uk
Chief Executive: Roy Clare CBE

National Alliance of Women's Organisations (NAWO)
Suite 405, Davina House
137–149 Goswell Road
London EC1V 7ET
Tel: 020 7490 4100
Fax: 020 7490 4100
Email: info@nawo.org.uk
Website: www.nawo.org.uk
Chair: Juliet Colman

NAWO is an independent infrastructure body, accountable to its diverse member organisations. It provides representation and advocacy on social policy and women's voluntary sector issues, particular policy expertise on Europe. It publishes a quarterly thematic newsletter and e-bulletin, regular new mailings, consultations and meetings for member organisations and others. It elects England's representative to the European Women's Lobby, Brussels.

National Association for Providers of Activities for Older People (NAPA)
Bondway Commercial Centre
5th Floor, Unit 5.12
71 Bondway
London SW8 1SQ
Tel: 0207 078 9375
Email: sylvie@napa-activities.co.uk
Website: www.napa-activities.co.uk
Membership Secretary: Sue Sangster
Strategic Director: Sylvie Silver
Chairman: Simon Labbett

National Centre for Language and Literacy
University of Reading
Bulmershe Court
Earley
Reading RG6 1HY
Tel: 0118 378 8820
Fax: 0118 378 6801
Email: ncll@reading.ac.uk
Website: www.ncll.org.uk
Resources Officer: Sue Abbas

National Extension College
The Michael Young Centre
Purbeck Road
Cambridge CB2 8HN
Tel: 01223 400200
Fax: 01223 400322
Email: info@nec.ac.uk
Website: www.nec.ac.uk
Chief Executive: Michael O'Toole
Chair: Dr Ann Limb

The College provides a range of services to adult learners and organisations which includes the design and publication of learning materials; the provision of distance learning courses for home-based students; co-ordination of a FlexiStudy Scheme in association with Further Education Colleges and CoNECt which is a collaborative partnership with colleges, enabling them to offer distance learning courses. Further information is available in the *NEC Resources Catalogue* and the *NEC Guide to Courses*, both available free of charge.

National Foundation for Educational Research
The Mere
Upton Park
Slough SL1 2DQ
Tel: 01753 574123
Fax: 01753 691632
Website: www.nfer.ac.uk
Director: Sue Rossiter

National Institute of Economic and Social Research
2 Dean Trench Street
Smith Square
London SW1P 3HE
Tel: 020 7222 7665
Fax: 020 7654 1900
Email: enquiries@niesr.ac.uk
Website: www.niesr.ac.uk
Director: Martin Weale
Email: mweale@niesr.ac.uk

National Literacy Trust
68 South Lambeth Road
London SW8 1RL
Tel: 020 7587 1842
Email: contact@literacytrust.org.uk
Website: www.literacytrust.org.uk
Head of Information: Sam Brookes

The National Literacy Trust is an independent charity that changes lives through literacy. It links home, school and the wider community to inspire learners and create opportunities for everyone. It supports those who work with learners through innovative programmes, information and research. Programmes supporting adult learners include Prison Reading Champions and the Vital Link reader development project, which links libraries and adult basic skills (delivered by The Reading Agency in partnership with the National Literacy Trust).

National Society for Education in Art and Design (NSEAD)

The Gatehouse
Corsham Court
Corsham
Wiltshire SN13 0BZ
Tel: 01249 714825
Fax: 01249 716138
Email: info@nsead.org
Website: www.nsead.org
General Secretary: Dr John Steers

The NSEAD is a professional association and trade union for teachers and lecturers of art and design in all phases of education. It publishes a quarterly newsletter and three issues of the *International Journal of Art and Design Education* (iJADE) annually, and START magazine for primary schools. The Society's website is extensive with many resources.

National Union of Students

2nd Floor, Centro 3
19 Mandela Street
London NW1 0DU
Tel: 08712 218 221
Fax: 08712 218 222
Email: nusuk@nus.org.uk
Website: www.nusonline.co.uk
Director of Campaigns and Strategy:
Jim Dickinson

National Youth Agency

Eastgate House
19–23 Humberstone Road
Leicester LE5 3GJ
Tel: 0116 242 7350
Fax: 0116 242 7444
Email: nya@nya.org.uk
Website: www.nya.org.uk
Chief Executive: Fiona Blacke

The National Youth Agency (NYA) aims to advance youth work to promote young people's personal and social development, as well as their voice, influence and place in society. Funded primarily by the Local Government Association and government departments it works to: improve and extend youth services and youth work; enhance and demonstrate youth

participation in society; and to promote effective youth policy and provision. It provides resources to improve work with young people and its management; creates and demonstrates innovation in services and methods; supports the leadership of organisations to deliver 'best value' and manage change; influences public perception and policy; and secures standards of education and training for youth work.

North West Skills for Life Research Forum

NW SfL RF@LLRC
Literacy Research Centre
Institute for Advanced Studies
Lancaster University
Lancaster LA1 4YD
Tel: 01524 510828
Fax: 01524 510855
Website:
www.literacy.lancs.ac.uk/links/
skillsforlife.htm
Contact: Kathryn James
Email: kathryn.james@lancaster.ac.uk

Linking research and practice has always been at the centre of Lancaster's literacy work and the North West Skills for Life Research Forum, set up in February 2003, is part of this. The Forum is the first Regional Research Forum in the country and as such presents an exciting opportunity to develop research, practice and theory in adult literacy, numeracy and language. Lancaster Literacy Research Centre was a founder member of the group whose members range from large organisations such as the LSDA and NIACE to individuals interested in both research and practice in Skills for Life in the NW. During 2003/2004 the Forum held regular seminars for discussion, information and debate. These covered a range of topics including ESOL and issues within Criminal Justice Settings. During 2005 it was decided to give the Research Forum some permanence within the Literacy Research Centre's new home at the Institute of Advanced Studies.

Open and Distance Learning Quality Council

16 Park Crescent
London W1B 1AH
Tel: 020 7612 7090
Fax: 020 7612 7092
Email: info@odlqc.org.uk
Website: www.odlqc.org.uk
Chief Executive: Dr David Morley

The Council, established in 1968, is the national organisation responsible for setting standards of tuition, education and training carried out by distance learning methods, for investigating these and, where appropriate, granting accreditation. It seeks to: protect the interests of students, colleges and the general public; further the development of distance education and training techniques; and, where appropriate, to link correspondence courses with other forms of further education and training. An information leaflet, listing the accredited colleges and the courses offered, is available from the above address, free of charge.

Open College of the Arts (OCA)

The Michael Young Arts Centre
Unit 1b, Redbrook Business Park
Wilthorpe Road
Barnsley S75 1JN
Tel: 01226 730495 or 0800 731 2116
Fax: 01226 730838
Email: open.arts@ukonline.co.uk
Website: www.oca-uk.com
Chief Executive Officer: Gareth Dent
Academic Director: George Apostoli
Operations Director: Katie Abbott

The Open College of the Arts (OCA), a charitable, educational trust, provides home-based arts education via postal or individual tuition by professional artists, using methods broadly similar to those of the Open University, to which the OCA is affiliated. Courses include photography, printmaking, creative writing, interior and garden design, art history, painting, drawing, sculpture, creative digital arts, textiles, calligraphy, music, singing and dance. OCA specialises in courses for students who want to develop their artistic skills but do not want a conventional college education. Most courses have university accreditation and credit points can be put towards university qualifications, including OCA's new BA Honours degree in Creative Arts.

Open Learning Foundation

3 Devonshire Street
London W1W 5BA
Tel: 020 7636 4186
Fax: 020 7631 0132
Email: olf2@btconnect.com
Website: www.olf.ac.uk
Managing Director: Prof. Colin Harrison

The Open Learning Foundation works closely with its university and college members to change the approach to learning and teaching. Open learning materials have been developed and made available to members as part of their annual subscription. Materials in business, nursing and social work as well as learning to learn, have been developed and constantly updated. The materials are available both as print-based and electronic versions. The latter can easily be used in modern learning management systems. The Foundation offers its members research and development into learning at a distance, by open learning and increasingly telematically. Specialist groups meet regularly to develop and publish educational concepts to further the delivery of learning to those who can attend member's sites and to reach out to those who, through personal or employment difficulties, find it impossible to attend courses personally. It supports members in the integration of open/flexible learning into established activities and in overcoming barriers to growth. It offers staff development courses and conferences to help establish new methods of teaching and learning into the mainstream of education. With its rapid response groups it is well able to react quickly to government initiatives at both UK and EU levels. It is part of the European Association of Distance Teaching Universities.

PCS Organising and Learning
160 Falcon Road
London SW11 2LN
Tel: 020 7801 2691
Fax: 020 7801 2630
Email: learningservices@pcs.org.uk
Website: www.pcs.org.uk/learning
Communications Officer: Anne Elliott-Day

Policy Studies Institute
50 Hanson Street
London W1W 6UP
Tel: 020 7911 7500
Fax: 020 7911 7501
Email: psi-admin@psi.org.uk
Website: www.psi.org.uk
Director: Malcolm Rigg

PRAGMA (Pre-Retirement Association of Greater Manchester)
Terry Dowling Centre
260 Brownley Road
Wythenshawe
Manchester M22 5EB
Tel: 0161 436 3335
Fax: 0161 436 3335
Director: Mark Bloomfield

Refugee Education and Training Advisory Service (RETAS)
3 Dufferin Street
London EC1Y 8NA
Tel: 020 7426 5800
Fax: 020 7251 1314
Email: info@education-action.org
Website: www.education-action.org
Advice Telephone Line: 020 7426 5801,
Thursday 2.00–5.00pm

Research and Practice in Adult Literacy Group (RaPAL)
Literacy Research Centre
Institute for Advanced Studies
Lancaster University
Lancaster LA1 4YD
Tel: 01524 510828
Fax: 01524 510855
Website: www.literacy.lancs.ac.uk/rapal
Contact: Kathyrn James

RaPAL is an independent network of learners, teachers, managers and researchers in adult basic education and literacy across the post-16 sector. Established in 1985, it is supported by membership subscription only. RaPAL encourages collaborative and reflective research that is closely linked with practice. It works in partnership with others committed to developing a learning democracy, campaigning for the rights of all adults to have access to the full range of literacies in their lives. RaPAL produces a journal three times a year and other occasional publications. It organises an annual conference and contributes to national debates about literacy, actively challenging public preconceptions and publicising alternative views.

Right to Write Ltd
Springfield House
71 Todmorden Road
Burnley
Lancashire BB11 3ES
Tel: 0870 240 4809
Fax: 0870 240 3197
Email: info@right2write.co.uk
Website: www.right2write.co.uk
Managing Director: Elaine Ferguson

Royal Institution of Great Britain
21 Albemarle Street
London W1S 4BS
Tel: 020 7409 2992
Fax: 020 7670 2920
Email: ri@ri.ac.uk
Website: www.rigb.org
Director: Baroness Susan Greenfield
Membership: Rhian Snook

For over 200 years, the Royal Institution (RI) has been 'diffusing science for the common purposes of life'. A range of activities takes place under one roof, from schools and public lectures to a heritage programme, research team and media centre. The recent redevelopment of the RI has now seen the creation of a café, bar, restaurant and exhibition spaces.

Membership of the RI is open to everyone interested in science, and information may be obtained by visiting the website or by contacting the Membership Team.

Publications include the *What's On* guide.

Royal Shakespeare Company
The Courtyard Theatre
Southern Lane
Stratford-upon-Avon
Warwickshire CV37 6BH
Tel: 01789 296655
Fax: 01789 272525
Website: www.rsc.org.uk
Head of Events and Exhibitions: Mark Ball

School of Everything
18 Victoria Park Square
Bethnal Green
London E2 9PF
Tel: 020 8980 8435
Email: hello@schoolofeverything.com
Website: www.schoolofeverything.com
Chief Executive Officer: Paul Miller

School of Everything is a website which
connects people who want to learn with
passionate teachers in their local area. The
service is free and has been developed with
the backing of Channel 4 Education and the
Young Foundation.

Skill: National Bureau for Students with Disabilities
Chapter House
18–20 Crucifix Lane
London SE1 3JW
Tel: 020 7450 0620
Fax: 020 7450 0650
Email: skill@skill.org.uk
Website: www.skill.org.uk
Chief Executive: Barbara Waters

Skill is a national voluntary organisation
that aims to develop opportunities for
people with disabilities and learning
difficulties in post-16 education, training,
employment and volunteering. It runs an
information service; provides good practice
advice and produces leaflets and
publications; runs conferences and events,
undertakes research and consultancy work;
and liaises with policy makers and other
service providers.
  Information Service (Tuesday
11.30am–1.30pm and Thursday
1.30–3.30pm), Tel: 0800 328 5050 or
020 7657 2337
Textphone: 0800 068 2422
Email: info@skill.org.uk

Social Care Institute for Excellence
1st Floor, Goldings House
Hays Lane
London SE1 2HB
Tel: 020 7089 6840
Fax: 020 7089 6841
Email: info@scie.org.uk
Website: www.scie.org.uk
Chief Executive: Julie Jones
Social Care Online website:
www.scie-socialcareonline.org.uk

Society for the Advancement of Games and Simulations in Education and Training (SAG SET)
c/o Mrs M H Godfrey
110 Liberton Brae
Edinburgh EH16 6LA
Website: www.sagset.org

SAGSET promotes and disseminates the use
of games and simulations in education and
training. It acts as a forum for ideas on the
challenges of the techniques or on the
practice of gaming and simulation in
education.

Southwark Muslim Women's Association
165 Bellenden Old School
Bellenden Road
London SE15 4DG
Tel: 020 7732 8053
Fax: 020 7732 9506
Email: smwasmwa@aol.com
Website: www.smwa.org.uk
Centre Director: Zafar Iqbal

SPELL (Supporting People into Employment and Lifelong Learning)
301 Buchanan Road
Parson Cross
Sheffield
South Yorkshire S5 8AU
Tel: 0114 249 8100
Fax: 0114 249 3933
Email: info@spelldirect.org
Website: www.spelldirect.org
Manager: Alan Chapman

Sport England
3rd Floor, Victoria House
Bloomsbury Square
London WC1B 4SE
Tel: 08458 508 508
Fax: 020 7383 5740
Email: info@sportengland.org
Website: www.sportengland.org
Chief Executive: Jennie Price

Sport England is committed to sustaining
and increasing participation in community
sport. It is a non-departmental public body
and a National Lottery distributor. Sport
England's ambition is to get two million
people doing more sport by 2012.

**Standing Conference on University
Teaching and Research in the
Education of Adults (SCUTREA)**
Centre for Continuing Education
Essex House
University of Sussex
Falmer
Brighton BN1 9RH
Tel: 01273 872 534
Fax: 01273 877 534
Website: www.scutrea.ac.uk
Secretary: Linda Morrice
Senior Lecturer: Dr Rob Mark
Treasurer: Anne-Marie Houghton

The object of SCUTREA is to enable those in
higher education who engage in the teaching
of, and research into the teaching of, adults
to express and share their academic
concerns. Membership is open to individuals
in the UK and overseas, whether or not they
are members of universities, who are
accepted as making contributions to the
study of, or research into, the education of
adults. SCUTREA also welcomes into
membership institutions which are accepted
on the grounds that they are furthering the
study of, or research into, the education of
adults. Publications include SCUTREA
Papers and a regular newsletter.

**TWICS (Training for Work
in Communities)**
284 Burgess Road
Swaythling
Southampton SO16 3BE
Tel: 023 8067 1111
Fax: 023 8067 2222
Email: admin@twics.org.uk
Website: www.twics.org.uk
Co-ordinator: Barbara Hancock

United Reformed Church
86 Tavistock Place
London WC1H 9RT
Tel: 020 7916 8635
Fax: 020 7916 2021
Website: www.urc.org.uk
Secretary for Education and Learning:
Revd Fiona Thomas

Venuemasters
The Workstation
Paternoster Row
Sheffield
South Yorkshire S1 2BX
Tel: 0114 249 3090
Fax: 0114 249 3091
Email: info@venuemasters.co.uk
Website: www.venuemasters.co.uk
Chief Executive Officer: Terry Billingham

Venuemasters offers a free finding service for
meeting and accommodation facilities
available at more than 84 universities and
colleges throughout Britain.

**Visual Impairment Centre for Teaching
and Research**
University of Birmingham
School of Education
Edgbaston
Birmingham B15 2TT
Tel: 0121 414 6733
Fax: 0121 414 4865
Email: victar-enquiries@bham.ac.uk
Website:
www.education.bham.ac.uk/research/victar
Administrative Secretary: Sofia Hansrod

Voluntary Service Overseas (VSO)
317 Putney Bridge Road
London SW15 2PN
Tel: 020 8780 7500
Fax: 020 8780 7300
Email: enquiry@vso.org.uk
Website: www.vso.org.uk
Communications Information Officer:
Alexandra Vernon

VSO is an international development charity
that works through volunteers. It enables
people aged 18–75 to share their
professional skills and experience with local
communities in the developing world.

Women Returners' Network
Chelmsford College
Moulsham Street
Chelmsford
Essex CM2 0JQ
Tel: 01245 263796
Website: www.women-returners.co.uk
Chief Executive: Joy MacMillan

The Work Foundation
21 Palmer Street
London SW1H 0AD
Tel: 020 7976 3500
Fax: 020 7976 3600
Website: www.theworkfoundation.com
Executive Vice-Chair: Will Hutton

YMCA George Williams College
199 Freemasons Road
Canning Town
London E16 3PY
Tel: 020 7540 4900
Fax: 020 7511 4900
Email: registry@ymca.ac.uk
Website: www.ymca.ac.uk
Principal: Mary Wolfe

The Young Foundation
18 Victoria Park Square
Bethnal Green
London E2 9PF
Tel: 020 8980 6263
Fax: 020 8981 6719
Email: reception@youngfoundation.org
Website: www.youngfoundation.org
Director: Geoff Mulgan

YWCA England and Wales
Clarendon House
52 Cornmarket Street
Oxford OX1 3EJ
Tel: 01865 304200
Fax: 01865 204805
Email: info@ywca.org.uk
Website: www.ywca.org.uk
Chief Executive Officer: Sarah Payne

YWCA England and Wales is the leading
charity working with young women facing
poverty, discrimination or abuse. It provides
them with support, information and the
oppurtunity to learn. YWCA is a force for
change in the lives of young women,
enabling them to work together to challenge
and overcome discrimination and
disadvantage.

Awarding Bodies – England

Regulatory Authorities

Qualifications and Curriculum Authority
83 Piccadilly
London W1J 8QA
Tel: 020 7509 5555
Fax: 020 7509 6975
Website: www.qca.org.uk
Chairman: Sir Anthony Greener
Email: greenera@qca.org.uk
Chief Executive: Dr Ken Boston AO

The Quality Assurance Agency for Higher Education
Southgate House
Southgate Street
Gloucester GL1 1UB
Tel: 01452 557000
Fax: 01452 557070
Email: comms@qaa.ac.uk
Website: www.qaa.ac.uk
Chairman: Sam Younger
Chief Executive: Peter Williams

The Quality Assurance Agency for Higher Education's (QAA's) mission is to safeguard the public interest in sound standards of higher education qualifications and to inform and encourage continuous improvement in the management of the quality of higher education. Established in 1997 to provide an integrated quality assurance service for UK higher education, QAA is an independent body funded by subscriptions from universities and colleges of higher education, and through contracts with the main funding bodies. QAA's core business is to review the quality and standards of higher education in universities and colleges of higher education. It does this by auditing institutional arrangements for managing quality and standards, including arrangements for collaboration with overseas partners, and by reviewing the quality and standards of higher education programmes offered in further education colleges. These activities result in reports that are available to the public on QAA's website. Other work carried out involves advising government on the applications for degree awarding powers and university title; licensing the agencies that validate Access to Higher Education provision in England, Wales and Northern Ireland, and reviewing their assurance mechanisms.

Unitary Awarding Bodies

Assessment and Qualifications Alliance (AQA)
31–33 Springfield Avenue
Harrogate
North Yorkshire HG1 2HW
Tel: 01423 840015
Fax: 01423 523678
Email: accesscourses@aqa.org.uk
Website: www.aqa.org.uk
Access to Higher Education Officer:
Dr Gill Yamin

Edexcel
190 High Holborn
London WC1V 7BH
Tel: 0870 240 9800
Website: www.edexcel.org.uk
Managing Director: Jerry Jarvis

OCR
1 Hills Road
Cambridge CB2 1PB
Tel: 01223 553998
Fax: 01223 552627
Email: general.qualifications@ocr.org.uk
Website: www.ocr.org.uk
OCR Customer Contact Centre
General qualifications email:
general.qualifications@ocr.org.uk
Vocational qualifications email:
vocational.qualifications@ocr.org.uk

Other Recognised Awarding Bodies

ABC Awards
Robins Wood House
Robins Wood Road
Aspley
Nottingham NG8 3NH
Tel: 0115 854 1616
Fax: 0115 854 1617
Email:
enquiries_nottingham@abcawards.co.uk
Website: www.abcawards.co.uk
Executive Director: Nigel Florence

ASDAN
Wainbrook House
Hudds Vale Road
St George
Bristol BS5 7HY
Tel: 0117 941 1126
Fax: 0117 935 1112
Email: info@asdan.org.uk
Website: www.asdan.org.uk
Director of Qualifications and
Accreditation: Brian Hobbs
Chief Executive: Roger White

ASET
International House
Siskin Parkway East
Middlemarch Business Park
Coventry CV3 4PE
Tel: 08707 202 909
Fax: 02476 516 505
Email: enquiries@ediplc.com
Website: www.aset.ac.uk
Chief Executive: Chris Daniel

BCS (The British Computer Society)
First Floor, Block D
North Star House
North Star Avenue
Swindon SN2 1FA
Tel: 0845 300 4417
Fax: 01793 417444
Email: BCSHQ@hq.bcs.org.uk
Website: www.bcs.org

Cambridge ESOL
University of Cambridge
ESOL Examinations
1 Hills Road
Cambridge CB1 2EU
Tel: 01223 553 355
Email: esol@ucles.org.uk
Website: www.ucles.org.uk

Chartered Institute of Personnel and Development
151 The Broadway
London SW19 1JQ
Tel: 020 8612 6200
Email: cipd@cipd.co.uk
Website: www.cipd.co.uk
Chief Executive Officer: Jackie Orme

The Chartered Institute of Personnel and
Development is the pre-eminent professional
body in the field of people management and
development with over 130,000 members.
The Institute was formed from the Institute
of Personnel Management and the Institute
of Training and Development, which were
united on 1 July 1994. It received its Royal
Charter in July 2000. The CIPD offers a
wide range of services including over 130
training events, various levels of
membership, a professional education
scheme, books, consultancy and a full
library and information service.

City & Guilds
1 Giltspur Street
London EC1A 9DD
Tel: 020 7294 2800
Fax: 020 7294 2400
Email: learnersupport@cityandguilds.com
Website: www.cityandguilds.com
Director General: Chris Jones

ConstructionSkills
Bircham Newton
Kings Lynn
Norfolk PE31 6RH
Tel: 01485 557 557
Fax: 01485 577 793
Email: call.centre@cskills.org
Website: www.constructionskills.net

CACDP
Durham University Science Park
Block 4
Stockton Road
Durham DH1 3UZ
Tel: 0191 383 1155
Fax: 0191 383 7914
Email: durham@cacdp.org.uk
Website: www.cacdp.org.uk
Chief Executive: Jim Edwards

EDI (Educational Development International)
International House
Siskin Parkway East
Middlemarch Business Park
Coventry CV3 4PE
Tel: 02476 516500
Fax: 02476 516505
Email: enquiries@ediplc.com
Website: www.ediplc.com
Chief Executive: Nigel Snook

ECITB (Engineering Construction Industry Training Board)
Blue Court
Church Lane
Kings Langley
Hertfordshire WD4 8JP
Tel: 01923 260000
Fax: 01923 270969
Email: ecitb@ecitb.org.uk
Website: www.ecitb.org.uk

English Speaking Board (International) Ltd
26a Princes Street
Southport PR8 1EQ
Tel: 01704 501730
Fax: 01704 539637
Email: admin@esbuk.org
Website: www.esbuk.org
Company Secretary: Veronica Swift

EPIC Training and Consulting Services Limited
Alban Row
27–31 Verulan Road
St Albans
Hertfordshire AL3 4DG
Tel: 01727 869008
Fax: 01727 843318
Email: info@epicltd.co.uk
Website: www.epicltd.com
Financial and Systems Manager: Lynda McKill
Senior Training Advisor: Graham Crawshaw

National Open College Network
The Quadrant
Parkway Business Park
99 Park Avenue
Sheffield S9 4WG
Tel: 0114 227 0500
Fax: 0114 227 0501
Email: nocn@nocn.org.uk
Website: www.nocn.org.uk
Chief Executive: Jill Brunt

NCFE
Citygate
St James Boulevard
Newcastle upon Tyne NE1 4JE
Tel: 0191 239 8000
Fax: 0191 239 8001
Email: info@ncfe.org.uk
Website: www.ncfe.org.uk
Chief Executive: David Grailey

Open College of the North West
West Lodge
Quernmore Road
Lancaster LA1 3JT
Tel: 01524 845046
Fax: 01524 388467
Email: ocnw@lancaster.ac.uk
Website: www.ocnw.com
Chief Executive: Phil Wilkinson

Thames Valley University
St Mary's Road
Ealing
London W5 5RF
Tel: 020 8579 5000
Fax: 020 8566 1353
Website: www.tvu.ac.uk
Vice-Chancellor: Prof. Peter John
Pro-Vice-Chancellor: Lee Nicholls

Vocational Training Charitable Trust
3rd Floor, Eastleigh House
Upper Market Street
Eastleigh
Hampshire SO50 9FD
Tel: 02380 684500
Fax: 02380 651493
Website: www.vtct.org.uk
Chief Executive: Peter Wren

The Vocational Training Charitable Trust (VTCT) is a national awarding body devoted to the development of world-class qualifications for physical non-medical therapies. Since 1962 it has been a market leader for Holistic, Beauty, Health and Fitness and Sports Therapies. In support of these it offers National and Scottish Vocational Qualifications together with the NVQs in Key Skills and Customer Service. VTCT includes three subsidiary institutes: International Health and Beauty Council (IHBC), International Institute of Health and Holistic Therapies (IIHHT) and International Institute of Sports Therapy (IIST). All qualifications use the assessment and verification system, and all 80+ qualifications are offered internationally to the same standard.

Other Awarding Bodies

Federation of Authorised Validating Agencies (FAVA)
c/o OCN Oxford, Thames and Chiltern
Nash House
Repton Place
White Lion Road
Amersham
Buckinghamshire HP7 9LP
Tel: 0870 220 8250
Chair and Assistant Director for Quality and Development: Anne Rixson

FAVA is a collaboration between a number of leading Authorised Validating Agencies (AVAs) with the aim of promoting high-quality Access to Higher Education Provision. The current membership is:

- Cambridge Access Validating Agency
- Assessment and Qualifications Alliance
- Hampshire Authorised Validating Agency
- Open College Network Oxford Thames and Chiltern
- Open College of the North West.

In order to promote high-quality Access to Higher Education Provision FAVA is committed to:

- providing a mutually supportive forum for the discussion of issues that affect member AVAs
- sharing best practice and experiences between the member AVAs
- recognising and researching the national need of the member AVAs
- benchmarking performance on Access Programmes across the member AVAs
- promoting and sharing staff development activities between member AVAs.

All FAVA full members are licensed by the Quality Assurance Agency for Higher Education (QAA), which acts as the regulatory authority for Access to Higher Education Provision. FAVA speaks with a collective voice to the QAA and other agencies on policy matters relating to Access Provision. Furthermore, FAVA endeavours to keep the regulatory authority informed of significant issues affecting provider organisations and Higher Education institutions.

Assessment and Qualifications Alliance (AQA)
31–33 Springfield Avenue
Harrogate
North Yorkshire HG1 2HW
Tel: 01423 840015
Fax: 01423 523678
Email: accesscourses@aqa.org.uk
Website: www.aqa.org.uk
Access to Higher Education Officer:
Dr Gill Yamin

The Cambridge Access Validating Agency

Unit 8
Gwydir Street Enterprise Centre
Gwydir Street
Cambridge CB1 2LG
Tel: 01223 302148
Fax: 01223 302148
Email: a.morley@cava.ac.uk
Website: www.cava.ac.uk
Chief Executive Officer: Annabel Morley

Hampshire Authorised Validating Agency

University of Portsmouth
University House
Winston Churchill Avenue
Portsmouth
Hampshire PO1 2UP
Tel: 023 9284 3396
Fax: 023 9284 3082
Email: barbara.gander@port.ac.uk
Website: www.hava.ac.uk
Senior Officer: Barbara Gander

Open College of the North West

West Lodge
Quernmore Road
Lancaster LA1 3JT
Tel: 01524 845046
Fax: 01524 388467
Email: ocnw@lancaster.ac.uk
Website: www.ocnw.com
Chief Executive: Phil Wilkinson

National Open College Network

National Open College Network

The Quadrant
Parkway Business Park
99 Park Avenue
Sheffield S9 4WG
Tel: 0114 227 0500
Fax: 0114 227 0501
Email: nocn@nocn.org.uk
Website: www.nocn.org.uk
Chief Executive: Jill Brunt

National Open College Network (NOCN) is the leading credit and unit-based awarding body in the UK. There are 2,500 centres nationally offering NOCN qualifications, which collectively certificate around 600,000 successful learners every year. Its mission is to widen participation and access to high quality and flexible education, training and learning. It promotes social inclusion and works to ensure that learner achievement is recognised, valued and understood through a national framework of credit and qualifications. NOCN licenses nine regional Open College Networks in England, one in Wales and one in Northern Ireland, and together work in partnership with organisations to develop learning that will enable people to participate and succeed. NOCN's provision is relevant to learners and employers and is underpinned by robust standards, achievable goals and offers progression opportunities for all.

Open College Network North East Region (OCNNER)

1 Palmer Road
South West Industrial Estate
Peterlee
County Durham SR8 2HU
Tel: 0191 518 6550
Fax: 0191 518 6551
Email: admin@ocnner.org.uk
Website: www.ocnner.org.uk
Chief Executive: Dave Rippon

Open College Network North West Region

PO Box 58
Speke
Liverpool L24 8WW
Email: ocn@ocnnwr.org.uk
Website: www.ocnnwr.org.uk
Chief Executive: Tony Smith

Open College Network Yorkshire and Humber Region

OCN House
Lower Warrengate
Wakefield WF1 1SA
Tel: 01924 434600
Fax: 01924 364213
Website: www.ocnyhr.org.uk
Regional Director: Sarah Connell

Open College Network West Midlands Region

OCNWMR Building
Overstrand
Pendeford Business Park
Wolverhampton WV9 5HA
Tel: 01902 624230
Fax: 01902 624231
Email: wolverhampton@ocnwmr.org.uk
Website: www.ocnwmr.org.uk
Chief Executive Officer: Christine Assheton

Open College Network East Midlands Region (OCNEMR)

10 Newmarket Court
Newmarket Drive
Derby DE24 8NW
Tel: 01332 861 999
Fax: 01332 752 351
Email: ocnemr@ocnemr.org.uk
Website: www.ocnemr.org.uk
Regional Director: Linda Wyatt

Open College Network Eastern Region

University of Essex
Wivenhoe Park
Colchester
Essex CO4 3SQ
Tel: 01206 873023
Fax: 01206 873956
Email: enquiries@ocner.org.uk
Website: www.ocner.org.uk
Chief Executive: Keith Mogford

Open College Network South West Region

122 Bath Road
Cheltenham
Gloucestershire GL53 7JX
Tel: 01242 225511
Fax: 01242 225510
Email: info@ocnswr.org.uk
Website: www.ocnswr.org.uk
Chief Executive: Sandy de Vielle

Also office at:
Units 24/25
HQ
237 Union Street
Plymouth PL1 3HQ

Open College Network South East Region (OCNSER)

The Runnymede Centre
Chertsey Road
Addlestone
Surrey KT15 2EP
Tel: 01932 569894
Fax: 01932 564139
Website: www.ocnser.org.uk
CEO: Steve Babbidge
Finance and Operations Director: Pat Hand
Access and Business Development Director: David Gittins

Open College Network Oxford, Thames and Chiltern

Nash House
Repton Place
White Lion Road,
Amersham
Buckinghamshire HP7 9LP
Tel: 0870 220 250
Website: www.ocnotc.com
Assistant Director for Quality and Development: Anne Rixson

Open College Network London Region

15 Angel Gate
City Road
London EC1V 2SF
Tel: 020 7278 5511
Fax: 020 7833 8289
Email: enquiries@ocnlr.org.uk
Website: www.ocnlr.org.uk
Chief Executive: Maree Walker

Learning Guidance Providers – England

National Organisations

Association for Careers Education and Guidance (ACEG)
9 Lawrence Leys
Bloxham
Banbury
Oxfordshire OX15 4NU
Tel: 01295 720809
Fax: 01295 720809
Email: info@aceg.org.uk
Website: www.aceg.org.uk
General Secretary: Alan Vincent

CRAC: The Career Development Organisation
Sheraton House
Castle Park
Cambridge CB3 0AX
Tel: 01223 460277
Fax: 01223 311708
Email: enquiries@crac.org.uk
Website: www.crac.org.uk
Chief Executive: Jeffrey Defries
PA to Chief Executive: Suzi Fryer

Institute of Career Guidance
3rd Floor, Copthall House
1 New Road
Stourbridge
West Midlands DY8 1PH
Tel: 01384 376464
Fax: 01384 440830
Email: hq@icg-uk.org
Website: www.icg-uk.org
Executive Director: Chris Evans

Learndirect
PO Box 900
Manchester M60 3LE
Tel: 0800 100 900
Website: www.learndirect.co.uk
Head of Service: Lissa Davenport

Learndirect advice is a national information, advice and guidance helpline that supports adults in making appropiate decisions on the full range of learning, work and career opportunities. The service is free, impartial, confidential, and delivered by competent and qualified helpline staff that conform to equal opportunity practices, in accordance with the Guidance Council Code of Principles.

NAEGA (National Association for Educational Guidance for Adults)
c/o Meeting Makers Ltd
Jordanhill Campus
76 Southbrae Drive
Glasgow G13 1PP
Tel: 0141 434 1500
Fax: 0141 434 1519
Email: admin@naega.org.uk
Website: www.naega.org.uk
Secretary: Mo Osborne
Administrator: Fiona McGillivray

NAEGA is a UK-wide membership organisation committed to developing adult guidance practitioners in their locality through the provision of networked training events, regular news updates and information and support, whilst providing regular feedback to policy makers at a national level.

National Institute for Careers Education and Counselling (NICEC)
Sheraton House
Castle Park
Cambridge CB3 0AX
Tel: 01223 460277
Fax: 01223 311708
Email: nicec@crac.org.uk
Website: www.crac.org.uk
Director: Jeffrey Defries

Ufi Ltd
Dearing House
1 Young Street
Sheffield S1 4UP
Tel: 0114 291 5000
Fax: 0114 291 5001
Website: www.ufi.com
Chief Executive: Sarah Jones
Deputy Chief Executive: Pablo Lloyd
Chairman: John Weston

Ufi is the organisation behind learndirect –
the largest e-learning network of its kind in
the world. Established in 1999 to take
forward the concept of a 'university for
industry', Ufi's mission is to use technology
to transform the skills and employability of
the working population to improve the UK's
productivity. Through the three strands of its
service, learndirect courses, learndirect
business and learndirect advice, Ufi has
enabled millions of people across England,
Wales and Northern Ireland to access
learning and acquire new skills.

Nextstep Network

North East

Nextstep North East
CfBT Advice and Guidance
Suite 7, Wear Valley Business Centre
27 Longfield Road
South Church Business Park
Bishop Auckland DL14 6XB
Tel: 0800 027 7944
Fax: 01388 776914
Email: nextstep@cfbt.com
Website: www.nextstepnortheast.org.uk
Regional Manager in the North East:
Carole Smith

North West

Nextstep North West
Unit 2a/b Wavertree Technology Park
Wavertree Boulevard South
Liverpool L7 9PF
Freephone: 0800 434 6129
Regional Manager, Nextstep North West:
Peter Johnson

Yorkshire and Humberside

Nextstep Yorkshire and Humber
c/o Careers Yorkshire and Humber Ltd
Guidance House
York Road
Thirsk YO7 3BT
Tel: 0845 052 1040
Regional Manager: Christine Harper
Email: christine.harper@vtplc.com

West Midlands

Nextstep West Midlands
c/o CSWP Ltd
1st Floor, Tower Court
Foleshill Enterprise Park
Courtaulds Way
Coventry CV6 5QT
Tel: 08000 217 244
Email: nextstep@cswp.org.uk
Website: www.nextstepwestmidlands.org
Regional Manager: Jane Johnstone

East Midlands

Nextstep East Midlands
Guideline Career Services
159a Front Street
Arnold
Nottingham NG5 7EE
Tel: 0115 924 7277
Fax: 0115 920 6585
Website: www.nextstepeastmidlands.org.uk
Operations Manager – Adult IAG:
Penny Robinson

Guideline Career Services co-ordinates a
network of information, advice and
guidance (IAG) providers across the East
Midlands.

Eastern

Nextstep East of England
Tel: 0845 603 1059
Website: www.nextstepeastofengland.org.uk

South West

Nextstep South West
Head Office
Spread Eagle Court
Northgate Street
Gloucester GL1 1SL
Tel: 07825 145643
Email: b.billington@connexionswest.org.uk
Website: www.nextstepglos.org.uk
Lead Advisor: Brenda Billington

South East

Nextstep South East
662 North Row
Milton Keynes MK9 3AP
Tel: 01908 232808
Fax: 01908 208901
Website: www.nextstepmkob.org.uk
Regional Manager: Lyndsey Whitehead
Freephone: 0800 1954 700

London

Nextstep London
Prospects Services Ltd
7th Floor, Grosvenor House
125 High Street,
Croydon CR0 9XP
Tel: 020 8649 6409
Fax: 020 8649 6444
Email: charles.humphreys@prospects.co.uk
Website: www.nextsteplondon.org.uk
Regional Manager: Sue Mairis
Marketing and Communications Manager:
Charles Humphreys

Other Guidance Providers

North East

Connexions Tyne and Wear
New Pathways
Amber Court
William Armstrong Drive
Newcastle Business Park,
Newcastle upon Tyne NE4 7YA
Tel: 0800 073 0708
Fax: 0191 245 3481
Email: info@new-pathways.org.uk
Website:
www.nextstepnorthumberland.org.uk
Nextstep Northumberland Delivery
Co-ordinator: Mick Towers

New Pathways Tyne and Wear
c/o Connexions Hub Services
Interchange Centre
West Street
Gateshead NE8 1BH
Tel: 0191 443 4206
Fax: 0191 443 4224
Email: info@new-pathways.org.uk
Website: www.new-pathways.org.uk
Project Co-ordinator: Sue Reeve

North West

Connexions Cheshire and Warrington
Partnership Office
No 2 The Stables
Gadbrook Park
Rudheath
Northwich
Cheshire CW9 7RJ
Tel: 01606 305200
Fax: 01606 49158
Website: www.connexions-cw.co.uk
Development Manager: Gill Alderson

Connexions Cheshire and Warrington has
operational centres, all of which deliver
advice and guidance about learning, jobs
and training in the following locations
throughout Cheshire and Warrington:

Chester, Congleton, Crewe, Ellesmere Port, Macclesfield, Northwich, Warrington and Winsford.

Connexions Stockport
64 Chestergate
Stockport
Cheshire SK1 1NP
Tel: 0161 475 7700
Fax: 0161 476 6760
Email:
enquiries@connexions-stockport.org.uk
Website: www.connexions-stockport.org.uk

Greater Merseyside Connexions Partnership
Head Office
Unit 2A
Wavertree Boulevard South
Wavertree Technology Park
Liverpool L7 9PF
Tel: 0151 230 4436
Fax: 0151 254 6601
Chief Executive: Kieran Gordon
Adult Guidance Manager: Peter Johnson

Highway to Opportunities (H2O)
Brunswick House
Union Street
Oldham OL1 1DE
Tel: 0161 621 9200
Fax: 0161 621 9201
Email: h2o@positivestepsoldham.org.uk
Website: www.h-2-o.org.uk
IAG Manager: Sarah Bell

Wigan Council
Department of Adult Services
Information Advice and Guidance Team
Connexions Centre Wigan
London House
104–110 Standishgate
Wigan
Lancashire WN1 1XP
Tel: 01942 828912
Team Leader: Anthony Mohammed
Education Advice Worker: Rita Higginson
Education Advice Worker: Naina Kent
Information Support Worker:
Richard Creighton
Receptionist/Clerical Worker: Andrea Lewis

Yorkshire and Humberside

Adult Choices
Onward House
Baptist Place
Bradford
West Yorkshire BD1 2PS
Tel: 01274 829381
Fax: 01274 829401
Website: www.careersb.co.uk
Operations Director: Craig Williams

Calderdale and Kirklees Careers
78 John William Street
Huddersfield
West Yorkshire HD1 1EH
Tel: 01484 226700
Fax: 01484 226725
Email: careers@ckcareers.org.uk
Website: www.workabout.org.uk
H.R.D. Manager: Derran Sewell

EASA (Education Advice Service for Adults)
The Learning Shop
69 Godwin Street
Bradford
West Yorkshire BD1 2SH
Tel: 01274 433677
Email: mail@easabradford.co.uk
Manager: Marion Hamilton

Future Prospects
24 Swinegate
York
North Yorkshire YO1 8AZ
Tel: 01904 634748
Fax: 01904 634750
Email: admin@futureprospects.org.uk
Website: www.futureprospects.org.uk
Manager: Andrew Cambridge
Manager: Andy Bucklee

igen Limited
Coverdale House
15 East Parade
Leeds LS1 2BH
Tel: 0113 208 9000
Fax: 0113 209 1350
Email: philip.styan@futurepathways.co.uk
Website: www.igengroup.co.uk
Operations Manager (Adult Services):
Philip Styan

NEW Futures
Sheffield Futures
Star House
43 Division Street
Sheffield S1 4SL
Tel: 0114 201 2800
Fax: 0114 201 2757
Email: enquiries@sheffieldfutures.org.uk
Website: www.sheffieldfutures.org.uk
Senior Manager: Nigel Ball

For booked careers guidance appointments
please telephone 0114 201 2838.

West Midlands

Connexions Staffordshire
Foregate House
70 Foregate Street
Stafford ST16 2PX
Tel: 0808 1000 434
Fax: 01785 355 747
Email: info@cxstaffs.co.uk
Website: www.cxstaffs.co.uk
Chief Executive: Carol Jones
Operation Manager Adults: Susan Walmsley

East Midlands

Connexions Nottinghamshire
Heathcote Buildings
Heathcote Street
Nottingham NG1 3AA
Tel: 0115 912 6611
Fax: 0115 912 6612
Email: ask@cnxnotts.co.uk
Website: www.cnxnotts.co.uk
Information Services Manager:
Dianne Purdy

Eastern

Hertsmere Worknet
The Old Post Office
23 Shenley Road
Borehamwood
Hertfordshire WD6 1AU
Tel: 020 8236 7600
Fax: 020 8236 7609
Email: admin@worknet.org.uk
Website: www.worknet.org.uk
Business Manager: Allison Overington

Norfolk Guidance Service
Room B18, County Hall
Martineau Lane
Norwich NR1 2UA
Tel: 01603 223890
Fax: 01603 222422
Email: ngs@norfolk.gov.uk
Website:
www.norfolkguidanceservice.org.uk
Head of Service: Jennifer Holland

South West

Connexions Swindon and Wiltshire
1 Wicker Hill
Trowbridge
Wiltshire BA14 8JS
Tel: 01225 716450
Fax: 01225 716459
Email: cnx-trowbridge@wiltshire.co.uk
Website: www.connexions.org.uk
Centre Administrative Manager:
Jackie Skrebys

Information, Advice and Guidance at Connexions West of England
4 Colston Avenue
Bristol BS1 4ST
Tel: 0117 9074426
Fax: 0117 9872661
Email: enquiries@connexionswest.org.uk
Manager: Mike Griffiths

Prospects
Pearl House
Church Street
Bridgwater
Somerset TA6 5AT
Tel: 01278 422301
Fax: 01278 453775
Email: jenny.windsor@prospects.co.uk
Website: www.prospects.co.uk

Skills 4 Jobs
c/o Tribal Education
Suite 12, Pear Tree Business Centre
Cobhan Road
Ferndown Industrial Estate
Wimborne
Dorset BH21 7PT
Tel: 0845 437 8994
Email: info@skills4jobs.org
Website: www.skills4jobs.org
Business Development Manager:
Lindsey Burke

South East

The Bridge Consultancy
PO Box 501
Chichester
West Sussex PO19 9AA
Tel: 01983 292588
Fax: 01983 292588
Email: bridgeuk@aol.com
Website: www.thebridgeconsultancy.co.uk
Managing Consultant and Director of
Counselling: Mary Barker

Supporting individuals, couples, groups and
organisations to manage change effectively;
personal and professional workplace
counselling; current guidance (IAG);
redundancy, mentoring, coaching, training,
supervision working in secular and Christian
settings.

Connexions Centre
Enfield Careers Centre
59 Church Street
Enfield
Middlesex EN2 6AN
Tel: 020 8366 9546
Fax: 020 8366 9586
Email:
enfieldcc@connexions-northlondon.co.uk
Website: www.prospects.co.uk
Information Assistant: S Brown-Grant

New Start Adult Guidance Service – Oxford City
East Oxford Lifelong Learning Centre
Collins Street
Oxford OX4 1EE
Tel: 01865 798081
Email: city.newstart@oxfordshire.gov.uk
Website: www.oxfordshire.gov.uk
Guidance Adviser: Cecily Lee

London

Careers Management Capital
Head Office
3–4 Picton Place
London W1U 1BJ
Tel: 020 7487 9315
Fax: 020 7224 1702
Email: enquiries@capitalcareers.ltd.uk
Website: www.capitalcareers.ltd.uk

Other Offices:
Westminister Centre: Tel: 020 7487 4504
Camden Centre: Tel: 020 7482 3996
Hammersmith Centre: Tel: 020 8741 2441

Education Advice Service for Adults
The Learning Trust
1 Reading Lane
London E8 1GQ
Tel: 020 8820 7168
Fax: 020 8820 7174
Email: adult.EGSA@learningtrust.co.uk
Website:
www.learningtrust.co.uk/adult_learning/
Adult Guidance Service Manager:
Lorna Ford-Panton

Greenwich Education and Training Advice for Adults (GRETA)
31 Herbert Road
Plumstead
London SE18 3SZ
Tel: 020 8331 5101
Fax: 020 8312 5122
Email: shaunagh.gwynn@prospects.co.uk
Nextstep Delivery Manager:
Shaunagh Gwynn
Manager, External Contracts: Mike Bowles

Lambeth Adult Guidance Service
Ivor House
1 Acre Lane
London SW2 5TB
Tel: 020 7926 3324
Fax: 020 7926 3301
Website: www.lambeth.gov.uk
Manager: Helen Sprogis

Channel Islands

Careers Jersey
PO Box 55
St Helier

Jersey JE4 8PE
Tel: 01534 449351 or 449440
Fax: 01534 449470
Email: careers@gov.je
Website: www.gov.je/careers
Head of Information, Advice and Guidance:
Andy Gibbs

Guernsey Adult Guidance Service
Education Department
PO Box 32
Grange Road
St Peter Port
Guernsey GY1 3AU
Tel: 01481 733044/057
Fax: 01481 713015
Email: rvivian@education.gov.gg
Website: www.careers.gg
Adult Guidance Manager: Richard Vivian

Wales – Education System

Government

Department for Children, Education, Lifelong Learning and Skills
Welsh Assembly Government
Cathays Park
Cardiff CF10 3NQ
Tel: 0845 0103300
Fax: 029 2082 5823
Email: DELLSwebteam@wales.gsi.gov.uk
Website: www.wales.gov.uk
Welsh Assembly Government First Minister:
Rhodri Morgan AM
Minister for Children, Education and
Lifelong Learning Skills: Jane Hunt AM
Permanent Secretary: Jon Shortridge
Director of Children, Lifelong Learning and
Skills: Steve Marshall
Head of Lifelong Learning and Skills Group:
Dr Dennis Gunning

Welsh Joint Education Committee (WJEC)
245 Western Avenue
Cardiff CF5 2YX
Tel: 029 2026 5000
Fax: 029 2057 5887
Email: info@wjec.co.uk
Website: www.wjec.co.uk
Chief Executive: Gareth E Pierce

Welsh Local Government Association
Local Government House
Drake Walk
Cardiff CF10 4LG
Tel: 029 2046 8600
Fax: 029 2046 8601
Website: www.wlga.gov.uk
Executive Director: Steve Thomas
Director of Lifelong Learning, Leisure and
Information:
Dr Chris Llewelyn
Email: chris.llewelyn@wlga.gov.uk

Inspection

Estyn
Anchor Court
Keen Road
Cardiff CF24 5JW
Tel: 029 2044 6446
Fax: 029 2044 6448
Website: www.estyn.gov.uk
Her Majesty's Chief Inspector in Wales:
Dr Bill Maxwell

Local Education Authorities

Blaenau Gwent County Borough Council
Community Services
Anvil Court
Church Street
Abertillery ND13 1DB
Tel: 01495 355262
Email:
education.department@blaenau-gwent.gov.uk
Corporate Director of Community Services:
Phil Hodgson
Head of Adult Education: Byron Jones
Adult Education Manager: Sheila Daycock
Adult Education Manager: Kathy Smith

Bridgend County Borough Council
Wellbeing Directorate
Sunnyside
Bridgend CF31 4AR
Tel: 01656 642211
Fax: 01656 766162
Website: www.bridgend.gov.uk
Corporate Director – Wellbeing:
Abigail Harris
Interim Principal, Office – Adult and
Community Learning: Donna Hooper

Caerphilly County Borough Council
Directorate of Education and Leisure
Council Offices
Caerphilly Road
Ystrad Mynach
Hengoed
Caerphilly CF82 7EP
Tel: 01443 864956
Fax: 01443 862153
Website: www.caerphilly.gov.uk
Director of Education and Leisure:
David Hopkins
Head of Community Education, Leisure and
Libraries: Peter Gomer
Principal Officer, Community Education and
Libraries: Steve Mason

Cardiff County Council
Schools and Lifelong Learning
County Hall
Atlantic Wharf
Cardiff CF10 4UW
Tel: 029 2087 2700
Fax: 029 2087 2705
Website: www.cardiff.gov.uk/schools
Chief Schools and Lifelong Learning Officer:
Chris Jones
Lifelong Learning Manager: Geraint Rees
Operational Manager: Gabi Taylor
County Community Education Officer
(Adult/Education): Mair Sims

Carmarthenshire County Council
Education and Community Services.
Room 300, Block 1
Parc Myrodin
Richmond Terrace
Carmarthen SA31 2NH
Tel: 01267 224501
Fax: 01267 221692
Website: www.carmarthenshire.gov.uk
Director of Education and Community
Services: Alun Davies
Lifelong Learning Manager: Matt Morden

Ceredigion County Council
Education Department
County Offices
Marine Terrace
Aberystwyth
Ceredigion SY23 2DE
Tel: 01970 633656
Fax: 01970 633663
Email: education@ceredigion.gov.uk
Website: www.ceredigion.gov.uk
Director of Education and Community
Services: Gareth Jones
Assistant Director: Dr Rhodri Morgan
Community Learning Officer: Mari Morgan

City and County of Swansea
Education Department
Lifelong Learning Service
Dynevor Information Centre
Dynevor Place
Swansea
West Glamorgan SA1 3ET
Tel: 01792 648081
Fax: 01792 653722
Director of Education: Richard Parry
Manager, Lifelong Learning:
Michael Hughes

Conwy County Borough Council
Education Department
Government Buildings
Dinerth Road
Rhos-on-Sea
Colwyn Bay LL28 4UL
Tel: 01492 575001
Fax: 01492 541311
Website: www.conwy.gov.uk/education
Statutory Head of Education Services:
Geraint James
Youth Services Manager: Jane Williams

Denbighshire County Council
Directorate of Lifelong Learning
Trem Clwyd
Canol Y Dre
Ruthin
Denbighshire LL15 1QA
Tel: 01824 708098
Fax: 01824 708029
Website: www.denbighshire.gov.uk
Corporate Director: Lifelong Learning:
Huw Griffiths
Principal Adult Education Officer:
Julian Molloy

Flintshire County Council
Directorate of Lifelong Learning
County Hall
Mold
Flintshire CH7 6ND
Tel: 01352 704010
Fax: 01352 754202
Email: education@flintshire.gov.uk
Website: www.flintshire.gov.uk
Director of Lifelong Learning: Ian Budd
Transition Years Co-ordinator: Justin Soper
Tel: 01352 704064
Lifelong Learning Librarian: Gina Maddison

Gwynedd Council
Council Offices
Caernarfon
Gwynedd LL55 1SH
Tel: 01286 672255
Fax: 01286 677347
Website: www.gwynedd.gov.uk
Strategic Director – Development:
Iwan Trefor Jones
Head of Youth and Community/Student
Support Services Unit: Peter Lunt Williams

Isle of Anglesey County Council
Education and Leisure Department
Park Mount
Glanhwfa Road
Llangefni
Anglesey LL77 7EY
Tel: 01248 752900
Fax: 01248 752999
Website: www.ynysmon.gov.uk
Corporate Director for Education and
Leisure: Richard Parry Jones
Email: rpjed@anglesey.gov.uk

Merthyr Tydfil County Borough Council
Integrated Adult Services
Ty Keir Hardie
Riverside Court
Avenue De Clichy
Merthyr Tydfil
Mid Glamorgan CF47 8XE
Tel: 01685 724602
Fax: 01685 384868
Email:
integratedadultservices@merthyr.gov.uk
Website: www.merthyr.gov.uk
Director of Integrated Adult Services:
Giovanni Isingrini
Head of Community Education:
Sheila Thompson
Adult Education Co-ordinator:
Jennifer Connolly

Monmouthshire County Council
Directorate of Lifelong Learning and Leisure
5th Floor, County Hall
Cwmbran
Monmouthshire NP44 2XH
Tel: 01633 644487
Fax: 01633 644488
Website: www.monmouthshire.gov.uk
Corporate Director of Lifelong Learning and
Leisure: Andrew Keep
Community Education Manager:
Carol Clammer

Neath Port Talbot County Borough Council
Education, Leisure and Lifelong Learning
Directorate
Civic Centre
Port Talbot
West Glamorgan SA13 1PJ
Tel: 01639 763333
Fax: 01639 763150
Email: education@neath-porttalbot.gov.uk
Website: www.neath-porttalbot.gov.uk
Director of Education, Leisure and Lifelong
Learning: Karl Napieralla
Adult Community Learning Manager:
Helen Matthews

Newport City Council
Community Learning and Libraries
John Frost Square
Newport
Gwent NP20 1PA
Tel: 01633 656656
Email: gill.john@newport.gov.uk
Website: www.newport.gov.uk
Community Learning and Libraries
Manager: Gill John
Head of Continuing Learning and Leisure:
Ffion Lloyd
Managing Director: Chris Freegard

Pembrokeshire County Council
Education Directorate
County Hall
Haverfordwest
Pembrokeshire SA61 1QZ
Tel: 01437 775121
Fax: 01437 775838
Director of Education and Community
Services: Gerson Davies
Lifelong Learning Manager, Adult Education
Service: Chris Birch

Powys County Council
People and Well-being
County Hall
Llandrindod Wells
Powys LD1 5LG
Tel: 01597 826422
Fax: 01597 826475
Website: www.education.powys.gov.uk
Executive Director: Phil Robson
Head of Schools and Pupil Inclusion:
Douglas Wilson
Email: douglas.wilson@powys.gov.uk
Principal Adult Education Officer:
Hywel Roberts

Rhondda Cynon Taf County Borough Council
Education and Lifelong Learning
Ty Trevithick
Abercynon
Mountain Ash
Mid Glamorgan CF45 4UQ
Tel: 01443 744000
Fax: 01433 744023
Email:
jacqui.elisabeth.hopkins@rhondda-cynon-taff.go
Website: www.rhondda-cynon-taff.gov.uk
Director of Education and Lifelong
Learning: Mike Keating
Head of Youth Service: Ron Jones

Torfaen County Borough Council
3rd Floor, County Hall
Cwmbran
Torfaen NP44 2WN
Tel: 01633 648804
Email: karen.padfield@torfaen.gov.uk
Website: www.torfaen.gov.uk
Head of Adult Education: Karen Padfield
Adult Education Officer: Jean Gaywood
Adult Education Officer: Linda Brown

Vale of Glamorgan Council
Civic Offices
Holton Road
Barry CF63 4RU
Tel: 01446 709148
Fax: 01446 709448
Website: www.valeofglamorgan.gov.uk
Head of Lifelong Learning: David Prosser
Director, Learning and Development:
Bryan Jeffreys
Principal Adult and Community Learning
Officer: Barbara Walters

Wrexham County Borough Council
Leisure, Libraries and Culture
Lambpit Street
Wrexham
Clwyd LL11 1AR
Tel: 01978 297431
Fax: 01978 297448
Website: www.wrexham.gov.uk
Chief Officer, Leisure, Libraries and Culture:
Alan Watkin
Email: alan.watkin@wrexham.gov.uk

Further Education

Fforwm (Association of Welsh Colleges)
The Quadrant Centre
Cardiff Business Park
Llanishen
Cardiff CF14 5WF
Tel: 029 2074 1800
Fax: 029 2074 1803
Email: secretariat@fforwm.ac.uk
Website: www.fforwm.ac.uk
Chief Executive: Dr John Graystone

Further Education Institutions

Barry College
Colcot Road
Barry
Vale of Glamorgan CF62 8YJ
Tel: 01446 725000
Fax: 01446 732667
Email: enquiries@barry.ac.uk
Website: www.barry.ac.uk
Chief Executive: Paul Halstead

Bridgend College
Cowbridge Road
Bridgend
Mid Glamorgan CF31 3DF
Tel: 01656 302302
Fax: 01656 663912
Email: enquiries@bridgend.ac.uk
Website: www.bridgend.ac.uk
Principal: Mark Jones
Head of Essential Skills: Roger Evans

Coleg Ceredigion
Llanbadarn Campus
Llanbadarn Fawr
Aberystwyth
Ceredigion SY23 3BP
Tel: 01970 639700
Fax: 01970 623206
Website: www.ceredigion.ac.uk
Principal: Andre Morgan
Vice-Principal: Jacqui Weatherburn
Basic Skills Co-ordinator: Theresa Davies
Heads of Faculty: Keith Jones, Greg Hill,
Theresa Jones

Coleg Glan Hafren
Trowbridge Campus
Trowbridge Road
Rumney
Cardiff CF3 1XZ
Tel: 029 2025 0250
Fax: 029 2025 0339
Website: www.glan-hafren.ac.uk
Principal: Malcolm Charnley
Director of Planning and Business
Development: Nigel Hallett

Coleg Gwent
Usk Campus
The Rhadyr
Usk
Gwent NP15 1XJ
Tel: 01495 333333
Fax: 01495 333526
Email: info@coleggwent.ac.uk
Website: www.coleggwent.ac.uk
Principal/Chief Executive: Howard Burton
Vice-Principal, Quality, Enterprise and
Planning: Nicola Gamlin

Coleg Llysfasi
Ruthin
Pentrecelyn
Denbighshire LL15 2LB
Tel: 01978 790263
Fax: 01978 790468
Email: admin@llysfasi.ac.uk
Website: www.llysfasi.ac.uk
Principal: Fred Cunningham

Coleg Meirion-Dwyfor
Ffordd Ty'n y Coed
Dolgellau
Gwynedd LL40 2SW
Tel: 01341 422827
Fax: 01341 422393
Email: coleg@meirion-dwyfor.ac.uk
Website: www.meirion-dwyfor.ac.uk
Principal: Dr Ian Rees
Email: ij.rees@meirion-dwyfor.ac.uk
Head of Faculty, SLDD:
Gwyn Owain Rowlands

Coleg Menai
Ffordd Ffriddoedd
Bangor
Gwynedd LL57 2TP
Tel: 01248 370125
Fax: 01248 370052
Email: access@menai.ac.uk
Website: www.menai.ac.uk
Principal: Dr Haydn E Edwards

Coleg Morgannwg
Ynys Terrace
Rhydyfelin
Pontypridd
Rhondda Cynon Taff CF37 5RN
Tel: 01443 662800
Fax: 01443 663028
Email: college@morgannwg.ac.uk
Website: www.morgannwg.ac.uk
Principal: Judith Evans
Head of School – Community Development
and Adult Basic Education: Lindsay Harris

Coleg Powys
Llanidloes Road
Newtown
Powys SY16 4HU
Tel: 0845 4086 205
Fax: 01686 622 246
Email: enquiries@coleg-powys.ac.uk
Website: www.coleg-powys.ac.uk
Principal: John L Stephenson
Head of School – General and Community
Education: Hala Hanschell
Head of School – IT, General and
Community Education: Dr Philippa Davies

Coleg Sir Gâr
Graig Campus
Sandy Road
Llanelli
Carmarthenshire SA15 4DN
Tel: 01554 748000
Fax: 01554 756088
Email: catherineharry@colegsirgar.ac.uk
Website: www.colegsirgar.ac.uk
Principal and Chief Executive:
Brian Robinson

Deeside College
Kelsterton Road
Connah's Quay
Deeside
Flintshire CH5 4BR
Tel: 01244 831531
Fax: 01244 814305
Email: enquiries@deeside.ac.uk
Website: www.deeside.ac.uk
Vice Principal, Curriculum and Quality:
Ian Dickson

Gorseinon College
Belgrave Road
Gorseinon
Swansea SA4 6RD
Tel: 01792 890700
Fax: 01792 898729
Email: admin@gorseinon.ac.uk
Website: www.gorseinon.ac.uk
Principal/Chief Executive: Nick Bennett
Manager, Lifelong Learning: Alison Pope

Llandrillo College
Llandudno Road
Rhos-on-Sea
Colwyn Bay LL28 4HZ
Tel: 01492 546666
Fax: 01492 543052
Email: admissions@llandrillo.ac.uk
Website: www.llandrillo.ac.uk
Principal: Huw Evans
Deputy Principal: Jean Smith

Merthyr Tydfil College
Ynysfach
Merthyr Tydfil CF48 1AR
Tel: 01685 726000
Fax: 01685 726100
Website: www.merthyr.ac.uk
Associate Dean and Head of College:
Jonathan Martin

Neath Port Talbot College
Dwr-y-Felin Road
Neath
West Glamorgan SA10 7RF
Tel: 01639 648000
Fax: 01639 648009
Email: enquiries@nptc.ac.uk
Website: www.nptc.ac.uk
Principal: Mark Dacey
Community Programme Manager:
Rosemary Royce

Pembrokeshire College
Merlin's Bridge
Haverfordwest
Pembrokeshire SA61 1SZ
Tel: 01437 753000
Fax: 01437 767279
Email: info@pembrokeshire.ac.uk
Website: www.pembrokeshire.ac.uk
Principal: Glyn Jones

Pengwern College of Further Education
Sarn Lane
Rhuddlan
Denbighshire LL18 5UH
Tel: 01745 590281
Fax: 01745 591736
Email: pengwern.college@mencap.org.uk
Deputy Principal: Lisa Duncalf

Royal Welsh College of Music and Drama
Castle Grounds
Cathays Park
Cardiff CF10 3ER
Tel: 029 2034 2854
Fax: 029 2039 1304
Email: info@rwcmd.ac.uk
Website: www.rwcmd.ac.uk
Principal: Hilary Boulding

St Davids Catholic College
Ty Gwyn Road
Penylan
Cardiff CF23 5QD
Tel: 029 2049 8555
Fax: 029 2047 2594
Principal: Mark Leighfield

Swansea College
Tycoch Road
Sketty
Swansea SA2 9EB
Tel: 01792 284000
Fax: 01792 284074
Email: delivery@swancoll.ac.uk
Website: www.swancoll.ac.uk
Principal and Chief Executive:
Jeff Gunningham
Assistant Principal, Finance and Resources:
Anthony Robertson
Deputy Principal: Sandra Hickman

Welsh College of Horticulture
Northop
Mold
Flintshire CH7 6AA
Tel: 01352 841000
Fax: 01352 841031
Email: admin@wcoh.ac.uk
Website: www.wcoh.ac.uk
Principal: Dr Mark Simkin
Head of Widening Participation:
Richard Lewis

Yale College
Grove Park Road
Wrexham
Clwyd LL12 7AB
Tel: 01978 311794
Fax: 01978 291569
Email: admissions@yale-wrexham.ac.uk
Website: www.yale-wrexham.ac.uk
Principal: Paul Croke

Ystrad Mynach College
Twyn Road
Ystrad Mynach
Hengoed
Caerphilly CF82 7XR
Tel: 01443 816888
Fax: 01443 816973
Email: enquiries@ystrad-mynach.ac.uk
Website: www.ystrad-mynach.ac.uk
Principal: Bryn Davies
Marketing Officer: Catherine Phillips

Higher Education

Bangor University
College of Education and Lifelong Learning
Dean Street
Bangor
Gwynedd LL57 1UT
Tel: 01248 383672
Fax: 01248 382044
Email: glenda.jones@bangor.ac.uk
Website: www.bangor.ac.uk
Vice-Chancellor: Prof. Merfyn Jones
Pro-Vice-Chancellor (Widening
Participation): Meri Huws

Cardiff University
Cardiff Centre for Lifelong Learning
Senghennydd Road
Cardiff CF24 4AG
Tel: 029 2087 0000
Fax: 029 2066 8935
Email: learn@cardiff.ac.uk
Website: www.cardiff.ac.uk
Vice-Chancellor: Dr David Grant
Dean of Lifelong Learning:
Dr Richard Evans

North East Wales Institute of Higher Education
School of Education and Community
Plas Coch Campus
Mold Road
Wrexham LL11 2AW
Tel: 01978 293053
Fax: 01978 290008
Email: a.osullivan@newi.ac.uk
Website: www.newi.ac.uk
Subject Leader, Informal and Continuing
Education: Alison O'Sullivan

The Open University in Wales
18 Custom House Street
Cardiff CF10 1AP
Tel: 029 2047 1019
Fax: 029 2038 8132
Email: wales@open.ac.uk
Website: www.open.ac.uk
Director: Rob Humphreys

Swansea Metropolitan University
Mount Pleasant
Swansea SA1 6ED
Tel: 01792 481000
Fax: 01792 481085
Email: enquiry@sihe.ac.uk
Website: www.smu.ac.uk
Vice-Chancellor: Prof. David Warner
Academic Secretary: Dr David Ashelby

Trinity College
College Road
Carmarthen SA31 3EP
Tel: 01267 676767
Fax: 01267 676766
Website: www.trinity-cm.ac.uk
Principal: Dr Medwin Hughes
Head of Student Services: Tom Evans

University of Glamorgan
Llantwit Road
Treforest
Pontypridd CF37 1DL
Tel: 01443 480480
Fax: 01443 480558
Website: www.glam.ac.uk
Vice-Chancellor: Prof. David Halton

University of Wales
University Registry
King Edward VII Avenue
Cathays Park
Cardiff CF10 3NS
Tel: 029 2037 6999
Fax: 029 2037 6983
Email: uniwales@wales.ac.uk
Website: www.wales.ac.uk
Head of the Academic's Office:
John McInally

University of Wales, Aberystwyth
Old College
King Street
Aberystwyth
Ceredigion SY23 2AX
Tel: 01970 623111
Fax: 01970 611446
Website: www.aber.ac.uk
Principal: Prof. Noel Lloyd
Head of Admissions and Recruitment:
Dr H M Davies
Lifelong Learning Officer: Dr Sue Pester
Head of School – Education and Lifelong
Learning: Prof. Peter Neil

University of Wales, Lampeter
College Street
Lampeter
Ceredigion SA48 7ED
Tel: 01570 424785
Fax: 01570 424990
Email: enquiries@volstudy.ac.uk
Website: www.volstudy.ac.uk
Vice-Chancellor: Prof. R A Pearce
Head of Department – Voluntary Sector
Studies: Conny Matera-Rogers

University of Wales, Newport
Lodge Road
Caerleon
Newport
Gwent NP18 3QT
Tel: 01633 432046
Fax: 01633 432006
Email: uic@newport.ac.uk
Website: www.newport.ac.uk
Vice-Chancellor: Dr Peter Noyes
Director – Centre for Community and
Lifelong Learning: Vivian Davies

University of Wales, Swansea
Department of Adult Continuing Education
Singleton Park
Swansea SA2 8PP
Tel: 01792 295277
Fax: 01792 295751
Email: adult.education@swansea.ac.uk
Website: www.swan.ac.uk/dace
Head of Department: Prof. Colin Trotman
Vice-Chancellor: Prof. Richard B Davies

University of Wales Institute, Cardiff (UWIC)
PO Box 377
Western Avenue
Cardiff CF5 2SG
Tel: 029 2041 6070
Fax: 029 2041 6286
Email: uwicinfo@uwic.ac.uk
Website: www.uwic.ac.uk
Vice-Chancellor and Principal:
Prof. A J Chapman
Dean of Academic Development and
Participation: Peter Treadwell

Open College Network

Open College Network Wales
North Wales
3–4 Llys Onnen
Parc Menai
Bangor
Gwynedd LL57 4DF
Tel: 01248 670011
Fax: 08700 519679
Email: croeso@ocn.org.uk
Website: www.ocnwales.org.uk
Chief Executive Officer: Janet Barlow

South Wales
1–2 Purbeck House
Cardiff Business Park
Llanishen
Cardiff CF14 5GJ
Tel: 02920 747866
Fax: 02920 741079

Residential Adult Education

Coleg Harlech WEA (North Wales)
Harlech
Gwynedd LL46 2PU
Tel: 01766 780363
Fax: 01766 780169
Email: info@fc.harlech.ac.uk
Website: www.harlech.ac.uk
Principal: Annie Williams
Deputy Director of Projects:
Catrin Lloyd Perry
Director of Studies: Trefor Fon Owen

Coleg Harlech WEAN is a specialist adult education provider offering community courses across North and Mid Wales, and residential provision at its site in Harlech, Gwynedd. The Association is particularly keen to recruit adult learners who may have experienced difficulties reaching their full potential in the past. A range of subject areas are offered at different levels. Creative art and design, music technology, social sciences and multimedia feature strongly in the curriculum.

The Hill Education and Conference Centre

Pen-y-Pound
Abergavenny
Gwent NP7 7RP
Tel: 01495 333777
Fax: 01495 333778
Email: hill@coleggwent.ac.uk
Website: www.thehillabergavenny.co.uk
Director: Linda Swanson
Deputy Director: Stuart Ford
Conference Manager: Allison Werner

The Hill is an adult education and conference centre set in delightful grounds on the edge of the Brecon Beacons National Park. The campus offers a wide variety of courses, including IT, horticulture, Welsh, management, hospitality, classroom assistant and teacher training. Weekend courses and summer schools are also provided in a range of leisure and vocational topics. With 48 en-suite bedrooms and six well equipped conference rooms it offers residential and conference facilities throughout the year at competitive rates. It has a Visit Wales 3 star grading.

Adult and Community Education Providers

Ebbw Vale Learning Action Centre

James Street
Ebbw Vale
Gwent NP23 6JG
Tel: 01495 303544
Email: kathy.smith@blaenau-gwent.gov.uk
Website: www.blaenau-gwent.gov.uk
Adult Education Manager: Kathy Smith

Pontypool Community Education Centre

The Settlement
Trosnant Street
Pontypool
Gwent NP4 8AT
Tel: 01495 742600
Email: the.settlement@torfaen.gov.uk
Community Education Manager:
Karen Padifield
Adult Education Officer: Linda Brown

Risca Community Education Centre

Oxford House
Grove Road
Risca
Caerphilly NP11 6GN
Tel: 01633 612245
Fax: 01633 615903
Email: oxfordhouse@caerphilly.gov.uk
Area Community Education Manager:
Gaynor Edmunds

Learning Guidance Providers

Careers Wales Cardiff and Vale Ltd

Cardiff Careers Centre
53 Charles Street
Cardiff CF10 2GD
Tel: 029 2090 6700
Fax: 029 2090 6799
Website: www.careerswales.com

Careers Wales Gwent

Ty Glyn, Unit 1, Brecon Court
William Brown Close
Llantarnam Park
Cwmbran
Gwent NP44 3AB
Tel: 01633 487600
Fax: 01633 487601
Email:
headoffice@careerswalesgwent.org.uk
Website: www.careerswales.com
Chief Executive: Trina Neilson
Adult Guidance Manager: Paty Wysom

Careers Wales Mid Glamorgan and Powys
10–11 Centre Court
Treforest Industrial Estate
Pontypridd CF37 5YR
Tel: 01443 842207
Fax: 01443 842208
Email: hqadmin@cwmg.co.uk
Website: www.careerswales.com
Chief Executive: Ann Evans

Careers Wales North East
Head Office
St Davids Building
Daniel Owen Square
Earl Road
Mold
Flintshire CH7 1DD
Tel: 01352 750456
Fax: 01352 756470
Email: enquiries@cwne.org
Website: www.careerswales.com
Chief Executive: Joyce M'Caw

Careers Wales North West
Head Office
5 Llys Castan
Parc Menai
Bangor
Gwynedd, LL57 4FH
Tel: 01248 627800
Fax: 01248 672801
Email: spencers@careers-gyrfa.org.uk
Website: www.gyrfacymru
Adult Guidance Manager: Emlyn Evans
Information and Marketing Manager: Sarah
Jones-Morris

For further information contact your local
Careers Centre:
Bangor – 01248 364682
Caernarfon – 01286 662930
Colwyn Bay – 01492 534079
Head Office – 01248 672800
Holyhead – 01407 762177
Llandudno – 01492 871900
Porthmadog – 01766 514501
Rhyl – 01745 330012

Careers Wales West
Head Office
Heol Nantyreos
Cross Hands
Carmarthenshire SA14 6RJ
Tel: 01269 846000
Fax: 01269 846001
Email: mail@cwwest.co.uk
Website: www.careerswales.com
Policy Manager, Skills and Economic
Regeneration: Andrew Kirby

For Adult Services contact:
Andrew Kirby
William Knox House
Britannic Way
Llandarcy SA10 6EL
Tel: 01792 352015

Education-related and Other Organisations

Age Concern Cymru
Ty John Pathy
13–14 Neptune Court
Vanguard Way
Cardiff CF24 5PJ
Tel: 029 2043 1555
Fax: 029 2047 1418
Email: enquiries@accymru.org.uk
Website: www.accymru.org.uk
Director: Robert Taylor
Healthy Ageing Manager: Mark Allen

All Wales Ethnic Minority Association (AWEMA)
1st Floor, Suite 2
St Davids House
Wood Street
Cardiff CF10 1ES
Tel: 029 2066 4213
Fax: 029 2023 6071
Email: enquiries@awema.org.uk
Website: www.awema.org.uk
Chief Executive: Naz Malik

Amgueddfa Cymru – National Museum Wales
National Museum Cardiff
Cathays Park
Cardiff CF10 3NP
Tel: 029 2039 7951
Fax: 029 2057 3321
Email: post@museumwales.ac.uk
Website: www.museumwales.ac.uk
Director: Michael Houlihan
Head of Learning: Ceri Black
Operations Manager: Llinos Thomas

Amman Valley Enterprises
Education and Training Centre
Tairgwaith
Ammanford
Carmarthenshire SA18 1UD
Tel: 01269 826267
Fax: 01269 826267
Lifelong Learning Co-ordinator:
Susan Morgan

Arts Council of Wales
Holst House
9 Museum Place
Cardiff CF10 3NX
Tel: 029 2037 6500
Fax: 029 2022 1447
Email: information@artswales.org.uk
Website: www.artswales.org.uk
Head of Planning and Development:
Diane Hebb

Bridgend Learning and Skills Network
Children's Directorate
Sunnyside Offices
Sunnyside
Bridgend
Mid Glamorgan CF31 4AR
Tel: 01656 642697
Fax: 01656 642646
Chair: John Bevan OBE
Co-ordinator: Kath Durbin

Ceredigion Lifelong Learning Thematic Group
c/o Coleg Ceredigion
Park Place
Cardigan
Dyfed SA43 1AB
Tel: 01239 612032
Fax: 01239 622339
Email: weatherburnj@ceredigion.ac.uk
Chair: Jacqui Weatherburn
Contact: Maureen Stamper –
PA to Jacqui Weatherburn

Cyfanfyd
Temple of Peace
Cathays Park
Cardiff CF10 3AP
Tel: 029 2066 8999
Fax: 029 2064 0333
Email: info@cyfanfyd.org.uk
Website: www.cyfanfyd.org.uk
Co-ordinator: Dominic Miles

Cyngor Gofal Cymru/Care Council for Wales
South Gate House
Wood Street
Cardiff CF10 1EW
Tel: 029 2022 6257
Fax: 029 2038 4764
Email: info@ccwales.org.uk
Website: www.ccwales.org.uk
Chair: Mutale Nyoni
Chief Executive: Rhian Huws-Williams
Minicom: 029 2078 0680

Equality and Human Rights Commission
3rd Floor, Callaghan Square
Cardiff CF10 5BT
Tel: 029 20 447710
Fax: 029 20 447712
Website:
www.wales@equalityhumanrights.com
Director: Kate Bennett

GMB – Britain's General Union
Williamson House
17 Newport Road
Cardiff CF24 0TB
Tel: 029 2049 1260
Fax: 029 2046 2056
Email: allan.garley@gmb.org.uk
Regional Secretary: Allan Garley

Merthyr Learns
Ty Keir Hardie
Riverside Court
Avenue De Clichy
Merthyr Tydfil
Mid Glamorgan CF47 8XD
Tel: 01685 724621
Fax: 01685 721965
Director of Integrated Adult Services:
Giovanni Isingrini
Senior Manager for Adult Learning:
Sue Hughes

Minority Ethnic Women's Network, Swansea
24 Mansel Street
Swansea SA1 5SQ
Tel: 01792 467722
Fax: 01792 455031
Website: www.mewnswansea.org.uk
Chief Executive: Yvonne Jardine

MEWN Swansea intends to achieve its aims
in different ways: through work in training
and childcare, by sharing of information and
networking, through helping women to
participate in public and community life,
including business and enterprise, and by
informing and influencing policy makers.

National Federation of Women's Institutes (NFWI)
19 Cathedral Road
Cardiff CF11 9HA
Tel: 029 2022 1712
Fax: 029 2038 7236
Email: walesoffice@nfwi-wales.org.uk
Website: www.thewi.org.uk
Head of Wales Office: Rhian Connick

North Wales Race Equality Network Ltd
The Equality Centre
Bangor Road
Penmaenmawr
Conwy LL34 6LF
Tel: 01492 622233
Email: info@nwren.org
Website: www.nwren.org
Director: Mary Holmes

Pembrokeshire Association of Voluntary Services (PAVS)
36–38 High Street
Haverfordwest
Pembrokeshire SA61 2DA
Tel: 01437 769422
Fax: 01437 769431
Email: training@pavs.org.uk
Website: www.pavs.org.uk/training
Chief Officer: Sue Leonard

South East Wales Racial Equality Council (SEWREC)
St David's House
137 Commercial Street
Newport NP20 1LN
Tel: 01633 250006
Fax: 01633 264075
Email: info@sewrec.org.uk
Chief Executive: David Phillips

Sports Council for Wales
Welsh Institute of Sport
Sophia Gardens
Cardiff CF11 9SW
Tel: 0845 045 0904
Fax: 0845 846 0014
Email: scw@scw.org.uk
Website: www.sports-council-wales.org.uk
Information Officer: John Hinton

Swansea Bay Racial Equality Council
3rd Floor, Grove House
Grove Place
Swansea SA1 5DF
Tel: 01792 457035
Fax: 01792 459374
Email: director@sbrec.org.uk
Website: www.sbrec.org.uk
Director: Taha Idris

Swansea Learning Partnership
c/o City and County of Swansea
County Hall
Oystermouth Road
Swansea SA1 3SN
Tel: 01792 637259
Fax: 01792 636642
Swansea Learning Partnership Steering
Group Chair: Richard Parry

The National Trust Wales Office
16 Trinity Square
Llandudno
Conwy LL30 2DE
Tel: 01492 860 123
Fax: 01492 860 233
Website: www.nationaltrust.org.uk
Community, Learning and Volunteering
Manager: Susan Roberts

Ufi Cymru
Priory House
Beignon Close
Ocean Way
Cardiff CF24 5PB
Tel: 029 2049 4540
Fax: 029 2049 4262
Email: wales2@ufi.com
Operations Director, Wales and Northern
Ireland: Jeff Greenidge

UNISON
Unison House
Custom House Street
Cardiff CF10 8AP
Tel: 029 2072 9414
Fax: 029 2038 7531
Email: g.john@unison.co.uk
Website: www.unison-cymruwales.org.uk
Regional Education Organiser: Gareth John

Vale Learning Network
Barry College
Colcot Road
Barry
Vale of Glamorgan CF62 8YJ
Tel: 01446 725075
Email: davidgiles@valelearning.net
Website: www.valelearning.net
VLN Co-ordinator: David Giles

**Workers' Educational Association
South Wales**
Unit 7
Coopers Yard
Curran Road
Cardiff CF10 5NB
Tel: 029 2023 5277
Fax: 029 2023 3986
Email: weasw@swales.wea.org.uk
Website: www.swales.wea.org.uk
General Secretary: Maggi Dawson MBE

Northern Ireland – Education System

Government

Department for Employment and Learning
Adelaide House
39–49 Adelaide Street
Belfast BT2 8FD
Tel: 028 9025 7777
Fax: 028 9025 7778
Email: private.office@delni.gov.uk
Website: www.delni.gov.uk
Minister for Employment and Learning:
Sir Reg Empey MLA

Education and Library Boards

Belfast Education and Library Board
40 Academy Street
Belfast BT1 2NQ
Tel: 028 9056 4000
Fax: 028 9033 1714
Website: www.belb.org.uk
Chief Executive: David Cargo

North Eastern Education and Library Board
County Hall
182 Galgorm Road
Ballymena
County Antrim BT42 1HN
Tel: 028 2565 3333
Fax: 028 2564 6071
Website: www.neelb.org.uk
Chief Executive: Gordon Topping OBE

South Eastern Education and Library Board
Grahamsbridge Road
Dundonald
Belfast BT16 2HS
Tel: 028 9056 6200
Fax: 028 9056 6267
Website: www.seelb.org.uk
Chief Executive: SG Sloan

Southern Education and Library Board
3 Charlemont Place
The Mall
Armagh
County Armagh BT61 9AX
Tel: 028 3751 2200
Website: www.selb.org
Chief Officer: Helen McClenaghan

Western Education and Library Board
1 Hospital Road
Omagh
County Tyrone BT79 0AW
Tel: 028 8241 1411
Fax: 028 8241 1400
Email: info@welbni.org
Website: www.welbni.org
Chief Executive: Barry Mulholland

Teacher Training Colleges

St Mary's University College
191 Falls Road
Belfast BT12 6FE
Tel: 028 9032 7678
Fax: 028 9033 3719
Website: www.stmarys-belfast.ac.uk
Principal: Peter Finn
Email: p.finn@smucb.ac.uk

Stranmillis University College
Stranmillis Road
Belfast BT9 5DY
Tel: 028 9038 1271
Fax: 028 9066 4423
Website: www.stran.ac.uk
Principal: Dr Anne Heaslett

Further Education

Belfast Metropolitan College
Brunswick Street
Belfast BT2 7GX
Tel: 028 9026 5000
Fax: 028 9026 5101
Email: central_admissions@belfast.ac.uk
Website: www.belfast.ac.uk

Northern Regional College
Antrim Campus
Fountain Street
Antrim
Co Antrim BT41 4AL
Tel: 028 9446 3916
Fax: 028 9446 5132
Email: info@nrc.ac.uk
Website: www.nrc.ac.uk

North West Regional College
Derry/Londonderry Campus
Strand Road
Londonderry BT48 7AL
Tel: 028 7127 6000
Fax: 028 7126 0520
Website: www.nwrc.ac.uk

South Eastern Regional College
Ballynahinch Campus
Church Street
Ballynahinch
Co Down BT24 8LP
Tel: 028 4461 5815
Fax: 028 9756 5637
Email: info@serc.ac.uk
Website: www.serc.ac.uk

Southern Regional College
Arnagh Campus
Lonsdale Building
College Hill
Armagh
Co Down BT61 7HN
Tel: 028 3752 2205
Fax: 028 3751 2844
Email: info@src.ac.uk
Website: www.src.ac.uk

South West College
Cookstown Campus
Burn Road
Cookstown
Co Tyrone BT80 8DN
Tel: 028 8676 2620
Fax: 028 8676 1818
Email: dungannon@swc.ac.uk
Website: www.swc.ac.uk

Universities

Queen's University of Belfast
Open Learning School of Education
20 College Green
Belfast BT7 1LN
Tel: 028 9097 5058
Fax: 028 9097 1084
Email: openlearning.education@qub.ac.uk
Website: www.qub.ac.uk/education
Head of School: Tony Gallagher

The Open University in Ireland
40 University Road
Belfast BT7 1SU
Tel: 028 9024 5025
Fax: 028 9023 0565
Email: Ireland@open.ac.uk
Website: www.open.ac.uk
Director: Rosemary Hamilton

University of Ulster
Institute of Lifelong Learning
Shore Road
Newtownabbey
County Antrim BT37 0QB
Tel: 028 9036 6059
Fax: 028 9036 8634
Email: lll@ulster.ac.uk
Website: www.ulster.ac.uk
Vice-Chancellor and President:
Prof. Richard Barnett
Director of Access and Distributed Learning:
Sylvia Alexander
Executive Assistant Professional
Development Unit: Bob Forsythe

Education Providers in the Voluntary Sector

Northern Ireland Council for Voluntary Action
61 Duncairn Gardens
Belfast BT15 2GB
Tel: 028 9087 7777
Fax: 028 9087 7799
Email: nicva@nicva.org
Website: www.nicva.org
Chief Executive: Seamus McAleavey

Open Arts
Crescent Arts Centre
2–4 University Road
Belfast BT7 1NH
Tel: 028 9031 2515
Email: openarts@aol.com
Website: www.openarts.net
Director: Kate Ingram

Ulster People's College
1 Lower Crescent
Belfast BT7 1NR
Tel: 028 9033 0131
Fax: 028 9024 1016
Website: www.ulsterpeoplescollege.org.uk
Director: Ian Savage

WEA Northern Ireland
1–3 Fitzwilliam Street
Belfast BT9 6AW
Tel: 028 9032 9718
Fax: 028 9023 0306
Email: info@wea-ni.com
Website: www.wea-ni.com
Director: Colin Neilands

Education-related and Other Organisations

Arts Council of Northern Ireland
MacNeice House
77 Malone Road
Belfast BT9 6AQ
Tel: 028 9038 5200
Fax: 028 9066 1715
Email: info@artscouncil-ni.org
Website: www.artscouncil-ni.org
Chief Executive: Roisin McDonough

Association of Northern Ireland Colleges (ANIC)
Millenium Community Outreach Centre
Springfield Educational Village
400 Springfield Road
Belfast BT12 7DU
Tel: 028 9090 0060
Chief Executive: John D'Arcy
Email: john.darcy@anic.ac.uk

BBC Learning, Northern Ireland
Broadcasting House
Ormeau Avenue
Belfast BT2 8HQ
Tel: 028 9033 8000
Fax: 028 9033 8761
Website: www.bbc.co.uk/ni/learning
Editor, Learning BBC Northern Ireland:
Jane Cassidy

The British Council
2nd Floor, Norwich Union House
7 Fountain Street
Belfast BT1 5EG
Tel: 028 9024 8220
Fax: 028 9023 7592
Email: nireland.enquiries@britishcouncil.org
Website: www.britishcouncil.org/education
Director: Gillian Belben
Head of Educational Programmes:
Mary McGeown
Local website address:
www.britishcouncil.org/nireland.htm

City & Guilds Northern Ireland (CGLI)
Montgomery House
29–31 Mongomery Street
Belfast BT1 4NX
Tel: 028 9044 2350
Fax: 028 9044 2350
Email: belfast@cityandguilds.com
Website: www.cityandguilds.com
National Manager: Helen Bready

EGSA Connecting Adults with Learning
(Educational Guidance Service For Adults)
4th Floor
40 Linenhall Street
Belfast BT2 8BA
Tel: 028 9024 4274
Fax: 028 9027 1507
Website: www.connect2learn.org.uk
Director: Eileen Kelly

For advice and information on any aspect of adult learning in Northern Ireland, including essential skills, call the Learners Line on 0845 602 6632 or email info@egsa.org.uk

Engineering Training Council
Interpoint
20–24 York Street
Belfast BT15 1AQ
Tel: 028 9032 9878
Fax: 028 9031 0301
Email: info@etcni.org.uk
Website: www.etcni.org.uk
Chief Executive: William Brown

Irish Congress of Trade Unions
Carlin House
4–6 Donegall Street Place
Belfast BT1 2FN
Tel: 028 9024 7940
Fax: 028 9024 6898
Email: info@ictuni.org
Website: www.ictuni.org

Learning and Skills Development Agency Northern Ireland
2nd Floor, Alfred House
19–21 Alfred Street
Belfast BT2 8ED
Tel: 028 9044 7700
Fax: 028 9031 9077
Email: tcarson@lsda.org.uk
Website: www.lsdani.org.uk
Director: Trevor Carson

National Museums Northern Ireland
c/o Ulster Folk and Transport Museum
Bangor Road
Holywood
County Down BT18 0EU
Tel: 028 9042 8428
Fax: 028 9042 8728
Email: uftm.info@magni.org.uk
Website: www.nmni.com
Chief Executive: Tim Cooke

Northern Ireland Association for the Care and Resettlement of Offenders
Amelia House
4 Amelia Street
Belfast BT2 7GS
Tel: 028 9032 0157
Fax: 028 9023 4084
Email: niacro@niacro.co.uk
Website: www.niacro.co.uk
Training Services Manager: Heather Reid

Northern Ireland Community of Refugees and Asylum Seekers
Unit 2
129 Ormeau Road
Belfast BT7 1SH
Tel: 02890 246699
Fax: 02890 248855
Email: nicras@hotmail.co.uk
Website: www.nicras.org.uk
Volunteer Development Worker: Moira McCombe

Northern Ireland Council for the Curriculum, Examinations and Assessment (CCEA)
Clarendon Dock
29 Clarendon Road
Belfast BT1 3BG
Tel: 028 9026 1200
Fax: 028 9026 1234
Email: info@ccea.org.uk
Website: www.rewardinglearning.org.uk
Chief Executive: Neil Anderson

Northern Ireland Local Government Association
Philip House
123 York Street
Belfast BT15 1AB
Tel: 028 9024 9286
Fax: 028 9023 3328
Email: office@nilga.org
Website: www.nilga.org
Chief Executive: Heather Moorhead

Northern Ireland Screen
3rd Floor, Alfred House
Alfred Street
Belfast BT2 8ED
Tel: 028 9023 2444
Fax: 028 9023 9918
Email:
education@northernirelandscreen.co.uk
Website: www.northernirelandscreen.co.uk

Northern Ireland Social Care Council
7th Floor, Millennium House
19–25 Great Victoria Street
Belfast BT2 7AQ
Tel: 028 9041 7600
Fax: 028 9041 7601
Email:
info@info@nisocialcarecouncil.org.uk
Website: www.niscc.info
Chief Executive: Brendan Johnston

OCR
Riverwood House
54 New Forge Lane
Belfast BT9 5NW
Tel: 028 9066 9797
Fax: 028 9066 2343
Email: ocr-ireland@ocr.org.uk
Website: www.ocr.org.uk

Open College Network Northern Ireland
Building 3
212–218 Upper Newtownards Road
Belfast BT4 3ET
Tel: 028 9065 0200
Fax: 028 9065 5200
Email: info@ocnni.org.uk
Website: www.ocnni.org.uk
Chief Executive: Brendan Clarke
Operations Manager: Martin Flynn

Qualifications and Curriculum Authority Northern Ireland
2nd Floor, Glendinning House
6 Murray Street
Belfast BT1 6DN
Tel: 028 9033 0706
Fax: 028 9023 1621
Email: infoni@qca.org.uk
Website: www.qca.org.uk/ni
Manager (NI): Joan Gormley

Sports Council for Northern Ireland
House of Sport
20 Upper Malone Road
Belfast BT9 5LA
Tel: 028 9038 1222
Fax: 028 9068 2757
Email: info@sportni.net
Website: www.sportni.net
Chief Executive: Eamonn McCartan

TWN Ltd
Unit 10b, Weavers Court
Linfield Road
Belfast BT12 5GH
Tel: 028 90319 888
Fax: 028 90311 166
Email: info@twnonline.com
Website: www.twnonline.com
Chief Executive: Norma Shearer

UCU University and College Union
94 Malone Road
Belfast
County Antrim BT9 5HP
Tel: 028 9066 5501
Fax: 028 9066 9225
Website: www.ucu.org.uk
Regional Official: James McKeown
Email: jmckeown@ucu.org.uk

Women's Resource and Development Agency
6 Mount Charles
Belfast BT7 1NZ
Tel: 028 9023 0212
Fax: 028 9024 4363
Email: info@wrda.net
Director: Dr Margaret Ward

UTV plc
Havelock House
Ormeau Road
Belfast BT7 1EB
Tel: 028 9032 8122
Fax: 028 9024 6695
Website: www.utvplc.com
Group Chief Executive: John McCann

Scotland – Education System

Government

Scottish Executive
5th Floor, St Andrews House
Regent Road
Edinburgh EH1 3DG
Tel: 0131 556 8400
Fax: 0131 244 2312
Email:
scottish.ministers@scotland.gsi.gov.uk
Website: www.scotland.gov.uk
Cabinet Secretary for Education and
Lifelong Learning: Fiona Hyslop

Scottish Executive Education and Training
St Andrews House
Regent Road
Edinburgh EH1 3DG
Tel: 0131 556 8400/08457 741741
Fax: 01397 795001
Email:
ceu@scotland.gsi.gov.uk/Topics/Education
Website: www.scotland.gov.uk
Cabinet Secretary for Education and
Lifelong Learning: Fiona Hyslop
Minister for Schools and Skills:
Maureen Watt

National Government Agencies

Scotland's Colleges (formerly Scottish Further Education Unit)
Argyll Court
Castle Business Park
Stirling FK9 4TY
Tel: 01786 892000
Fax: 01786 892001
Email: sfeu@sfeu.ac.uk
Website: www.sfeu.ac.uk
Chief Executive: Chris Travis

The Scottish Further Education Unit (SFEU)
is part of Scotland's Colleges brand. It is the
key development agency for Scotland's
colleges. In undertaking this primary role in
the college sector, it contributes to the work
of a wide range of national committees and
delivers a range of high-quality services
which promote and support changes in
Scotland's 43 colleges leading to excellence
in learning effectiveness and in college
development.
It achieves this through working in close
partnership with the colleges and by
maintaining a high level of understanding of
the developmental needs they face. In
addition to work supported by core funding,
it undertakes a number of project-based
activities in curriculum and staff
development designed to maintain the
position of Scotland's college sector at the
forefront of lifelong learning.
Among the many services which it is able to
provide are expert advice, research and
development, consultancy and customised
training; professional development and
training for colleges and their staff through
conferences, workshops and seminars
focusing on topical issues which enable
individuals and groups to explore common
challenges and share ideas.

Scottish Further and Higher Education Funding Council
Donaldson House
97 Haymarket Terrace
Edinburgh EH12 5HD
Tel: 0131 313 6500
Fax: 0131 313 6501
Email: info@sfc.ac.uk
Website: www.sfc.ac.uk
Interim Chief Executive: Laurence Howells

YouthLink Scotland
Rosebery House
9 Haymarket Terrace
Edinburgh EH12 5EZ
Tel: 0131 313 2488
Fax: 0131 313 6800
Website: www.youthlink.scotland.co.uk
Chief Executive: James Sweeney

Local Education Authorities

Aberdeen City Council
Strategic Leadership
St Nicholas House
Broad Street
Aberdeen AB10 1BW
Tel: 01224 522000
Fax: 01224 523075
Website: www.aberdeencity.gov.uk
Corporate Director for Strategic Leadership:
Abigail Tierney

Aberdeenshire Council
Education, Learning and Leisure Service
Woodhill House
Westburn Road
Aberdeen AB16 5GB
Tel: 01224 664095
Fax: 01224 664615
Website: www.aberdeenshire.gov.uk
Community Learning and Development
Manager: Anne Simpson

Angus Council
Angus House
Orchardbank Business Park
Forfar
Angus DD8 1AE
Tel: 01307 476300
Email: education@angus.gov.uk
Website: www.angus.gov.uk
Director of Education: Jim Anderson

Argyll and Bute Council
Community Services: Education
Argyll House
Alexandra Parade
Dunoon PA23 8AJ
Tel: 01369 704000
Fax: 01369 708584
Email: suzanne.kerr@argyll-bute.gov.uk
Website: www.argyll-bute.gov.uk
Director of Community Services:
Douglas Hendry

City of Edinburgh Council
Children and Families Department
Community Learning and Development
1–4 Waverley Court
4 East Market Street
Edinburgh EH8 8BG
Tel: 0131 469 3373
Fax: 0131 529 6214
Website:
www.edinburgh.gov.uk/adultcourses
Senior Community Learning and
Development Worker: Pat Brechin

Clackmannanshire Council
Services to People
Education Community Services
Lime Tree House
Alloa
Clackmannanshire FK10 1EX
Tel: 01259 450000
Fax: 01259 452440
Email: contactcentre@clacks.gov.uk
Website: www.clacksweb.org.uk/learning/
Head of Service: Jim Goodall

Comhairle Nan Eilean Siar
Education and Leisure Services
Sandwick Road
Stornoway
Isle of Lewis HS1 2BW
Tel: 01851 703773
Fax: 01851 705796
Website: www.cne-siar.gov.uk
Chief Executive: Malcolm Burr
Director of Education: Murdo Macleod
Director, Department for Sustainable
Communities: Munro Gold

Dumfries and Galloway Council

Education, Social Work and Community
Services
30 Edinburgh Road
Dumfries DG1 1NW
Tel: 01387 260419
Fax: 01387 260453
Website: www.dumgal.gov.uk
Director of Education: Colin Grant
Email: colin.grant@dumgal.gov.uk

Dundee City Council

Mitchell Street Centre
Mitchell Street
Dundee DD2 2LJ
Tel: 01382 435820
Fax: 01382 435805
Email: marie.dailly@dundeecity.gov.uk
Website: www.dundeecity.gov.uk
Director of Leisure and Communities:
Stewart Murdoch
Adult Learning Manager: Marie Dailly

East Ayrshire Council

Rennie Street
Kilmarnock
East Ayrshire KA1 3AR
Tel: 01563 578127
Fax: 01563 578102
Website: www.east-ayrshire.gov.uk
Principal Officer, Community Learning and
Development: Dot Grieve
Email: dot.grieve@east-ayrshire.gov.uk

East Lothian Council

John Muir House
Haddington
East Lothian EH41 3HA
Tel: 01620 827596
Fax: 01620 827291
Website: www.eastlothian.gov.uk
Head of Education: Don Ledingham
Head of Community Wellbeing:
Tom Shearer

Community Services Department
9–11 Lodge Street
Haddington EH41 3DX
Tel: 01620 827606
Fax: 01620 824295

East Renfrewshire Council

Education Department
Council Offices
211 Main Street
Barrhead G78 1SY
Tel: 0141 577 3239
Fax: 0141 577 3343
Email:
eric.whitfield@eastrenfrewshire.gov.uk
Website: www.eastrenfrewshire.gov.uk
Director of Education: John Wilson

Falkirk Council

Education Service
McLaren House
Marchmont Avenue
Polmont
Falkirk FK2 0NZ
Tel: 01324 506600
Fax: 01324 506601
Email: director.educ@falkirk.gov.uk
Website: www.falkirk.gov.uk
Director of Education: Julia Swan

Fife Council

Community Services
Town House
Kirkcaldy
Fife KY1 1XW
Tel: 08451 555555 ext 471788
Email: janice.laird@fife.gov.uk
Website: www.fifedirect.org.uk
Service Manager – Lifelong Learning:
Janice Laird

Glasgow City Council

Culture and Sport Glasgow
20 Trongate
Glasgow G1 5ES
Tel: 0141 287 5058
Fax: 0141 287 5151
Website: www.csglasgow.org
Chief Executive, Culture and Sport
Glasgow: Bridget McConnell

Highland Council
Education Culture and Sport Service
Glenurquhart Road
Inverness IV3 5NX
Tel: 01463 702000
Fax: 01463 711177
Email: ecs@highland.gov.uk
Website: www.highland.gov.uk
Director of Education, Culture and Sport:
Hugh Fraser
Lifelong Learning Manager:
Christopher Phillips

Midlothian Council
Education Division
Fairfield House
8 Lothian Road
Dalkeith EH22 3ZG
Tel: 0131 271 3718
Fax: 0131 271 3751
Email:
education.services@midlothian.gov.uk
Website: www.midlothian.gov.uk
Director of Education: Donald S MacKay
Email: lorraine.brown@midlothian.gov.uk

Moray Council
Community Learning and Development
23a High Street
Elgin
Morayshire IV30 1EE
Tel: 01343 563603/4
Fax: 01343 563335
Email: ian.todd@moray.gov.uk
Website: www.moray.org
Community Learning and Development
Team Leader: Ian Todd

North Ayrshire Council
Cunninghame House
Irvine
Ayrshire KA12 8EE
Tel: 01294 324 400
Fax: 01294 324 444
Email: education@north-ayrshire.gov.uk
Corporate Director (Educational Services):
Carol Kirk

North Lanarkshire Council
Municipal Buildings
Kildonan Street
Coatbridge
North Lanarkshire ML5 3BT
Tel: 01236 812222
Fax: 01698 403020
Email: education@northlan.gov.uk
Website: www.northlan.gov.uk
Executive Director, Learning and Leisure
Services: Christine Pollock

Orkney Islands Council
Community Learning and Development
Department of Education and Recreation
Services
Council Offices
Kirkwall
Orkney KW15 1NY
Tel: 01856 873535
Fax: 01856 870302
Email: community.education@orkney.gov.uk
Community Learning and Development
Manager: Dr Malcolm Graves
Email: malcolm.graves@orkney.gov.uk

Perth and Kinross Council
Pullar House
Kinnoull Street
Perth PH1 5GD
Tel: 01738 476211
Fax: 01738 476210
Website: www.pkc.gov.uk
Executive Director, Education and
Children's Services: John Fyffe

Renfrewshire Council
Education and Leisure
Renfrewshire House
Cotton Street
Paisley
Renfrewshire PA1 1UJ
Tel: 0141 842 5663
Fax: 0141 842 5655
Email: els@renfrewshire.gov.uk
Website: www.renfrewshire.gov.uk
Director of Education and Leisure:
John Rooney

Scottish Borders Council
Community Learning and Development
Langlee Complex
Marigold Drive
Galashiels
Selkirkshire TD1 2LP
Tel: 01896 755110
Fax: 01896 756535
Website: www.scotborders.gov.uk
Community Learning and Development
Officer: Oonagh McGarry
Email: omcgarry@scotborders.gov.uk

Shetland Islands Council
Adult Learning Service
Old Library Centre
Lower Hillhead
Lerwick
Shetland ZE1 0EL
Tel: 01595 743888
Fax: 01595 744430
Email: adult.learning@shetland.gov.uk
Website: www.shetland.gov.uk
Adult Learning Manager: Nancy Heubeck

South Ayrshire Council
County Buildings
Wellington Square
Ayr KA7 1DR
Tel: 0845 601 2020
Fax: 01292 612258
Website: www.south-ayrshire.gov.uk
Director of Education, Culture and Lifelong
Learning: Michael McCabe OBE

South Lanarkshire Council
Almada Street
Hamilton
South Lanarkshire ML3 0AE
Tel: 01698 454452
Fax: 01698 454465
Email: education@southlanarkshire.gov.uk
Website: www.southlanarkshire.gov.uk
Executive Director (Education Resources):
Larry Forde
Head of Inclusion: Andrea Batchelor

Stirling Council
Viewforth
Stirling FK8 2ET
Tel: 01786 443388
Fax: 01786 442538
Email: info@stirling.gov.uk
Website: www.stirling.gov.uk
Head of Libraries, Learning, Communities
and Culture: Susan Carragher
Adult Learning and Strategic Support
Manager: Lynne Gibbons

West Dunbartonshire Council
Garshake Road
Dumbarton
West Dunbartonshire G82 3PU
Tel: 01389 737 309
Fax: 01389 737 348
Email:
education.centralregistry@west-dunbarton.gov.
Website: www.west-dunbarton.gov.uk
Director of Educational Services:
Terry Lanagan

West Lothian Council
West Lothian House
Almondvale Boulevard
Livingston
West Lothian EH54 6QG
Tel: 01506 776000
Fax: 01506 777029
Email: education@westlothian.gov.uk
Director of Education and Cultural Services:
Gordon Ford

Universities

University of Aberdeen
Centre for Lifelong Learning
King's College
Aberdeen AB24 3FX
Tel: 01224 273528
Fax: 01224 272478
Email: lifelonglearning@abdn.ac.uk
Website: www.abdn.ac.uk/lifelonglearning/
Director of Centre for Lifelong Learning:
Dr Peter Murray

University of Abertay Dundee
Bell Street
Dundee
Angus DD1 1HG
Tel: 01382 308000
Fax: 01382 308877
Website: www.abertay.ac.uk
Principal and Vice-Chancellor: Prof. Bernard
King CBE

University of Dundee
Principal's Office
Nethergate
Dundee DD1 4HN
Tel: 01382 345559
Fax: 01382 229948
Email: j.calderhead@dundee.ac.uk
Website: www.dundee.ac.uk
Vice-Principal: Prof. James Calderhead

The University of Edinburgh
Office of Lifelong Learning
11 Buccleuch Place
Edinburgh EH8 9LW
Tel: 0131 650 4400
Fax: 0131 667 6097
Email: oll@ed.ac.uk
Website: www.lifelong.ed.ac.uk
Director: Dr Cornelius Gillen
Email: c.gillen@ed.ac.uk

University of Glasgow
Department of Adult and Continuing
Education
St Andrew's Building
11 Eldon Street
Glasgow G3 6NH
Tel: 0141 3301835
Fax: 0141 3301821
Email: enquiry@ace.gla.ac.uk
Website: www.gla.ac.uk/dace
Head of Department: Rod Purcell

Glasgow Caledonian University
Learner Support
70 Cowcaddens Road
Glasgow G4 0BA
Tel: 0141 273 1180
Fax: 0141 273 1183
Website: www.gcal.ac.uk
Director of Learner Support: Tom Finnigan

Heriot-Watt University
Riccarton
Edinburgh EH14 4AS
Tel: 0131 451 4624
Website: www.hw.ac.uk
Deputy Principal Learning and Teaching:
Prof. Bob Craik

Napier University
Lifelong Learning
The Forum
Bankhead Crossway North
Edinburgh EH11 4BP
Tel: 0131 455 2969
Email: info@napier.ac.uk
Website: www.napier.ac.uk
Director of Lifelong Learning:
Prof. Sam Allwinkle

The Open University in Scotland
Jennie Lee House
10 Drumsheugh Gardens
Edinburgh EH3 7QJ
Tel: 0131 226 3851
Fax: 0131 220 6730
Email: scotland@open.ac.uk
Website: www.open.ac.uk/scotland
Director: Peter Syme

University of St Andrews
St Andrews Extension Programmes
St Katharines West
The Scores
St Andrews
Fife KY16 9AX
Tel: 01334 462211
Fax: 01334 463300
Website: www.st-andrews.ac.uk
Director of Continuing Education:
Alex Rougvie
Email: ar6@st-andrews.ac.uk

University of Stirling
Adult Learning and Teaching
Stirling Institute of Education
Pathfoot Building
Stirling FK9 4LA
Tel: 01786 467 940
Fax: 01786 466 131
Email: alt@stir.ac.uk
Website: www.ioe.stir.ac.uk
Head of Section: Dr Richard Dockrell

University of Strathclyde
Centre for Lifelong Learning
Graham Hills Building
40 George Street
Glasgow G1 1QE
Tel: 0141 553 4183
Fax: 0141 553 1270
Email: learn@cll.strath.ac.uk
Website: www.cll.strath.ac.uk
Director of Lifelong Learning:
Lesley Hart MBE
Email: l.hart@strath.ac.uk

University of the West of Scotland
Paisley
Renfrewshire PA1 2BE
Tel: 0141 848 3193
Fax: 0141 848 3191
Email: lifelonglearning@paisley.ac.uk
Website: www.lifelonglearning.paisley.ac.uk
Dean, Lifelong Learning:
Dr Anne McGillivray

Residential Adult Education

Newbattle Abbey College
Newbattle Road
Dalkeith
Midlothian EH22 3LL
Tel: 0131 663 1921
Fax: 0131 654 0598
Email: office@newbattleabbeycollege.ac.uk
Website: www.newbattleabbeycollege.ac.uk
Principal: Ann Southwood
Deputy Principal: Norah Fitzcharles

Education-related and Other Organisations

Association of Scotland's Colleges
Argyll Court
The Castle Business Park
Stirling FK9 4TY
Tel: 01786 892100
Fax: 01786 892109
Email: enquiries@ascol.org.uk
Website: www.ascol.org.uk
Acting Chief Executive: Howard McKenzie

British Council Scotland
3rd Floor, The Tun
4 Jackson's Entry
Holyrood Road
Edinburgh EH8 8PJ
Tel: 0131 524 5700
Fax: 0131 524 5701
Email: scotland.enquiries@britishcouncil.org
Website: www.britishcouncil.org/scotland

Church of Scotland
Church and Society Council
121 George Street
Edinburgh EH2 4YN
Tel: 0131 225 5722
Fax: 0131 220 3113
Email:
churchandsociety@cofscotland.org.uk
Website: www.churchofscotland.org.uk
Secretary: Ewan Aitken

Convention of Scottish Local Authorities (COSLA)
Rosebery House
9 Haymarket Terrace
Edinburgh EH12 5XZ
Tel: 0131 474 9200
Fax: 0131 474 9292
Email: carol@cosla.gov.uk
Website: www.cosla.gov.uk
Chief Executive: Rory Mair

Educational Institute of Scotland
46 Moray Place
Edinburgh EH3 6BH
Tel: 0131 225 6244
Fax: 0131 220 3151
Email: enquiries@eis.org.uk
Website: www.eis.org.uk
General Secretary: Ronald A Smith

General Teaching Council for Scotland
Clerwood House
96 Clermiston Road
Edinburgh EH12 6UT
Tel: 0131 314 6000
Fax: 0131 314 6001
Email: gtcs@gtcs.org.uk
Website: www.gtcs.org.uk
Director of Educational Policy:
Tom Hamilton

Highlands and Islands Enterprise
Cowan House
Inverness Retail and Business Park
Inverness IV2 7GF
Tel: 01463 234171
Fax: 01463 244469
Email: hiegeneral@hient.co.uk
Website: www.hie.co.uk
Chief Executive: Sandy Cumming CBE

Lead Scotland (Linking Education and Disability)
Princes House
5 Shandwick Place
Edinburgh EH2 4RG
Tel: 0131 317 3439
Email: enquiries@lead.org.uk
Website: www.lead.org.uk
Director: Rona Connolly

Learning and Teaching Scotland
The Optima
58 Robertson Street
Glasgow G2 8DU
Tel: 08700 100297
Email: enquiries@ltscotland.org.uk
Website: www.ltscotland.org.uk
Chairman: John Mulgrew
Chief Executive: Bernard McLeary

Also at: Level 9
City House
Overgate
Dundee DD1 1UH
Tel: 01382 443600
Fax: 01382 443645

Quality Assurance Agency for Higher Education (QAA)
183 St Vincent Street
Glasgow G2 5QD
Tel: 0141 572 3420
Fax: 0141 572 3421
Website: www.qaa.ac.uk
Director, QAA Scotland: Norman Sharp

Scotland's Learning Partnership
22 Hill Street
Edinburgh EH2 3JZ
Email: salp@salp.org.uk
Website: www.salp.org.uk
Director: Fiona Boucher

Scotland's Learning Partnership is a multi-agency partnership open to all adult learning providers and learners who can sign up to its mission: "To support and encourage those adults who do not traditionally participate within our education system to become involved in community-based learning in Scotland."

Scottish Arts Council
Education Department
12 Manor Place
Edinburgh EH3 7DD
Tel: 0131 226 6051
Fax: 0131 225 9833
Email: help.desk@scottisharts.org.uk
Website: www.scottisharts.org.uk
Head of Education: Joan Parr

Scottish Catholic Education Service
75 Craigpark
Glasgow G31 2HD
Tel: 0141 556 4727
Fax: 0141 551 8467
Email: mail@sces.uk.com
Website: www.sces.uk.com
Secretary: Margaret Lavery

Scottish Council for Development and Industry
Campsie House
17 Park Circus Place
Glasgow G3 6AH
Tel: 0141 332 9119
Email: enquiries@scdi.org.uk
Website: www.scdi.org.uk
Membership Relations Manager:
Vince McKeown

Scottish Council for Voluntary Organisations
Mansfield Traquair Centre
15 Mansfield Place
Edinburgh EH3 6BB
Tel: 0131 556 3882
Fax: 0131 556 0279
Email: enquiries@scvo.org.uk
Website: www.scvo.org.uk
Chief Executive: Martin Sime
Learning Team Manager: Celia Carson

Scottish Education and Action for Development (SEAD)
20 Graham Street
Edinburgh EH6 5QR
Tel: 0131 555 5550
Email: sead@gn.apc.org
Website: www.sead.org.uk
Co-ordinator: Karen Grant

Scottish Enterprise
150 Broomielaw
Atlantic Quay
Glasgow G2 8LU
Tel: 0141 248 2700
Email: network.helpline@scotent.co.uk
Website: www.scotent.co.uk
Chief Executive: Jack Perry

Scottish Qualifications Authority
The Optima Building
58 Robertson Street
Glasgow G2 8DQ
Tel: 0845 279 1000
Fax: 0141 242 2244
Email: customer@sqa.org.uk
Website: www.sqa.org.uk
Customer Operations Manager:
Mary Donnelly

Scottish Trades Union Congress
333 Woodlands Road
Glasgow G3 6NG
Tel: 0141 337 8100
Fax: 0141 337 8101
Email: info@stuc.org.uk
Website: www.stuc.org.uk
General Secretary: Grahame Smith

Scottish Women's Rural Institutes
42 Heriot Row
Edinburgh EH3 6ES
Tel: 0131 225 1724
Fax: 0131 225 8129
Email: swri@swri.demon.co.uk
Website: www.swri.org.uk
General Secretary: Anne Peacock

Senior Studies Institute
University of Strathclyde
40 George Street
Glasgow G1 1QE
Tel: 0141 548 4828
Fax: 0141 553 1270
Email: brian.mckechnie@strath.ac.uk
Website: www.cll.strath.ac.uk/ssi.html
Programmes Manager: Brian Mckechnie

Skills Development Scotland (learndirect scotland)
Alhambra House
45 Waterloo Street
Glasgow G2 6HS
Tel: 0141 285 6000
Fax: 0141 285 6001
Email: info@learndirectscotland.com
Website: www.learndirectscotland.com
Chief Executive: David Yeates
Director of Partnerships and Marketing:
Liz Mullen

sportscotland
Caledonia House
South Gyle
Edinburgh EH12 9DQ
Tel: 0131 317 7200
Fax: 0131 317 7202
Email: library@sportscotland.org.uk
Website: www.sportscotland.org.uk
Chief Executive: Stewart Harris

WEA Scotland
Riddle's Court
322 Lawnmarket
Edinburgh EH1 2PG
Tel: 0131 226 3456
Fax: 0131 220 0306
Email: hq@weascotland.org.uk
Website: www.weascotland.org.uk
Director: Joyce Connon

YMCA Scotland
11 Rutland Street
Edinburgh EH1 2DQ
Tel: 0131 228 1464
Fax: 0131 228 5462
Email: info@ymcascotland.org
Website: www.ymcascotland.org
National General Secretary: Peter Crory

YWCA Scotland
7b Randolph Crescent
Edinburgh EH3 7TH
Tel: 0131 225 7592
Fax: 0131 225 1052
Email: info@ywcascotland.org
Website: www.ywcascotland.org
Chief Executive: Gill Martin

International

Worldwide Organisations

The Commonwealth of Learning
1055 West Hastings Street, Suite 1200
Vancouver BC V6E 2E9
Canada
Tel: 001 604 775 8200
Fax: 001 604 775 8210
Email: info@col.org
Website: www.col.org
President and Chief Executive Officer:
Sir John Daniel
Communications Manager: Dave Wilson

International Council for Adult Education (ICAE)
General Secretariat
Av 18 de Julio 2095/301
11200 Montevideo
Uruguay
Tel: 005982 409 79 82
Fax: 005982 409 79 82
Email: secretariat@icae.org.uy
Website: www.icae.org.uy
President: Paul Bélanger
Secretary General: Celita Eccher

International Federation of Workers' Educational Associations
7 Community House
41 Salt River Road
Salt River 7925
Cape Town
South Africa
Tel: 0027 21 447 1677
Fax: 0027 21 447 9244
Email: dave.spooner@ifwea.org
Website: www.ifwea.org
General Secretary: Sahra Ryklief

International Labour Organisation
4, Route des Morillons
CH-1211 Geneva 22
Switzerland
Tel: 0041 22 799 6111
Email: ilo@ilo.org
Website: www.ilo.org

International Literacy Institute
University of Pennsylvania
3910 Chestnut Street
Philadelphia, PA 19104 3111
USA
Tel: 001 215 898 2100
Fax: 001 215 898 9804
Email: boyle@literacy.upenn.edu
Website: www.literacy.org
Director: Dr Daniel A Wagner

International Reading Association
Public Information Office
800 Barksdale Road
PO Box 8139
Newark, DE 19714 8139
USA
Tel: 001 302 731 1600
Fax: 001 302 731 1057
Email: pubinfo@reading.org
Website: www.reading.org
Executive Director: Alan E Farstrup

Organisation for Economic Co-operation and Development (OECD)
2 Rue André-Pascal
F-75775 Paris Cedex 16
France
Tel: 0033 1 45 24 82 00
Fax: 0033 1 45 24 85 00
Email: webmaster@oecd.org
Website: www.oecd.org
Senior Analyst CERI: David Istance

The World Bank
1818 H Street, N.W.
Washington, DC 20433
USA
Tel: 001 202 473 1000
Fax: 001 202 477 6391
Website: www.worldbank.org

UNESCO Education Section
Division of Basic Education
7 Place de Fontenoy
75352 Paris 07 SP
France
Tel: 0033 1 45 68 10 00
Fax: 0033 1 45 68 56 27
Website: www.unesco.org

UNESCO Institute for Lifelong Learning
Feldbrunnenstrasse 58
D20148 Hamburg
Germany
Tel: 0049 40 44 80 410
Fax: 0049 40 41 07 723
Email: uil@unesco.org
Website: www.unesco.org/uil
Director: Adama Ouane

World Education
44 Farnsworth Street
Boston
Massachusetts 02210
USA
Tel: 001 617 482 9485
Fax: 001 617 482 0617
Email: wei@worlded.org
Website: www.worlded.org
President: Joel Lamstein

Africa

African Women's Development and Communication Network (FEMNET)
(Reseau de Developpement et de
Communications des Femmes Africaines)
PO Box 54562
00200 Nairobi
Kenya
Tel: 00254 20 3741 301
Fax: 00254 20 3742 927
Email: admin@femnet.or.ke
Website: www.femnet.or.ke
Executive Director: Nora Matovu

Pan African Association for Literacy and Adult Education (PAALAE)
B P 10358
Dakar
Senegal
Tel: 00221 825 4850
Fax: 00221 824 4413

UNESCO Office in Dakar and Regional Bureau for Education in Africa
12 Avenue L S Senghor
B P 3318
Dakar
Senegal
Tel: 00221 849 23 23
Email: dakar@unesco.org
Website: www.dakar.unesco.org

Ethiopia

Adult and Nonformal Education Association in Ethiopia
PO Box 14578
Addis Ababa
Ethiopia
Tel: 00251 1112 48634
Fax: 00251 1112 48638
Email: anfeae@ethionet.et
Website: www.anfeae.org
Managing Director: Alemayehu Hailu Gebre

Namibia

Namibian Association for Literacy and Adult Education
Box 4118
Windhoek
Namibia
Tel: 00264 61 211 722
Fax: 00264 61 210 256
Secretary: Job K Tjiho

Senegal

ANAFA
BP 10358
Dakar
Senegal
Tel: 00 221 855 9450
Secretary-General: Ousmane Faty Ndongo

Sierra Leone

Sierra Leone Adult Education Association
90 Sanders Street
PMB 705
Freetown
Sierra Leone
Tel: 00232 22 242276
Fax: 00232 22 224439 or 241620
Executive Secretary: S K Mansaray
Additional telephone numbers are 232 30 215714 or 232 76 794525

South Africa

DVV International (IZZ-DVV)
9, Scott Road
Observatory, 7925
Cape Town
South Africa
Tel: 0027 21 447 4828 or 4898
Fax: 0027 21 447 4878
Email: iiz-dvv@iafrica.com
Website: www.aldsa.org
Project Director: Wolfgang Leumer

UMTAPO Centre
PO Box 2792
Durban 4000
South Africa
Tel: 0027 31 309 3350
Fax: 0027 31 309 8189
Email: info@umtapo.co.za
Website: www.umtapo.co.za
Executive Director: Deena Soliar

University of the Western Cape
Division for Lifelong Learning
Private Bag X17
Bellville
Cape Town 7535
South Africa
Tel: 0027 21 959 3339
Fax: 0027 21 959 3788
Email: lifelong@uwc.ac.za
Website: www.uwc.ac.za/dll
Director: Prof. Shirley Walters

Sudan

National Council of Literacy and Adult Education
PO Box 2588
Khartoum
Sudan
Tel: 00249 11 770744
Fax: 00249 11 776030
Secretary General: Abdul Aziz Abdul Latif

Sudan Open Learning Organisation
PO Box 8370
Khartoum
Sudan
Tel: 00249 9123 91168
Fax: 00249 8347 1059
Literacy and Adult Education Consultant:
Hashim Abuzeid El Safi

Swaziland

Swaziland Association of Adult Education
c/o DMS, UNISWA
P/B Kwaluseni
Swaziland
Tel: 00268 84011
Fax: 00268 55270
Secretary: B T N Ngwenya

Tanzania

National Adult Education Association of Tanzania (CHEWATA)
PO Box 7484
Dar-es-Salaam
Tanzania
Tel: 00255 22 211 0092
Email: halimalukale@yahoo.com
Secretary General: Halima L Zinga

Uganda

National Adult Education Association of Uganda
PO Box 8174
Kampala
Uganda
National Secretary: Joy Kirenga

Uganda Literacy and Adult Learners Association (ULALA)
PO Box 22439
Kampala
Uganda
Tel: 00256 0772 465909
Fax: 00256 414 530160
Email: ulalaki@netscape.net
National Co-ordinator: Kasiita Ismail

Zimbabwe

African Development Education Network
PO Box A 1969
Avondale
Harare
Zimbabwe
Tel: 00263 4 667912
Email: info@aden.org.zw
Website: www.aden.org.zw

Middle East

Arab League Educational, Cultural and Scientific Organisation (ALECSO)
Mohamed V Avenue
PO Box 1120
Tunis
Tunisia
Tel: 00216 71 785 751
Fax: 00216 71 784 965
Email: alesco@alesco.org.tn
Website: www.alecso.org.tn
Director General: Dr Mongi Bousnina

Arab Network for Literacy and Adult Education
90d Ahmed Orabi St
al Mohandseen
Giza
Egypt
Tel: 002 02 7311007 or 002 02 7295042
Fax: 002 02 7295042
Email: women_society@yahoo.com
or email: adult_education_net@hotmail.com
Secretary General: Seham Negm

UNESCO Regional Office for Education in the Arab States
PO Box 11–5244
Cite Sportive Avenue
Beirut
Lebanon
Tel: 00961 1 83 00 13
Fax: 00961 1 82 48 54
Email: beirut@unesco.org
Website: www.unesco.org/beirut

Egypt

General Authority for Literacy and Adult Education (GALAE)
1 Gomhuria Street
Gesr El-Suez
POB 13, 11595
Qupa
Cairo
Egypt
Tel: 00202 294 0021
Fax: 00202 294 0024
Email: info_galae@afmic.com

Jordan

General Union of Voluntary Societies
PO Box 910254
11191 Amman
Jordan
Tel: 00962 6 463 4001
Fax: 00962 6 465 9973
Website: www.guvs-jordan.com
President: Dr Abdullah El-Khatib

Asia and the Pacific Region

Asian South Pacific Bureau of Adult Education (ASPBAE)
c/o MAAPL
9th Floor, Eucharistic Congress Building
No.3
5 Convent Street
Colaba
Mumbai – 400 039
India
Tel: 0091 22 2202 1391/2281 6853
Fax: 0091 22 2283 2217
Email: aspbae@vsnl.com
Website: www.aspbae.org
Secretary General:
Maria Lourdes Almazan Khan

UNESCO Asia and Pacific Regional Bureau for Education
920 Sukhumvit Road
Prakanong
Klongtoey
Bangkok 10110
Thailand
Tel: 0066 2 391 0879
Fax: 0066 2 391 0866
Email: bangkok@unescobkk.org
Website: www.unescobkk.org

Australia

Adult Learning Australia Inc
GPO Box 826
CIT Southside Campus,
Canberra ACT 2601
Australia
Tel: 0061 2 6215 9500
Fax: 0061 2 6282 0042
Email: info@ala.asn.au
Website: www.ala.asn.au
Chief Executive Officer: Peter Peterson

Australian Council for Adult Literacy
PO Box 2283
Canberra ACT 2601
Australia
Tel: 0061 3 9546 6892
Fax: 0061 3 9546 0421
Email: info@acal.edu.au
Website: www.acal.edu.au
President: Margaret McHugh

National Centre for Vocational Education Research Ltd (NCVER)
PO Box 8288
Station Arcade
Adelaide SA 5052
Australia
Tel: 0061 8 8230 8400
Fax: 0061 8 8212 3436
Email: ncver@ncver.edu.au
Website: www.ncver.edu.au

Bangladesh

Bangladesh Literacy Society (BLS)
House No C-10, Road No 5a
Arambagh (Eastern Housing)
Pallabi
Dhaka 1216
Bangladesh
Tel: 00880 2 801 7751
Email: iilbls@citechco.net
Secretary General (Founder) and Executive
Director: Prof. Md. Osman Ghani

Campaign for Popular Education
5/14 Humayun Road
Mohamadpur
Dhaka -1207
Bangladesh
Tel: 00880 2 913 0427 or 811 5769
Fax: 00880 2 811 8342
Email: info@campebd.org
Website: www.campebd.org

Dhaka Ahsania Mission
House No 19, Road No 12 (New)
Dhanmondi
Dhaka-1209
Bangladesh
Tel: 00880 2 811 5909 or 811 9521/22
Fax: 00880 2 811 3010 or 811 8522
Email: dambgd@bdonline.com
Website: www.ahsaniamission.org
Executive Director: Kazi Rafiqul Alam

National Association for Non-Formal Adult Education (NANFAE)
GPO Box 2305
Ramna
Dhaka-1000
Bangladesh
Tel: 00880 2 861 0089
Fax: 00880 2 861 3958
Email: sangjog@bangla.net
Secretary General:
Mohammed Shafiqur Rahman
Programme Co-ordinator: Syeda Ismat Ara

SANGJOG/Connection
GPO Box 2305, Ramna
Dhaka-1000, Bangladesh
Tel: 0088 02 8610089
Fax: 0088 02 8613956
Email: sangjog@bangla.net
Secretary General:
Mohammed Shafiqur Rahman
Office Manager: Md. Rezaul Karim
or email: sangjog_ngo@yahoo.co.uk

China

Caritas Community and Higher Education Service
Room 506, Caritas House
2 Caine Road
Hong Kong
Tel: 00852 2843 4660
Fax: 00852 2530 3065
Email: headoffce@cches.edu.hk
Website: www.cches.edu.hk
Head: Yau Sun Kit

China Association for Adult Education
35 DaMucang Hotong
Xidan 100816
Beijing
China
Tel: 0086 10 6609 7119

Hong Kong Association for Continuing Education
Room 1401, Parkes Commercial Centre
2–8 Parkes Street
Tsim Sha Tsui
Kowloon
Hong Kong
Tel: 00852 2375 1618
Fax: 00852 2375 1683

Macau Association for Continuing Education
Beco do Goncalo No 1 – 'C'
Ground Floor, PO Box 3031
Macau SAR
China
Tel: 00853 616 8166
Fax: 00853 795 2188
Email: tsuipf@macau.ctm.net
Chair: Lawrence Tsui

India

ASTHA Sansthan
39 Kharol Colony
Udaipur
Rajasthan 313 004
India
Tel: 0091 294 2451 348
Fax: 0091 294 2451 391
Email: astha39@sancharnet.in
Website: www.astha.org
Co-ordinating Director:
Bhanwar Singh Chadana

Indian Adult Education Association
Shafiq Memorial
17 B Indraprastha Estate
Ring Road
New Delhi 110002
India
Tel: 0091 11 2337 9282/306
Fax: 0091 11 23378206
Email: info@iaea-india.org
Website: www.iaea-india.org
President: Shri K C Choudhary

Society for Participatory Research in Asia (PRIA)
42, Tughlakabad Institutional Area
New Delhi-110 062
India
Tel: 0091 11 299 60931/32/33
Fax: 0091 11 299 55183
Email: info@pria.org
Website: www.pria.org
President: Rajesh Tandon

Japan

Japan Association for Promotion of Social Education
19 Tsukiji-cho
2F Ono Building
Shinjuku-ku
Tokyo 162–0818
Japan
Tel: 0081 3 3235 4143
Fax: 0081 3 3235 4143
Email: japse@nifty.com
Website: www.japse.txt-nifty.com
Contact for International Affairs:
Prof. Yoko Arai

Japan Society for the Study of Adult and Community Education (JSSACE)
c/o School of Education
Waseda University
Shinjuku-ku Nishi-waseda 1-6-1
Tokyo 169–8050
Japan
Tel: 0081 90 3875 5096
Fax: 0081 3 3318 4032
Email: jssace_intl@yahoo.co.jp
Website: wwwsoc.nii.ac.jp/jssace
Contact: Dr Miho Tokiwa-Fuse

National Federation of Social Education
No. 15–10, Akamidai 4-chome
Kounosu
Saitama 365–0064
Japan
Director: Makoto Yamaguchi

New Zealand

ACE Aotearoa
Adult and Community Education,
Aotearoa Inc
Box 12114,Wellington
New Zealand
Tel: 0064 4 4736622
Fax: 0064 4 4994947
Email: director@aceaotearoa.org.nz
Website: www.aceaotearoa.org.nz
Chief Executive: Margie Scotts

Pakistan

Pakistan Association for Continuing and Adult Education (PACADE)
101 J Block Model Town
Postal Code 54700
Lahore
Pakistan
Tel: 0092 42 583 0148
Fax: 0092 42 583 0148
Email: pacade@brain.net.pk
President: Mr Inayatullah

Philippines

Association for Non-Traditional Education in the Philippines (ANTEP)
PO Box 12824
Ortigas Centre Post Office
Pasig City
Metro Manila
Philippines
Tel: 00632 631 2605
Fax: 00632 633 8418
Executive Director: Frank B Lopez

Education For Life Foundation, Phillipines
No. 13 Dao Street Brgy. Quirino 3A
Project 3, Quezon City
Manila
Philippines
Tel: 00632 434 1368
Fax: 00632 435 2891
President: Edicio de la Torre

Singapore

Singapore Association for Continuing Education (SACE)
PO Box 0395
Singapore
Website: www.sace.org.sg
President: Thomas Kuan
1st Vice-President: Naren Krishan
2nd Vice-President: Ramli Wong

Singapore Workforce Development Agency
1 Marina Boulevard # 16–01
Singapore 018989
Tel: 0065 6512 1212
Fax: 0065 6512 1111
Email: wda_enquiry@wda.gov.sg
Website: www.wda.gov.sg
Deputy Chief Executive:
Dr Gary Willmott OAM

Institute for Adult Learning
1 Kay Siang Road
Tower Block Level 6
Singapore 248922
Tel: 0065 6579 0300
Fax: 0065 6579 0400
Email:info@ial.edu.sg
Website: www.ial.edu.sg
Executive Director: Dr Gary Willmott OAM

Sri Lanka

National Association for Total Education (NATE) Sri Lanka
47b Railway Avenue
Nugegoda
Sri Lanka
Email: natesrilanka@yahoo.com
President: Lalita Gunasekara

Taiwan

Chinese Adult Education Association – Taipei
PO Box 7–764
Taipei 106
Taiwan
Tel: 00886 2 8369 2860
Fax: 00886 2 8369 2861
Email: caeat@ms9.hinet.net
President: Prof. Fu-Shun Huang

Thailand

Ministry of Education
Office of the Non-Formal and Informal
Education (ONIE)
Ratchadamnoen Road
Bangkok 10300
Thailand
Tel: 0066 2 282 2673/281 5162
Fax: 0066 2 280 1688
Email: onie-eng@nfe.go.th
Website: www.nfe.go.th/en
Secretary-General: Apichart Jeerawuth
Chief, Foreign Relations Section:
Parichart Yenjai

Vietnam

National Organisation for Community Education, Continuing Education and Development NOCEAD (Vietnam)
Box 152
IPO Hanoi
Vietnam
Executive Vice Director: Dr Ngo Quang Son

Europe

ERDI – Consortium of European Research and Development Institutes for Adult Education
VOCB
Kardinaal Mercierplein, 1
B-2800 Mechelen
Belgium
Tel: 0032 15 44 65 00
Fax: 0032 15 44 65 01
Email: lattke@die-bonn.de
Website: www.erdi.info
President: Vida Mohorčič Špolar
Vice President (UK): Alastair Thomson

European Association for the Education of Adults (EAEA)
Rue de la Concorde 60
B-1050 Brussels
Belgium
Tel: 0032 2 513 52 05
Fax: 0032 2 513 57 34
Email: eaea-office@eaea.org
Website: www.eaea.org
President: Sue Waddington
Secretary General: Gina Ebner
Email: gina.ebner@eaea.org

EAEA Link Office Budapest
Wesselényi utca 13II/5
1077 Budapest
Hungary
Tel: 00 36 1 411 1459
Fax: 00 36 1 411 1460
Email: eaea-services@eaea.org
Website: www.nepfoiskola.hu/eaea
Contact: Zsófia Fesztbaum

EAEA Link Office Helsinki
c/o Finnish Adult Education Association
Annankatu 12 A 15
FIN-00120
Helsinki
Finland
Tel: 00358 9 612 03 712
Fax: 00358 9 646 504
Email: eaea-info@eaea.org
Website: www.eaea.org
International Affairs Secretary:
Johanni Larjanko

EAEA Mediterranean Office
c/o FEUP
Calles Los Madrazo 3, 1
28014 Madrid
Spain
Tel: 0034 915 219 108
Fax: 0034 915 231 087
Email: eaea-support@eaea.org
Website: www.feup.org
Contact: Isabel Garcia-Longoria

European Centre for the Development of Vocational Training (CEDEFOP)
PO Box 22427
GR-55102 Thessaloniki
Greece
Tel: 0030 2310 490 111
Fax: 0030 2310 490 102
Email: info@cedefop.europa.eu
Website: www.cedefop.europa.eu
See also www.trainingvillage.gr

European Commission
Directorate General for Education and Culture
Unit B3
B-1049 Bruxelles
Belgium
Tel: 0032 2 2991111 or 2963988
Fax: 0032 2296 8602
Email: adam.pokorny@ec.europa.eu
Website:
www.europa.eu.int/comm/education/
index_en.html
Head of Unit: Adam Pokorny

European Prison Education Association
c/o Drammen videregående skole
Danvikgata 25
N-3045 Drammen
Norway
Tel: 00 353 1 8302818
Fax: 00 353 1 8301175
Website: www.epea.org
Chairperson: Dr Anne Costelloe

European Society for Research on the Education of Adults (ESREA)
Secretariat
c/o Dr Andreas Fejes
Department of Behavioural Sciences and Learning
Linköping University
581 83 Linköping
Sweden
Website: www.esrea.org
Dr Andreas Fejes

European University Continuing Education Network (EUCEN)
EUCEN Executive Office
Balmes 132
08008 Barcelona
Spain
Tel: 0034 93 542 18 25
Fax: 0034 93 542 29 75
Email: executive.office@eucen.org
Website: www.eucen.org
Executive Officer, Administrator:
Carme Royo

Austria

Verband Österreichischer Volkshochschulen
Weintraubengasse 13
A-1020 Wien
Austria
Tel: 0043 1 216 42 26
Fax: 0043 1 214 38 91
Email: voev@vhs.or.at
Website: www.vhs.or.at
Secretary General: Dr Wilhelm Filla

Belgium

Ministère de la Communauté Francaise
Service de l'Education Permanente
Boulevard Léopold II 44
B-1080 Brussels
Belgium
Tel: 0032 2 413 2311
Email: education.permanente@cfwb.be
Website: www.cfwb.be
Director: France Lebon

SoCiuS – Steunpunt voor Sociaal-Cultureel Werk
Gallaitstraat 86 Bus 4
1030 Brussel
Belgium
Tel: 0032 2 215 2708
Fax: 0032 2 215 8075
Email: welkom@socius.be
Website: www.socius.be
Director: Fred Dhont
Staff Member International Affairs:
Theo Van Malderen
Email: theo.van.malderen@socius.be

Bulgaria

Federation of Societies for Support of Knowledge
123, ap 1 Dondukov Blvd
Sofia
Bulgaria
Tel: 00359 2 9434 149
Email: fssk@spnet.net
Website: www.fssk-bg.com

Croatia

Croatian Association for the Education of Adults
10000 Zagreb
Vlaška 65
Croatia
Tel: 00385 1 45 51 614
Fax: 00385 1 45 53 628
Website: www.hzpou.hr
President: Damir Matkovic

Cyprus

Cyprus Adult Education Association
PO Box 4019
Nicosia 24019
Cyprus
Tel: 00357 99470810
Fax: 00357 22486 714
Email: klitossy@cytanet.com.cy
President: Klitos Symeonides

Denmark

Dansk Folkeoplysnings Samråd
(Danish Adult Education Association)
Gl. Kongevej 39E
2.tv
DK 1610 København V
Denmark
Tel: 0045 33 151 466
Fax: 0045 33 150 983
Email: dfs@dfs.dk
Website: www.dfs.dk
Organisational Officer: Flemming Gjedde

Estonia

**Association of Estonian Adult
Educators 'ANDRAS'**
Valge 10
Tallinn 11413
Estonia
Tel: 00372 6 211 671
Fax: 00372 6 211 670
Email: andras@andras.ee
Website: www.andras.ee
Manager: Ene Kapp
Project Co-ordinator: Kerttu Taidre
Project Manager: Sirje Plaks

**Estonian Non-formal Adult
Education Association**
Rännaku pst. 12
10917 Tallinn
Estonia
Tel: 00 372 677 6293
Email: evhl@vabaharidus.ee
Website: www.vabaharidus.ee
Secretary General: Maire Salundi

Finland

Finnish Adult Education Association
Annankatu 12 A 15
00120 Helsinki
Finland
Tel: 00358 9 612 03 70
Fax: 00358 9 646 504
Email: taimisto@vsy.fi
Website: www.vsy.fi
International Affairs Secretary:
Johanni Larjanko

**Finnish Association of Adult
Education Centres**
Annankatu 25 A
00100 Helsinki
Finland
Tel: 00358 9 6122 430
Fax: 00358 9 6122 4351
Email: helja.nurmela@ktol.fi
Website: www.ktol.fi
Executive Director: Heljä Nurmela

Germany

**Deutsches Institut für
Erwachsenenbildung (DIE)**
Friedrich-Ebert-Allee 38
53113 Bonn
Germany
Tel: 0049 228 3294–0
Fax: 0049 228 3294 399
Email: info@die-bonn.de
Website: www.die-bonn.de
Director: Prof. Ekkehard Nuissl von Rein

**Institute for International Co-operation
of the German Adult
Education Association**
DVV international
Obere Wilhelmstrasse 32
53225 Bonn
Germany
Tel: 0049 228 975 690
Fax: 0049 228 975 6955
Email: info@dvv-international.de
Website: www.dvv-international.de
Contact: Prof. (H) Heribert Hinzen

Greece

Association for Adult Education
Gedeon 18
Paiania
Athens
Greece
Tel: 0030 210 9624 012
Website: www.aae.org.gr

Ergon KEK
123 Vas. Sofias Avenue
Athens 115 21
Greece
Tel: 0030 210 646 1482
Fax: 0030 210 646 1597
Email: ergonkek@otenet.gr

General Secretariat for Adult Education
417, Acharnon Street
GR-111 43 Athens
Greece
Tel: 0030 210 253 03 98
Fax: 0030 210 253 03 98
Email: magda@gsae.edu.gr
Website: www.gsae.edu.gr
Contact: Magda Trantallidi-Papadimitriou

Hungary

Hungarian Folk High School Society
Wesselényi utca 13 II/5
Budapest 1077
Hungary
Tel: 0036 1 411 14 59
Fax: 0036 1 411 14 60
Email: mnt@nepfoiskola.hu
Website: www.nepfoiskola.hu
Managing President: János Sz. Tóth Ph.D.

Iceland

Leikn, The National Association for Adult Education in Iceland
Skólavegur 1
Rekjanesbær 230
Iceland
Tel: 00354 421 7500
Fax: 00354 421 7503
Email: leikn@leikn.is
Website: www.leikn.is

Ireland

AONTAS, National Association for Adult Education
2nd Floor, 83–87 Main Street
Ranelagh
Dublin 6
Ireland
Tel: 00353 1 406 8220/1
Fax: 00353 1 406 8227
Email: mail@aontas.com
Website: www.aontas.com
Director: Berni Brady

National Adult Literacy Agency (NALA)
76 Lower Gardiner Street
Dublin 1
Ireland
Tel: 00353 1 855 4332
Fax: 00353 1 855 5475
Email: literacy@nala.ie
Website: www.nala.ie
Director: Inez Bailey

Israel

Israel Adult Education Association
Seminar Ef'al
1 Hayasmin Street
Ramath Ef'al
52960 Israel

Italy

Forum permanente per l'educazione degli Adulti
Via del Parione 11/B
I-50123 Firenze
Italy
Tel: 0039 055 218 348
Fax: 0039 055 238 2098
Email: forumeda@unifi.it
Website: www.edaforum.it
Director: Dr Paolo Sciclone

Unione Nazionale per la Lotta contro l'Analfabetismo (UNLA)
Corso Vittorio Emanuele II
217 Palazzo Sora
00186 Roma
Italy
Tel: 0039 6688 04301
Fax: 0039 6688 04302
Email: sedecentrale@unla.it
Website: www.unla.it

Latvia

Latvian Adult Education Association (LAEA)
11 Merkela str.
LV-1050, Riga
Latvia
Tel: 00371 7 222 411
Fax: 00371 7 222 411
Email: laea@laea.lv
Website: www.laea.lv
Director: Ingrīda Mikiško

Liechtenstein

Liechtenstein Adult Education Foundation
Postfach 824
Lettstrasse 4
FL-9490 Vaduz
Liechtenstein
Tel: 00423 232 9580
Fax: 00423 232 0750
Email: stiftung@erwachsenenbildung.li
Website: www.erwachsenenbildung.li

Lithuania

Lithuanian Association of Adult Education (LAAE)
Geležinio vilko 12
LT-01112 Vilnius
Lithuania
Tel: 00370 5 2312309
Fax: 00370 5 2312309
Email: lssavilnius@takas.lt
Website: www.lssa.smm.lt
Secretary General: Dalia Cymbaliuk

Malta

Foundation for Educational Services
PO Box 1
Rabat
Malta
RBT02
Tel: 00356 2145 5600
Fax: 00356 2145 5625
Email: fes@gov.mt
Website: www.fes.org.mt

The Netherlands

Bond van Nederlandse Volksuniversiteiten
Karel Doormanstraat 24
3012 GJ Rotterdam
The Netherlands
Tel: 0031 10 281 0106
Fax: 0031 10 281 0115
Email: info@volksuniversiteit.nl
Website: www.volksuniversiteit.nl
Manager: Paul Hensen
Manager: Rosa Verhoeff

CINOP
Postbus 1585
5200 BP 's-Hertogenbosch
The Netherlands
Tel: 0031 736 800 800
Fax: 0031 736 123 425
Email: info@weekvanhetleren.nl
Website: www.cinop.nl

Norway

Lifelong Learning Research Centre
Norwegian University of Science and Technology (NTNU)
No-7491 Trondheim
Norway
Tel: 0047 73 59 28 00
Fax: 0047 73 59 28 01
Email: vill@svt.ntnu.no
Website: www.ntnu.no/vill/english
Head of Department: Astrid M Solvberg

Norwegian Association for Adult Learning (NAAL)
PO Box 9339
Gronland
N-0135
Oslo
Norway
Tel: 0047 22 41 0000 (Office)
Fax: 0047 22 41 0001
Email: vofo@vofo.no
Website: www.vofo.no
Secretary General: Sturla Bjerkaker
(Board Member for ICAE)
Vice Director/Vice Secretary General:
Ellen Stavlund

Vox – Norwegian Institute for Adult Learning
Box 6139 Etterstad
N-0602 Oslo
Norway
Tel: 0047 2338 1300
Email: postmottak@vox.no

Poland

Association of Polish Adult Educators
ul Ogrodowa 47
Częstochowa 42–200
Poland
Tel: 0048 34 324 1517
Email: wshit@wshit.edu.pl
Website: www.wshit.edu.pl/

Romania

Asociatia Nationalã a Universitatĭlor Populare – ANUP
Bd. N Bãlcescu nr. 18
Sector 1
Bucharest
Romania
Tel: 0040 1 314 6637
Fax: 0040 1 314 0063
Email: updalles@pcnet.ro
Website: www.updalles.ro
Director: Dr Nicolae Sãcãliş

Romanian Institute for Adult Education
Calea Bogdanestilor, no 32a, room 205, 206
300389 Timisoara
Timis
Romania
Tel: 0040 256 592 658
Fax: 0040 256 592 658
Email: irea@irea.uvt.ro
Website: www.irea.uvt.ro
Scientific Director and Manager:
Simona Sava

Russia

All-Russia 'ZNANIE' Society (KNOWLEDGE)
3–4 Novaya Ploschad
RF-101990 Moscow
Russia
Tel: 007 095 921 9058
Fax: 007 095 925 4249
Email: znanie@znanie.org
Website: www.znanie.org
Chairman of the Board: Victor Rybalko

International Association 'ZNANIE'
2 Khoroshevsky proesd 3-A
Moscow 123 00
Russia
Tel: 007 095 941 22 91
Fax: 007 095 941 23 53
Email: yefim@malitikov.ru
Website: www.malitikov.ru
President: Prof. Dr Yefim Malitikov

Slovakia

Academy of Education/Akadémia Vzdelávania
Gorkeho str. 10
SK – 815 17 Bratislava
Slovakia
Tel: 00421 2 544 100 37
Fax: 00421 2 544 100 39
Email: sekretariat@aveducation.sk
Website: www.aveducation.sk
Managing Director: Ivan Janicina

Slovenia

Slovenian Institute for Adult Education (SIAE)
Šmartinska 134a
1000 Ljubljana
Slovenia
Tel: 00386 01 5842 560
Fax: 00386 01 5842 550
Email: info@acs.si
Website: www.acs.si
Acting Director: Andrej Sotosek MSc
Head of Information Unit:
Zvonka Pangerc Pahernik MSc

Spain

Federación de Asociaciones de Educación de personas Adultas (FAEA)
Paseo Fernando el Católico 29
1 Iizda
E-50006 Zaragoza
Spain
Tel: 0034 976 553 773
Fax: 0034 976 552 842
Email: faea@faea.es
Website: www.faea.es

Federación Española de Universidades Populares
Calles Los Madrazos 3, 1
28014 Madrid
Spain
Tel: 0034 915 219 108
Fax: 0034 915 231 087
Email: info@feup.org
Website: www.feup.org
General Co-ordinator:
Isabel Garcia-Longoria
General Co-ordinator:
Montserrat Morales

Sweden

Folkbildningsrådet (Swedish National Council of Adult Education)
Box 380 74
S-10064 Stockholm
Sweden
Tel: 0046 8 412 4800
Fax: 0046 8 21 8826
Email: fbr@folkbildning.se
Website: www.folkbildning.se
Secretary General:
Britten Mansson-Wallin

Switzerland

SVEB – Schweizerischer Verband fur Weiterbildung
FSEA- Fédération suisse pour la formation continue
Oerlikonerstrasse 38, PO Box 270
CH-8057 Zurich
Switzerland
Tel: 0041 44 311 6455
Fax: 0041 44 311 6459
Email: sveb@alice.ch
Website: www.alice.ch
Director: André Schläefli
Deputy Director: Ruth Jermann

Latin America and the Caribbean Region

Caribbean Regional Council for Adult Education (CARCAE)
c/o Adult Education Unit
51 Frederick Street
Port of Spain
Trinidad and Tobago
Tel: 001 868 625 4091
Fax: 001 868 627 3359
Email: carcae@usa.net
Chair: Vilma McClenan

Consejo de Educación de Adultos de América Latina (CEAAL)
Via Cincuentenario No 84B
Coco del Mar, San Francisco
Apartado 0831–00817, Paitilla
Ciudad de Panamá
Republica de Panamá
Tel: 00 507 270 1084
Email: info@ceaal.org
Website: www.ceaal.org
President: Pedro Pontual
Secretary General: Carlos Zarco Mera

Barbados

Barbados Adult Education Association
Esperanza
Welches Terrace
St Michael
Barbados
Email: rjcbarak@yahoo.com
President: Rosaline Corbin

Belize

Society for the Promotion of Education and Research (SPEAR)
5638 Gentle Avenue
PO Box 1766
Belize City
Belize
Tel: 00501 223 1668
Fax: 00501 223 2367
Email: spear@btl.net
Website: www.spear.org.bz

Bolivia

Asociación de Instituciones de Promoción y Educación (AIPE)
Calle Macario Pinilla 525
La Paz
Bolivia
Tel: 00591 241 9723
Fax: 00591 241 0242
Email: aipe@aipe.org.bo
Website: www.aipe.org.bo
Executive Director:
Dr Alfonso Camacho Pena

Guyana

Adult Education Association of Guyana
88 Carmichael Street
North Cummingsburg
PO Box 101111
Georgetown
Guyana
Tel: 00592 225 0758

Jamaica

Jamaican Council of Adult Education (JACAE)
PO Box 60
47B South Camp Road
Kingston 4
Jamaica
Tel: 001 876 928 5181
Fax: 001 876 928 5392

Jamaican Foundation for Lifelong Learning
PO Box 60
47B South Camp Road
Kingston 4
Jamaica
Tel: 001 876 928 5181
Fax: 001 876 928 5392
Email: eshakes@jfll.org.jm
Executive Director: Edward Shakes
Director, Technical Servicing and Field Operations: Sandra Prince

Uruguay

Instituto de Promoción Económico Social del Uruguay (IPRU)
PO Box Casilla des Correos 10690
Distribution 1
11200 Montevideo
Uruguay
Tel: 00598 2 408 9158
Fax: 00598 2 409 2343
Email: ipru@chasque.apc.org
General Co-ordinator: Alicia Canapale

North America

Canada

Canadian Association for the Study of Adult Education
Suite 204, 260 Dalhousie Street
Ottawa
Ontario K1N 7E4
Canada
Tel: 001 613 241 0018
Fax: 001 613 241 0019
Email: casae.aceea@csse.ca
Website: www.oise.utoronto.ca/CASAE

Institut de cooperation pour l'Education des Adultes (ICEA)
5225 Rue Berri, Bureau 300
Montreal
Quebec H2J 2S4
Canada
Tel: 001 514 948 2044
Fax: 001 514 948 2046
Email: icea@icea.qc.ca
Website: www.icea.qc.ca
Director General: Dominique Ollivier

USA

American Association for Adult and Continuing Education (AAACE)
10111 Martin Luther King Jr Highway
Suite 200C
Bowie, MD 20720
USA
Tel: 001 301 459 6261
Fax: 001 301 459 6241
Email: aaace10@aol.com
Website: www.aaace.org

American Association of Community Colleges
One Dupont Circle
NW, Suite 410
Washington, DC 20036
USA
Tel: 001 202 728 0200
Fax: 001 202 833 2467
Email: jirwin@aacc.nche.edu
Website: www.aacc.nche.edu

Learning Resources Network (LERN)
PO Box 9
River Falls, WI 54022
USA
Tel: 001 800 678 5376
Fax: 001 888 234 8633
Email: info@lern.org
Website: www.lern.org

National Community Education Association
3929 Old Lee Highway Ste. 91-A
Fairfax, VA 22030
USA
Tel: 001 703 359 8973
Fax: 001 703 359 0972
Email: ncea@ncea.com
Website: www.ncea.com

Pro Literacy Worldwide
1320 Jamesville Avenue
Syracuse, NY 13210
USA
Tel: 001 315 422 9121
Fax: 001 315 422 6369
Email: pwaite@proliteracy.org
Website: www.proliteracy.org
Executive Director: Peter A Waite

Media

National Media Organisations

BBC Learning
White City, 201 Wood Lane
London W12 7TS
Tel: 020 8752 5252
Email: learning@bbc.co.uk
Website: www.bbc.co.uk/learning
Controller: Liz Cleaver
Head of Interactive Learning:
Myles Runham
Head of Learning Campaigns:
Elizabeth McKay
Head of Policy and Public Affairs:
Wendy Jones

BBC Wales
Broadcasting House
Llandaff
Cardiff CF5 2YQ
Head of Education and Learning:
Dr Eleri Wyn Lewis

BBC Northern Ireland
Broadcasting House
Ormeau Avenue
Belfast BT2 8HQ
Editor, Learning: Jane Cassidy

BBC Scotland
Broadcasting House
5 Queen Street
Edinburgh EH2 1JF
Head of Learning: Nick Simons

BBC Learning plays a central part in meeting the BBC's purpose of supporting education and building knowledge, providing specialist learning content for children and adults, and stimulating audiences to develop interest in – and knowledge of – a wide range of subjects.

Using the best of the BBC – its content, channels of communication, talent and creative skills – BBC Learning offers resources and activities designed to meet real needs and complement the formal education process. Through interactive media, such as broadband internet and mobile devices, BBC Learning can offer people powerful learning experiences in their own time and at their own pace.

BBC Learning supports people in acquiring the skills essential to life and work in the 21st century, including literacy, numeracy, communication and computer skills through initiatives such as BBC Skillswise and RaW. The BBC's biggest ever literacy campaign, RaW, has targeted the estimated 12 million people in the UK who have limited reading and writing skills. Its approach is entertainment-led, with links to broadcast programmes, games and features on its interactive website and a wide range of activities with partner organisations throughout the UK.

BBC Learning campaigns offer opportunities for learning in the broadest sense, with the emphasis on active participation. Building on the interest generated by broadcast programmes, these campaigns encourage and enable people in communities throughout the UK to learn more through taking part in events and activities developed with expert partners.

Breathing Places is a campaign which inspires people to create and care for green spaces in their local area. *Headroom* encourages the widest possible audience to understand more about mental health and to take simple steps to look after their own mental well-being. The *Headroom* website aims to be one of the most accessible and comprehensive multimedia resources for mental well-being on the web.

The BBC also provides community-based learning support alongside television, radio and online output. Project managers work locally with libraries, businesses and other partners to assist the understanding and use of the BBC's learning output.
Website: www.bbc.co.uk/learningoverview

Bss

International House
7 High Street
Ealing
London W5 5DB
Tel: 0845 600 1317
Fax: 020 8799 9099
Email: marketing@bss.org
Website: www.bss.org
Chief Executive: Peter Calderbank

Bss is a charity providing information and
advice services to viewers and listeners of TV
and radio programmes covering education
and social welfare. Bss also works with
charities and public sector organisations
providing similar support using phones,
web, fulfilment and donation processing, as
well as running the learndirect helpline for
England and Northern Ireland, which gives
information and advice on all aspects of
learning.

International Broadcasting Trust

CAN Mezzanine
32–36 Loman Street
London SE1 0EH
Tel: 020 7922 7940
Email: mail@ibt.org.uk
Website:www.ibt.org.uk
Director: Mark Galloway

The International Broadcasting Trust (IBT)
is an educational and media charity working
to promote broadcast coverage of the
developing world, its people and the issues
which affect their lives. IBT was set 30 years
ago by a consortium of over fifty aid and
development agencies, educational bodies,
churches and trades unions, as a unique
partnership between non-governmental
organisations and broadcasters,
educationalists and film makers. IBT's
principal activities include lobbying
Government and regulators, dialogue with
broadcasters and publishing research.

OFCOM – Office of Communication

Riverside House
2a Southwark Bridge Road
London SE1 9HA
Tel: 020 7981 3000
Fax: 020 7981 3333
Email: contact@ofcom.org.uk
Website: www.ofcom.org.uk

Press Association

292 Vauxhall Bridge Road
London SW1V 1AE
Tel: 020 7963 7000
Fax: 020 7963 7192
Email: tim.ross@pa.press.net
Website: www.thepagroup.com
Education Correspondent: Tim Ross

Teletext Ltd

Building 10
Chiswick Park
566 Chiswick High Road
London W4 5TS
Tel: 0870 731 3000
Fax: 0870 731 3001
Website: www.teletext.co.uk

Press

National Press

Daily Express

10 Lower Thames Street
London EC3R 6EN
Tel: 08714 341010
Website: www.express.co.uk

Daily Mail, The Mail on Sunday, Evening Standard, Metro, Loot, Ireland on Sunday

Northcliffe House
2 Derry Street
Kensington
London W8 5TT
Tel: 020 7938 6000
Fax: 020 7938 4626
Website: www.dmgt.co.uk

Daily Mirror
Trinity Mirror
1 Canada Square
Canary Wharf
London E14 5AP
Tel: 020 7293 3000
Email: feedback@mirror.co.uk
Website: www.mirror.co.uk

Daily Star
The Northern and Shell Building
10 Lower Thames Street
London EC3R 6EN
Tel: 08714 341010
Website: www.dailystar.co.uk
Associate Editor: Kieron Saunders

Daily Telegraph
111 Buckingham Palace Road
London SW1W 0DT
Tel: 020 7931 2000
Website: www.telegraph.co.uk
Education Editor: Graeme Paton

Financial Times
1 Southwark Bridge
London SE1 9HL
Tel: 020 7873 3000
Website: www.ft.com
Education Correspondent: Jon Boone

Guardian Education
119 Farringdon Road
London EC1R 3ER
Tel: 020 7239 9913
Website: www.educationguardian.co.uk
Website Editor: Donald MacLeod
Further Education Editor: Peter Kingston
Tel: 020 7239 9929
Editor, Education Guardian : Claire Phipps
Tel: 020 7713 4723

The Independent
Independent House
191 Marsh Wall
London E14 9RS
Tel: 020 7005 2880
Fax: 020 7005 2933
Email: r.garner@independent.co.uk
Website: www.independent.co.uk
Education Editor: Richard Garner
Education Correspondent: Sarah Cassidy

Morning Star
William Rust House
52 Beachy Road
Bow
London E3 2NS
Tel: 020 8510 0815
Fax: 020 8986 5694
Website: www.morningstaronline.com
Education Correspondent: Daniel Coysh

Observer Newspaper
119 Farringdon Road
London EC1R 3ER
Tel: 020 7278 2332
Fax: 020 7837 7817
Website: www.observer.guardian.co.uk
Education Correspondent: Anushka Asthana

Sunday Telegraph
111 Buckingham Palace Road
London SW1W 0DT
Tel: 020 7931 3569
Email: julie.henry@telegraph.co.uk
Website: www.telegraph.co.uk
Education Correspondent: Julie Henry

Sunday Times
1 Pennington Street
Wapping
London E98 1ST
Tel: 020 7782 5000
Fax: 020 7782 5731
Email:
geraldine.hackett@Sunday-times.co.uk
Website: www.timesonline.co.uk
Education Correspondent: Sian Griffiths

The Times
1 Pennington Street
Wapping
London E98 1TT
Tel: 020 7782 5000
Website: www.timesonline.co.uk
Editor: Robert Thomson

Times Educational Supplement

Admiral House
66–68 East Smithfield
London E1W 1BX
Tel: 020 7782 3000
Fax: 020 7782 3202
Website: www.tes.co.uk
Editor: Gerard Kelly
Further Education Editor: Steve Hook

Times Higher Education

26 Red Lion Square
London WC1R 4HQ
Tel: 020 3194 3000
Website: www.thes.co.uk
Editor: Ann Mroz

Regional Press

Birmingham Post and Mail

Weaman Street
Birmingham B4 6AT
Email: thepost@mrn.co.uk
Website:
www.icbirminghamicnetwork.co.uk
Education Correspondent: Shahid Naqvi
Email: shahid-naqvi@mrn.co.uk

Lancashire Evening Post

Editorial Education Department
Oliver's Place
Fulwood
Preston PR2 9ZA
Tel: 01772 254841
Fax: 01772 880173
Email: newsdesk@lep.co.uk
Website: www.lep.co.uk
Education Correspondent: Sonja Astbury
Tel: 01772 838160
Email: sonja.astbury@lep.co.uk

Liverpool Daily Post and Echo

PO Box 48
Old Hall Street
Liverpool L69 3EB
Tel: 0151 227 2000
Fax: 0151 472 2474
Education Correspondent: Ben Turner
Features Editor (Echo): Dawn Collinson

London Evening Standard

Northcliffe House
2 Derry Street
Kensington
London W8 5TT
Tel: 020 7938 6000
Website: www.thisislondon.co.uk
Education Correspondent: Tim Ross

Manchester Evening News

1 Scott Place
Hardman Street
Manchester M3 3RN
Tel: 0161 832 7200
Website: www.manchesteronline.co.uk
Education Correspondent: Yakub Qureshi

South Wales Echo

Six Park Street
Cardiff CF10 1XR
Tel: 029 2024 33634
Email: moira.sharkey@mediawales.co.uk
Website: www.icwales.com
Education Correspondent: Moira Sharkey

Western Mail

Six Park Street
Cardiff CF10 1XR
Tel: 029 2022 3333
Fax: 029 2058 3652
Email: newsdesk@mediawales.co.uk
Website: www.icwales.co.uk
Education Correspondent: Abbie Wightwick

Yorkshire Post

PO Box 168
Wellington Street
Leeds
West Yorkshire LS1 1RF
Tel: 0113 243 2701
Fax: 0113 238 8521
Website: www.yorkshirepost.co.uk
Education Correspondent: John Roberts

Radio

BBC Local Radio Stations

BBC Radio Berkshire
PO Box 104.4
Reading RG4 8FH
Tel: 0118 946 4200
Fax: 0118 946 4555
Email:
radio.berkshire.actiondesk@bbc.co.uk
Website: www.bbc.co.uk/berkshire
Social Action Producer: Anna Jackson

BBC Radio Bristol
PO Box 194
Bristol BS99 7QT
Tel: 0117 974 1111
Fax: 0117 923 8323
Email: radio.bristol@bbc.co.uk
Website: www.bbc.co.uk/bristol
Managing Editor: Tim Pemberton
Assistant Editor: Jason Dean

BBC Radio Cambridgeshire
BBC Learning
Broadcasting House
104 Hills Road
Cambridge CB2 1LD
Tel: 01223 259696
Fax: 01223 589840
Email: madeleine.forrester@bbc.co.uk
Website: www.bbc.co.uk/learning
BBC Learning Project Manager, Eastern
Region: Madeleine Forrester

BBC Radio Cornwall
Phoenix Wharf
Truro
Cornwall TR1 1UA
Tel: 01872 275421
Fax: 01872 240679
Email:.cornwall@bbc.co.uk
Website: www.bbc.co.uk/cornwall

BBC Coventry and Warwickshire
Priory Place
Coventry CV1 5SQ
Tel: 024 7655 1000
Email: coventry.warwickshire@bbc.co.uk
Website: www.bbc.co.uk/coventry
Senior Broadcast Journalist: Sue Curtis

BBC Radio Cumbria
Annetwell Street
Carlisle
Cumbria CA3 8BB
Tel: 01228 592444
Fax: 01228 511195
Email: radio.cumbria@bbc.co.uk
Website: www.bbc.co.uk/cumbria
Editor: Nigel Dyson

BBC Radio Derby
PO Box 104.5
Derby DE1 3HL
Tel: 01332 361111
Fax: 01332 290794
Email: radio.derby@bbc.co.uk
Website: www.bbc.co.uk/derby
Editor: Simon Cornes

BBC Radio Devon
Broadcasting House
Seymour Road
Plymouth
Devon PL3 5BD
Tel: 01752 229201
Fax: 01752 234564
Email: radio.devon@bbc.co.uk
Website: www.bbc.co.uk/devon
News Editor: Olivia Pearce

BBC Essex
PO Box 765
Chelmsford
Essex CM2 9XB
Tel: 01245 616000
Fax: 01245 492983
Email: claire.ziwa@bbc.co.uk
Action Desk Producer: Chris Penhall
BBC Essex Action Desk – responsible for
promoting lifelong learning
Tel: 01245 616081
Email: chris.penhall@bbc.co.uk

BBC Radio Gloucestershire
London Road
Gloucester GL1 1SW
Tel: 01452 308585
Fax: 01452 309491
Email: radio.gloucestershire@bbc.co.uk
Website: www.bbc.co.uk/gloucestershire

BBC Greater Manchester Radio
New Broadcasting House
Oxford Road
Manchester M60 1SJ
Tel: 0161 200 2000
Fax: 0161 244 3122
Email: radiomanchester@bbc.co.uk
Website: manchesteronline@bbc.co.uk
Managing Editor: John Ryan
News Editor: Mark Elliott

BBC Radio Guernsey
Broadcasting House
Bulwer Avenue
St Sampsons
Guernsey GY2 4LA
Tel: 01481 200600
Fax: 01481 200361
Email: bbcguernsey@bbc.co.uk
Website: www.bbc.co.uk/guernsey

BBC Hereford and Worcester –
Local Radio
Hylton Road
Worcester WR2 5WW
Tel: 01905 748485
Fax: 01905 748006
Email: bbchw@bbc.co.uk
Website: www.bbc.co.uk/worcester
Editor: James Coghill

The address for BBC Hereford is:
43 Broad Street
Hereford HR4 9HH
Tel: 01432 355252
Fax: 01432 356446
Website: www.bbc.co.uk/hereford
Local Radio Administrator: Julia Haywood

BBC Radio Humberside
Queen's Court
Queen's Gardens
Hull HU1 3RH
Tel: 01482 323232
Fax: 01482 314403
Email: radio.humberside@bbc.co.uk
Website: www.bbc.co.uk/humber

BBC Radio Jersey
18–21 Parade Road
St Helier
Jersey JE2 3PL
Tel: 01534 870000
Fax: 01534 732569
Email: jersey@bbc.co.uk
Website: www.bbc.co.uk/radiojersey
Managing Editor: Denzil Dudley

BBC Radio Kent
The Great Hall
Mount Pleasant Road
Tunbridge Wells
Kent TN1 1QQ
Tel: 01892 670000
Fax: 01892 549118
Email: radio.kent@bbc.co.uk
Website: www.bbc.co.uk/kent
Managing Editor: Paul Leaper

BBC Radio Lancashire
22–26 Darwen Street
Blackburn BB2 2EA
Tel: 01254 262411
Email: radio.lancashire@bbc.co.uk
Website: www.bbc.co.uk/lancashire

BBC Radio Leicester
9 St Nicholas Place
Leicester LE1 5LB
Tel: 0116 251 6688
Fax: 0116 251 1463
Email: radioleicester@bbc.co.uk
Website: www.bbc.co.uk/leicester
Editor: Kate Squire

BBC Radio Lincolnshire
Radion Buildings
PO Box 219
Newport
Lincoln LN1 3XY
Tel: 01522 511411
Fax: 01522 511058
Email: radio.lincolnshire@bbc.co.uk
Website: www.bbc.co.uk/lincolnshire

BBC London 94.9FM
35c Marylebone High Street
London W1M 4AA
Tel: 020 7224 2424
Email: yourlondon@bbc.co.uk
Website: www.bbc.co.uk/london
News Editor: Dipy Chaudhary

BBC Nottingham
London Road
Nottingham NG2 4UU
Tel: 0115 955 0500
Fax: 0115 902 1983
Email: emt@bbc.co.uk
Website: www.bbc.co.uk/nottingham

BBC Radio Merseyside
PO Box 95.8
Hanover Street
Liverpool L69 1ZJ
Tel: 0151 708 5500
Fax: 0151 794 0988
Email: liverpool@bbc.co.uk
Website: www.bbc.co.uk/liverpool

BBC Radio Newcastle
Broadcasting Centre
Barrack Road
Newcastle upon Tyne NE99 1RN
Tel: 07711 912704
Fax: 0191 232 5082
Website: www.bbc.co.uk/learningoverview
BBC Learning Project Manager:
Paul Corcoran

BBC Radio Norfolk
The Forum
Millennium Plain
Norwich NR2 1BH
Tel: 01603 617411
Fax: 01603 633692
Email: norfolk.@bbc.co.uk
Website: www.bbc.co.uk/norfolk
Social Action Producer: Gary Standley

BBC Radio Northampton
Broadcasting House
Abington Street
Northampton NN1 2BH
Tel: 01604 239100
Fax: 01604 230709
Email: northampton@bbc.co.uk
Website: www.bbc.co.uk/northamptonshire

BBC Radio Oxford
PO Box 952
269 Banbury Road
Oxford OX2 7DW
Tel: 08459 311444
Fax: 08459 311555
Email: oxford@bbc.co.uk
Website: www.bbc.co.uk/oxford

BBC Radio Sheffield
54 Shoreham Street
Sheffield S1 4RS
Tel: 0114 273 1177
Fax: 0114 267 5454
Email: radio.sheffield@bbc.co.uk
Website: www.bbc.co.uk/southyorkshire

BBC Radio Shropshire
2–4 Boscobel Drive
Shrewsbury SY1 3TT
Tel: 01743 248484
Fax: 01743 237018
Email: radio.shropshire@bbc.co.uk
Website: www.bbc.co.uk/shropshire
Editor: Tim Beech

BBC Radio Solent
Broadcasting House
Havelock Road
Southampton SO14 7PW
Tel: 02380 631311
Fax: 02380 339648
Email: radio.solent@bbc.co.uk
Website: www.bbc.co.uk/radiosolent

BBC Southern Counties Radio
Broadcasting Centre
Guildford
Surrey GU2 7AP
Tel: 01483 306306
Fax: 01483 304952
Email: scr.news@bbc.co.uk
Website: www.bbc.co.uk/southerncounties
News Editor: Mark Carter

BBC Radio Stoke

Cheapside
Hanley
Stoke-on-Trent ST1 1JJ
Tel: 01782 208080
Fax: 01782 289115
Email: radio.stoke@bbc.co.uk
Website: www.bbc.co.uk/stoke
News Editor: James O'Hara

BBC Radio Suffolk

Broadcasting House
St Matthew's Street
Ipswich IP1 3EP
Tel: 01473 250000
Fax: 01473 210887
Email: radiosuffolk@bbc.co.uk
Website: www.bbc.co.uk/radiosuffolk
Managing Editor: Peter Cook

BBC Radio Swindon and BBC Radio Wiltshire

Broadcasting House
56–58 Prospect Place
Swindon SN1 3RW
Tel: 01793 513626
Fax: 01793 513650
Website: www.bbc.co.uk/wiltshire

BBC Tees

PO Box 95FM
Broadcasting House
Newport Road
Middlesbrough TS1 5DG
Tel: 01642 225211
Fax: 01642 211356
Website: www.bbc.co.uk/radiocleveland
Managing Editor: Mathew Barraclough

BBC Three Counties Radio

1 Hastings Street
Luton
Bedfordshire LU1 5XL
Tel: 01582 637400
Fax: 01582 401467
Email: 3cr.news@bbc.co.uk
Website: www.bbc.co.uk/threecounties

BBC WM

The Mailbox
102–108 Wharfside Street
Birmingham B1 1AY
Tel: 0121 567 6000
Fax: 0121 567 6001
Email: bbcwm@bbc.co.uk
Website: www.bbc.co.uk/birmingham
Managing Editor: Keith Beech

BBC Radio York

20 Bootham Row
York YO30 7BR
Tel: 01904 641351
Fax: 01904 610937
Email: northyorkshire.news@bbc.co.uk
Website: www.bbc.co.uk/northyorkshire

Television

National Television Companies

BBC Learning

White City, 201 Wood Lane
London W12 7TS
Tel: 020 8752 5252
Email: learning@bbc.co.uk
Website: www.bbc.co.uk/learning
Controller: Liz Cleaver
Head of Interactive Learning:
Myles Runham
Head of Learning Campaigns:
Elizabeth McKay
Head of Policy and Public Affairs:
Wendy Jones

BBC Learning plays a central part in meeting the BBC's purpose of supporting education and building knowledge, providing specialist learning content for children and adults, and stimulating audiences to develop interest in – and knowledge of – a wide range of subjects.

Using the best of the BBC – its content, channels of communication, talent and creative skills – BBC Learning offers resources and activities designed to meet real needs and complement the formal education process. Through interactive media, such as broadband internet and mobile devices, BBC

Learning can offer people powerful learning experiences in their own time and at their own pace.

BBC Learning supports people in acquiring the skills essential to life and work in the 21st century, including, literacy, numeracy, communication and computer skills through initiatives such as BBC Skillswise and RaW. The BBC's biggest ever literacy campaign, RaW, has targeted the estimated 12 million people in the UK who have limited reading and writing skills. Its approach is entertainment-led, with links to broadcast programmes, games and features on its interactive website and a wide range of activities with partner organisations throughout the UK.

BBC Learning campaigns offer opportunities for learning in the broadest sense, with the emphasis on active participation. Building on the interest generated by broadcast programmes, these campaigns encourage and enable people in communities throughout the UK to learn more through taking part in events and activities developed with expert partners.

Breathing Places is a campaign which inspires people to create and care for green spaces in their local area. *Headroom* encourages the widest possible audience to understand more about mental health and to take simple steps to look after their own mental well-being. The *Headroom* website aims to be one of the most accessible and comprehensive multimedia resources for mental well-being on the web.

The BBC also provides community-based learning support alongside television, radio and online output. Project managers work locally with libraries, businesses and other partners to assist the understanding and use of the BBC's learning output.

Website: www.bbc.co.uk/learningoverview

Channel Four Television (Education)

124 Horseferry Road
London SW1P 2TX
Tel: 020 7396 4444
Fax: 020 7306 5630
Website: www.channel4.com
Head of Education and Managing Editor, Channel 4: Janey Walker
Commissioning Editor, Education New Media: Matt Locke

Commissioning Editor, Education:
Alice Taylor
Commissioning Editor, New Media:
Adam Gee

Channel 4 is a statutory corporation with its own board under the chairmanship of Luke Johnson. Under the 1990 Broadcasting Act, Channel 4 is required to ensure that a suitable proportion of its programmes are of an educational nature, designed to appeal to a wide range of adult interest. Priority areas for adults: health, relationships, multicultural issues, leisure, disability, active citizenship, careers, entrepreneurship, creative industries and media literacy. Many areas of Channel 4 programming serve educational aims through the provision of websites, interactive services, mobile services, publications and helplines. These encourage viewers to develop their interests both informally and through formal education. Channel 4 is also required to broadcast 330 hours of schools programmes a year. Channel 4 values its continuing education links and will continue to develop these in the future. Its Education department aims to make a real difference to people's lives through learning.

Regional Television Companies

Border Television
The Television Centre
Carlisle CA1 3NT
Tel: 0844 88 15850
Head of News: Steve Lambdon

Channel Television
Television Centre
La Pouquelaye
St Helier
Jersey
Channel Islands JE1 3ZD
Tel: 01534 816816
Fax: 01534 816817
Email: broadcast@channeltv.co.uk
Website: www.channelonline.tv
Director of Administration and Finance:
Martin Maack

GMTV
The London Television Centre
Upper Ground
London SE1 9TT
Tel: 020 7827 7000
Fax: 020 7827 7001
Website: www.gm.tv
Human Resources Director: Craig Thomas

ITV Anglia
Anglia House
Norwich
Norfolk NR1 3JG
Tel: 01603 615151
Fax: 01603 631032
Website: www.itv.com/anglia

ITV Central
Central Court
Gas Street
Birmingham B1 2JT
Tel: 0844 88 14150
Fax: 0844 88 14198
Email: dutyoffice@itv.com
Website: www.itv.com/central

ITV Granada
Quay Street
Manchester M60 9EA
Tel: 0161 832 7211
Fax: 0161 827 2180
Website: www.itv.com/granada
Head of Documentaries: Sarah Murch

ITV London
London Television Centre
Upper Ground
London SE1 9LT
Tel: 020 7620 1620
Fax: 020 7261 8163
Website: www.itvlocal.com/london

ITV Tyne Tees
Televison House
The Watermark
Gateshead
Tyne and Wear NE11 9ZS
Tel: 0844 88 15069
Fax: 0844 88 15010
Email: brenda.mitchell@itv.com
Website: www.itvlocal.com/tynetees

ITV Wales
The Television Centre
Culverhouse Cross
Cardiff CF5 6XJ
Tel: 0844 8810101
Website: www.itvregions.com/wales
Community Affairs Manager: Shone Hughes

ITV West Country
Western Wood Way
Langage Science Park
Plymouth
Devon PL7 5BQ
Tel: 0844 881 4800
Fax: 0844 881 4878
Website: www.itvregions.com/westcountry
Chief News Editor: Sarah Norman

ITV West Studios
470 Bath Road
Brislington
Bristol BS4 3HG
Tel: 0844 88 12345
Fax: 084 88 12346
Email: itvwestnews@itv.com/west
Website: www.itvlocal.com
Head of News: Liz Hannam

ITV Yorkshire
Television Centre
Kirkstall Road
Leeds
West Yorkshire LS3 1JS
Tel: 0113 243 8283
Fax: 0113 244 5107
Website: www.itvlocal.com/yorkshire
Community Affairs Manager: Jo Hargreaves

STV Central Ltd
Pacific Quay
Glasgow G51 1PQ
Tel: 0141 300 3000
Website: www.stv.tv
Public Relations Executive: Kirstin Elsby

UTV plc
Havelock House
Ormeau Road
Belfast BT7 1EB
Tel: 028 9032 8122
Fax: 028 9024 6695
Email: info@utvplc.com
Website: www.utvmedia.com
Group Chief Executive: John McCann

Glossary of organisation acronyms

AAACE — American Association for Adult and Continuing Education

ABCC — Association of British Correspondence Colleges

ABPI — Association of the British Pharmaceutical Industry Institute

ACEG — Association for Careers Education and Guidance

ACER — Association of Colleges in the Eastern Region

ACM — Association for College Management

ACRE — Action with Communities in Rural England

ACVO — Assessment Centre for Voluntary Organisations

AIPE — Asociación de Instituciones de Promoción y Educación (Bolivia)

ALA — Adult Learning Australia Inc (Australia)

ALECSO — Arab League Educational, Cultural and Scientific Organisation

ALM — Adults Learning Maths

ALP — Association of Learning Providers

ALT — Association for Learning Technology

ALW — Adult Learners' Week

ANAFA — Association Nationale pour l'Alphabétisation et la Formation Adultes (Senegal)

ANIC — Association of Northern Ireland Colleges

ANTEP — Association of Non-Traditional Education in the Philippines

ANUP — Asociatia Nationalā a Universitătilor Populare (Romania)

AoC — Association of Colleges

AOSEC — Association of South East Colleges

AQA — Assessment and Qualifications Alliance

ARCA — Adult Residential Colleges Association

ARVAC — Association for Research in the Voluntary and Community Sector

ASCOL — Association of Scotland's Colleges

ASE — Association for Science Education

ASLEF — Associated Society of Locomotive Engineers and Fireman

ASPBAE — Asia South Pacific Bureau of Adult Education

ATL — Association of Teachers and Lecturers

AWEMA — All Wales Ethnic Minority Association

BAC — British Accreditation Council for Independent Further and Higher Education

BALID — British Association for Literacy in Development

BASSAC — British Association of Settlements and Social Action Centres

BCA — Berkshire College of Agriculture

BECTA — British Educational Communications and Technology Agency

BECTU — Broadcasting, Entertainment, Cinematograph and Theatre Union

BILD — The British Institute for Learning and Development

BILD — British Institute of Learning Disabilities

BIMA	British Interactive Media Association	CRAC	Careers Research and Advisory Centre
BLS	Bangladesh Literacy Society	CROW	Centre for Research into the
BSS	Broadcasting Support Services		Older Workforce
BTEG	Black Training and Enterprise Group	CSIE	Centre for Studies on Inclusive Learning
CACDP	Council for the Advancement of Communication with Deaf People	DCSF	Department for Children, Schools and Families
CARCAE	Caribbean Regional Council for Adult Education	DEA	Development Education Association
CASAE	Canadian Association for the Study of Adult Education	DEFRA	Department for Environment, Food and Rural Affairs
CAVA	The Cambridge Access Validating Agency	DELNI	Department for Employment and Learning (Northern Ireland)
CBI	Confederation of British Industry	DfID	Department for International Development
CCEA	Northern Ireland Council for the Curriculum, Examinations and Assessment	DIE	Deutsches Institut für Erwachsenbildung (Germany)
		DIUS	Department for Innovation, Universities and Skills
CCPR	Central Council of Physical Recreation	DSC	Directory of Social Change
		DWP	Department for Work and Pensions
CEAAL	Consejo de Educación de Adultos de América Latina	EAEA	European Association for the Education of Adults
CEDEFOP	European Centre for the Development of Vocational Training	EASA	Education Advice Service for Adults
CESI	Centre for Economic and Social Inclusion	ECA	Educational Centres Association
		ECITB	Engineering Construction Industry Training Board
CfA	Council for Administration	EFA	Employers' Forum on Age
CHEWATA	National Adult Education Association of Tanzania	EGAS	Educational Grants Advisory Service
CILIP	Chartered Institute of Library and Information Professionals	EGSA	Educational Guidance Service for Adults (Northern Ireland)
CILT	Centre for Information on Language Teaching and Research	ELATT	East London Advanced Technology Training
CIPD	Chartered Institute of Personnel and Development	EMFEC	East Midlands Further Education Council
CLMG	Campaign for Learning through Museums and Galleries	EMIE	Education Management Information Exchange
COVER	Community and Voluntary Forum for the Eastern Region	EMDA	East Midlands Development Agency
COSLA	Convention of Scottish Local Authorities	EMUA	East Midlands Universities Association
CPI	Confederation of Paper Industries	EPSRC	Engineering and Physical Sciences Research Council

ERDI	Consortium of European Research and Development Institutes for Adult Education	JSSACE	Japan Society for the Study of Adult and Community Education
ESRC	Economic and Social Research Council	LAAE	Lithuanian Association of Adult Education (Lithuania)
ESREA	European Society for Research on the Education of Adults	LAEA	Latvian Adult Education Association (Latvia)
EUCEN	European University Continuing Education Network	LCN	Learning Communities Network
FACE	Forum for Access and Continuing Education	LERN	Learning Resources Network (USA)
FAEA	Federación de Asociaciones de Educación de personas Adultas	LET	Learning from Experience Trust
FAVA	Federation of Authorised Validating Agencies	LFHE	Leadership Foundation for Higher Education
FERA	Further Education Research Association	LGA	Local Government Association
FSC	Field Studies Council	LLUK	Lifelong Learning UK
GALAE	General Authority for Literacy and Adult Education (Egypt)	LSC	Learning and Skills Council
GO	Government Office	LSDA	Learning and Skills Development Agency (Northern Ireland)
GRETA	Greenwich Education and Training Advice for Adults	LSIS	Learning and Skills Improvement Service
H2O	Highway to Opportunities	LSN	Learning and Skills Network
HABIA	Hair and Beauty Industry Authority	MEWN	Minority Ethnic Women's Network (Swansea)
HEFCE	Higher Education Funding Council for England	MLA	Museums, Libraries and Archives Council
IBT	International Broadcasting Trust	MoD	Ministry of Defence
ICAE	International Council for Adult Education	NAAL	Norwegian Association for Adult Learning (Norway)
ICEA	Institut de cooperation pour l'Éducation des Adultes (Canada)	NAEGA	National Association for Educational Guidance for Adults
IdeA	Improvement and Development Agency for Local Government	NALA	National Adult Literacy Agency (Ireland)
IDEA	Institute for the Development and Education of Adults (Switzerland)	NAMSS	National Association for Managers of Student Services
IFWEA	International Federation of Workers' Educational Associations	NANFAE	National Association for Non-Formal Adult Education (Bangladesh)
ILO	International Labour Organisation	NAPA	National Association for Providers of Activities for Older People
IPPR	Institute for Public Policy Research	NASO	National Adult School Organisation
JACAE	Jamaican Council for Adult Education	NASUWT	National Association of Schoolmasters/Union of Women Teachers
		NATE	National Association for Total Education (Sri Lanka)

NATECLA National Association for Teaching English and other Community Languages to Adults

NATSPEC Association of National Specialist Colleges

NAVCA National Association for Voluntary and Community Action

NAWO National Alliance of Women's Organisations

NCLL National Centre for Language and Literacy

NCVER National Centre for Vocational Educational Research (Australia)

NCVO National Council for Voluntary Organisations

NCWE National Council for Work Experience

NEC National Extension College

NFER National Foundation for Educational Research

NFWI National Federation of Women's Institutes

NIACE National Institute of Adult Continuing Education

NIACRO Northern Ireland Association for the Care and Resettlement of Offenders

NICEC National Institute for Careers Education and Counselling

NIESR National Institute of Economic and Social Research

NILTA National Information and Learning Technologies Association

NLT National Literacy Trust

NOCEAD National Organisation for Community Education, Continuing Education and Development (Vietnam)

NOCN National Open College Network

NRDC National Research and Development Centre for Adult Literacy and Numeracy

NSEAD National Society for Education in Art and Design

NUJ National Union of Journalists

NUM National Union of Mineworkers

NUS National Union of Students

NUT National Union of Teachers

NYA National Youth Agency

OCA Open College of the Arts

OCNEMR Open College Network East Midlands Region

OCNNER Open College Network North East Region

ODLQC Open and Distance Learning Quality Council

OECD Organisation for Economic Co-operation and Development

OFCOM Office of Communication

OFFA Office for Fair Access

OFSTED Office for Standards in Education, Children's Services and Skills

OLF Open Learning Foundation

OU Open University

PAALAE Pan African Association for Literacy and Adult Education

PACADE Pakistan Association for Continuing and Adult Education (Pakistan)

PAVS Pembrokeshire Association of Voluntary Services

PRAGMA Pre-Retirement Association of Greater Manchester

PRIA Society for Participatory Research in Asia

PSI Policy Studies Institute

QAA Quality Assurance Agency for Higher Education

QCA Qualifications and Curriculum Authority

RaPAL Research and Practice in Adult Literacy Group

RAISE Regional Action and Involvement South East

RDA Regional Development Agency

RETAS Refugee Education and Training Advisory Service

RNIB Royal National Institute of Blind People

RNID Royal National Institute for Deaf People

SACE	Singapore Association of Continuing Education
SAGSET	Society for the Advancement of Games and Simulations in Education and Training
SCDI	Scottish Council for Development and Industry
SCUTREA	Standing Conference on University Teaching and Research in the Education of Adults
SCVO	Scottish Council for Voluntary Organisations
SEAD	Scottish Education and Action for Development
SEDA	Staff and Educational Development Association
SEEDA	South East England Development Agency
SEMTA	Science, Engineering and Manufacturing Technologies Alliance
SEWREC	South East Wales Racial Equality Council
SFC	Scottish Further and Higher Education Funding Council
SFEU	Scottish Further Education Unit
SIAE	Slovenian Institute for Adult Education
SITC	Scottish Interactive Technology Centre
SPEAR	Society for the Promotion of Education and Research (Belize)
SPELL	Supporting People into Employment and Lifelong Learning
SQA	Scottish Qualifications Authority
SRHE	Society for Research into Higher Education
SSC	Sector Skills Council
SSDA	Sector Skills Development Agency
STAN	Second Tier Advisors Network
STUC	Scottish Trades Union Congress

SVEB	Schweizerischer Verbund für Weiterbildung (Switzerland)
SWRDA	South West Regional Development Agency
SWRI	Scottish Women's Rural Institutes
TAEN	The Age and Employment Network
TUC	Trades Union Congress
TWICS	Training for Work in Communities
UALL	Universities Association for Lifelong Learning
UCAS	Universities and Colleges Admissions Service
UCU	University and College Union
Ufi	University for Industry
UKCES	UK Commission for Employment and Skills
ULALA	Uganda Literacy and Adult Learners Association
UNLA	Unione Nazionale per la Lotta contro l'Analfabetismo (Italy)
USDAW	Union of Shop, Distributive and Allied Workers
UWIC	University of Wales Institute, Cardiff
VOCOLLS	Voluntary and Community Sector Opportunities for Learning in Leicestershire
VONNE	Voluntary Organisations' Network North East
VSO	Voluntary Service Overseas
VTCT	Vocational Training Charitable Trust
WEA	Workers' Educational Association
WJEC	Welsh Joint Education Committee
YALP	Young Adult Learners' Partnership
YMCA	Young Men's Christian Association
YWCA	Young Women's Christian Association

Subject index

Organisation index